INDUSTRY AND BUSINESS IN JAPAN

INDUSTRY AND BUSINESS IN JAPAN

日本の産業

Edited with an introduction by Kazuo Sato

M. E. SHARPE, INC. White Plains, New York
CROOM HELM London

Copyright © 1980 by M. E. Sharpe, Inc.
901 North Broadway, White Plains, New York 10603

First published in Great Britain 1980 by Croom Helm Ltd
2-10 St John's Road, London SW11

British Library Cataloguing in Publication Data

Industry and Business in Japan.
    1. Industrial organization — Japan —
    Addresses, essays, lectures
    I. Sato, Kazuo
    338.7'0952   HD70.J3   79-91904
    ISBN 0-7099-0207-7

Library of Congress Catalog Card Number: 79-91904
M. E. Sharpe, Inc. ISBN: 0-87332-152-9

Printed in the United States of America

CONTENTS

IV. Industrial Policy

V. Bibliographic Studies

ACKNOWLEDGMENTS

This volume gathers twelve essays written by Japan's leading experts on Japanese industrial organization. All but two of the essays appeared originally in Japanese in Japanese economic journals and books. Eight of them were translated and published in Japanese Economic Studies, a quarterly translation journal under my editorship. For reasons of space, some of these versions have been abridged. Two essays (Nos. 1 and 12) have been translated into English for the present volume, and two essays (Nos. 2 and 3), already available in English, are reprinted.

The editor and the publisher of the present volume wish to thank all the authors and the original publishers for generously granting their permission to reproduce these essays here.

The editor wishes to thank the translators who translated the eight essays for Japanese Economic Studies although he accepts full responsibility for the edited final version. Lastly, he wishes to express his gratitude to Douglas Merwin and other members of the editorial staff of M. E. Sharpe, Inc. for expert management of editorial details involved in producing this volume.

K. S.

INTRODUCTION

Kazuo Sato

Japan's economic growth was spectacular through the 1960s, with real GNP increasing at more than ten percent per annum. Even in the 1970s when all other major Western economies suffered from decelerated growth, Japan continued to maintain an annual economic growth rate of five to six percent. Thus, from the war-ravaged economy of the late 1940s, Japan has come to be one of the world's leading industrial powers. In 1978, in industrial exports Japan was second only to West Germany, having surpassed the United States for the first time in history.

The dynamic force behind this tremendous economic growth over more than three decades is Japan's modern industry run by large Japanese businesses and supported by the Japanese government. A great deal has been said about Japan, Incorporated in the popular press of the seventies, but when it comes to hard, solid analysis of Japan's business and industry, relatively little is available in English apart from journalistic descriptions based largely on stereotypes. Two exceptions are Eleanor Hadley, Antitrust in Japan (Princeton: Princeton University Press, 1970), and Richard Caves and Masu Uekusa, Industrial Organization in Japan (Washington, D.C.: The Brookings Institution, 1976). (1) But worthy studies are so few that the subject faces the danger of becoming as much of a myth as many other things about Japan.

This does not mean that Japanese scholars have done no significant studies on the subject. On the contrary, there has been a large outpouring of important studies conducted by Japanese economists. Unfortunately, they are available only in Japanese and remain inaccessible to the Western reader. (2) The present volume is designed to help fill this gap by gathering a number of important Japanese articles written by eminent Japanese specialists in the field of industrial organization. Topics covered in the volume range across industrial growth, the dual structure, industry studies, business groupings, capital concentration, and industrial policy. Yet this volume alone cannot do full justice to Japanese scholarship since the field is vast and outstanding studies are so numerous. It is intended only as a sampling of what goes on in Japanese economic studies in Japan. To aid the interested reader in search of the original literature, two bibliographical studies are included in the volume.

The dozen papers in this volume are grouped into five major sections and are introduced and summarized here.

I. Japan's Industrial Organization: Historical Perspective

Japanese Marxian economists used to believe that capitalism in Japan would follow the inevitable path of captialist development toward monopoly capitalism and rising exploitation of labor. Monopoly capital would command high profit rates and the distribution of income would become increasingly unequal. The policy of income redistribution would be needed. This sort of a contention had become common wisdom in Japan without its veracity ever being tested.

Ryutaro Komiya challenged this popular myth in a series of papers he wrote in the early 1960s. He examined corporations' rates of profits on assets and equity as reported in the Annual Report of Corporate Enterprise statistics and discovered that smaller corporations had higher profit rates than giant corporations in the late 1950s. Having found an apparent contradiction in the Monopoly Capital thesis, Komiya used it to full advantage. (3) Essay 1 of the present volume is a Komiya article that appeared in the March 1961 issue of the Sekai magazine. Komiya's papers are regarded as marking the beginning of

serious academic studies of industrial organization in Japan.
Since they have not been available in English, Essay 1 is included here for its historical significance.

In this essay, Komiya first notes the inverse relation between
firm size and profitability and then attempts to draw its policy
implications. It is obvious that labor cannot expect any appreciable benefit from the redistribution of property income since
property income is already low enough in Japan as compared
with other advanced countries. Rather, as Komiya sees it, the
inequality of income distribution is in that large firms are able
to pay much higher wages than smaller firms. Monopoly Capital distributes its high surplus value not to capital but to labor.
Thus, the class confrontation is not between property owners
and workers but within the working class. In particular, a
small coterie of power elites who manage big businesses is
given disproportionately large power in society. The dual
structure between large and small businesses that preserves
large wage differentials among workers must be resolved if
the inequality of income distribution is to be eliminated, and
education must be popularized. These measures, however, are
long-term in nature. For short-term income redistribution,
the antimonopoly policy cannot be effective. Improvements in
the social security system and in the tax system are required.

The dual structure of large and small businesses manifests
itself not only in wages but also in technology, capital intensity, financing, and so on. Large firms adopted modern and advanced technology, while small firms relied upon traditional or less advanced
technology. Such size-related differences among firms are loosely
called the dual structure, which has been regarded as a particularly
salient feature of the Japanese economy. (However, unlike the case
in contemporary less developed countries, there has been no
sharp discontinuity between large and small firms.)

This feature is given a clear-cut measurement by Ken'ichi
Miyazawa in a research project he supervised at the Institute
of Economic Research of the Economic Planning Agency in the
late 1950s. The project report was published as Shihon Kozo
to Kigyokan Kakusa [Capital Structure and Interfirm Differen-

xii   Industry and Business in Japan

tials] (Tokyo: Government Printing Office, 1960), which is
No. 6 of the Institute's Report Series. Essay 2 is an English
summary of this monograph. (4) It gives a concise summary of
Miyazawa's quantitative examination of the size structure of
Japanese manufacturing toward the end of the 1950s, just as the
Japanese economy was about to burst into economic expansion.

The dual structure was most prominent in technology-related
factors in manufacturing. As firm size increased, techniques
changed from premodern to modern and capital intensity, capital-output ratio, labor productivity, and wage rate were all
raised. The wage differential was as much as three to one between large and small firms. Miyazawa's production-function
analysis attributes these characteristic differentials to the fact
that smaller firms were on lower production functions. This
fact in turn is explained by two factors related to the supply of
labor and of capital. In large firms, on the one hand, lifetime
employment was prevalent so that labor mobility was low.
Wages were dependent on seniority of workers. On the other
hand, the excess supply of labor in the economy exerted a downward pressure on wages offered by small firms. Thus, the wage
differential between large and small firms developed. As regards the capital supply, there was a significant difference in
firms' accessibility to the capital market. As a firm's ability
to borrow depends a great deal on how much capital it owns,
large firms were able to borrow large volumes of funds from
city banks and long-term credit banks as well as from other
financial institutions at relatively low interest rates, while
small firms had to rely on friends, relatives, moneylenders
and small local banks for their funds at relatively high interest
rates. The interest differential may be attributed to differences
in risks and in the degree of financial market competitiveness.
Under these circumstances, large firms were able to increase
their capital intensity and to adopt more advanced technology.
Large banks tended to lend to large firms and the tendency toward capital concentration was fostered. However, small firms
were able to survive on account of low wages and via subcontracting to large firms.

Low profit rates realized by large firms suggest that market competition was intense among large firms. In the postwar period of rapid economic expansion, their competition was directed to increasing their market shares. To achieve this objective, firms were forced to step up their capital accumulation. This led to "excessive" competition among large firms. At the same time, these firms had to depend more and more on large banks to secure investable funds. The ties became stronger between banks and firms. Thus, a number of firms formed themselves into a group financially tied together with a major bank. Such a group of financially related firms is called a keiretsu, as distinct from the prewar zaibatsu, a group of firms controlled by a holding company of the parent zaibatsu family. In Essay 3, Yoshikazu Miyazaki defines keiretsu as "a closely tied complex of industrial and financial corporations." Keiretsu groups were particularly prominent in heavy and chemical industries, which were expanding most actively in the postwar period.

Miyazaki points out that the financial dependence of Japanese big businesses on external fund supply was very high as compared with large corporations abroad. In other words, the indirect financing method was much more important in Japan for corporate finances. City banks assumed a particularly significant position here as major suppliers of credit to keiretsu firms.

Miyazaki then proposes his celebrated hypothesis on the one-set principle of keiretsu behavior, according to which each keiretsu group attempts to establish a "complete set of all industries related to one another by having at least one firm of its group participate in an industry each," apparently because this sort of behavior is conducive to improving profitability of member firms of the keiretsu. Group banks are involved in financing the keiretsu investment required for setting up firms in new industries. Thus, intense competition breaks out among firms of different keiretsu. This intergroup competition was not observed in the zaibatsu days, since zaibatsu tended to specialize themselves so as to avoid competition. Miyazaki gives a number of reasons why this sort of keiretsu behavior emerged. Though his one-set principle has been criticized in the literature, it remains an influential hypothesis.

The first three essays pioneered the field of industrial organization. In the two decades since they first appeared, many follow-up studies have been published, advancing the level of scholarship by leaps and bounds. In the meantime, industrial organization itself has undergone a great many changes. Ken'-ichi Imai, among others, has energetically pushed research forward in this field. His recent book, Gendai Sangyo Soshiki [Contemporary Industrial Organization] (Tokyo: Iwanami Shoten, 1976), is a compendium of his many studies, and its high quality indicates how far Japanese scholarship has come since 1960. Essay 4, the introductory chapter of Imai's book, is a convenient summary of his views.

Imai first describes the historical background of industrial development after World War II. The Japanese government, particularly the Ministry of International Trade and Industry (MITI), wished to have Japan catch up with the West in productivity so as to be able to compete internationally. Business circles were enthusiastic about this industrial policy since it promised the satisfaction of the profit motive. Rapid economic growth resulted from the government's growth policy, which placed priority on expanding supply capacity. However, as firms competed to increase their market share by expanding their investment, the government had to control excessive competition by enforcing "voluntary" investment adjustments and depression cartels. A policy-induced investment cycle began to appear.

From input-output analysis, Imai finds that the competitive segment of the economy depends heavily on its own final demand, while the oligopolistic segment of the economy benefits from the competitive segment's final demand as well as its own final demand. In other words, the oligopolistic segment is closed to the rest of the economy. This is one salient feature of the Japanese industrial structure.

Imai's examination of individual firms' growth reveals that

large firms did not necessarily expand at the highest rates and
that medium-sized firms often did better than large firms. For
changes in market concentration, Imai takes note of several important phenomena, including development of loose combinations
of firms, formation of cartels, keiretsu control of distribution
channels particularly in the consumer goods industries, business groupings, and rising diversification of firms.

II. Industry Studies

Significant changes have taken place in Japan's industrial
structure since World War II. Old industries waned and new
industries emerged. At the forefront of industrial expansion
were many heavy and chemical industries, including iron and
steel, automobile, electronics, petrochemicals, and so on.
Many of them began with the hothouse protection in the early
1950s and attained maturity strong enough to compete with
foreign producers in the international market by the late 1960s.
This is indeed a remarkable record of achievement.

Such tremendous industrial growth prompted researchers
to look carefully into individual industries. How did they develop in the postwar period? What sort of an industrial policy
was directed toward them? How did they perform? Was the
market mechanism efficient and efficacious? If not, what sort
of public policy is now needed? Industry studies are expected
to answer these and other questions. The most notable of such
industry studies is the three-volume study edited by Hisao
Kumagai, Nihon no Sangyo Soshiki [Industrial Organization of
Japan] (Tokyo: Chuo Koron Sha, 1973, 1973, 1976). In it an
array of seventeen industries has been impressively scrutinized
by top-ranking economists. (5) Essays 5 and 6 below present
two of them, iron and steel and the automobile industry, because of their representativeness and their strategic importance in Japan's exports. (6)

In Essay 5, Hiroya Ueno and Hiromichi Muto examine Japan's automobile industry, which has been one of Japan's star
industries. Even though the automobile industry existed before

World War II, it was small in scale and weak in competitive power. When Japan had to rebuild its industry in the late 1940s, it had to decide whether the automobile industry ought to be developed in Japan or not. From the static principle of comparative advantage, it might be asserted that Japan should avoid specializing in automobile production since it lacked the necessary capital resources and technological expertise. Indeed this was the position taken by the Bank of Japan. The dynamic principle of comparative advantage, however, let the MITI insist that Japan had to build up the automobile and other heavy industries so that it could eventually compete with advanced industrial countries in the international market. The MITI won the policy debate and the Japanese government adopted full-scale industrial protection over infant industries through measures involving tariffs, excise taxes, import restrictions, and control of capital inflows. Industrial funds were supplied at low interest rates to these industries. Subsidies were given, liberal depreciation allowances were permitted, and duties on imported machines were exempted.

Consequently, the automobile industry grew at a very rapid rate. The domestic demand for automobiles expanded at a fast rate as domestic income grew and automobile prices began to fall in relative terms. Motorization swept the country. Highway construction began all over the country. The automobile industry became strong enough to withstand international competition by 1965 when import restrictions on automobiles were removed. While imports of automobiles did not increase, Japan's exports of automobiles started to rise in great strides in Southeast Asia, the United States, and elsewhere in the world.

Having taken a look at the postwar development of the automobile industry, the authors then examine the industrial organization of the industry, which can be characterized as an oligopoly with product differentiation. The authors take note of low barriers of entry despite high production concentration in the industry. There has been a movement toward administered pricing in order to suppress interfirm competition. As for the performance of the industry, the authors point out that it has enjoyed high excess profits. This may be attributed partly to the absence of foreign competition. Even after import restrictions were removed, the list prices of imported autos have remained quite high. They are about three times as high as the price of domestic cars, particularly because of a high excise tax on autos and dealers' margins. The authors then examine the efficiency of the industry, its keiretsu control and subcontracting practices, and finally evaluate the MITI's industrial policy.

Another star industry of postwar Japan has been iron and steel. Imai examines this industry in Essay 6. (7) In 1950, Japan's steel industry was considerably behind the American steel industry. But in the next two decades, the former not only caught up with the latter but even came to excel it by a large margin. While this progress can be regarded as a brilliant success of the MITI's industrial policy, it has also been getting criticism for its negative impact on economic welfare. The steel industry is an oligopoly without product differentiation. At the same time, strong economies of scale make the minimum plant size large enough to allow the presence of only a few oligopolies in the industry surrounded by a competitive fringe. Thus, the industry is characterized by competition among the few. Acute price competition breaks out from time to time, especially at the time of a recession. Oligopolies try to restrain competition among themselves by making some cartel arrangements. Thus, "voluntary" investment adjustments took place under the MITI's administrative guidance. In order to ensure no loss of market shares, however, such investment adjustments force oligopolistic firms to enlarge their investments to create excess capacity. The result is renewed efforts to curtail production when a recession comes. Since demand for steel products fluctuates widely over business cycles, prices tend to become volatile, reflecting intense price competition among steel producers. Arguments were proposed by steel producers to reduce the variability of steel prices by forming price cartels. Imai gives a careful review of such arguments in his paper.

III. Big Business and Business Groups

For better or worse, big businesses always attract public attention in any country. By sheer size they acquire a significant
part of the country's economic power. Since the primary interest of big businesses is the pursuit of profits, they make the
most of the economic power under their control. Their interest often does not coincide with that of the public at large.

In Japan, the zaibatsu became notorious for their powerful
control of Japanese economic life till the end of World War II.
The deconcentration of economic power became the first item
on the agenda of the American occupation forces. A number of
large firms were disbanded (though the final tally fell far short
of the initial intentions), influential business executives were
purged from public posts, and shareholdings of the zaibatsu
families were virtually confiscated.

Such sweeping reforms notwithstanding, big businesses came
back into power as the Japanese economy recovered from wartime ravages and regained its autonomy. New forms of combinations emerged. A number of firms banded together, albeit
loosely, particularly around major banks. Their ties were sup-
posedly through financial interrelations. These groups are called
keiretsu as we noted earlier. There is supposed to be cooperation or collusion among firms within the same keiretsu group
and competition among groups. The collusion is reinforced
through the group's subjugation of many smaller firms through
subcontracting practices. The competition has expressed itself
in the so-called excessive rivalry among the groups. These
are the topics of the three essays included in this section.

In Essay 7, Tadao Kiyonari and Hideichiro Nakamura present a study of in what manner and in what form the Big Business System was established in Japan. The authors first review the exchange between Kazuji Nagasu and Ryutaro Komiya
in the early 1960s. As a practical-minded Marxist, Nagasu
was not bound by the dogmatic schema of Marxist ideology in
looking at the realities of the Japanese economy, and yet he insisted that the Big Business Establishment dominated Japanese

economic life by exploiting the people. A handful of large firms subjugated smaller firms through subcontracting and established keiretsu control. It was as a challenge to Nagasu that Komiya presented his view discrediting the control by Monopoly Capital in Essay 1 and other papers.

Kiyonari and Nakamura then examine whether or not the keiretsu grouping is a revival of the zaibatsu control. They observe that individual large banks have relatively limited control over keiretsu firms because the latter borrow from many banks and that there are two types of keiretsu groups, one that developed from former zaibatsu groups and the other that was created anew in heavy and chemical industries mostly without strong financial tie-ups. No monopolization has been in force via finances and technology. Competition has been supplied by new entrants into industry. The authors thus regard Japan's Big Business System as a competitive oligopoly system.

As regards Miyazaki's one-set principle presented in Essay 3, the authors raise a number of questions on the grounds that financial control by keiretsu banks is not strong enough, that the indirect financing method which Miyazaki makes much of began to decline in popularity in the 1960s, that the Miyazaki hypothesis neglects the intra-group competition that has become stronger in recent years, and that there are business groups without keiretsu financing. Unlike Miyazaki, the authors think that firms are only loosely tied within individual keiretsu groups.

The authors then go on to examine the fact the Japanese business has now been under managerial capitalism with managerial control increasing in power. They take note of rising criticisms of the bad effects of managerial control since managers began to treat businesses as their own private property. As regards the trend toward concentration, the authors emphasize the viability of smaller firms which outgrew large firms. This observation led one of the authors, Nakamura, to his well-known thesis that leading medium-sized enterprises contribute to keeping the Big Business System flexible and fluid.

Keiretsu, or business groupings, have attracted public attention because of the belief that these groups exercise their economic power to their own advantage and against the public interest. The antimonopoly policy is supposed to keep vigil upon such tendencies. While it is difficult to measure abuses of economic power, it is relatively simple to quantify the extent of monopolistic or oligopolistic control of the markets. Concentration ratios are one such indicator. (8) However, business interrelationships are multidimensional, and more than one indicator is needed to measure them properly. The structure of business ownership is important. The increase in interlocking stock ownership is a recent phenomenon that ought to be noted. Yoshikazu Miyazaki has been engaged in this kind of fact-finding research for many years. (9) In Essay 8, he presents some of his important research findings for nonspecialists.

Miyazaki cites a few instances of anti-public behavior of big businesses in recent years as an indication of growing evils of the Big Business System in Japan. He then goes on to document his statistics about what he regards as the Japanese-type structure of big business. First, he notes that 464 top corporations held a 55 percent share in paid-in capital of all Japanese corporations as of 1966. Concurrently, private stockholders have been becoming less and less important, their share falling from 61 percent in 1950 to 40 percent in 1970. They have been taken over by financial institutions, investment trusts, and domestic corporations. At the same time, an international comparison indicates that Japanese businesses depend a great deal on funds supplied by financial institutions. This indirect financing method has resulted in a very poor equity-asset ratio and liquidity ratio of Japanese firms.

By comparing the capital concentration ratio of four major business groups, prewar and postwar, Miyazaki finds that the postwar keiretsu has become as important as the prewar zaibatsu. At the same time, interlocking share ownership within keiretsu groups has been rising. The share of intragroup financing through keiretsu banks has also risen. Thus, the interdependence of big businesses within each keiretsu group has been intensified.

It has been argued that managerial control tends to be neutral to the interest of capital owners since management is insulated from ownership. However, when stock ownership becomes interlocked among big businesses instead of being dispersed over a large number of individuals, managers must serve the interest of owning corporations. The business for business' sake attitude may prevail among managers of big businesses, who care less about the social cost of their actions as witnessed in recent examples.

Interfirm relationships may be examined in terms of the distribution of equity ownership, which is Miyazaki's approach. However, when equity accounts for only a small part of total assets of firms, more attention should be paid to the distribution of firms' indebtedness. Intragroup financing through keiretsu banks is emphasized because financial ties and linkages are expected to bind member firms close together. Since firms within a keiretsu group are supposed to develop stronger connections in extending trade credit, it becomes necessary to develop a more sophisticated model of analysis than merely taking a look at firms' indebtedness statistics. In Essay 9, Yusaku Futatsugi provides such a model and presents quantitative analysis that gives more secure footing to the analysis of the keiretsu phenomenon.

Consider n firms including banks and nonbank firms. Firm i's balance sheet gives

$$\sum_{j \neq i} X_{ij} + E_i + G_i + D_i = S_i (i = 1,...,n)$$

where X_{ij} is firm i's indebtedness to firm j, E_i firm i's surplus, G_i firm i's indebtedness to individuals, D_i outstanding deposits of banks (> 0 if firm i is a bank and $= 0$ if not), and S_i firm i's total assets. $a_{ij} = X_{ij}/S_j$ is the percentage of firm j's total assets which are lent to firm i. Imagine that a's are fixed constants. Then, we have a matrix of equations

$$AS + E + G + D = S$$

where A is a $n \times n$ matrix $[a_{ij}]$ and E, G, D, and S are $n \times l$ vectors. Inverting the equation, we get

$$(I - A)^{-1}(E + G + D) = S.$$

This equation enables us to decompose firms' total assets to parts due to E, G, and D respectively. For instance, given outstanding deposits of bank k, we can compute the amount of firm i's assets which are owed to the former. Let this be denoted by S_i^k and define $\rho_{ik} = S_i^k/S_i$. The author calls it the total asset dependence coefficient of firm i on outstanding deposits of bank k. It shows how strongly firm i depends on bank k. In addition, the author proposes other indicators such as the inter-firm linkage coefficient, which is the sum $b_{ij} + b_{ji}$ where b's are elements of $(I - A)^{-1}$. When both i and j refer to nonbank firms, this coefficient indicates the strength of financial linkage between the two firms.

The author takes 112 nonbank firms and 10 financial groups (combining a few related financial institutions into a group) in 1964 and conducts the quantitative analysis as outlined above. The author identifies financial affiliation of nonbank firms to respective financial groups. He finds three major patterns in this respect. In the first pattern, member firms depend very heavily upon and among themselves in addition to their dependence on group banks. This pattern is observed among three major keiretsu groups, namely, Mitsui, Mitsubishi, and Sumitomo. In the second pattern, member firms depend heavily on banks but not on each other. Yasuda and Sanwa are found to be such groups. In the third pattern, two major business groups are connected together through financial intermediation of a financial group. This is the case with the Kawasaki and Furukawa business groups joined together through the Daiichi Financial Group. Analysis of this sort proves to be highly informative. (10)

IV. Industrial Policy

The very active role that Japan's industrial policy played in promoting Japan's industrial growth in the postwar period is by now well known. The popular name Japan, Incorporated is an apt expression for the cooperation between the government

and business. (11) How did this policy emerge in postwar
Japan? Who was responsible for it? What were the concrete
and specific measures of the policy? What were the achievements of the policy? Has the policy completed its role now
that Japanese industry has matured? Does Japan need to de-
vise new policy instruments to cope with the defects of industrial organization that have become apparent in recent years?
These are a few questions related to Japan's industrial policy.
In Essay 10, Hiroya Ueno responds to some of them. And he
examines the merits and demerits of the policy. (12)

Ueno first observes that Japan had to weigh dynamic comparative advantages very seriously before its industrial policy
was formulated in the postwar reconstruction period. Which
industries should Japan be specialized in in view of the scarcity
of land, natural resources, and capital? The only abundant factor of production was well-educated labor. It was believed by
the government and business leadership that Japan should develop those industries that could create value added upon imported materials. Such industries should have a strong growth
potential. They must be promoted and protected until they became strong enough to compete internationally. Thus, the MITI
laid out a policy of promoting capital- and technology-intensive
industries. These key industries, mostly heavy and chemical
industries, exhibited increasing returns to scale, which justified the government intervention on usual infant-industry
grounds. The MITI assumed leadership in pursuing its industrial policy with priority financing and various means of incentives.

Going beyond usual qualitative discussions, Ueno statistically
documents government intervention in the sphere of industrial
policy with regard to administrative guidance, legislation, selective fund allocation, protective policy measures, and so on.

The successful outcome of the industrial protection policy
was a reduction of production cost and an improvement of product quality. By 1965, when Japanese industry was internationally competitive, the protective policy should have been
dismantled, but it was kept on for the time being. Some after-

effects of the policy began to appear in the 1970s, particularly in the form of environmental pollution, oligopolization of industry, unbalanced productivity developments among industries, and interfirm collusions through recession cartels.

V. Bibliographic Studies

Our volume concludes with two surveys of the literature in Japanese so as to help the reader in search of original sources in that literature.

In Essay 11, Toshimasa Tsuruta gives a historical account of how industry studies themselves changed in character in the course of postwar industrial development. A few major works are singled out by the author as reflecting changing views of the profession and of the general public.

Up to the late 1950s, popular attention was riveted on the issues of improving productivity in existing industries and of creating new industries. Modernization and improved productivity were given great emphasis. Technologists thus dominated discussions of industrial development at this time. The most representative of the writings in this subperiod is the eight-volume compendium edited by Hiromi Arisawa, Gendai Nihon Sangyo Koza [A Course on Contemporary Industry of Japan] (Tokyo: Iwanami Shoten, 1959).

By the mid-1960s Japanese industry had come to possess sufficiently strong international competitive power. At this time, foreign trade was significantly liberalized. The public focus shifted to this new feature, particularly on how to defend itself against the impending liberalization of capital. Modernization and development of Japanese industry in the international setting were called for as a major item on the agenda of Japan's industrial policy. Representative of the views that prevailed at the time is the nine-volume study Gendai no Sangyo [Contemporary Industry] (Tokyo: Toyo Keizai Shimpo Sha, 1967).

No single point of view has dominated public opinion since the end of the 1960s. Many ill effects of industrialization have come into the open and a number of serious economic problems

have begun to appear, such as excessive accumulation of foreign exchange, increasing oligopolization, pollution and industrial diseases, resources problems, and industrial adjustments.
At the same time, more down-to-earth industry studies have
begun to be produced by economists applying orthodox tools of
economic analysis. The market structure has been studied,
market performances have been evaluated, and policy recommendations have been put forth. The most worthy of this new
wave is the three-volume study edited by Hisao Kumagai, Nihon
no Sangyo Soshiki (Tokyo: Chuo Koron Sha, 1973-76), which has
already been referred to in section II above.

Essay 12, by Kazunori Echigo, is a straightforward literature
survey that provides the reader with detailed bibliographic cita-
tions in the field of industrial organization up to the mid-1970s.
The article appeared in the Survey of the State of Economic
Studies in Japan (in Japanese) (Tokyo: Toyo Keizai Shimpo Sha,
1975) in commemoration of the twenty-fifth anniversary of the
Union of the National Economic Associations in Japan. In the
text of Essay 12, Echigo says a few words about the state of
Japanese economic studies in industrial organization. He notes
that the subject of industrial organization established itself as
a discipline in Japan in the mid-1960s. Until then, academic
discussions were conducted mostly by Marxists, who talked
about the dual structure, keiretsu, and so on from their characteristic point of view of monopoly capitalism. It was only in
the 1960s that the Japanese economics profession came to ap-
preciate the significance of the price mechanism as a regulator
of economic activity. In the rest of the essay, the author refers
to a number of popular topics such as excessive competition
among oligopolies, merger movements and economists' reactions to them, economies of scale measurements, price behaviors, econometric studies, antimonopoly policy, the role of
small and medium-sized firms, and industry studies.

Notes

1) A summary of this book appears in Hugh Patrick and

Henry Rosovsky, eds., Asia's New Giant, How the Japanese Economy Works (Washington, D.C.: The Brookings Institution, 1976), chapter 7, pp. 459-523. For a review, see E. M. Hadley, " 'Industrial Organization' by Caves and Uekusa: A Review Article," Japanese Economic Studies, V (Winter 1976-77), 64-82.

2) The reader may consult Masao Baba and Yoshihiro Taguchi, eds., Sangyo Soshiki [Industrial Organization] (Tokyo: Nihon Keizai Shimbun Sha, 1970), a Japanese readings volume with 21 articles, most of which were published in the late 1960s.

3) Before writing this series of papers, Komiya insisted that Japanese economists should spend more effort in examining empirical data than merely speculating in theory. The approach taken in this paper is very typical of his subsequent writings which exerted significant influence upon Japanese economic thinking. See Yasukichi Yasuba, "Modern Economists' Views on the Japanese Economy — A Survey," Japanese Economic Studies, I (Winter 1972-73), 3-46, esp. 26-27, for an evaluation of Komiya's contributions.

4) It was originally published in Developing Economies, 2 (June 1964).

5) These industries are as follows: I (consumer electronics, pharmaceuticals, automobile, shipbuilding, bearings, bankings), II (iron and steel, aluminum, camera, synthetic fibers, housing, distribution of rice), III (computer, beer, foods, life insurance, medical services).

6) For banking, see Shunsaku Nishikawa, "The Banking Sector: Competition and Control," Japanese Economic Studies, II (Spring 1974), 3-52.

7) This paper is included as chapter 4 of Imai's aforementioned book.

8) For changes in concentration ratios, see Yoshihige Higuchi and Kazuo Watanabe, "General Concentration in Japan — Status and Trends," Japanese Economic Studies, II (Summer 1974), 3-61.

9) The most recent of Miyazaki's quantitative research appears in Yoshikazu Miyazaki, Sengo Nihon no Kigyo Shudan [Business Groups in Postwar Japan] (Tokyo: Toyo Keizai Shimpo Sha, 1976).

10) For further research of the author along this line, see
Yusaku Futatsugi, Nihon no Kigyo Shudan [Japan's Business
Groups] (Tokyo: Toyo Keizai Shimpo Sha, 1976).

11) See Hideichiro Nakamura, "Japan, Incorporated and
Postwar Democracy," Japanese Economic Studies, VI (Spring-
Summer 1978), 68-109

12) This paper is included in Hiroya Ueno, Nihon no Keizai
Seido [Japan's Economic Institutions] (Tokyo: Nihon Keizai
Shimbun Sha, 1978), chapter 1, pp. 3-117.

I.

JAPAN'S INDUSTRIAL ORGANIZATION: HISTORICAL PERSPECTIVE

1

"MONOPOLY CAPITAL" AND INCOME REDISTRIBUTION POLICY

Ryutaro Komiya*

Introduction

Many Marxian economists regard the contemporary Japanese economy as being at the stage of Monopoly Capitalism or State Monopoly Capitalism. They assert that Monopoly Capital, which dominates Japan, intensifies capitalist contradictions and that its exploitation of labor is the most inequitable facet of contemporary income distribution. However, non-Marxian economists like us have a number of fundamental questions about these Marxian assertions. This paper asks a few frank questions about the Marxian view of Monopoly Capital and, at the same time, intends to examine a number of important problems in the policy of income redistribution in Japan. Non-Marxian economics sets economic policy to two major tasks: first, ensuring production with high efficiency in the economy as a whole and, second, realizing an "equitable" income distribution. Though Marxian and non-Marxian economists are divided on how to look at the problem of efficiency in the contemporary Japanese economy, the problem of efficiency is set aside in this paper.

Let me enumerate a few highlights of this paper.

*Ryutaro Komiya, " 'Dokusen Shihon' to Shotoku Saibumpai Seisaku" ["Monopoly Capital" and Income Redistribution Policy], Sekai, March 1961, pp. 124-134. Translated by permission of the publisher and author. Translated by Kazuo Sato.

1) It is difficult to support the assertion that all big businesses are monopolistic and earn higher profit rates than
medium-sized and small enterprises do. In fact, the net rate of
return on equity is higher in smaller firms than in large firms.

2) The share of property income in national income distributed is not only considerably lower in postwar Japan than in prewar Japan but also much lower than in the United States, the
United Kingdom, and elsewhere.

3) The power elite that controls Japan consists typically of
managers, whose interests are not so strongly tied with property
income earners. Moreover, it seems almost inevitable that
power elites like this are found in socialist societies as well.

4) There are many conflicts of interest within the group that
is popularly lumped together as the working class. It is difficult to say that the confrontation between property owners and
workers is the fundamental one in contemporary Japan.

5) The greatest inequity in income distribution in present-day
Japan is found in the fact that executives and employees of big
businesses are paid inordinately high incomes as compared
with incomes of the public at large. Basic measures for eliminating this inequity are the elimination of the dual structure
and the popularization of education.

6) The most effective short-term measures for income redistribution are found in improving the social security system
and increasing direct taxes such as the income and inheritance
taxes. Little can be expected from the redistributional effect of
the antimonopoly policy.

This paper outlines my own ideas without intending to provide
detailed explanations or rigorous proofs. I hope that I can supplement or modify them on other occasions after the readers'
critical comments benefit me.

What Is Monopoly Capital?

Monopoly Capital, a term used in Marxian economics, is
hardly ever defined clearly. I myself am ignorant of its concept.
In his recent best-selling book, Introduction to the Japanese

Economy [Nihon Keizai Nyumon], Professor Kazuji Nagasu
seems to use the term interchangeably with Big Business.

Non-Marxian economics confronts monopoly, oligopoly, or
imperfect competition against competition. Monopoly describes
a situation in which a single firm controls a commodity market
or an industry, while oligopoly is a case where a few firms are
in command.

Monopolies and oligopolies bring about undesirable effects.
Above all, a monopolistic firm can exert a direct influence on
the commodity price, in order to earn monopoly profits by
raising it over and above the level that would correctly reflect
the relative strength of demand and supply under competitive
conditions. This is an undesirable state of affairs from the point
of view of establishing equitable income distribution. Second,
the higher price under monopoly reduces demand and reduces
production, thereby distorting the optimum allocation of national
resources such as labor, capital, and land and deteriorating the
national efficiency of production.

It goes without saying that these evils of monopoly must be
evaluated from the long-term point of view. On the one hand,
monopolistic firms may delay the development of new production techniques or the introduction of new products since they
are not challenged by competitors. This would impede economic
development in general. On the other hand, however, we must
note that a firm may have a higher profit rate because it has
been pursuing technological innovations to improve its productivity much more actively than other firms. To restrict unnec-
essarily such progressive firms from their technical innovation
activities is to impede economic development against the interest of the general public. It is therefore not easy to judge
whether evils of monopoly are apparent in any industry.

Theory of Industrial Organization and the Importance of Antimonopoly Policy

Non-Marxian economics has an important applied field in industrial organization which examines whether industrial or mar-

ket organization in specific industries is in a desirable state or
not. In this field, workable competition is defined as the state in
which a market is operated generally in an optimal manner from
the point of view of optimal resource allocation. When this state
is not realized because evils of monopolies or oligopolies are
evident or, conversely, because repetitions of unstable competition among a large number of small firms prevent firms from
attaining the optimal scale, the government must intervene in
the market mechanism in order to improve market and industrial organization. Antimonopoly policy addressed to this particular objective is regarded in the United States as a public policy.

In the United States, studies of industrial organization and antimonopoly policy are given special emphasis. Any university
economics department offers a course in industrial organization
just like other popular applied fields such as money, public finance, and international trade. Based on these studies, the government enforces very stringent antimonopoly policy. In Japan,
I regret to say, both the economics profession and the general
public are uninterested in industrial organization and antimonopoly measures. I would give 50 points to the Japanese government in its pursuance of antimonopoly policy as against, say, 80
points to the U.S. government.

At the same time, I cannot agree very much with Marxian
economists in their analysis of evils of monopoly in Japan. They
are fond of presenting statistics on market shares such as the
four-company concentration ratios in production and of describ-
ing interfirm relations such as the extent of the group control
of zaibatsu and banks over a number of firms, but seldom take
the trouble of analyzing market performances such as the monopoly power that monopolies or oligopolies exercise in raising
market prices, the monopoly-caused stagnation of technological
innovations, the amount of monopoly profits, or the restraints on
production. To be fair, I have to note that non-Marxian economists have not produced too many studies worth noting on Japanese industrial organization. I believe that there are a number
of industries apparently subject to evils of monopoly or oligopoly. But, on the other hand, there are other industries which,

though controlled by large firms, exhibit broadly desirable performances from the long-range point of view as a result of considerable competition in them.

One point that I want to mention in connection with the view that identifies Big Business with Monopoly is that the evils of monopoly do not appear in an industry whose domestic production is controlled by a few firms if they have to compete with imports. Suppose a firm "monopolizes" domestic production of a commodity in Japan. This firm is not able to raise the product price monopolistically so long as trade is liberalized and the international market of this commodity is substantially competitive. This is a reason why trade liberalization is important. In such industries as automobiles and chemicals with the optimum factory size considerably large in relation to the size of domestic markets, measures to facilitate concentration of production in a few firms so as to realize this optimum size, while maintaining competition with foreign firms, will help to bring the optimum production scale into being without realizing evils of monopoly.

Should evils of monopoly or oligopoly be inevitable in an industry even after trade liberalization, the government ought to place the operation of the industry under direct public regulation or nationalize it as a public body even though the industry is not a type usually regarded as a public utility.

Big Businesses Are Less Profitable

If big businesses are ipso facto monopoly capital, the profit rate should be higher in larger enterprises than in smaller enterprises. But facts are not likely to verify this proposition.

While it is necessary to take due caution in deciding what ratio is to be taken as the profit rate, the rate of operating profits to total assets was about 8% on average for all enterprises regardless of firm size according to the 1958 Corporate Enterprise Statistics. At the same time, the rate of net profits to equity tends to be higher in enterprises with smaller equity; it is the lowest in the biggest firms. More specifically, the rate was 22.7% in the smallest size group of firms with equity less

than 2 million yen, 25.5% and 22.3% in the two intermediate size
groups (equities with 5 to 10 million yen and 10 to 50 million
yen), and only 14.1% in the largest firms with equity of more
than 100 million yen. While small enterprises with equity less
than 5 million yen tend to have unstable and volatile profits,
medium-sized enterprises with equities from 5 to 50 million yen
tend to have stabler profits and to realize always the highest
profit rate among enterprises of different sizes. A similar pattern is observed in American firms, too.

    Results differ between profitabilities measured against total
assets and equities, largely because owned capital (equity) is
a smaller proportion of total capital in smaller corporations.
It is often stated that smaller enterprises tend to be financially
discriminated against. As far as statistics go, smaller enterprises tend to have a larger ratio of borrowed capital to owned
capital and, consequently, to have a much higher profit rate on
capitalists' own capital than big businesses do after payments
of interest (at possibly far higher interest rates than big firms
pay) and of taxes。

Japan's Property Income

    Next, let us depart from Monopoly Capital for the time being
and pay attention to the problem of income distribution between
capital and labor. A salient feature of the postwar Japanese
economy is the very low share of property income in national
income. The share of property income, namely, rental, interest, and dividend incomes of individuals, was 22.4% of national
income on average between 1934 and 1936. The share fell virtually to zero immediately after the war. Though it has been
rising gradually, it was still 6.0% in 1957 and 6.8% in 1958, not
only much below the prewar level but far less than the shares
observed in the United States (12.3%), the United Kingdom
(10.4%), and elsewhere. Of the 6.8% (in 1958), 1.5 percentage
points are rental income, the most of which was rent imputed
to 70% of people who live in their own houses, i.e., income which
can hardly be called that of the small affluent class. Further-

more, one-third of interest income, which accounts for 3.6 percentage points, is imputed interest, another special item in national income statistics that does not accrue to individuals. Dividend income, which may be most directly related to profits of
Monopoly Capital, is merely 1.7% of national income. Moreover, incomes of unincorporated individual proprietors are more
of the character of labor or managerial incomes. Generally
speaking, the propensity to save out of property income is very
high. Also, corporations' retained earnings, which are 3.3% of
national income, are wholly saved. Thus, even if the part that
is consumed out of these unearned incomes is confiscated from
the propertied class and redistributed to the general public, the
standard of consumption of the general public is to be raised by
a couple of percentage points at best. It is naïve to believe that
Monopoly Capital earns hugh monopoly profits by exploiting the
nation at large so that people's livelihood can be improved tre-
mendously if these monopoly profits are redistributed. The idea
is nothing but a fantasy. Such gains from income redistribution
is far less than the gains of annual economic growth.

The Japan Socialist Party insists that Japan was able to save
more, i.e., accumulate more, because the low wages in Japan
led to high profits. In other words, "the high postwar growth
rate of the Japanese economy is nothing but a manifestation of
Monopoly Capital's strong exploitation and low wages." But this
statement is utterly fallacious, as clearly indicated by national
income statistics. The causal chain, low wages → high profits
→ strong accumulation → rapid growth, may have applied to
prewar Japan but is completely alien to postwar Japan.

Japan's Power Elite Is Managers

In his Introduction to the Japanese Economy, Professor Nagasu states that some one million people (3% of the labor force)
control contemporary Japan. The top-ranking class of this million is 20,000 to 30,000 high-ranking bureaucrats and executives
of corporations with more than 100 million yen of equity. While
the number is small, the controlling class is extremely power-

ful, is in full control of the power machinery of Japan's economy and politics, and is in a position to exercise power over the complex contemporary economy. So far, I agree with him in broad terms. But I cannot agree with his conclusion that the remaining 97% of the nation which should be defined as the working class as against the 3% which is the capitalist class should unite themselves for improving the structure of the Japanese economy.

The ruling class of contemporary Japan consists typically of managers, not of capitalists. Managers, in cooperation with politicians, bureaucrats, and technocrats, form Japan's power elite. But is such a class nonexistent in socialist society?

Now is the time when science is so far advanced that mankind can be destroyed by the push of a single button of nuclear weaponry. Similarly, any contemporary economy is based on extremely complex interrelations, and decisions of economic policy-makers have inestimably large influences on a great many people, whether in a capitalist or in a socialist society. There is only a handful of top-ranking members in the economic and political power structure in any socialist society. It is almost inevitable that the power elite be given such huge power that a great many people depend on its pushing a button. Non-Marxian economists believe that it is more rational to operate a socialist economy based on a competitive price mechanism than to run a centralized, planned economy, but the power elite will gain more power if the socialist economy is to be operated centrally instead of relying on the price mechanism.

In the event that socialism is established by a revolution, a new power elite takes over. But there is no guarantee that the new power elite is more exemplary in the sense that it has more concern for the interests of the common people. In contemporary Japan in particular, an individual must go through a highly competitive process to achieve membership in the power elite. Most managers in Japan have come from the middle class. They have no background of inherited wealth. Moreover, Japan is now highly homogeneous as far as social classes go. Even though the revolution may change a little the rule of competition that selects members of the power elite, it seems probable that roughly the same people will emerge as members of the power elite.

The power elite in contemporary Japan does not have much interest in property income, which is 6.8% of national income. First of all, business executives' salaries are included in the miscellaneous item of earned incomes just like Diet members' compensation; salaries of junior executives are included in the item "salaries and wages." Indeed, there is no hard-and-fast boundary between the power elite and the public at large. There is a continuum in the power structure ranging from section chiefs to division heads to directors. Nor is there any discontinuity from small to big firms. In other words, one can define the ruling class narrowly or broadly as one likes, whether one looks at Japan or any socialist society. It is virtually meaningless to say that 20,000 or 30,000 people control the Japanese economy in order to exploit all others.

Members of the power elite enjoy many privileges in addition to their fat paychecks. They help each other on many occasions and take every opportunity to ensure that their offspring become members of the elite class. These privileges and good salaries are expected to survive in socialist society.

Managers are on average more competent than non-managers. Therefore, it is natural that they get paid better. Whether their higher pays are reasonable or not is a question that can be answered with value judgement alone. Before one gets infuriated over the "unreasonably" high pay of Japanese managers, one should ponder how "equitably" managers' pay is determined in a socialist society and how high a plant manager's salary is relative to a rank-and-file operative in a nationalized factory.

The "inequitableness" of income distribution depends solely on personal value judgements, beyond the scope of any objective and scientific evaluation.

Second, the rentier class, which receives interest income amounting to 3.6% of national income (including, however, imputed interest, which was mentioned above), a little over a half of property income which is 6.8% of national income, is represented only by a very weak political power in Japan. At present,

big businesses have been bringing pressure to bear upon the
government for a low-interest policy which enhances their own
profits. Consequently, it seems that bank deposits and other interest rates are sooner or later to be reduced by policy action.
There is almost no opposition from the rentier class to this
move. In other words, the power elite, mainly composed of
managers of big businesses, holds the reins of the economy,
while rentiers have almost no influence on economic and political decision making.

Contradictions in Policy Proposals of the Socialist Party

Conflicts of interest are complex among the majority of the
people who are usually lumped together as the working class.
This complexity is reflected in policy proposals of the Socialist
Party, which is supposed to represent interests of the working
class. Let us take the following three points in this connection.

The first point refers to the fact that the Socialist Party is
almost silent about how to resolve wage differentials between
large and small businesses. Property income is only a very
small fraction of national income. Thus, if wage differentials
are to be resolved, it becomes vitally important to check further
rises in wages and other income emanating from large firms so
that a greater part of the gains from economic growth can be
directed toward improving the income level of other people.
Outside of this channel, there is very little in redistributing incomes within the economy. When the Socialist Party insists
that it is more important to raise lower wages drastically than
to check higher wages since the current wage level itself is
very low, where is this increase supposed to come from? It is
not illogical if the Party suggests reduction of annual capital
accumulation in favor of consumption of workers. But this is
apparently not its suggestion because the Socialist Party wishes
to raise the economy's growth rate over and above what the
Liberal-Democratic Party wants. But, in a certain sense, it is
quite natural that the Socialist Party cannot put forth a proposal
for the redistribution of wage incomes between large and small

businesses in order to resolve wage differentials, since the
Party depends a great deal on the organized labor of big businesses for electoral votes.

Second, we must note that there is almost no difference between the agricultural policies of the Socialists and the Liberal-
Democrats. A salient feature of Japan's current policy of agricultural protection is the price-support system of rice and other
agricultural products. This protective policy results in a higher
rice price. On the one hand, people at large have to consume
rice at a high price and pay for deficits in the Food Control Account out of their taxes; on the other hand, benefits of the protective policy are enjoyed by the top one-quarter or, at most,
one-third wealthiest farmers. This is because it is those
wealthier farmers alone who can sell rice in a considerable
amount to the government. Farmers below the average can sell
almost nothing. Some farmers even have to buy rice for their
own consumption. These poor farmers cultivate such small
plots that they can hardly benefit from the government investment in land improvement. Thus, for the sake of more equitable
income redistribution, it is far more rational to decontrol rice,
to let rice prices be determined in a free market, and to allocate
the money that has been paid by people for the rice price support at a high level to really poor farmers in the form of direct
subsidies or financial aid to assist them to change their occupa-
tions. Whenever an election comes, however, both the Socialists
and the Liberal-Democrats go first, for the sake of vote getting,
to wealthy farmers who are bosses of farm villages or of farmers' cooperatives. It is therefore out of the question for these
political parties to propose the decontrol of rice, thereby making
the agricultural policies of the Socialists and the Liberal-Democrats almost indistinguishable from one another.

Third, for the same political reason, in elections the Socialist
Party proves itself to be highly sympathetic to small firms. It
presents a policy proposal giving a preferential exemption up to
the annual income of 5 million yen for small incorporated firms.
This income level corresponds to corporations up to the equity
size of 10 to 50 million yen, which have the highest net rate of

return, as we already noted. From the standpoint of income redistribution, there is, I think, no reason why incomes of medium
and small enterprises should be given preferential treatment
ahead of workers in these enterprises. The explanation that
small enterprises tend to keep wages low in order to compen-
sate for their business difficulties does not stand up in the light
of the above-mentioned statistics on corporate profitability.

In this way, the Socialists' policy proposals are largely influenced by interests of politically vociferous labor unions of big
businesses, wealthy farmers, and small firm owners at the expense of the really poverty-stricken low-income class. As I see
it, incomes of those economically and politically strong groups
such as organized workers of big businesses and managers of
small enterprises are expected to increase at the same rate as
or even at a faster rate than the rate of economic growth. But
there is a question about incomes of those at the bottom of society, namely, below-average farmers, employees of small enterprises, temporary workers of big businesses, itinerant mer-
chants, day laborers, live-in workers, and handicraft workers.
They are quite different from wage earners at large and have
not been able to share very much in economic growth.

Big Businesses Are the Privileged Class

Thus, there is doubt about, one, the assertion that Monopoly
Capital controls the Japanese economy and, two, the assertion
that the capital-labor confrontation is the most fundamental confrontation in the contemporary Japanese economy. Though there
are many conflicts and confrontations among interests in society,
non-Marxian economists do not believe that the confrontation between the owners of capital and the workers is so serious in
Japan or the United States.

In my view, the most serious inequity in income distribution
in present-day Japan is the fact that 10% or at most 20% of the
people, i.e., those who belong to the power elite or who are employees of big businesses, have much higher incomes than all
other people. Moreover, their incomes have been rising at a

faster rate than national income per capita. However, what differentials can be "equitably" allowed to incomes of managers
and employees of big businesses is a difficult question that involves a value judgement, as we already observed. Government
employees' salaries have been considerably less than those of
big businesses' employees when bonuses, housing, and other
fringe benefits are taken into account. Nonetheless, government
employees are paid better than workers of small businesses who
perform the same tasks. Therefore, we may be justified in including government employees, both high-ranking and rank-and-
file, in the privileged group consisting of big businesses' workers. While rentiers who receive large dividend and interest incomes are another inequitous presence in income distribution,
it is wrong to exaggerate the size of their incomes.

Let us now ponder what measures should be taken in income
redistribution in order to realize an equitable distribution of
income in contemporary Japan.

Inequity of the Dual Structure

First of all, though this is beyond the usual scope of income
redistribution policy, one measure is to eliminate wage differentials or the so-called dual structure that is peculiar to Japan.
Wage differentials can exist in many forms, e.g., between agriculture and industry, between different industries, between
males and females, or between number of years of service. The
most inequitable among these is that the same job is paid widely
different wages among firms of different sizes. Relative to the
wages paid by establishments with 5 to 30 employees, establishments with 30 to 100 workers pay 1.3 times more, those with
100 to 500 workers pay 1.6 times more, and those with 500 or
more workers pay as much as 2.3 times more. These wage differentials may arise because of differences in years of school
attended, in skills, in years of continued service, and so on between large and small firms. But when we consider the fact
that workers of large firms are given more fringe benefits in
kind such as company housing or recreational facilities and are

free of the risk of unemployment, it is not too far off the mark
to regard the figures we have cited as broadly indicating pay differentials for the same kind of work between large and small
enterprises.

We observed that large firms are not more profitable than
small firms. This, however, does not necessarily reject the existence of monopoly firms. While further study is needed, I conjecture that in the sense of modern economic theory there are
quite a few monopolistic firms, namely, those firms which are
capable of administering prices. These monopolistic or oligopolistic firms may enjoy higher profitability, but they pay higher
wages, too. In other words, monopoly profits which these firms
extract from buyers through their monopoly power are distributed partly to their employees as wages and salaries. This
proposition is corroborated by the fact that establishments with
500 or more employees pay annual bonuses equivalent to 3.1
months of regular pay, whereas those with 5 to 30 workers pay
only 0.9 month of regular wages as bonuses. Surely, large firms
are given much preferential treatment in the government's economic policy. But their gains seem not to be reflected in the
firms' profit rates but passed on mostly to higher wages if all
industries are taken as a whole.

I am not saying that wage differentials in Japan are entirely
due to the monopoly element and the government's preferential
treatment. Witness the fact that big businesses in highly competitive industries also pay high wages similar to those paid in
less competitive industries.

The most fundamental cause of wage differentials is in the extremely low mobility of labor in Japanese enterprises as well
as in the government and academe under the dominant influence
of the lifetime employment or seniority systems. Managers of
big businesses believe that in order to be worthy of their size
their firms ought to maintain traditional paternalism by treating
their employees well under the lifetime employment or seniority
systems and by paying wages as good as those paid by other big
firms. In addition, enterprise unions, also peculiar to Japan,
which appeared after the war applied a further momentum to en-

larging wage differential far beyond what existed before the war.
It is very difficult, socially and politically, to eliminate these
differentials. For instance, many big businesses employ regular
workers and temporary workers. While they do the same work,
working side by side in the same workshop of the same factory,
the latter are paid less than a half of the former. Regular employees are subject, in principle, to lifetime employment, but
temporary workers are employed on an understanding that they
can be discharged at a moment's notice. They are not allowed
to join regular workers' unions. Because of the extreme convenience of the system of temporary workers who can be fired
any time and paid far lower wages, it seems that big businesses
have been expanding employment of temporary workers rather
than regular workers. Regular workers do nothing to rectify
this situation even though both regular and temporary workers
are members of the working class. Judging from this factor
alone, we must anticipate a large impediment in the way of eliminating wage differentials and the dual structure because those
who want them eliminated have little say in the whole affair.
Unless the labor market becomes free and competitive to the
extent that it is not unusual for blue-collar and white-collar
workers to move from one firm to another once in every five
or ten years just as in the United States and Europe, wage differentials are not likely to be resolved.

Popularization of Education

Second, while this measure, too, is not included in usual measures of income redistribution, we note that managers, engineers, and more-educated workers are paid higher salaries,
primarily because there are not too many people who have acquired professional knowledge and skills through higher education. Consequently, when education is more popularized (also,
rectifying the present situation in which only a few universities
are capable of giving qualified instruction) so that there are
more well-educated workers, the income gap between managers,
engineers, and professionals on the one hand and rank-and-file

workers on the other tends naturally to narrow. The recent emphasis on economics of higher education in the United States and
Europe reflects this sort of view.

For the time being, it is important in Japan to increase the
government expenditure on education, particularly on universities and vocational high schools, as well as training of skilled
workers, and to improve the scholarship system. It may be
noted that scholarships need not be given gratis. Since those
who have received more education get higher incomes than those
who received less education, they should be required to pay back
scholarships given by the nation (with proper interest charges
if need be).

Financial Sources of Social Security

Third, it must be noted that measures to eliminate the dual
structure and to popularize education cannot serve immediate
purposes because they can become effective only after a long
lapse of time. Therefore, what is immediately needed is improvement of the social security system. But social security
is costly. Though some suggest that expenditures on defense or
public investment should be curtailed to expand the expenditure
on social security, the expenditures on defense, education, and
the like should be dispensed with first of all if not needed, regardless of the necessity of social security, and be maintained
if needed. We must find means to finance social security. A
large increase in tax revenue will be needed if social security
is to be established on a reasonably satisfactory scale instead
of merely patching up the current very imperfect system.

Lately there has been a strong demand for reducing taxes.
In last year's general election, both the Socialists and the
Liberal-Democrats advanced virtually identical tax-cut proposals. A tax reduction is expected to come into effect this January. Frankly speaking, I am against the tax reduction. Those
who benefit from the cut in income taxes are in the top income
quartile. There is little merit in a policy that favors the
wealthiest. Instead of the tax cut, the expenditure on social

security should have been increased. One can understand why
the Liberal-Democrats call for a tax cut. But how can the Socialists propose a tax cut just for the sake of getting votes in the
election? Japan's Socialist Party may be the only one among
all socialist parties in advanced nations to raise such a proposal.

I foresee that the ratio of tax revenue or public finance to
GNP tends naturally to increase as society advances. To have
a dream of cheap government is nothing but a poor vision of
economic progress. As for tax policy, we should emphasize the
equitable burden of direct taxes, centering on income taxes,
which are defrayed by individuals.

Those who are critical of Monopoly Capital often insist on increasing the corporation tax to be paid by big businesses. The
corporation tax, however, is similar in a way to indirect taxes.
As it may tend to be imposed on the public at large, it is not
very significant in the income redistribution policy.

Equitable Burden of the Income Tax

Fourth then, it is important to make the burden of the income
tax more "equitable." Two loopholes must be eliminated from
the present tax system. The first is concerned with capital
gains, the most inequitable element of the present income tax
code.

In Japan, of capital gains arising from changes in asset valuation, those of securities, including corporate stocks, are excluded from taxation for the express purpose of promoting capital accumulation. But this exclusion leads to an extreme inequity and is often used for tax evasion. If capital gains of corporate stocks are roughly equal to corporate retained earnings,
their total is about 3.3% of national income or twice as large as
dividend income. Though it is difficult to tax capital gains of
this kind, it is not impossible to do so in Japan since it is done
in the United States. Taxing these capital gains is expected to
lower the saving rate to some extent, but Japan has been saving
a great deal, for example, as much as 36% of GNP in 1959 for
capital formation. I believe that the average growth rate of 8

to 10% per annum can be maintained even at a somewhat lower rate of capital accumulation. I also feel that equitable income redistribution should be given more emphasis than economic growth.

Another inequity is found in the very favorable tax treatment accorded to employees of big businesses. These firms maintain many welfare and recreational facilities such as company-owned hospitals, housing, stores, or mountain villas. They are tax-free pay in kind. As these hidden allowances to employees greatly differ among enterprises, they should all be treated as income and all company expenses involved should be taxed. Individual employees should be taxed for housing and the like, while the expenditures on welfare facilities which cannot be allocated to individual employees should be taxed at a uniform rate of, say, 30 or 40% for the sake of reducing inequity. The same applies to company expenses on entertainment.

Another measure to reduce wage differentials between large and small businesses to some degree is to impose heavy taxes on bonuses. As mentioned earlier, big businesses pay three months' regular pay as bonuses, while small businesses pay less than a month's pay for them. Also, within a single firm, employees at lower ranks are paid less than those at higher ranks. This makes bonuses more like distributed profits. Therefore, we may suggest that bonuses be treated like executives' bonuses which are taxed twice, first as part of corporate income and second as personal income. No labor-income exemption is to be allowed on workers' bonuses. This can be an effective way to eliminate wage differentials between large and small firms. Though there is no strong political power that backs up this sort of a proposal, there is also no reason why it should be objected to in the name of reducing inequity.

Fifth, the income tax must be "equitable." It is another difficult problem to determine what degree of progressiveness is the most "equitable." Also, it is often mentioned that excessively progressive taxation impairs workers' willingness to work or to save, thereby hindering the optimum allocation of resources. Non-Marxian economists believe that they cannot

disregard the adverse effects of the income tax upon the allocation of resources just as they cannot ignore the evils of indirect
taxation. In contrast, increasing inheritance and gift taxes has
very little adverse effect and may be supported by many persons
regardless of their value judgments. Farmers in particular
probably object strongly to the 100% inheritance taxation. But
it would be difficult to try to object to the 100% taxation on inheritances from parents to children, apart from that between
spouses, provided that people can easily find jobs even though
they have no property and that there is a well-established
scholarship system.

Finally, the antimonopoly policy is also important in redistributing income. But its real effect must be very limited because, as we already observed, monopoly profits are partially
paid to workers as wages and salaries. It is very doubtful as to
how much of dividend income (currently 1.7% of national income)
and executives' remunerations (currently 0.4%) can be reduced
by strengthening the antitrust policy. If there are no wage differentials and if the extent of monopoly is directly reflected in
the profit rate, profits of more profitable monopoly firms can be
for the most part extracted as taxes by applying progressive
corporate taxation on the basis of profit rates, namely, setting
a certain corporate tax rate on profits of corporations whose
profit rates are between, say, 10 and 15%, and so on. According
to the profit data of the Corporate Enterprise Statistics, however, it seems that in Japan small enterprises are the ones that
would be most heavily hit by this kind of taxation.

Thus, I find the significance of the antimonopoly policy in
Japan chiefly in its power to improve industrial organization and
consequently improve efficiency of the economic system as a
whole. The income redistribution policy, therefore, has to depend primarily on direct taxes like personal income and inheritance taxes and on social security.

2

THE DUAL STRUCTURE
OF THE JAPANESE ECONOMY
AND ITS GROWTH PATTERN

Ken'ichi Miyazawa*

I. Introduction

The coexistence of premodern and modern economic forms is a
"dualistic" character commonly found in developing countries,
not only in production and distribution methods but also in the mode
of life. In this article, the dualistic character, mainly in the
sphere of production methods, will be considered.

As far as the coexistence of premodern and modern methods of production is concerned, Japan and underdeveloped countries in Asia have something in common. In Japan, however,
premodern and modern branches are unified in a national economy, whereas in Asia's underdeveloped countries they remain
marked by the colonial economy and the mono-culture economy.
In the case of underdeveloped countries, the term "dualistic
state" or "dualism," employed by A. O. Hirschman (1) should
be used, as opposed to the "dual structure," a concept which
applies to Japan.

*Ken'ichi Miyazawa, "The Dual Structure of the Japanese
Economy and Its Growth Pattern," The Developing Economies,
2 (June 1964), 147-170, reprinted in Ken'ichi Miyazawa, Input-
Output Analysis and the Structure of Income Distribution, Lecture Notes in Economics and Mathematical Systems No. 116
(Berlin: Springer-Verlag, 1976), chapter 6, pp. 100-128, with
minor revisions. Reprinted by permission of the author and
the publisher.

22

Unlike industrial development in Western Europe, where modernization delivered a frontal attack on premodern techniques, in Asian countries modernization may keep them alive for a long period. This particular tendency has been pointed out by A. O. Hirschman; in contradiction to many other authors, he maintains that dualism is "the reason for dualistic development" (2), which has some compensating advantages and which represents in a way an attempt by an underdeveloped country to make the best of its resources during a transitional phase. So long as wage differentials exist between the modern and premodern branches, "premodern" industries will probably have an opportunity of prolonging their life and thus creating a valuable period for transition to "modern" operation. On the other hand, existing premodern enterprises run little danger of being eliminated, since new enterprises usually emerge in an industrial group which is entirely different from the current native industry. This "dualistic state" could certainly be retained and utilized, but, as Hirschman concedes, premodern branches will sooner or later succumb to modern production methods. It is, however, characteristic of Japan that not only did the above-mentioned adaptation in utilizing the dualistic state develop, but the process of adaptation in organizing complementary relations within the framework of the whole national economy developed as well.

Differentials in modern and premodern branches, which are found in Asian underdeveloped countries, produce a polarization involving high income and low income. Moreover, these two branches have a strong tendency to coexist in a heterogeneous and unincorporative form. It is a main feature of underdeveloped countries, considered as a stereotype, that traditional and modern branches coexist without being mixed, like water and oil. However, in Japan, modern branches include premodern branches in the working mechanism of the national economy: large modern enterprises and traditional medium and small enterprises are in a complementary relation, the latter depending on the development of the former; on the other hand, large enterprises use the cheap-labor products of medium

and small enterprises and regard them as a cushion against
business fluctuations.

II. Economic Growth and Differentials in Capital Intensity by Size of Firm

1) Schema of Capital Concentration and Growth of Enterprises

Let us refer to R. F. Harrod's famous "fundamental equation
of economic growth," $GC = S$ (3), and apply it to the problem of
the growth of enterprises by size of firm. As is proved by many
statistical analyses, the larger the scale of an enterprise, the
higher the capital-output ratio (C), whereas the smaller the
scale, the lower the ratio. Consequently, even in the case where
medium and small enterprises would grow at the same rate as
large enterprises, the capital accumulation ratio (S) required
for the realization of the growth rate (G) will be small because
of the low capital-output ratio, while on the other hand, the high
capital-output ratio of large enterprises makes the required
capital accumulation ratio extremely large. This means that
large enterprises cannot meet the high required capital accumulation ratio with retained earnings, even though they have a
large amount of owned capital. As a result, they must depend
upon outside capital to a considerable extent.

Such a tendency is of special relevance in an economy where,
as in Japan, the ratio of owned capital to total capital is particularly low as compared with the international level. Moreover,
the high rate of growth continued after the war has strengthened this tendency. Large enterprises must now rely on outside funds to a greater degree than medium and small enterprises. Here we find a prime motive for the close connection
between large enterprises and banks, and the consequent concentration of bank loans and discounts in enterprises of larger
scale. However, there are some factors necessary for the
realization of this motive. It is a fact that larger enterprises
have a strong borrowing power as a result of their privileged
position in regard to capital accessibility. This capital acces-

sibility depends, after all, upon the power of owned capital in large enterprises. Generally speaking, the greater the owned capital, the better the credit rating, and large enterprises enjoy a favorable position especially in regard to borrowing long-term funds. Indeed, statistical data indicate that owned capital of large enterprises is greater than medium and small enter-prises not only in absolute amount, but also in the ratio of owned-capital to working capital (the debit side in the balance sheet).

Even though large enterprises are thus able to actualize a high required capital-accumulation ratio, the high capital-output ratio itself constitutes an unfavorable condition. It means that capital efficiency or capital productivity is relatively unfavor-able, and also that the depreciation cost and interest charge are high. However, these disadvantages are eliminated by a high productivity of labor.

In order to explain high labor productivity in the simplest form, let us consider a "fundamental equation of productivity," $yc = k$, corresponding to Harrod's equation of economic growth. In this equation, y denotes the amount of output per worker, c the capital-output ratio (the average capital-output ratio) and k the capital intensity (that is, the amount of capital stock per worker). (4)

In order to improve in large enterprises the relationship of the capital-output ratio (c) and high labor productivity (y) which progresses at a greater rate than in medium and small enter-prises, production methods must be adopted so that capital in-tensity (k) more than offsets the progress of (c) , as indicated by the fundamental equation of productivity. Only then can higher productivity be achieved. In large enterprises the adop-tion of high capital intensity means at the same time a high ac-cumulation of capital stock; it corresponds to capital concentra-tion on the financial side.

In sum, a high capital-output ratio in large enterprises has two aspects, financial and material/technical, and these can be disposed in a schema of capital concentration in larger enter-prises (Figure 1).

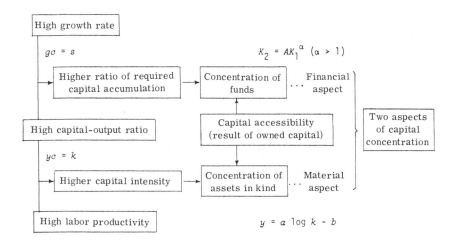

Figure 1. Schema of capital concentration in large enterprises.

In regard to finances, the high capital-output ratio means an increase in the ratio of required capital accumulation, and this provokes a concentration of funds. On the other hand, in regard to the technical aspect of production, the high capital-output ratio means an increase in capital intensity needed for achieving higher productivity, which leads to a concentration of capital stock. This double concentration is made possible because large enterprises enjoy capital accessibility. Mathematical formulas can be used, but first more elements of analysis are required.

2) Differentials in Wages and Capital Intensity

Looking at capital concentration from the technical aspect, what is the basic underpinning of the dual structure of the Japanese economy? Various economic, social, institutional, and historical factors with different influences are at play. If one is omitted, the remaining factors are insufficient to give the full picture. Although there is a real danger in going to extremes, let us concentrate on two fundamental factors: (1) the pressure of excess supply of labor or of potential unemployment, and (2) the unequal distribution of capital accessibility.

It is a well-known fact that wage differentials in Japan are greater than in other countries, and the explanation is mostly given from the viewpoint of the special character of the labor market. On the supply side of labor, there exists the pressure of excess supply, causing a search for employment at low wages. On the demand side, medium and small enterprises plan production with low-wage labor, whereas large enterprises are able to obtain better labor at wages relatively higher than the difference in quality. On the labor market itself, labor immobility is characteristic of large enterprises; they have a seniority wage system with automatic increment as years of service lengthens, on the premise of life-long employment. There is some turnover from large enterprises to medium and small enterprises, but the reverse movement is out of the question. Under these circumstances, wages in medium and small enterprises subjected to the pressure of excess supply of labor are low, and their employees cannot receive the same wages as in large enterprises, even in cases of long service. The result is a structure of wage differentials by size of firm.

This view certainly grasps one of the key points of the problem. However, it has not taken into consideration the conditions of production which give large enterprises the capacity to pay higher wages, nor does it explain Japan's high rate of economic growth and the permanence of the dual structure. Differentials in productivity and the underlying differentials in the composition of capital accumulation must be examined. (5)

Table 1 gives a summary of the main indicators; their relationship is corroborated in Figure 2.

The upper part of this figure indicates that by locating capital intensity (tangible fixed assets per employee) by size of firm on the horizontal axis, and labor productivity (value added per employee or turnover per employee) on the vertical axis, correlating points (represented by white or black points on the curves) can be plotted according to the size of firm.

In enterprises of the smallest size (employing less than 10 persons), value added productivity is ¥180,000 and capital in-

tensity ¥ 70,000, while in the largest (employing 1,000 or more
persons), value added productivity is ¥900,000 to ¥1,000,000
and capital intensity ¥600,000 to ¥700,000. The difference in
capital intensity is 9 to 10 times, causing a difference in productivity of 5 to 6 times. Between these extremes, enterprises
of the sizes 2,3,4,... in order of capital intensity form a con-
vex curve of productivity moving from the lower left to the upper right. As shown in the figure, the semi-logarithmic formula $y = a \log k - b$ fits the productivity curve, and the Cobb-
Douglas logarithmic formula is also satisfactorily verified,
but the curve fits the semi-logarithmic type better. The realization of high productivity in large enterprises is assured by
a greater increase in capital intensity than an increase in the
capital-output ratio with the enlargement of size (as illustrated
in the lower part of the figure).

Wage differentials are also found in Figure 2. Locating average annual wages per employee on the vertical axis, the amount
is ¥100,000 in the smallest class and ¥300,000 in the largest,
the difference being 3 times. When the average annual wages
are correlated with capital intensity in a linear form (black
points on the straight dotted line), a clear linear correlation
appears. Thus, considerable differentials in productivity are
a cause of wage differentials, and differentials in capital intensity are a cause of differentials in productivity. As shown
by the linear correlation formula indicated in the figure, in
marginal terms, when the differential in capital intensity increases by ¥100,000 as a result of an increase in scale, wage
differentials increase by ¥28,000 and more. The strong capital accessibility of large enterprises makes possible the adoption of high capital-intensive production methods, which in turn
make possible high productivity and high-wage capacity. On
the other hand, medium and small enterprises are forced to
adopt labor-intensive methods with a low technical level (or
low capital intensity), due to their weakness in regard to capital accessibility; this disadvantage is compensated by low
wages, due to the pressure of an excess labor force and potential unemployment.

Table 1

Productivity, Capital Intensity, Capital-Output Ratio and Wage Rate by Size of Firm (1957)

| Size by number of employees | Number of firms | Productivity | | Capital intensity K/L (thousand yen per employee) | Capital-Output ratio | | Wage rate W/L (thousand yen per employee) |
		Value added O/L (thousand yen per employee)	Turnover T/L (thousand yen per employee)		Value added K/O	Turn-over K/T	
1 1- 9	300,374	186	541	69	0.371	1.128	114
2 10- 29	77,644	289	904	78	0.270	0.086	136
3 30- 49	13,332	348	1,140	91	0.261	0.080	145
4 50- 99	8,460	420	1,392	120	0.285	0.086	157
5 100- 199	3,146	492	1,548	166	0.337	0.107	172
6 200- 299	981	564	1,716	209	0.371	0.122	187
7 300- 499	645	696	2,088	309	0.445	0.148	205
8 500- 999	441	780	2,328	408	0.523	0.175	230
9 1,000-1,999	222	922	2,886	589	0.639	0.204	259
10 2,000-4,999	135	1,078	2,872	687	0.669	0.245	301
11 5,000-9,999	46	866	2,393	558	0.729	0.233	287
12 10,000 or more	28	897	2,643	651	0.727	0.245	329
Total	405,424	516	1,560	289	0.560	0.185	194

Source: The data are taken from Ministry of International Trade and Industry, Chusho-Kigyo Sogo Kihon Chosa (Basic Survey on Medium and Small Enterprises), 1957.

Note: Manufacturing industry only. Includes both incorporated and unincorporated firms.

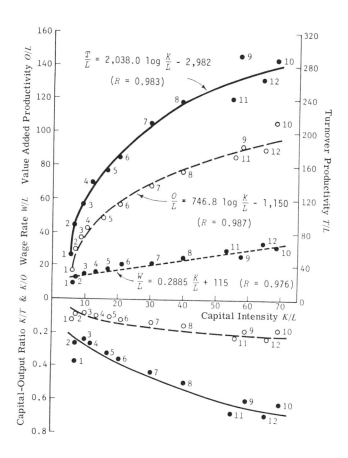

Figure 2. Relation between capital intensity and productivity by size of firm. Source: Figure 2 is based on the analysis conducted by the author at the Economic Research Institute, Economic Planning Agency. See K. Miyazawa and others, "Capital Structure by Firm-Size," Economic Bulletin (in English), No. 6, edited by the Economic Research Institute, Economic Planning Agency, Tokyo, 1961. For original data, see Table 1. Note: The numbers represent the size of the firm based on the number of employees: the size increases as one goes up from 1 to 12.

3) Permanence of the Dual Structure

A hypothetical interpretation of the above situation is given in Figure 3, where differentials in the sphere of production are indicated by the distance between two dotted curves, namely, the production function in large enterprises (f_a) and the production function in small enterprises (f_b). For the sake of simplicity, differentials in cost are assumed to be represented mainly by wage differentials. Wage rates of large and small enterprises are given on the vertical axis by points a and b respectively, the difference ab representing the wage differential.

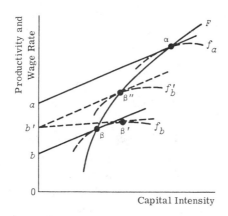

Figure 3. Hypothetical graph of the permanence of differentials.

In this case, the production point of the maximum profit rate in large enterprises (obtained by drawing a tangent line from a to the production function f_a) is α, and in small enterprises β. Consequently, the observed productivity curve is F (solid curve); it is considered to correspond to the actually observed productivity curve by size of firm illustrated in Figure 2. In Figure 3, the profit rates of large and small enterprises (the slope of the tangent line) are supposed to be equal; but even if differentials in the profit rate are supposed, there is no change in the situation.

If we suppose that, for some reason or another, wage differentials are narrowing, the distance of cost points ab declines to ab'. In this case, the production point of small enterprises shifts from β to β', resulting in a decline in the profit rate (the slope of the tangent line). Consequently, if small enterprises intend, under the new wage rate, to obtain the same rate of profit as in the past, there is no other alternative but to adopt high-grade production techniques f_b', and raise the production point to β''. If the wage differential ab' narrows to "zero," and f_b' coincides with f_a as all enterprises achieve an almost identical level of production, this level would coincide with the production function of the original J. Robinson type. (6) The reason why J. Robinson succeeded in producing a productivity curve for the economy as a whole is due to the fact that she tacitly presupposed a homogeneous economy where various differentials are almost negligible. The actual conditions in Japan, however, do not warrant such a presupposition.

The first fundamental condition to be considered in the existence of differentials in capital accessibility. Owing to their extreme weakness in capital accessibility, small enterprises relying on their own strength cannot raise their capital intensity to a point corresponding to β'', nor adopt new techniques (f_b'). Under such circumstances, and though many more complex factors will be at work, in substance there are four possibilities: (1) to survive, being contented with a low profit rate at point β', and generating differentials in the profit rate; (2) remain at point β or thereabout by hiring new cheap labor, and failing to narrow the wage differentials; (3) when the above two cases are impossible, small enterprises may disappear or (4) receive assistance, financial and technical, by subcontracting for large enterprises, and adopting new techniques β''.

Which of these possibilities has the highest probability? The disappearance of small enterprises, possibility (3), is of common occurrence; their survival at the cost of a low profit rate, possibility (1), can also be expected in many cases. But in view of the pressure of excess supply of labor, as obtained for a long period after the war, the survival of small enterprises

at a low production point, possibility (2), can be said to have
been the most probable case.　Another trend, however,
points toward possibility (4).　In some categories of industry,
large enterprises undergoing technical innovation tend to develop subcontracting medium and small enterprises, by giving
them assistance in raising funds, providing technical guidance,
lending idle machinery, etc.　This results in an improvement
in the dual structure.　However, two qualifications must be
added here.　Technical innovations are introduced into the large
enterprises themselves which provoke the development of the
subcontracting system.　The result is that, according to Figure 3, a shift to the upper right of the production function in
large enterprises f_a precedes the shift to the upper right of f_b
caused by the modernization of medium and small enterprises.
Consequently, the trend toward possibility (4) will not necessarily be sufficient to bridge the gap in the dual structure.　Furthermore, there are second, third, and more subcontractors.
When large enterprises force a reduction of unit price, the
burden will be passed on further down the line.

　　Thus, even if possibility (4) becomes prevalent, differentials
will never be improved as a whole, as long as the unequal distribution of capital accessibility and pressure of excess supply
of labor remain.　The slowing down of the rate of labor population increase and the increasing trend of demand for labor due
to capital formation are favorable factors, and worthy of attention.　Let us, however, turn to the problem of capital accessibility.

III. Differentials in Composition of Funds and Interest Rates

1) Funds of Enterprises and Capital Accessibility

　In Figure 3, capital accessibility related to the owned capital
of the enterprise is presented as one of the shift parameters
of the productivity curve f_a, f_b.　Based on available data in
Table 2, the correlation between owned capital K_1 and long-

Table 2

Differentials of Capital Intensity, Owned Capital
and Long-term Borrowings by Size of Firm

Size of firm (total assets) (¥ million)	Long-term capital per employee $K_1 + K_2$	Owned capital per employee K_1	Long-term borrowing per employee K_2	Capital intensity (tangible fixed assets per employee)
0- 2	70.2	65.6	4.6	58.7
2- 5	68.3	60.2	8.1	60.2
5- 10	95.7	83.9	11.8	102.0
10- 30	167.7	143.2	24.5	142.6
30- 50	186.0	121.0	65.0	182.2
50- 100	226.9	188.8	38.1	186.0
100- 500	459.7	375.8	85.2	334.8
500- 1,000	640.7	425.8	214.9	533.0
1,000- 5,000	1,014.8	685.7	329.1	739.9
5,000-10,000	1,589.2	1,186.6	402.6	1,018.6
10,000	1,316.7	1,015.3	301.4	988.9
Average	708.0	529.9	178.1	525.3

Source: Data are based on Ministry of Finance, Hojin Kigyo
Tokei Nempo [Yearbook of Corporate Enterprise Statistics],
1957. Manufacturing industry only. Unincorporated firms
are not included.

Note: Long-term capital = Owned capital + Long-term borrowings. Owned capital = Capital + Capital surplus + Earned
surplus (including net profit and loss for the current term).
Long-term borrowings = Corporate debenture + Long-term
borrowings from financial institutions.

term debt K_2 (the amount per person based on the number of
workers by size of firm) is found to be $K_2 = 0.0667K_1^{1.303}$
The elasticity of the long-term debt to owned capital is 1.30.
An elasticity greater than 1.00 means that an expansion of
owned capital to enlarge firm size is accompanied by a greater

increase in long-term debts than owned capital. In other words, when owned capital rises by one percent following enlargement of size, long-term debts increase by 1.3 percent. It may be concluded that, for an enterprise, the size of owned capital indicates its degree of capital accessibility (7), and that the competitive position of a firm in the capital market is limited by the amount of owned capital.

Since the size of owned capital is the fundamental factor for capital accessibility, the larger the amount of owned capital, the more capital-intensive methods of production are adopted due to the realization of high productivity and inclination towards high capital accumulation. Such a view is not sufficient to explain the high capital intensity in large enterprises. If in Japan the low wage-level is due to the pressure of excess supply of labor, the adoption of labor-intensive methods of production would be profitable even to large enterprises, or at least differentials would not be as large as actually experienced. Nevertheless, capital intensity in large enterprises is high. Why? Various factors must be considered. For instance, Japanese enterprises manifest a strenuous drive to attain the advanced technical levels of developed countries. However, on the financial side, a cause is the fact that the price of capital (interest rate) is relatively cheap for large enterprises.

2) Differentials in Interest Rates on Borrowed Funds and Cost of Funds

Adequate data of differentials in interest rates by size of enterprises are not easily available. In 1958, small enterprises with a capitalization of ￥5 million and less bore an average interest rate of 17 percent, while large enterprises with a capitalization of ￥100 million and over used borrowed funds bearing the relatively low average interest rate of 11 percent as shown in Table 3.

Figure 4 gives the cost schedule of raising funds. Attention is given mainly to the solid curve I in the center. The imputed cost of funds is measured on the vertical axis. On the horizon-

Table 3

Average Level of Interest Rates on Borrowings
by Size of Firm

Years	— Size classified by paid-in capital — (unit: percent)					
	-¥2 million	¥2-5 million	¥5-10 million	¥10-50 million	¥50-100 million	¥100 million
1956	15.36	14.52	14.28	14.19	13.35	12.24
1957	12.79	15.11	14.40	14.79	12.59	10.23
1958	17.38	17.80	16.49	13.84	13.62	11.15

Source: Based on published data in Ministry of Finance, Hojin Kigyo Tokei Nempo [Yearbook of Corporate Enterprise Statistics], 1956-58. Figures are obtained by dividing yearly interest payments by the outstanding amount of borrowed funds at the end of the year (long- and short-term borrowings plus corporate debentures).

Note: The average interest rate in the manufacturing industry = the sum of interest payment discount ÷ (short-term borrowings from financial institutions + long-term borrowings + corporate debentures).

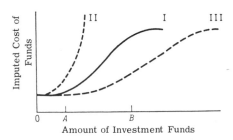

Figure 4. Cost schedule for investment funds.

tal axis, total funds employed are measured, being put in the order of advantageous sources of investment funds, namely

(a) internal funds (retained net earnings, depreciation allowances, etc.), (b) borrowings of various kinds, and (c) equity
issues.

1. Since internal funds may be used freely by the enterprise,
their investment does not incur any cash cost. However, if
these funds are invested outside, earnings corresponding to the
interest rate would be obtained. In this sense, the internal investment of these funds means the sacrifice of such external
earnings, the so-called opportunity cost. If the enterprise has
internal funds to the amount of $0A$, the accumulation would be
made with a nearly perfect elasticity to its opportunity cost.

2. In case an enterprise is forced to raise external funds,
the use of funds raised through borrowings from financial institutions and the issue of debentures is accompanied by a cash
cost in terms of interest payments, as well as imputed costs.
This brings about a rise in cost per unit of funds raised up to
the point B. Real interest rates (cash cost plus imputed cost)
rise with the increase in the amount of debts, because risk
premiums are charged.

3. The raising of funds through the issue of stock costs
more than other sources of funds, because of the expenses for
issuing, the care taken to protect the market prices of the existing stock, the disadvantages as to taxation, etc. However,
as long as enterprises accept this high cost, the raising of
funds through the issue of equities would not be so inelastic
as in the case of borrowed funds; it may even be considered
as quite elastic. The shape of the curve I on the right side of
point B represents this fact.

This is the graph of the cost schedule for investment funds
as shown by J. Dusenberry. (8) It must, however, be revised
in an economy with a dual structure, because the cost schedule
for investment funds shows a great difference according to
size of enterprise.

Going back to Figure 4, in medium and small enterprises,
owned capital is small in absolute amount; therefore, as indicated by the broken curve II on the left side, the gradual increase begins early. In addition, the weakness of medium and

small enterprises in raising funds results in a rapid advance
of imputed costs of borrowing, and will steepen the upward
slope. Further, the raising of funds through the issue of stock
and debentures runs into prohibitive difficulties, due to peculiarities of the Japanese capital market. Consequently, the
cost schedule for investment funds II ends by being entirely
inelastic.

The cost schedule for investment funds of large enterprises
is represented by the broken curve III on the right side of Figure 4. The amount of internal funds and the slope of the upward
curve are not independent of one another. It may be said that
the larger the internal funds, the slower the slope of the upward
curve, because, owing to the capital power of large enterprises,
funds can be borrowed at lower cost. Moreover, as large enterprises in Japan have little risk attached to their borrowing
of external funds, it must be considered that this upward part
is actually more elastic than is illustrated, being nearly horizontal. Further, under the existing circumstances, the cost
of expanding net worth through the issue of stocks being fairly
high for large enterprises, it is plausible that the right-hand
part of the curve III, rather than being continuous as in Figure 4, will in fact be discontinuous and jump to a certain higher
level. At any rate, it is clear from Figure 4 that the difference
between large and small enterprises in the cost schedule for
investment funds causes a marked disparity in the average
cost of raising funds per unit of total capital employed. Relatively higher interest rates are paid by small enterprises, and
relatively lower rates by large enterprises.

In Japan, an almost institutionalized relationship exists between the different sizes of enterprise and various types of financial institutions in accordance with the capital accessibility
of the enterprise. Figure 5 establishes the fact.

This Figure may be called the X-type intersection of borrowed funds of enterprises by size of firm. Enterprises by
size of firm are measured on the horizontal axis, and various
ratios of borrowed funds by lenders to total borrowed funds on
the vertical axis. The ratio a (city banks) can be considered

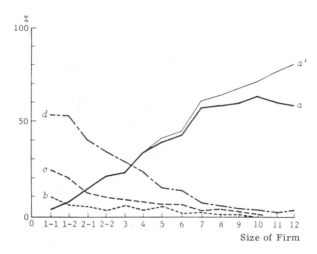

Figure 5. Composition of borrowed funds. Source: Same as
Figure 2. Notes: 1. The size of enterprises on the horizontal
axis is measured by the number of employees, increasing
from 1 (1-10 employees) to 12 (10,000 and more employees).
2. This chart shows the ratio of loans from each lending institution to total loans:
  a - city banks
  a' - city banks plus long-term credit banks and trust banks
  b - customers
  c - b plus money-lenders, relatives, and acquaintances
  d - c plus financial institutions for medium and small en-
         terprises.

as an indicator of the borrowing power of enterprises in each
size group: it increases monotonically as the size of the enterprise becomes larger, except for a small decline at the largest
size, but if borrowed funds from long-term credit banks and
trust banks are added (a'), it exhibits a smooth upward line.
   The ratio b (funds borrowed from customers) can be considered as an indicator reflecting in part the subcontracting relationship. The curve is high in the case of medium firms as a

reflection of the tendency of medium and small enterprises to come under the control of large ones. The ratio c (funds borrowed from money-lenders, relatives, and acquaintances) and the ratio d (funds borrowed from various medium and small financial institutions) follow a smooth downward curve. The weak borrowing power of medium and small enterprises is manifested by their high degree of dependence on these small financial institutions. The X-type intersection of the curves a and d is a clear reflection of the dual structure viewed from the financial angle. In other words, small enterprises survive by depending for a considerable part of their funds on money lenders, customers, relatives and acquaintances, who can be termed "marginal suppliers of funds." On the other hand, large enterprises subsist in dependence on the role of the Bank of Japan as a "marginal supplier of funds," namely by its advances through the intermediary of city banks to the extent corresponding to the firms' liquidity position. Such a situation is practically an institutional feature of Japan.

3) Differentials in Interest Rates and Unequal Distribution of Loans

Differentials in interest rate and composition of funds, examined above from the borrowing side, must now be investigated from the lending side.

Table 4 indicates the average rates of interest by type of financial institutions. The average interest rate of financial institutions for medium and small enterprises (mutual loans & savings banks, credit associations) are considerably higher than those of city banks and local banks for loans (loans on deeds, loans on bills) and discounts (discount of bills): differentials spread from 7.98 percent p.a. for city banks to 12.47 percent p.a. for credit associations. These are averages, of course; rates vary also according to borrowers.

Large enterprises are able to select the lender banks, which are then forced to put up with interest rates at nearly "competitive prices," while for medium and small enterprises lenders

Table 4

Differentials in Average Rates of Interest
by Type of Lending Institutions (1957)

	Loans % p.a.	Discounts % p.a.
City banks	7.98	8.42
Local banks	8.54	9.10
Long-term credit banks	9.41	7.87
Trust banks	8.03	8.11
Mutual loans & savings banks	10.75	10.40
Credit associations	12.47	12.47

Source: The Bank of Japan, Hompo Keizai Tokei [Economic
Statistics of Japan], 1957.

are in a monopolistic position, selecting borrowers and charg-
ing interest at "monopolistic prices." If it were possible to
imagine some "equilibrium interest rate" which equates supply of and demand for total funds of all financial institutions,
banks as a whole would extend loans to large enterprises at
lower interest rates than the equilibrium rate, and make up the
deficits thus incurred by higher rates on loans to medium and
small enterprises. However, as regards loans to medium and
small enterprises, there is an economic law that the cost to an
individual financial institution of making a loan is higher when
the risk is greater and the amount smaller.

Returning again to Table 4, let us compare the average rate
of interest on loans and the average rate of discount. The textbook argument would be that loans are credit of longer terms
than discounts; therefore rates are to be higher in the former
than in the latter. However, we find that the average rate of
discount is higher than the average rate of interest on loans
in the case of city banks, local banks, and trust banks. We may
call this a "reverse phenomenon," to be explained as follows.
The proportion of loans of these banks to large enterprises is

high, and these loans are extended at relatively low interest
rates, while as to discounts, the weight of medium and small
enterprises is high, and these discounts are made at relatively
high interest rates. Such a tendency is strongly reflected in
the general average. Thus, large banks are able to extend
loans to large enterprises at relatively low interest rates, because of the high interest rates on loans to medium and small
enterprises. Furthermore, banks can maintain their liquidity
of assets by offering only short-term loans to medium and
small enterprises. On the other hand, the average rate of interest in long-term credit banks, mutual loans and savings
banks, and credit associations is higher for loans than for discounts, as textbooks usually maintain. The reason is that customers of these financial institutions are limited mainly to
either larger enterprises (in the case of long-term credit
banks) and medium and small enterprises (in the case of mutual
loans and savings banks and credit associations). In this case
there is no reverse phenomenon.

Thus, loans of long-term credit banks and others to large
enterprises form one pole, and loans of small financial institutions to medium and small enterprises another; in the middle,
discriminatory loans of city banks and local banks to large and
small enterprises produce the above-mentioned reverse phenomenon. This situation can be ascertained by the difference
in the distribution pattern of loans by various types of financial
institutions.

Figure 6 shows the distribution of loans to different sizes of
enterprise by various types of financial institutions, based on
data used for Figure 5. The curve marked "average" is the
cumulative frequency curve for total loans of all financial institutions, including small financial institutions such as money-
lenders and government financial institutions, which are not
listed in the Figure. The uneven downward development indicates that the distribution of funds as a whole is unequal.

Since loans of long-term credit banks and trust banks cannot
be separated, Figure 6 is regrettably inconsistent with the data
of Table 4. However, it appears that the curves of city banks

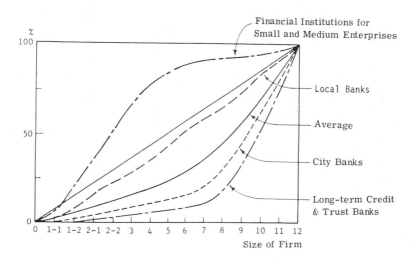

Figure 6. Degree of cumulative concentration of loans by
size of firm. Source: Same as Figure 2. Note: The vertical
axis indicates the cumulative frequency curve, and the horizontal axis the size of enterprises by the number of employees.

and of local banks are located between the most uneven curve
of long-term credit banks and trust banks inclining towards
large enterprises and the curve of financial institutions for
medium and small enterprises (mutual loans & saving banks,
credit associations, credit co-operatives, etc.). The above-
stated argument on the "reverse phenomenon" in differentials
in the interest rate on loans corresponds perfectly to such a
distribution.

IV. Structural Peculiarities of Capital Concentration

1) Factor Proportion and Differentials in Wages and Interest Rates

So far, a series of differentials in wages, productivity, capital intensity and the interest rate have been observed on the

ground of unequal distribution of capital accessibility. Let us
now reexamine the facts from the technical side of the production structure.

The decision concerning the degree of combination of the two
factors of production, capital and labor (capital intensity) depends on their relative price which an individual enterprise
faces in the factor markets. In Figure 3, a theoretical graph
of the permanence of differentials, each enterprise's capital
intensity is a function of factor prices. Medium and small enterprises choose labor-intensive methods of production with a
low capital intensity, in order to cope with relative high interest rates and relatively low wages. On the other hand, large
enterprises adopt capital-intensive methods of production with
a high rate of capital intensity to cope with relatively low interest rates and high wages. This situation can be analyzed by
the method of "isoquant curve of production."

Let us suppose that the production of enterprises of different
sizes is enlarged to the production level of the largest enterprises (with assets of over ¥ 10 billion), and the same magnifi-
cation applies to capital (tangible fixed assets) and labor (the
number of employees) without change in the initial ratio of factor combination. The resulting combination of labor and capital is shown in Figure 7.

Starting from the most labor-intensive combination 1 (enterprise with less than ¥ 2 million assets), various combinations
2, 3, 4 .... are determined up to the highest capital-intensive
combination 11. If enterprises of different size are acting under the principle of minimum cost with a production curve
identical to the observed isoquant curve, the ratio at the tangent
line to the various production points on the curve should indicate relative prices of capital and labor. The textbook argument would be that the greater the slope of the tangent line,
the smaller the capital cost (interest rates), and the more advantageous it is to replace labor by capital, and vice versa.
Nevertheless, the isoquant curve in Figure 7 is an observed
curve of production; it is not the schedule faced by enterprises
of different size as the basis for their behavior. The tangent
line ought to apply to an individual schedule, but not to the ob-

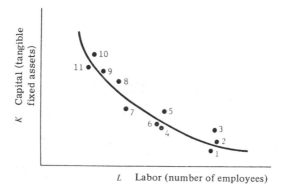

Figure 7. Isoquant curve of production. Source: Data are based on Ministry of Finance, Hojin Kigyo Tokei Nempo [Yearbook of Corporate Enterprise Statistics], 1957. Covering manufacturing industry only. Note: Enterprises are classified by asset holdings:

1. less than ¥2 million	7. ¥100-500 million
2. ¥2-5 million	8. ¥500-1,000 million
3. ¥5-10 million	9. ¥1,000-5,000 million
4. ¥10-30 million	10. ¥5,000-10,000 million
5. ¥30-50 million	11. over ¥10,000 million.
6. ¥50-100 million	

served curve. Consequently, it is meaningless to measure the ratio of relative prices of labor and capital by size of firm from this observed curve. (9) The conclusion is the following: enterprises of different size have different isoquant curves, as schedules, and the contact points of these respective isoquant curves and the price lines of each size of enterprise generate the observed isoquant curve shown in Figure 7. This interpretation is identical to that of the observed productivity curve illustrated in Figure 2.

Since measurement of the schedule isoquant curves is difficult, the structure of the ratio of labor and capital prices by size of firm must be obtained by other means. Table 5 shows that the differentials in the average rate of interest on bor-

Table 5

Disparity of Relative Prices of Wages and Interest Rates by Size of Firm

Size of firm (paid-in capital) (¥ million)	Differentials in wages	(1)	Differentials in the average rate of interest	(2)	Differentials in the ratio of wages and interest rate
	(¥1,000)		(%)		(3)
- 2	139	100.0	17.4	100.0	1.000
2- 5	172	123.5	17.8	102.3	0.828
5- 10	173	124.5	16.5	94.8	0.761
10- 50	200	143.5	13.8	79.3	0.553
50-100	231	165.9	13.6	78.2	0.471
100-	348	249.9	10.2	64.4	0.258

Source: Same as Table 3.
Notes: (1) Index number of the average wage per employee.
(2) Index number of the discount rate of interest expenses divided by the total of long-term and short-term borrowings from financial institutions plus debentures.
(3) (2) ÷ (1).

rowed funds (see Table 3) can be converted into an index number taking the interest rate of the smallest enterprises as 100. The same can be done for the differentials in wages. (10) The ratio of both indices is given as the difference in relative prices.

The difference in the ratio of relative prices is evident; the ratio of interest rates to wages is 0.258 for the largest enterprises with a paid-in capital of over ¥100 million, whereas it is 1 for the smallest enterprises with a capital of less than ¥2 million. Considering the difference in relative prices in connection with Figure 7, it may be supposed that the price line of the ratio of interest rates and wages (as the reciprocal) grows steeper from small to large enterprises.

Different in this from wage differentials, differentials in interest rates are also common in other advanced countries, because of the risk connected with the borrower. In Japan, however, structural aspects are more important. A fairly evident type of combination is found between different sizes of enterprise and various types of financial institutions. Secondly, the interest rate has an important connection with a special feature of capital concentration in Japan, namely, that a firm depends on outside capital rather than on owned capital as in other advanced countries. Consequently, differentials in interest rates influence considerably and directly the formation of the dual structure. The 1.00 to 0.258 disparity in relative prices of interest rates and wages (see Table 5) is fairly large, and it may be concluded that it contributes to the further widening of differentials in capital intensity.

The analysis of factor ratios in terms of relative prices is a static endeavor. There are also dynamic factors causing differentials in prices and in capital intensity.

2) Structural Peculiarities of Capital Concentration in Japan

Returning again to general points of view, one aspect has remained untouched in the above analysis. Since capital concentration is a phenomenon common to all capitalist economies, what are the peculiarities of the Japanese case?

Pressure of excess supply of labor and unequal distribution of capital accessibility have already been pointed out as the two fundamental underpinnings of Japan's dual structure; they cannot be separated. As a result, capital concentration in Japan presents three peculiarities: capital concentration in a capital-short economy, the stimulus of the international environment, and the coexistence of large and small business.

1. That capital concentration is related to the pressure of excess supply of labor means that capital is short in comparison to labor. Existing capital is insufficient in relation to the quantity necessary for the whole economy. As is often pointed out, the shortage of capital has been one of the fundamental factors restricting development of the Japanese economy. Capital shortage means an inadequacy of enterprises to internally generate capital and a need to raise funds indirectly. Funds scattered in the private individual sector are collected through banks, postal savings and other financial institutions, which act as intermediaries between individuals and enterprises. Such an "indirect financing method," characteristic of the Japanese money and credit situation, finds its fundamental cause in the shortage of capital. Thus, the rationale for financial institutions is established, and an institutional background is provided for differentials in interest rates related to credit-standing of the borrower.

2. If low wages are due to the pressure of excess supply of labor, the adoption of labor-intensive methods of production would be advantageous even to large enterprises. This is a widely accepted economic principle. Nonetheless, differentials in interest rates to the advantage of large enterprises exist, and are a reason for them to adopt high capital intensity. This fact alone does not explain, however, the existing marked differentials in capital intensity. Also important is a strong expansionary mood and an active inclination towards investments that tend to make up for the shortage of capital and which are stimulated by the international environment in which the Japanese economy has to catch up rapidly with the technical level

of developed countries. This peculiarity is supported in turn
by the combination of large banks and large holdings of capital
through loans to related enterprises; differentials in interest
rates advantageous to large enterprises can be considered as
a cause or an effect. In an economy short of capital, the greater
the degree of concentration of loans to large enterprises, the
wider the differentials in capital intensity between large and
small enterprises. Moreover, large enterprises, in the case
of emergency, can depend heavily on the Bank of Japan as a
"marginal supplier of funds" through large banks.

3. But what is the situation in regard to small enterprises?
In theory, when capital concentration proceeds, small business
will disappear in the generality of cases. In Japan, however,
numerous businesses with small capital continue to exist. Several factors are at play. Medium and small enterprises offer
a means of absorbing excess labor. Large and small enterprises are in a complementary relation: large ones utilize materials manufactured by cheap labor in smaller enterprises
through the subcontracting system and the formation of related
enterprises under their control, and use medium and small enterprises as a cushion against business fluctuations. There is
also, as already pointed out, the support that "marginal suppliers of funds" can offer medium and small enterprises. The
higher interest rate, due to the greater risk, is a disadvantage
compensated by cheap labor. The last factor would be the high
weight of "trade credit" in the composition of the total funds of
medium and small enterprises which have much recourse to
bills and accounts payable. (11)

V. Conclusion

In Japan, differentials in wages and interest rates, manifested
by the utilization of relatively cheap labor in medium and small
enterprises, and relatively low interest rates for large enterprises have solidified the dual structure of the Japanese economy. An anticipated slowing-down of growth in the labor supply, the increasing trend of demand for labor due to capital

formation, and the promotion of foreign trade liberalization are putting pressure on the premodern sectors. These facts have started a trend towards the abolition of the dual structure. It appears imminent that systematization and reorganization of medium and small enterprises will be pushed forward. Success depends greatly upon the adaptation and reorganization of capital accessibility and of the institutional structure of capital.

In Asia's underdeveloped countries, differentials in income and wages appear as an extreme difference between the upper and lower classes, somewhat as the division between two poles. In Japan, differentials are not as bipolar but moves from a high stratum to a middle stratum and from a middle stratum to a low stratum, forming a "continuous differential structure." (12) The concept of Japan's "dual structure" must, therefore, be clearly distinguished from the "dualism" found in Asian underdeveloped countries.

Limiting ourselves to economic factors, the following points are of importance:

1. Duality may characterize the initial stage of development, and be limited to the formation and utilization of the dualistic development explained by Hirschman, namely, the polarized coexistence of modern and premodern branches. However, after the "take-off," described by Rostow (13) and especially in the case of rapid progress, premodern branches are to be combined with modern branches in a complementary fashion. This is the case of Japan, where indigenous conditions have also effectively contributed to the adaptation of such a combination.

2. Considering the national economy as a whole, concentrated utilization of scarce capital requires the promotion of capital-intensive and modern methods of production, while low wages due to an abundant supply of labor favor the existence of medium and small enterprises. But here again all depends on the stage of development. That underdeveloped countries in Asia have a relationship between capital and labor resources different from that of developed countries is clearly reflected in the fact that modern production methods are shut out from various

branches of commerce and industry. To invest scarce capital in already existing production activities is too expensive; for an effective use of capital, hope is placed in investment in industries which introduce new products.

Quite differently, at a more advanced stage of development, as in Japan, the introduction of capital-intensive methods is required only for the improved efficiency of existing production, and if capital is scarce, its distribution among enterprises will be unbalanced.

3. In the case of Japan, shortage of capital as compared to labor has two aspects. From the international viewpoint, although capital intensity in large enterprises is said to be high, the level is still lower than in developed countries. Therefore, these enterprises use a system whereby they complement productivity relatively lower than the international level by low wages in subcontracting medium and small enterprises. From the national viewpoint, the scarcity of capital brings about capital concentration in large enterprises in order to use more efficiently the scarce resource, and at the same time, it brings about the dependence of medium and small enterprises on labor-intensive methods of production, as well as an incentive to be subordinated to large-scale enterprises as subcontractors in order to escape the instability of management resulting from poor and outmoded methods of production. In this case, the permanence of premodern production branches is fundamentally different from what happens in underdeveloped countries in Asia.

4. Until the end of the 1950s (or the beginning of the 1960s) the Japanese economy was characterized by excess supply of labor, and wages in the premodern small enterprises tended to be given by the low level but with some upward trend and cyclical fluctuations. As a result of the high rate of economic growth during the 1960s, the demand for labor had an increasing trend due to rapid capital formation and technological progress, and thus decreasing the wage differentials. One of the major effects of these developments is the transition from a labor surplus to a labor shortage economy, which will stimu-

late the process of adaptation and abolition of the dual structure.

Notes

1) A. O. Hirschman, The Strategy of Economic Development (New Haven: Yale University Press, 1958), p. 126.

2) Ibid., pp. 125-132.

3) R. F. Harrod, Towards a Dynamic Economics (London: Macmillan, 1949), in particular Lecture 3, esp. pp. 77ff.

4) If O indicates net output, L labor, and K capital, then $yc = O/L \cdot K/O = K/L = k$.

5) See Miyohei Shinohara, Growth and Cycles in the Japanese Economy (Tokyo: Kinokuniya, 1962), pp. 103-109.

6) J. Robinson, "The Production Function and the Theory of Capital," Review of Economic Studies, 21 (1953-54), 81-106, and also The Accumulation of Capital (London: Macmillan, 1956), pp. 101 ff.

7) This kind of view is also maintained by M. Kalecki, Theory of Economic Dynamics (London: G. Allen and Unwin, 1954), pp. 91-95 and J. Steindl, Maturity and Stagnation in American Capitalism (Oxford: Basil Blackwell, 1952), pp. 40 ff.

8) J. Duesenberry, Business Cycles and Economic Growth (New York: McGraw Hill, 1958), pp. 93-99.

9) Such measurement has been tried: the Douglas type production function was measured from the basic data of Figure 7, and the condition of minimum cost added. Then, the values of differentials in interest rates were arrived at by substituting the values of differentials in wages obtained from data using the minimization equation. However, the values thus obtained could not be judged significant compared with the actual ones.

10) The differentials in wages are obtained from the Corporate Enterprise Statistics cited in Table 3.

11) This fact is confirmed by various business statistics.

12) Kazushi Ohkawa, "The Differential Employment Structure in Japan," The Annals of the Hitotsubashi Academy, 9 (April 1959), pp. 205-217.

13) W. W. Rostow, "The Take-Off into Self-Sustained Growth," Economic Journal, 66 (March 1956), pp. 25-48.

3

EXCESSIVE COMPETITION AND THE FORMATION OF KEIRETSU

Yoshikazu Miyazaki *

I. Three Aspects of the Post-War Japanese Economy

In the ten years from 1954 to 1963 Japan's real national product rose by more than 2.2 times, showing an annual average growth rate of 9.4%. In the light of the fact that during this period the annual average growth rate of real national product was 7.4% in West Germany, 6.5% in Austria, 6.1% in Norway, 6% in Italy, 4.9% in France and, in particular, 2.8% in the United States and 2.5% in the United Kingdom, we see that Japan's growth rate was of remarkable order.

The economic bodies which actually attained this high economic growth are, of course, individual enterprises. The growth of Japanese enterprises in the post-war period has been such as to fit the word "miraculous" exactly. For example, sales and profits of the Matsushita Electric Industrial, a representative manufacturer of domestic electrical appliances in Japan, increased by as much as thirteen times in the ten years from 1954 to 1963. Even in its most flourishing ten-year period (during the 1920s) the Ford Motors, famous for its mass-

*Yoshikazu Miyazaki, "Rapid Economic Growth in Post-War Japan — With Special Reference to 'Excessive Competition' and the Formation of 'Keiretsu'", The Developing Economies, V (June 1967), 329-350. Sections IV and V of the paper are omitted. Reprinted by permission of the author and the publisher.

production "Ford system," proved incapable of exceeding an increase of the order of ten times. In post-war Japan, however, not only Matsushita but also such manufacturers of domestic electrical appliances as the Sanyo Electric, SONY, and the Hayakawa Electric have all realized sales increases of ten to twenty times in the last ten years, while the Toyota Motor and the Nissan Motor are also no exceptions to this phenomenon.

Nevertheless, it is well known that behind the splendid spectacle afforded by this rapid growth there has developed a fierce market-sharing competition among various enterprises. The large enterprises of Japan have been vying desperately with one another, competing fiercely in the introduction of foreign technology, in investment in equipment in their factories, and in advertising and sales. The term "excessive competition" secured immediate acceptance throughout the country as an expression of this state of affairs. The situation is exemplified by the following facts: 64 Japanese trading companies are engaged in business in New York and 38 in Hong Kong; 53 Japanese manufacturers have been importing electronic technology from the Radio Corporation of America, and 17 Japanese companies have been paying patent fees for the Sanforizing process to the Peabody Company.

Thus, because the Japanese economy grew at a rapid rate it provoked "excessive competition" among enterprises, and the "high economic growth rate" and "excessive competition," being, as it were, the two sides of a coin, have been the driving force of the post-war economy with "excessive competition" acting as the driving force for the attainment of the high growth rate. From the point of view of the relations between various enterprises this economic situation has tended to strengthen large-scale enterprises. As is well known, there used to be the Mitsui, Mitsubishi, Sumitomo, and other zaibatsu, the enterprise groups which ruled pre-war Japan, but these zaibatsu were dissolved under the post-war Occupation policy. Recently, however, the companies formerly affiliated to the zaibatsu have come to be reintegrated anew as enterprise groups known by the name of "keiretsu" (a word signifying a closely tied complex of industrial and financial corporations).

Viewing this development from "zaibatsu" to "keiretsu" as a whole, the following two points seem characteristic. First, in the pre-war zaibatsu the links in the enterprise groups were centered on the commercial sector of their businesses. (Consider, for example, the influence wielded by Mitsui & Company (Mitsui Bussan) in the pre-war Mitsui zaibatsu and by the Mitsubishi Shoji in the Mitsubishi zaibatsu.) But in the post-war "keiretsu" the enterprise groups are centered on the heavy and chemical industry sector. Second, the pre-war zaibatsu took the form of "family konzerns" linked vertically and topped by a holding company for the whole group. On the other hand, the post-war "keiretsu" are centered on financial institutions, and take the form of konzerns in which the enterprises are linked horizontally.

The post-war "keiretsu" include not only enterprise groups formerly affiliated to the Mitsui, Mitsubishi, Sumitomo and other zaibatsu, but also newly formed enterprise groups such as the Toyota, Hitachi, Toshiba, and Yawata Groups. All of these are making unceasing efforts to strengthen their own groups, and at the frontiers of the new industries which have been developed in Japan since the war, they have been competing against one another in equipment investment. When, for example, the Mitsubishi Group built a petrochemical refinery at Yokkaichi, competition was pressed forward to construct a similar plant by the Mitsui Group at Iwakuni, and the Sumitomo Group at Niihama, then by the Nippon Oil Group at Kawasaki, and lastly by the Idemitsu Kosan at Tokuyama. At present no less than nine petrochemical refineries are producing within the narrow confines of Japan. This is so not only in the case of the petrochemical industry. In the field of motor vehicles, too, nine manufacturers in addition to Toyota and Nissan are competing to increase their shares in the market. Similar competition is being carried on in all other industries from iron and steel to food processing. As a result, Japan's productive potential has risen rapidly and she has realized a degree of rapid growth which is literally the highest in the world.

In the above account we have likened the "high economic
growth rate" and "excessive competition" to the two sides of
a coin, but in fact there is another aspect to the Japanese economy. It would be more accurate to say that the "high economic
growth rate," "excessive competition," and "the keiretsu form
of organization" are the three aspects which built up three-
dimensionally the reality of the Japanese economy in the 1950s.
Thus, in order to reveal the secret of rapid economic growth
in post-war Japan, it is necessary to reveal the process by
which "excessive competition" developed among the large enterprises of Japan, i.e., to explain the method of capital accumulation in the various "keiretsu" and the process by which the
enterprises were organized in the form of "keiretsu."

The key to the secret of rapid economic growth in the postwar period, particularly since 1955, is to be found in the following four questions: First, how did large enterprises get the
necessary funds? Second, how did they get the necessary labor?
Third, what instigated the enterprises to invest so furiously?
And fourth, to what extent were the policies adopted by the government effective? The labor question can be answered quite
simply. Until quite recently (or at least up to 1956), a continual
supply of superior labor, both of good quality and readily adap-
table to modern technology, was available, and the enterprises'
propensity to invest was never subject to restriction from this
aspect. Consequently, in the following sections we shall consider the remaining three questions in some detail.

II. The Establishment of Indirect Financing

First, we must consider the method of obtaining funds for an
enterprise. The following three main methods are normally
employed: Under direct financing when an enterprise is about
to embark on an undertaking it issues debentures or shares
and obtains funds directly from the public. Under indirect financing it does not obtain funds directly from the public but
indirectly in the form of a loan from some financial institutions
which have collected funds from the general public in the form

of deposits. This method is characterized by the existence of
a financial institution standing between the public, the providers
of the funds, and the enterprise, the source of demand for funds.
Lastly, under internal financing the funds needed by the enterprise are provided out of the internal funds of the enterprise
itself, for example, out of depreciation funds or retained profits.

Table 1 shows the percentages of funds obtained by enterprises in Japan, the United States, England, and West Germany

Table 1

Percentages of Funds Obtained by Enterprises
in Various Countries (%)

Source of Funds	Japan 1958-62 Average	United States 1958-62 Average	England 1958-60 Average	West Germany 1958-62 Average
Internal Funds				
Depreciation	20	39	28	50
Retained Profits	4	26	34	5
Shares	13	14	15	11
Debentures	7	} 11	6	} 34
Bank Loans	34		4	
Others	22	10	13	
Principal Method Employed	Indirect financing	Internal financing	Internal financing	Internal financing

Source: Statistics Department, Bank of Japan, Nippon Keizai
wo Chushin to suru Kokusai Hikaku Tokei [Japan and the World:
A Comparison by Economic and Financial Statistics], March
1964.

in the last five years. As we see from the table, the advanced
countries were practically wholly dependent on internal financing, and Japan alone is conspicuous for having adopted indirect
financing. We would expect there to be some relation between

this method of obtaining funds and the highest growth rate in the world.

In what way, then, did this indirect financing come into being? That it was not, of course, of natural origin will be apparent from the fact that West Germany, which, like Japan, made a recovery after the defeat in war, adopted a method different from that adopted by Japan. To state our conclusion in advance, an important factor is that in the post-war measures for currency reform — the ending of war subsidies, the dissolution of the zaibatsu, and the dispersal of concentration of economic power — more care was taken in Japan than in West Germany to see that the city banks would always be in an advantageous position.

First, in the change to the new yen currency in Japan carried out in February 1946 (the Emergency Financial Measures) the new yen was given in exchange for the old yen at par only up to a sum which was insufficient even for a month's living expenses. All remaining yen assets were compulsorily paid into savings accounts, which, furthermore, were frozen and free withdrawals from the banks were stopped. For the city banks, which had on their books vast sums in bad debts owed by munitions firms which were bankrupt due to the defeat in war, this freeze of deposits was, needless to say, a welcome measure promising recovery from a desperate situation. In contrast to this, the currency reform effected in West Germany in June 1948 was a measure extremely unfavorable to the creditor banks, since it provided for the exchange of old Reichsmarks for new Deutsche Marks at the rate of 10 to 1, and debts in the old Reichsmarks were in principle also scaled down to one-tenth. Conversely, this may be said to have been a measure very much in favor of borrower enterprises. Nor was this all, for in West Germany measures were also taken to evaluate firms' assets at market prices and to grant a temporary exemption from taxation for capital gains resulting from this reevaluation, so that extraordinarily convenient conditions were provided for manufacturers directly participating in industrial production. In Japan the ground was made firm for the banks, but on the

other hand, in the course of the subsequent inflation the manufacturers were obliged to suffer inroads made in their capital
through lack of redemption funds, because the re-evaluation of
their assets was delayed. Here we find the earliest instance
of the banks being given preferential treatment over industry.

Second, we must consider the ending of wartime subsidies.
In West Germany no particular problem arose regarding wartime subsidies, since all debts were reduced to one-tenth. In
Japan problems arose over bad debts owed to the banks and the
disposal of the rights on them. In this matter, too, the banks
enjoyed favorable treatment. The "special losses" of the munitions firms resulting from the ending of wartime subsidies
were not charged to the account of the banks, the former creditors, but a fair proportion of them was charged to the account
of the shareholders of the munitions firms. In particular it is
worthy of note that before anything was charged to the account
of the creditors (chiefly the banks) an amount of up to 90% of
capital funds chargeable to the account of the shareholders was
first calculated, and only if this were insufficient was anything
ever charged to the account of the creditors. Thus the banks
which in the previous instance found themselves in a favorable
position at the time of the change to the new yen currency as
debtors of their depositors now received preferential treatment
as creditors of the munitions firms.

Third, it is a well-known fact that, as a part of the measures
for the dissolution of the zaibatsu, private enterprises or combinations of such enterprises which either (a) had large assets,
(b) had many employees, (c) were engaged in branches of activity unrelated to one another, (d) exercised managerial control
over other enterprises, or (e) supplied a greater part of important products, were designated as enterprises in which "an excessive concentration of economic power in private hands" was
present, and measures for deconcentration were taken in respect to them. While there was a fair number of companies in
the manufacturing and mining, and the commerce and services
sectors which were designated as subject to deconcentration
under these measures and which were actually split up and

their factories disposed of (257 companies were designated in the manufacturing and mining sector and 68 in the commerce and services sectors, but only 18 companies were made subject to action), the main banks, headed by the city banks, were not designated either as holding companies or as companies subject to deconcentration, and they survived unscathed.

Finally, the point that the banks were consistently afforded preferential treatment due to the success of some measures and the failure of others was a great factor in the development of the Japanese indirect financing method. These measures included such things as the collapse of the movement for the democratization of securities holdings which aimed at the promotion of direct financing, the collapse of the Shoup Recommendations (measures for preferential treatment of dividends as opposed to interest on deposits in tax policy), and the revival of the debenture-issuing banks which had been prohibited by the Occupation authorities.

The term "indirect financing," however, does not adequately describe the methods of obtaining funds employed in the postwar Japanese economy. This is because, though we speak of "indirect financing," it is not true that enterprises of different sizes are all equally being financed by financial institutions.

Next, let us go further into the matter and see what concrete forms indirect financing took after 1955.

First, in Table 2 we can see, within the funds supplied for the purposes of industry, the breakdown of the funds obtained from sources outside the enterprise and the relative importance of each source. The most conspicuous fact would seem to be that, after 1955, the importance of government financial institutions declined greatly while the proportion of funds supplied by private financial institutions, in particular by the city banks, rose.

A closer examination of the content of this advance on the part of the city banks throws into relief the fierce competition in loans among the city banks, and the consequent competition for deposits to be used for this purpose. Table 3 lists the banks in order of their loan balances at the end of each year from March, 1955.

Table 2

Sources of Funds Supplied to Industry (%)

Year	Total external funds supplied	Securities market		Private financial institutions				Government financial institutions	Government loans and investment special account
		Shares	Debentures	Total	City banks	Long-term credit banks	Others		
1954	100.0	23.23	3.01	66.21	14.96	9.79	41.45	16.35	2.67
1955	100.0	14.12	3.92	68.91	17.68	7.47	43.76	11.07	3.32
1956	100.0	12.53	4.06	76.78	40.87	3.94	31.97	4.98	2.33
1957	100.0	15.89	2.91	73.36	33.90	4.87	34.59	6.08	1.94
1958	100.0	14.28	3.54	72.44	24.82	8.30	39.32	7.29	2.46
1959	100.0	11.17	6.88	73.06	24.78	6.94	41.34	6.42	2.48
1960	100.0	16.12	5.22	71.19	24.83	6.34	40.02	5.46	2.01

Source: Compiled from Statistics Department, the Bank of Japan, Hompo Keizai Tokei [Economic Statistics of Japan], 1962.

Table 3

City Banks in Order of Outstanding Loan Balances
in the Last Ten Years, 1955-1964
(as of March of each year)

Banks	1955	1956	1957	1958	1959	1960	1961	1962	1963	1964
Fuji	1	1	1	1	2	2	1	1	1	2
Mitsubishi	2	2	2	2	1	1	2	2	2	1
Sanwa	3	3	4	3	3	3	3	3	3	3
Sumitomo	4	4	3	4	4	4	4	4	4	4
Kangyo	5	5	5	6	5	7	6	5	7	6
Mitsui	6	6	6	5	6	6	5	6	6	7
Tokai	7	7	7	8	8	5	7	8	5	5
Dai-Ichi	8	8	8	7	7	8	8	7	8	8
Kyowa	9	9	9	9	9	10	10	11	11	11
Daiwa	10	11	12	11	11	11	11	10	9	9
Kobe	11	12	11	12	12	12	12	12	12	12
Tokyo	12	10	10	10	10	9	9	9	10	10
Hokkaido Takushoku	13	13	13	13	13	13	13	13	13	13

Source: Compiled from an analysis of financial statements
published by the Japanese banks.

All the banks show spectacular increases of up to five times
in the last ten years, but we can see from the figures how
fierce the competition for loans was among the city banks, as
was exemplified in the struggle for the first place between the
Fuji Bank and the Mitsubishi Bank, and the Tokai Bank's ascent
to a higher place in the table. The figures for March 1964
show that the loan balances of the four great A-class banks,
Mitsubishi, Fuji, Sanwa, and Sumitomo, were all over ¥600 billion, with the B-class banks, Tokai, Kangyo, Mitsui, and Dai-
Ichi, in ¥400 billion, and the remainder below ¥300 billion.
Fierce lending competition among the city banks is thus one

of the characteristics of recent times, but this is not all. It is
an important point that over two-thirds of loans have been extended to large enterprises by the city banks as is clear from
Table 4. If we add to these loans those made by the long-term

Table 4

Borrowings by Large Manufacturing Enterprises
(with more than 1,000 Employees)

(%)

	City banks	68.68
	Local banks	36.61
	Long-term loan and trust banks	86.39
Private financial institutions	Financial institutions for medium and smaller enterprises	10.31
	Total	70.75
	Development Bank	34.31
Government financial institutions	Small Business Finance Corporation	0.12
	People's Finance Corporation	12.20
	Total	37.64
Business associates		16.39
Professional moneylenders		—
Relatives and acquaintances		0.78
Others		59.44
Grand Total		58.04

Source: Chushokigyo Chosa Saishukei Shiryo [Recompiled
Data from Surveys of Medium and Smaller Enterprises] , loan
balances on 31st December 1957.

credit banks, the trust banks, and the development banks, we
see that an immense sum in capital funds is being supplied entirely for the purpose of financing large enterprises.

What is more, carrying our analysis of loans from the city banks to large enterprises one step further, we can draw attention to a most singular tendency. This is the fact that these loans are supplied predominantly to enterprises belonging to the same keiretsu by these banks. This is shown statistically in Table 5.

Table 5

Proportion of Keiretsu Financing in Loans Made by the Principal Banks (1956-60 Averages)

	(%)			(%)	
Bank	$\dfrac{b}{a}$	$\dfrac{b}{c}$	Bank	$\dfrac{b}{a}$	$\dfrac{b}{c}$
Fuji	13.27	24.21	Sumitomo	9.73	19.33
Mitsubishi	19.23	21.97	Mitsui	24.27	17.16
Sanwa	10.05	25.08	Dai-Ichi	16.65	18.11

Note: (a) denotes total loans, (b) loans made to enterprises in the keiretsu, and (c) total borrowings by the enterprises in the keiretsu.
Source: Compiled from Negotiable Securities Reports.

In the table, $\dfrac{b}{a}$ indicates the percentage of loans made by city banks to enterprises belonging to their respective keiretsu, and $\dfrac{b}{c}$ indicates, from the point of view of the enterprises belonging to the respective keiretsu, the percentage of the funds required by the enterprises borrowed brom banks belonging to their own keiretsu. Generally speaking, $\dfrac{b}{c}$ is greater than $\dfrac{b}{a}$. This shows that the lending power of the city banks is the greater, and that they easily have more than enough funds with which to meet the requirements of the keiretsu enterprises. An exception is the Mitsui Bank. In spite of the fact that 24% of the loans made by the bank are to enterprises in the Mitsui keiretsu, the bank is not supplying to the full the funds demanded by the keiretsu enterprises because an extremely large sum in funds is required by the Mitsui keiretsu. We may say that this reveals most strikingly one of the weaknesses of the post-war Mitsui keiretsu.

To summarize, we have made clear: (1) that after 1956 the importance of Government financial institutions declined and the indirect financing centered on private financial institutions, particularly the city banks, was established; (2) that fierce competition in loans occurred among the city banks; (3) that a greater part of loans made by the city banks went to finance large enterprises, and (4) that keiretsu financing was particularly conspicuous. These are the characteristics of indirect financing peculiar to the economy of post-war Japan.

III. The Principle of "Set Control" (1) of New Enterprises

What raised the enterprises' propensity to invest? In a word we may say that it was "investment behavior aiming at control by the keiretsu" of a complete set of all industries related to one another.

While he was still president of the Mitsubishi Bank, Makoto Usami, the President of the Bank of Japan, spoke as follows regarding the principle of set control:

> We are not doing it under any definite principle of aiming at set control. Within our group alone there are a large number of undertakings and if, for example, it happens that we have to go into business in, say, the petrochemical industry, the Mitsubishi Rayon has connections with petrochemicals, and so does the Mitsubishi Chemical Industries. As a result it appears as though we had a general principle of getting set control of industries. I think the truth is not that we have the idea of getting a complete set of everything there is, but that these things happen out of the necessities of business. (2)

This may indeed be so. When we speak of set control, we, too, do not mean an irrationality of "getting a complete set of everything there is." It is no doubt natural that these events should have taken place under the pressure of necessity, but what were these necessities? Why did they result in the principle of set control? This is what I wish to analyze.

As we have seen above, indirect financing has been prevalent in post-war Japan. What is more, through the pipelines of the giant pre-war zaibatsu banks and the other city banks have passed the funds for the post-war recovery and for modernization investment. The companies which were in an advantageous position for obtaining funds were those backed by the powerful banks, headed by the companies formerly affiliated to the zaibatsu and connected with these pipelines. That is to say, in the natural course of events funds were supplied in the form of long- or short-term loans by the Mitsui Bank to the Mitsui keiretsu, by the Mitsubishi Bank to the Mitsubishi keiretsu, by the Sumitomo Bank to the Sumitomo keiretsu, by the Fuji Bank to the Yasuda keiretsu and the former Asano keiretsu, and by the Dai-Ichi Bank to the Kawasaki Dockyard, Kobe Steel, etc. It is nevertheless true that investment in coal and other mining, shipbuilding, marine transport, and other industries which have had difficulty in paying their way since the war, as well as in electricity, roads, railways, airways, telecommunications, and other branches of the basic industrial sector, has been increasingly dependent on state capital financed by the Development Bank or direct investment out of government funds.

Thus the companies backed by powerful banks, such as those formerly affiliated to the zaibatsu and in possession of advantageous positions for obtaining funds, took steps to rebuild and expand themselves. It was not merely the rebuilding, rehabilitation, and expansion of enterprises which has existed from the war years that took place. All of the keiretsu, backed by funds from the banks, eagerly entered new fields, including some with which they had no connection before the war. For example, up to 1952 integrated steel manufacturers were confined to the so-called "three integrated companies" — the

Yawata Iron & Steel and the Fuji Iron & Steel (the two companies which were formerly the Nippon Iron & Steel) and the Nippon Kokan. Recently Kawasaki Steel, Sumitomo Metal Industries, Amagasaki Iron & Steel, Kobe Steel, Nakayama Steel, Nisshin Steel, and Osaka Iron & Steel have been added to the number of steel manufacturers, making a total of ten large producers.

In the automobile industry the situation is the same. In 1949 all small four-wheeled vehicles were produced by the three firms Toyota, Nissan, and Ota Motors. Since that date Prince (formerly the Fuji Precision Machinery), Hino, Isuzu, Shin Mitsubishi, Toyo Kogyo, Daihatsu Motor, Honda Motors, Fuji Heavy Industries and others have joined the field and by 1964 had expanded their production by as much as forty times in their efforts to overtake Toyota and Nissan. On the other hand, Ota Motors and Tokyu Kurogane bacame entirely eclipsed by the rise of these new companies. In the paper industry, Oji Paper, which before the war produced 72% of all paper output (excluding Japanese paper) in Japan, was not only divided up into three companies (Jujo Paper, Oji Paper, and Honshu Paper) but also came into competition with Daishowa Paper Mfg., Kokusaku Pulp Industries, Tohoku Pulp, Kanzaki Paper Mfg., Chuetsu Pulp Industries, Mitsubishi Paper Mfg., etc.

In addition to these, similar relations are to be found both in synthetic fibres and in electric refrigerators, typical consumer durables. This will be clear from production concentration ratios in industries conspicuous for the number of new enterprises, as shown in Table 6.

What we can read from this table, however, is not merely the large numbers of new enterprises entering these fields but that practically all these new enterprises, as a closer inspection will show, had the backing of such powerful banks as the following:

    (1) Mitsui Bank: Hino Motors, Kanegafuchi Spinning
        (Kanebo)
    (2) Mitsubishi Bank: Honda Motors, Shin Mitsubishi
        Heavy Industries
    (3) Sumitomo Bank: Nippon Electric, Daishowa Paper Mfg.,

Table 6

Production Concentration Ratios in Industries
Conspicuous for their Number of New Enterprises (%)

(A) Iron & Steel		1937	1949	1958	1960	1963
Name of Company						
Former {Yawata Iron & Steel		83.9	65.9	29.8	33.2	25.8
Nippon Iron & Steel {Fuji Iron & Steel				28.2	26.6	23.7
Nippon Kokan {Nippon Kokan		10.1	22.6	13.8	13.4	13.8
{Tsurumi Iron & Steel		3.8				
Kawasaki Steel				7.9	8.0	11.0
Sumitomo Metal Industries (3)				4.8	4.9	9.1
Kobe Steel (6)					3.2	4.8
Amagasaki Iron & Steel (5)				4.7	4.4	3.2
Nakayama Steel (5)				5.0	4.0	2.3
Nisshin Steel (5)					−	2.3
Osaka Iron & Steel (5)					0.8	1.0
Others		2.2	11.5	5.8	1.5	3.0

(B) Small Four-wheeled Vehicles	1949	1954	1958	1960	1963
Name of Company					
Toyota Motor	34.5	47.7	45.7	33.3	39.6
Nissan Motor	52.7	28.9	33.5	41.9	34.8
Prince Motors		13.7	9.4	8.4	8.7
Isuzu Motors (6)			2.3	5.9	7.4
Hino Motors (1)			2.9	5.2	4.7
Shin Mitsubishi Heavy Industries (2)				4.8	2.6
Toyo Kogyo (3)			3.1		1.4
Daihatsu Motor (5)			0.6		0.4
Honda Motor (2)					0.2
Fuji Heavy Industries				0.4	0.1
Ota Motors	12.8	9.3			
Tokyu Kurogane			0.9		
Others	0	0.4	1.6	0.1	0.1

Table 6 (cont.)

(C) Paper and Pulp						
Name of Company		1937	1949	1958	1960	1962
Oji Paper	Jujo Paper		25.0	19.1	15.5	15.8
Oji Paper	Oji Paper	71.7	27.0	8.4	13.0	15.3
Oji Paper	Honshu Paper		10.7	8.1	6.1	4.2
Daishowa Paper Mfg (3)			2.9	7.4	8.0	8.8
Kokusaku Pulp Industries					2.6	5.0
Tohoku Pulp (7)				2.9	3.7	4.6
Kanzaki Paper (3)				3.5	4.7	3.9
Chuetsu Pulp Industries				4.6	3.9	2.9
Mitsubishi Paper		6.0	4.8	3.1	3.1	2.8
Hokuetsu Paper		5.4	6.9	3.6	3.2	2.6
Daio Paper				3.3		
Others		16.9	22.7	35.6	36.2	34.1

(D) Synthetic Fibres			
Name of Company	1950	1955	1958
Toyo Rayon	22.0	1.3	45.6
Kurashiki Rayon	57.4	3.8	21.9
Nippon Rayon (5)			8.9
Dai Nippon Spinning	3.4	5.2	5.6
Teikoku Rayon (5)			4.9
Asahi-Dow		7.0	3.9
Kanegafuchi Spinning (Kanebe)	16.9	0.1	2.2
Japan Exlan			2.9
Others	0.3	2.6	4.1

(E) Electric Refrigerators			
Name of Company	1956	1957	1958
Hitachi	27.3	25.7	28.8
Tokyo Shibaura Electric	28.2	28.4	22.2
Matsushita Electric Industrial	24.2	28.5	20.4
Mitsubishi Electric	17.1	14.0	15.8
Nippon Electric Industry (3)		0.4	2.5
Sanyo Electric (3)		0.8	5.2
Fuji Electric (6)			1.2
Hayakawa Electric (4)		1.1	0.5
Yaou Electric		1.1	0.4
Others	3.2		3.0

Note: The numbers in parentheses following the names of companies refer to the keiretsu listed in the text, pp. 67, 70.

Sources: Up to 1958, Fair Trade Commission (ed.), Shuyo Sangyo ni okeru Seisan Shuchudo [Concentration of Production in Principal Industries], 1960. For 1960, 1962, and 1963, Toyo Keizai Tokei Geppo.

Sumitomo Metal Industries, Toyo Kogyo, Kanzaki
Paper Mfg., Sanyo Electric
(4) Fuji Bank: Hayakawa Electric
(5) Sanwa Bank: Teikoku Rayon, Amagasaki Iron & Steel,
Nisshin Steel, Nakayama Steel, Nippon Rayon, Osaka
Iron & Steel, Daihatsu Motor
(6) Dai-Ichi Bank: Isuzu Motors, Fuji Electric, Kobe Steel
(7) Nippon Kangyo Bank: Tohoku Pulp.

Large business organizations in competition against one another in entering new industries and connected in keiretsu on
the finance side were also seen in pre-war Japan. These were
the zaibatsu. The differences between the pre-war zaibatsu
and these keiretsu do not consist merely in the fact that the
pre-war zaibatsu had holding companies as their nuclei while
the post-war keiretsu have certain principal banks at their centers. Each of the pre-war zaibatsu had its own sphere of activity, the Mitsui zaibatsu in paper, synthetic dyes, coal and foreign trade, the Mitsubishi zaibatsu in heavy industries centered
on shipbuilding, in marine transportation and plate glass, and
the Sumitomo zaibatsu in metal manufacturing industries centered on rolled copper and aluminum. They made their principal investments in these fields, each adopting a system which
secured for it fairly stable markets, and each sought monopolistic control of the industries in which it was involved.
    The post-war situation differs from this. A good example
of this fact is provided by the moves made by large enterprises
in relation to the petrochemical industry and the atomic energy
industry. From the very first the giant financial keiretsu —
Mitsui, Mitsubishi, Sumitomo, Fuji, and Dai-Ichi — lined up in
competition in equipment investment.
    Thus the immense sums of capital funds supplied through the
city banks since the war were not invested selectively, as in
the pre-war period, in the principal industries in which the
various zaibatsu had their interests. Investment has been carried out in such a way that each of the keiretsu, accepting the
fact that it will come into rivalry with its fellows, contrives

to get under its own control a complete set of all new industries.
This being so, why has investment behavior aiming at set control by each keiretsu appeared in the post-war Japanese economy? In this regard we can think of the following four circumstances.

(1) It goes without saying that one important factor was the
splitting-up of undertakings under the Economic Deconcentration Law, as in the cases of the integrated steel manufacturers
and the paper industry. The ability to maintain control over
markets which until then had been more or less stable collapsed,
and entry into new industries in the form of new enterprises
was facilitated.

(2) If keiretsu were not to fall behind in taking advantage of
the recent wave of technical innovation they could not afford to
stand pat, each holding on to its own field of activity and relying only on its traditional "stable" markets. They were obliged
to get under their control as many of the new industries as they
could, enlarging the scope of their field, and strengthening the
links between their industries in a multilateral and comprehensive manner.

(3) The above two circumstances may be said to be typical
of Japanese business in general, whether organized as a part
of a keiretsu or not. Why, then, is it that, in spite of this, practically all the new enterprises which we have listed above are
connected with the financial keiretsu of some powerful bank?
In the modern heavy and chemical industries, where sweeping
technical innovation has occurred, enlargement of the scale of
operations through the integration and diversification of production (as in the case of the petrochemical refinery) is required, if only for technical reasons, and there is a strong
tendency for the needed capital funds to assume immense pro-
portions. Because of this it is only large enterprises which
can accumulate or obtain elsewhere large sums of capital and
which have the backing of big financing banks that can enter
these industries. In sum, entry of new enterprises into these
industries did in fact occur, but there was a great difference
between this and the "free entry" spoken of in economics text-

books. The firms which entered these industries were no more than a very limited élite of large enterprises backed by powerful banks which could easily supply the immense sums needed for investment in equipment.

(4) We cannot ignore what is known in economics textbooks as "the internalization of external economies." The term refers to those benefits accruing which are given to the enterprise in a fortuitous manner by changes in the whole body of the industry of which the enterprise is a part and in the national economy as a whole, as opposed to benefits accruing as a result of efforts made within the enterprise itself. For example:

> Let us consider the case in which a new subway line is opened and a new subway station built at an intersection in a city. There is no doubt that, thanks to this, the intersection will be twice as busy a place as before and the shops already established at the four corners of the street can be expected to receive a windfall in the form of a great increase in the number of customers. This clearly owes to "external economies." (3)

Similarly, as the automobile industry is established and developed in the Japanese economy, the manufacturers of thin steel plate, tires, piston rings, ball-bearings, electrical fittings and other automobile parts will naturally benefit from it. The establishment of the automobile industry has just the same effect as the "subway station at the intersection." By its essential nature this kind of "external economies" produces effects on the generality of industries through the intermediacy of the element of complementary production, through the relations existing among the goods produced.

In the post-war Japanese economy, however, investment plans have been drawn up with the intention of blocking, as far as possible, the general effects produced by "external economies" and of confining such effects within the bounds of one's own keiretsu; in other words, of aiming at the "internalization of external economies." Good examples of this are the estab-

lishment of the Mitsubishi Monsanto Chemicals as a market
for the carbide produced by the Mitsubishi Chemicals, the establishment of the Aichi Steel for the purpose of manufacturing
special steel for the Toyota Motor, the establishment of the
Nippon Denso as an independent company for the specialized
production of electrical parts for the Toyota Motor, and the
establishment of the Toyota Motor Sales for the purpose of
integrating the sales branch of the Toyota Motor. Such plans
to "internalize external economies" are also one of the factors
leading to the adoption of investment behavior aiming at set
control of new industries by each of the keiretsu.

Once this principle of aiming at set control is adopted by all
the keiretsu the result is that all keiretsu become rivals in each
of the industries in which they are involved. Competition is intensified. According to usual economics textbooks, competition
among the enterprises is developed in accordance with "the
principle of maximizing profits." But when we consider the
competition among the keiretsu in post-war Japan we find it
more appropriate to regard it as having been carried on in accordance with "the principle of maximizing sales" with the aim
of enlarging the keiretsu's share of the market, rather than in
accordance with "the principle of maximizing profits." That is
to say, in order not to be left behind by the others, each keiretsu
has taken steps to enlarge its market share in each industry
whenever it can, and has frantically competed with its rivals in
equipment investment. This kind of investment behavior aiming
at set control has also been a driving force in Japan's spectacular economic growth since the war. On the other hand, it has
also been a cause of "excessive competition."

Notes

1) Elsewhere in this volume, this term is translated as the
"one-set" principle. — K.S.

2) "Zaibatsu Kaitai no Kozai" [The Merits and Demerits of
the Dissolution of the Zaibatsu], Ekonomisuto, August 18, 1964.

3) Shigeto Tsuru, "Nihon no Toshi o do suru?" [What Is to
Be Done about Japan's Cities], Asahi Journal, vol. 4, no. 2.

4

JAPAN'S INDUSTRIAL ORGANIZATION

Ken'ichi Imai*

What was the foundation of the Japanese industrial organization which supported Japan's postwar economic development?
On the one hand, Japan's industrial organization positively contributed to high economic growth, but, on the other hand, it created friction between the market and the environment, which
has become the cause as well as the consequence of the fragility
of public action and social welfare. The Japanese economy is
often said to possess outstanding adaptability. If so, its industrial organization should also possess corresponding characteristics. In a dynamic economy, industrial organization is always in the process of change and evolution. Then, how can
Japanese industrial organization convert itself from the one
that has been formed primarily to contribute to economic
growth to the one that can bring the genuine fruit of economic
activities to the people?

---

*Ken'ichi Imai, "Josho — Nihon no Sangyo Soshiki" [Intro-
duction — Japan's Industrial Organization]. Chapter I of K.
Imai, Gendai Sangyo Soshiki [Contemporary Industrial Organi-
zation] (Tokyo: Iwanami Shoten, July 1976), pp. 1-51. Translated by permission of the author and publisher. Translated
by Hirokatsu Ogasawara.

This translation originally appeared in Japanese Economic
Studies, VI (Spring-Summer, 1978), 3-67 (54-57 omitted from
this reprint).

This introductory chapter is devoted to presenting a bird's-eye view of Japan's industrial organization with the above point in mind.

1. Formation of the Market Structure and Its Institutional Framework

The foundation of Japan's postwar industrial organization was laid when the zaibatsu were dissolved. The holding companies, which had been at the center of the zaibatsu control, were dissolved by the Holding Company Liquidation Commission, and the Law for the Elimination of Excessive Concentrations of Economic Power was enacted as a special law. For the purpose of expediting the formation of a competitive market structure and increasing opportunities for entry into the market, eleven large corporations, including Nippon Steel, Mitsubishi Heavy Industries, Mitsui Mining, Mitsubishi Mining, Oji Paper Mill, and Dai-Nippon Beer, were respectively divided into two to four companies (or ordered to separate specific business divisions), and seven other corporations, including Hitachi Works, Tokyo Shibaura Electric, Teikoku Oil, Shochiku and Toho, also had to divert their plants or transfer their stocks. (1) The Deconcentration Law was regarded as "the surgical procedure necessary for the economy in order for it to be turned over to the safekeeping of the Antimonopoly Law." "[S]taff of the Antitrust and Cartels section of [GHQ] hoped to see the economy turned over in deconcentrated form to the Fair Trade Commission, the administrative body for the permanent antimonopoly legislation. Otherwise, the Antimonopoly Law was regarded as likely to be either ignored or scuttled as soon as the nation once again became independent." (2)

The efforts in the Japanese business society to ignore or scuttle the Antimonopoly Law to date indicate that what they feared was no illusion at all. It is only by this surgical operation that competitive business practices and industrial organization were, for the first time in history, incorporated into the Japanese industry, finance, and commerce which had fallen into the "hands of the few" (3) in the 1920s and the 1930s.

One salient feature of the postwar economic democratization measures centering on the zaibatsu dissolution is that they not only disconnected linkages of capital through the dissolution of holding companies and the division of large corporations but also severed interlocks of personnel through the purge of business leaders. The prewar zaibatsu, despite their limited stock ownership of affiliated companies except for a few special ones (4), could maintain virtually complete control over them because the zaibatsu had another powerful means in the form of personnel control. The zaibatsu families either directly or indirectly appointed all of the executives of core companies, while prohibiting them with agreements or affidavits from taking any independent action. Many of these executives, concurrently assigned to a number of enterprises, kept contact and surveillance among themselves. In order to convert the zaibatsu-affiliated enterprises into independent and free enterprises, it was indispensable to eliminate this personnel control. Therefore, 245 companies which had been deemed to be "extremely monopolistic" were obligated to purge top-level executives.

It seems that the purge that severed the zaibatsu personnel ties was of considerable significance to the growth and development of Japanese business in the postwar period. Advantages of competitive enterprises can be given full play when individual enterprises can freely invest in plant and equipment and freely decide on outputs and prices. And, the newly appointed managers after the purge of senior executives could fully use such advantages. At the same time, through the above process, the separation of ownership and management was achieved at this juncture, thus fully opening the door for the age of managerial control.

Thus, the zaibatsu dissolution, together with the agrarian land reform and the emancipation of the labor movement, was the fundamental pillar of economic democratization and the basis of industrial organization in postwar Japan.

In the international sphere, the regime of free trade was reorganized around the GATT-IMF system and Japan could fully enjoy its merits. For some time after the war, its lack of the capacity to export forced Japan to rely on its domestic resources alone. Eventually, however, Japan was able to expand exports under the new postwar free trade system with no limitations on market shares, unlike under the prewar cartel system, and thus to purchase resources overseas freely and to enjoy the benefits of lowered maritime transportation cost, a particularly significant postwar innovation. This development turned the lack of domestic resources to be even an advantage to Japan as an oceanic nation. As for technology, which is the foundation of production, it became feasible for Japan to introduce new technology from abroad, especially the United States, thus encouraging the new corporate managers to undertake aggressive investment programs in plant and equipment. This led to erecting new production frontiers in Japanese industry, thus creating the physical foundation of economic growth.

Although postwar Japan's industrial organization was given a fresh start under highly competitive conditions in terms of the human and physical environment of business, the economy itself was managed not by the price mechanism but rather by economic control.

While Japan was still in the process of its postwar economic rehabilitation, it was necessary to adopt the so-called priority production formula by implementing the Reconstruction Finance Corporation loans and to control the allocation of resources under the Provisional Materials Arrangement Law. However, even after the rehabilitation was completed, Japan continued to control the allocation of industrial materials and to maintain industrial policy which was enforced under bureaucratic control in the name of administrative guidance directed to individual industries. One of the important themes of this book is to probe the factors that gave rise to this policy and defects which were created by them in Japanese industrial organization. Basically speaking, however, as E. M. Hadley (5), who took part in the dissolution of zaibatsu, had already clearly perceived, "In Japan . . . , there was no awareness of the extent to which market forces are capable of directing production and distribution," and a belief prevailed that "the market mechanism is regarded as incapable of providing direction to the economy." Among the bureaucrats in general, there was almost no consideration for leaving the allocation of resources to the market mechanism, as they had been accustomed to forming the industrial order and deciding on introduction of new products and technology only from the national point of view.

Therefore, up until the late 1950s, the Mining and Industrial Production Five-Year Plan (1951) of the Economic Stabilization Board and the specific industrial plans of the Industrial Rationalization Council had provided the guidelines to Japanese industries. In this respect, the government could exercise such authority as authorization of foreign exchange allocation for imports and approval of technology imports with a view to influencing the behavior of individual firms. (6) As the means of forming industrial order under bureaucratic guidance, a series of laws was enacted for the purpose of rationalizing specific industries with the legal grounds provided for justifying exceptions from the Antimonopoly Law. In other words, the special legislation for administrative guidance gradually eroded the effects of the general statute in forming industrial order. (7)

Without reference to the pros and cons of such an approach, this is a widely recognized fact. Then, has industrial organization in Japan been formed exactly in accordance with such bureaucratic plans? The answer is no. New industrial organization has been formed by market forces which grew up along with economic growth beyond the administrative framework, breaking through the network of the old system. We shall statistically clarify developments of this process in the next section. At this point, we want to give emphasis to the fact that contradictions between the administrative and institutional frameworks and market forces notwithstanding, the latter surmounted such contradictions to create competitive industrial organization.

But this does not mean that these contradictions were brought to an end. They persisted, albeit covertly, through the subsequent process of rapid growth, and have now been brought into the open in the form of confrontation between the Antimonopoly Law and administrative guidance.

The Process of High Economic Growth and the Framework of Industrial Organization

When the postwar high economic growth of Japan started still remains a question for debate. From the point of view of systematization of the Japanese economy and society, however, one must find special significance in the formation of a stable power elite group composed of the triad of the Liberal-Democratic Party, the bureaucratic machinery, and the business community, exercising check and balance with one another, following the establishment of the Liberal-Democratic Government upon the conservative merger in 1955, which had superseded the preceding fragile coalition government. It made it easier for the government target of quickly catching up with the advanced industrial nations and the profit-motivated business target of rapid growth to agree, join forces, and develop into a political target in the form of the income-doubling program to lead Japan to national consensus of a sort along the way toward high economic growth.

In the process of high economic growth, the Industrial Structure Investigation Committee [Sangyo Kozo Chosakai], an advisory body to the Minister of International Trade and Industry, played the role of a road-builder for organizing the industries. This committee was composed of subcommittees on specific industries, with committee members from the representative firms in each specific industry to compile the respective industrial rationalization plan by harmonizing big business interests and bureaucratic views. And, the members of its General Committee lined up big business leaders, serving as a pipeline connecting the bureaucratic machinery, the business community, and the political circles.

The trinity of the Liberal-Democratic Party, bureaucracy, and the big business was complemented by the centralization of political power due to the increased reliance of local finance upon the National Treasury. Though the strengthening of local autonomy was, along with economic democratization, one of the main objectives of Japan after the war, the local self-governing system virtually became subordinate to the Central Government. It is on this basis that regional development plans were incorporated into centralized development planning like the Comprehensive National Land Development Plan, which enabled private firms to rely substantially upon government and public appropriations in securing industrial land, industrial water, transportation facilities, housing land, school and welfare facilities and so on in building new factories in any of the newly developed industrial areas.

What lay behind such a policy was the basic concept that a strong industrial foundation is the basis of the development of private enterprises, which would expedite the growth and development of the national economy, thus eventually benefiting the entire society. However, granted that such a policy might ultimately bring forth public benefits, one must question the propriety of the government, which, in neglect of its duty to coordinate interests among private persons, accords absolute advantages to specific parties and endows specific private firms with apparently private gains up to the last stage leading to public welfare. It certainly is vulnerable to the criticism that this concept justifies the government's offer of extra benefits to private firms which have not been granted to common citizens and restriction of civil rights on the pretext of achieving public interests. (8)

Then what special features has the formation of industrial order under the bureaucratic initiative and administrative guidance attributed to industrial organization in Japan? This is a main theme of this book, which shall be amplified later. Here, let me sum up a few main points as an introduction to this theme.

As an objective of its industrial policy in the process of high economic growth, the MITI oft-emphasized improving international competitive power. Though it is hard to define what the international competitive power is, it was generally accepted at that time that this meant to organize an efficient, top-level production system in the world. This is somewhat similar to the U.S. space development project as a national goal to achieve in which the U.S. government itself embarked on a program for building up a production system. The market mechanism cannot effectively steer such forced development, and the bureaucratic planning must take over.

However, planning did not take such an explicit form in the case of Japan. The Japanese government covertly exercised the administrative guidance, while paying lip service to the independence of individual firms. (9)

The government justified the administrative guidance ostensibly to prevent excessive competition. In building up a physically effective production system, competition always seems excessive, causing waste and duplication. Besides, the administrative guidance inclines by nature toward assigning quotas, either overtly or covertly. Thus, as a matter of fact, firms were engaged in excessive competition for those quotas.

The postwar industrial policy which had incorporated elements of economic control into the market mechanism in a complex form led to the creation of a growth accelerating system of producer sovereignty. In this system of industrial organization unique to Japan, an important role was played by the administrative guidance in the name of fixed-investment adjustment. This is essentially an authorized investment cartel in the form of coordination panels, one in each industry, organized on the basis of the Industrial Structure Investigation Committee's recommendation, in order to adjust investment programs of individual enterprises through their mutual consultations.

We shall later explain the situation which gave rise to such a cartel. However, the November 1966 agreement between the MITI and the Fair Trade Commission on "Operation of the Antimonopoly Law concerning the Promotion of Improvements in the Industrial Structure" provided an institutional justification for exempting most of investment adjustments from the

Antimonopoly Law. Together with the antirecession cartel system, this has been responsible for creating the system of producer sovereignty, while giving rise to the following defects in Japanese industrial organization.

An investment adjustment — be it through administrative guidance or through voluntary coordination — eventually results in some sort of quotas. A firm which has begun investment earlier can hold a larger production capacity than its competitors, thus establishing advantages over the others. This prompts firms to compete for capacity expansion. Thus, the investment adjustment which has been intended to eliminate excess capacity stimulates, on the contrary, capacity expansion beyond what is economically needed. Moreover, under this system, individual firms are not free to decide on when to implement investment so that they have to begin and stop investment at the same time, thus eliminating time lags that usually arise between individual firms' investment spendings. This gives rise to unnatural ups and downs in investment expenditure, which make it difficult to balance supply and demand smoothly.

If all firms compete all at once for capacity expansion substantial excess capacity is inevitable at a time of recession, and a cartel of one sort or another has to be organized. If firms are to be called into account for their own deeds, a checking mechanism should come into being against excessive investment even under the aforementioned system. However, a safeguard that surfaced in Japan was a cartel. At first, it took the form of MITI recommendations on curtailment of operation. However, their legitimacy was questioned under the Antimonopoly Law, and industries began filing formal applications for antirecession cartels, which were usually authorized with virtually no objection. (10) And, the guaranteed presence of such a cartel as the safeguard at the times of recession relaxed the firms' vigilance toward excessive investment, thus creating another cause for their excessive competition for capacity expansion. In short, this resulted in a vicious circle between investment adjustment and an antirecession cartel.

The demand for investment, which was initially quite normal to meet anticipated expansion of demand in the growth process of the Japanese economy, turned into a blind pursuit of capacity expansion for its own sake under the aforementioned system. Thus, investment tended to grow on its own momentum. Consequently, business behaviors grew extremely abnormal, responding little to the needs of consumers but a great deal to changes in firms' market shares. The competition among firms was less for supplying high-quality products by giving full play to what they are best at but more for strengthening their potential bargaining power in securing more investment quotas.

On the other hand, it is also undeniable that the driving force that supported the competition for investment from within firms was entrepreneurs' nationalistic aspirations for catching up with the advanced industrial nations in technology and their personal ambition for public success in achieving their aspirations. In other words, the individual desire for contributing to the national goal of catching up with the advanced industrial nations and for achieving it ahead of the others to attain a social fame seems to have been what mentally engineered their leadership over employees. (11)

Such unique features of competition based upon the aforementioned external and internal motives are undoubtedly elements of what is generally referred to as excessive competition among Japanese firms. In the early 1960s, there was a hypothesis of investment inviting further investment to explain the high growth of the Japanese economy. From our viewpoint of industrial organization, it is nothing but the aforementioned mechanism of letting investment expand on its own momentum.

The aforementioned producer-sovereignty, supply-first system is what makes up unique Japanese industrial organization in a number of industries like steel and petrochemicals, which do not allow much product differentiation. At the same time, the supply-first system has also been formed through a different mechanism in the consumer-good markets, where product differentiation is easy, as in the food and the household elec-

trical appliances industries. The result is the manufacturer-
controlled distribution system.

Manufacturers in postwar Japan organized a distribution system under their own control in place of the prewar system under wholesalers' control. This control progressively advanced
as the national economy expanded rapidly. In the economic
climate of postwar Japan, it was commonly accepted that manufacturers should control the distribution channels of their
products, and unfair practices in the phase of distribution such
as restrictive or exclusive dealings were usually left un-
policed in the operation of antimonopoly policy. For instance,
in the examination of the Matsushita resale case, the Matsushita Electric Industrial Company asserted the legitimacy
of its resale practices. It was only recently that the company
had decided to acquiesce in the judgment at the examination.

Needless to say, once a control of distribution is established
by an oligopolistic firm, a system of producer sovereignty
comes into being in the field of distribution too. Producers
can not only positively stimulate consumers' demand by means
of advertising and other sales promotion activities but also can
ostensively differentiate products under their initiative, turn
out slightly varied products in performance and appearance one
after another, and market these through their own distribution
channels, while creating consumer demand for new products on
the strength of false advertising.

Crudely speaking, competitive sales promotion within this
framework has very little to add to consumers' welfare. As
typically seen in oligopolists' nonprice competition, the effects
of advertising and sales promotion tend to offset each other,
thus only raising distribution cost in the entire economy. Advertising agencies are also tempted to compete with one another
for more sensual excitement as their clients, manufacturers,
compete more intensely, thus causing instead difficulties to
themselves in an excessive and futile competition. Excessive
advertising campaigns like this have bad effects socially and edu-
cationally. While not all of this is waste, it brings about, in the final
analysis, almost no substantial benefit to the entire nation.

It has been theoretically clarified (12) that oligopolistic
firms prefer sales promotion to price competition. The problem of how to tackle the nonprice competition under oligopoly
is not limited to Japan alone but is a universal basic problem
of capitalism today. At least the distribution system, however,
to date has been controlled by manufacturers more strongly in
Japan than in any other countries, thus providing another cause
for forming a system of producer sovereignty.

Industrial Organization and Environment

Within the aforementioned framework, the supply-first
mechanism of mass production and mass consumption was established in Japanese industrial organization, and it was the industrial foundation of the high economic growth of postwar
Japan. It is true that the high economic growth contributed to
raising the income level, increasing employment, and opening
up new opportunities both for enterprises and people. However, what are the aftereffects that have been left in Japan's
industrial organization and economic system by its growth
which has been accelerated by the above mechanism?

Accelerated investment in plant and equipment certainly contributed to rationalizing and modernizing Japanese firms,
strengthening competitive power on overseas markets, and pushing economic development forward. This process is ipso facto the
process of technological innovations. The adoption of up-to-
date equipment of large scale and large capacity helped to
lower production cost. Industrial organization has attained the
highest level of technical efficiency in the world today in many
of Japan's industries.

However, has such a thoroughgoing pursuit of bigness in
capacity and scale well matched the natural and cultural environment of Japan?

It is true that the continuation of investment on a high level
and the hugeness of individual investment projects are not a
phenomenon peculiar to Japan alone but a feature common to
any contemporary industrial society. The tide of technological

innovations which mushroomed after World War II concentrated in manufacturing, especially in heavy and chemical industries, and created large-scale technology. To go along with this tide was, in a way, to move along with the requirements of the times. It was probably a good economic strategy to have pushed up investment to meet potential demand expected to forthcome from the population of 100 millions. However, has sufficient thought been given to Japan's overcrowded environmental capacity and has sufficient consideration been paid to the social cost of Japan's environment inasmuch as such investment tends to concentrate industrial and housing areas in a few locations because of its geographical features? The answer to this question seems to have already been given in the presence of the environmental problem itself, notably in connection with industrial pollution. But one might attribute environmental pollution to the fault of administration. In any case, I am not emphasizing this particular point. What I want to emphasize here from the viewpoint of industrial organization is that Japan's industrial organization contained a mechanism which accelerated the supplier-oriented investment for the installation of large-capacity, oversize equipment. A heavily populated society and high-level investment are not necessarily incompatible. But, in order to make them compatible, it was necessary to provide sufficient precautions vis-à-vis the environmental conditions of investment as well as a framework which could accommodate investment to the environmental capacity. Nonetheless, the industrial organization policy of Japan unilaterally accelerated supplier-oriented investment while adapting the environmental conditions to the requirements of such investment. For instance, when investment in large-capacity oversize equipment led to a surplus in supply capacity, the government created effective demand by increasing public investment. If excess supply persisted, the government called for production cutbacks or antirecession cartels. When the demand management policy alone was not enough, the government promoted industrial reorganization through mergers and other measures, thus trying to accommodate industrial organization and even the environment to the needs of the industries.

Cost of production is certainly lowered by increasing the capacity and scale of plant. The minimum optimal plant size is determined at a level where production cost has been sufficiently lowered. However, this does not mean that plant size should be expanded to the point of minimum cost at the sacrifice of all other conditions. The minimum optimal size normally has a certain range, out of which a point should be chosen that meets best a number of conditions including demand fluctuations and environmental requirements. Nevertheless, the maximum plant capacity has been invariably adopted by every big enterprise in Japan. It has not infrequently been the case that a plant would be built in Japan with a scale in excess of those that are built in the United States or elsewhere, which was of the optimal size only in a place with enough land space and environmental capacity. A plant like that is unlikely to pass the criteria of technical efficiency in theory of industrial organization when environmental cost is taken into account as social cost under the environmental conditions of Japan. (In other words, the plant size is not at the lowest point of the cost curve, when social cost is included.) If strict environmental control were in force, cases would have been more numerous where firms constructed medium-sized plants in various localities, thus forming more flexible industrial organization well matched to the environmental requirements in Japan.

Large plant scale is certainly a manifestation of technological innovations, but it was an easygoing way as far as research and development is concerned in that it has not developed technology suited to the environmental needs of Japan and has not adapted it to environmental changes. Rather, technology has developed itself along the lines of increasing plant capacity, and forced enterprises to accommodate their environment to the requirements of technology. Take the automobile industry, for instance. The supply conditions of the mass production system were there first, and the environmental standards were moderated to meet them. And, this was done in the name of the industrial policy. As a result,

there have been few instances of new production technology developed by major automobile manufacturers in accordance with
the requirements of overcrowded Japanese society. Our automobile industry is not at all in harmony with the environmental
requirements in Japan.

When it comes to sales promotion, we have to reexamine
whether it is in harmony with the natural and cultural environment of Japan. The process of entry into the age of mass consumption is extremely important to the economy and culture of
any nation. Granted that Japan had no adequate and effective
tool to control its transition into the age of mass consumption
at an unprecedented speed, we must reexamine the following
facts: the manufacturer-controlled distribution networks intensified the supplier-led marketing; restraints and rules are
absent concerning advertising and other sales promotion activities and competition for sales allows whatever method to
be used in order to dominate the market; up until recently,
there has been no consideration at all for recycling the waste
arising from consumption; all of these facts contributed to
speeding up mass consumption. Needless to say, the direction
of policy must be turned from the one running from suppliers
to consumers to the one moving from consumers to suppliers,
that is, to establishing a framework by which goods and services are produced and supplied to meet the needs of consumers.

Contemporary industrial organization needs a machinery by
which the market mechanism can be controlled within the social and economic system — in other words, conditions that
allow economic activities within a given social system. The
task of this book is to seek the rule of industrial organization
for controlling the market mechanism within the environmental
capacity and to probe the adaptability in directions of the Japanese industries toward this end.

2. Changes in the Market Structure and Firm Behavior

Within the aforementioned institutional framework, Japanese

firms achieved rapid growth owing to vigorous demand, and
through this growth process, they accomplished various innovations, expanded their marketing areas, sophisticated the division of labor, and intensified competition in all fields. It
was precisely the Schumpeterian process of creative destruction, a revolutionary process which cannot be summed up in a
few sheets of statistical tables. But let us dare to present two
tables that symbolically represent dynamic changes in the
Japanese economy, namely, Table 1 on variation coefficients of
the industrial structure, and Table 2 on changes in the employment
structure. Table 1 presents an international comparison of the
variation coefficients of the industrial structure as an indicator
of the "adaptability" of the Japanese economy as discussed in
the 1964 White Paper on the Japanese Economy. Japan's variation coefficient was already high internationally at that time,
but grew even higher in the 1960-1970 period, thus indicating
that the industrial structure of the Japanese economy had undergone a remarkable change by giving full play to its shift-
ability.

Table 2 reveals a decline of employment in agriculture,
forestry and fisheries from 48.3% of total employment in 1950
to 19.3% in 1970 despite substantial governmental protection.
Employment in mining also declined from 1.7% in 1950 to 0.4%
in 1970. On the other hand, key industries covering chemicals,
iron and steel, and machinery doubled their employment from
6.7% in 1950 to 13.8% in 1970. Such a rapid change is really
noteworthy in the history of modern economic growth in view of
the fact that it took 40 years for Britain to reduce primary-
sector employment from 22.8% to 12.3%. Although various social and political forces tended to keep market forces in con-
tainment in the Japanese economic structure as mentioned
earlier, market forces were strong enough to cope with these
obstacles and to achieve such structural changes through the
evolutionary growth process.

This process also had a great impact upon Japanese industrial organization. In this section, I shall present a statistical
overview of the main features of Japanese industrial organization and the process of its formation.

Table 1

Variation Coefficients of Industrial Structure

	1954-1961	1960-1970
Japan	18.4	19.3
U.S.A.	5.6	10.9
U.K.	9.1	12.0
West Germany	7.0	10.6
France	5.4	12.9
Italy	14.3	11.4

Note: A variation coefficient is computed as follows: industrial compositions of GNP are computed for the beginning and end years of the period. Differences by industry in percentage points are taken between the two years. They are summed in absolute value to yield the coefficient under study.

Sources: For 1954-1961, see Keizai Hakusho, 1964, p. 58. For 1960-1970, figures are obtained from U.N., Yearbook of National Accounts Statistics, 1973.

Let me first show Table 3 to give the reader a bird's-eye view of the Japanese market structure. From the 1970 input-output table dividing the whole Japanese economy into 450 industries, we estimate values of production originating in the oligopolistic sector (13) and in the public utility and public works sector and attribute the remainder of domestic production to the competitive sector. This detailed interindustry table by market structure is thus consolidated into Table 3.

This table reveals that the oligopolistic sector holds a share of 21.6% of total value of domestic production covering the entire industrial spectrum from the primary to the tertiary industries, the public utility and public works sector, 13.1%, and the competitive sector supplies the rest, 65.2%. Needless to say, there is no assurance of the presence of fully competitive conditions even in the nonoligopolistic sector, which includes the markets with restricted competition due to their exemption

Table 2

Changes in the Employment Structure (millions)

Industry	1950 No.	%	1960 No.	%	1970 No.	%
1. Agriculture, forestry & fisheries	17.2	48.3	14.2	32.5	10.1	19.3
2. Mining	0.6	1.7	0.5	1.1	0.2	0.4
3. Food processing	0.8	2.2	0.9	2.1	1.1	2.1
4. Textile & apparel	1.3	3.7	1.8	4.1	2.2	4.2
5. Wood products & furniture	0.7	2.0	0.9	2.1	0.9	1.7
6. Pulp, paper, and printing-publishing	0.4	1.1	0.7	1.6	1.0	1.9
7. Leather & rubber products	0.1	0.3	0.3	0.7	0.4	0.8
8. Chemicals	0.4	1.1	0.5	1.1	0.6	1.1
9. Petroleum & coal products	0.03	0.1	0.04	0.1	0.05	0.1
10. Stone, clay, and glass	0.3	0.8	0.5	1.1	0.6	1.1
11. Iron & steel	0.3	0.8	0.5	1.1	0.6	1.1
12. Nonferrous metals and metal products	0.3	0.8	0.8	1.8	1.5	2.9
13. Nonelectrical machinery	0.4	1.1	0.7	1.6	1.1	2.1
14. Electrical machinery	0.2	0.6	0.7	1.6	1.5	2.9
15. Transport equipment	0.4	1.1	0.6	1.4	1.0	1.9
16. Precision instruments	0.1	0.3	0.2	0.5	0.3	0.6
17. Miscellaneous manufacturing	0.2	0.6	0.5	1.1	0.8	1.5
18. Construction	1.5	4.2	2.7	6.2	3.9	7.5
19. Electricity, gas & water	0.2	0.6	0.2	0.5	0.3	0.6
20. Wholesale & retail trade	4.0	11.2	6.9	15.8	10.1	19.3
21. Banking & insurance	0.3	0.8	0.7	1.6	1.1	2.1
22. Real estate	0.01	0.0	0.08	0.2	0.27	0.5
23. Transportation and communications	1.6	4.5	2.2	5.0	3.2	6.1
24. Services	4.4	12.4	6.6	15.1	9.4	13.0
25. Not elsewhere classified	0.04	0.1	0.01	0.0	0.02	0.0
Total	35.6	100.0	43.7	100.0	52.2	100.0

(Bracketed subtotals for items 12–16: 1950 = 6.7; 1960 = 10.3; 1970 = 13.8)

Source: Sangyo Betsu Shugyosha no Jikeiretsu Hikaku [Time-Series Comparison of Employment by Industry], 1975.

Table 3

Value of Production by Industry and by Market Structure (billion yen)

Industry	(1) Competitive sector	(2) Oligopolistic sector	(3) Public utility & public works sector	(4) Value of domestic production = (1) + (2) + (3)	Share of oligopoly (2)/(4)	Share of public utility & public works (3)/(4)
1. Agriculture, forestry & fisheries	5,206.9	—	1,906.7	7,113.6	—%	26.8%
2. Mining	808.3	150.9	—	959.2	15.7	—
3. Food processing	6,856.6	1,947.5	816.5	9,620.6	20.2	8.5
4. Textile & apparel	5,892.2	242.3	—	6,134.5	4.0	—
5. Wood products & furniture	3,399.2	—	—	3,399.2	—	—
6. Pulp, paper, and printing-publishing	3,450.3	1,023.2	—	4,473.5	22.9	—
7. Leather & rubber products	639.9	289.2	—	929.1	31.1	—
8. Chemicals	4,416.5	1,694.5	—	6,111.0	27.7	—
9. Petroleum & coal products	646.0	2,372.7	—	3,018.7	78.6	—
10. Stone, clay, and glass	1,742.2	927.7	—	2,669.9	34.7	—
11. Iron & steel	4,042.5	7,242.7	—	11,285.3	64.2	—
12. Nonferrous metals and metal products	4,433.2	1,200.0	—	5,633.2	21.3	—
13. Nonelectrical machinery	6,319.1	2,004.6	—	8,323.7	24.1	—

14. Electrical machinery	4,175.0	3,457.4	–	7,632.4	45.3	–
15. Transport equipment	2,633.5	4,990.4	–	7,623.9	65.5	–
16. Precision instruments	634.7	468.8	–	1,103.5	42.5	–
17. Miscellaneous manufacturing	2,088.6	131.1	–	2,219.7	5.9	–
18. Construction	10,392.9	–	5,865.8	16,258.7	–	36.1
19. Electricity, gas & water	–	–	2,627.9	2,627.9	–	100.0
20. Wholesale & retail trade	14,126.1	–	163.6	14,289.7	–	1.1
21. Banking & insurance	–	4,906.9	–	4,906.9	100.0	–
22. Real estate	5,907.7	–	–	5,907.7	–	–
23. Transportation and communications	1,442.3	946.0	5,055.6	7,443.9	12.7	67.9
24. Services	12,611.7	944.3	4,775.8	18,331.8	5.2	26.1
25. Not elsewhere classified	3,499.9	–	–	3,499.9	–	–
Total	105,365.3	34,940.4	21,212.0	161,517.8		
	65.2%	21.6%	13.1%	100.0%		

Notes: The oligopolistic sector in manufacturing follows the broad definition in note 13). Banking and insurance are assigned entirely to the oligopolistic sector in view of high concentration and institutional restrictions of competition. The oligopolistic sector in services is advertising. In agriculture, production of rice, wheat and barley is assigned to the public utility and public works sector; their marketing is treated likewise.

Source: Prepared from Administrative Management Agency et al., 1970 Sangyo Renkanhyo [1970 Interindustry Tables], Vol. I (1974).

from the Antimonopoly Law. However, by taking Table 3 as our first approximation, we are perhaps not too far off the mark when we conclude, as is commonly alleged, that nearly 70% of Japanese industry is operated in competitive markets. (14)

For manufacturing alone, however, the oligopolistic sector accounts for 35.2%. Moreover, its share is especially outstanding in heavy and chemical industries — e.g., 78.6%, 64.2%, and 65.5%, in petroleum and coal products, iron and steel, and transport equipment, respectively. I shall examine these changes in concentration in detail later.

Next, to show interrelations among the competitive sector, the oligopolistic sector, and the public utility and public works sector, let us present estimates of the degree of sectoral dependence on final demands. The result gives a basic characteristic of the Japanese economy. The degree of dependence of the competitive sector upon final demands in each of the three sectors is shown in Table 4, that of the oligopolistic sector in Table 5. (15)

As is evident from Table 4, the competitive sector depends a great deal on final demands in the competitive sector itself, with the average at 82.6%, but very little on final demands in the oligopolistic sector, with the average at 9.6%. Though the latter degree of dependence is the highest in the competitive sectors of iron and steel and leather and rubber products, it is no more than 22.6% and 22.1%, respectively.

On the other hand, the degree of dependence of the oligopolistic sector on final demands (Table 5) reveals that its production relies heavily on final demands in the competitive sector, with 45.4% of its total value of production indirectly induced by final demands in the competitive sector. At the same time, the oligopolistic sector in transport equipment, nonelectrical machinery, electrical machinery, and miscellaneous manufacturing is shown to rely very strongly on final demands in the oligopolistic sector.

These facts indicate that the oligopolistic sector of the Japanese economy has a structure such that its growth is induced by final demands in the competitive sector and the public utility

Table 4

Dependence of the Competitive Sector on Final Demands in the Three Sectors (1970)

	Dependence on final demands in the competitive sector	Dependence on final demands in the oligopolistic sector	Dependence on final demands in the public utility & public works sector	Total %
1. Agriculture, forestry & fisheries	86.9	6.9	6.3	100.0
2. Food	96.9	2.0	1.1	100.0
3. Textile & apparel	94.9	2.7	2.5	100.0
4. Wood products & furniture	88.1	4.0	7.9	100.0
5. Pulp, paper, & printing-publishing	83.5	8.8	7.7	100.0
6. Leather & rubber products	73.9	22.1	4.0	100.0
7. Chemicals	81.2	11.1	7.7	100.0
8. Petroleum & coal products	57.9	24.1	18.0	100.0
9. Stone, clay, & glass	65.0	6.4	28.6	100.0
10. Iron & steel	64.8	22.6	12.6	100.0
11. Nonferrous metals & metal products	75.6	12.5	12.0	100.0
12. Nonelectrical machinery	83.8	11.5	4.7	100.0
13. Electrical machinery	79.6	13.9	6.6	100.0
14. Transport equipment	82.2	5.5	12.3	100.0
15. Precision instruments	82.8	13.2	4.0	100.0
16. Miscellaneous manufacturing	82.8	12.3	4.8	100.0
17. Construction	97.4	1.0	1.6	100.0
18. Trade	89.1	5.8	5.1	100.0
19. Real estate & rental	94.2	3.2	2.7	100.0
20. Transportation & communications	79.7	8.5	11.8	100.0
21. Services	93.7	3.7	2.7	100.0
Average	82.6	9.6	7.8	100.0

Notes: Figures in this table show the degree by which the value of domestic production in the competitive sector of each industry is induced by the total final demands in the competitive sector, the oligopolistic sector, and the public utility and public works sector, respectively.
The mining industry is excluded from the table, as some of its figures turn negative due to its dependence on imports.

Table 5

Dependence of the Oligopolistic Sector on Final Demands in the Three Sectors (1970)

	Dependence on final demands in the competitive sector	Dependence on final demands in the oligopolistic sector	Dependence on final demands in the public utility & public works sector	Total %
1. Food	41.1	57.7	1.2	100.0
2. Textile & apparel	81.6	15.4	2.9	100.0
3. Pulp, paper, & printing-publishing	80.2	11.3	8.5	100.0
4. Leather & rubber products	34.7	60.6	4.7	100.0
5. Chemicals	66.7	28.6	4.8	100.0
6. Petroleum & coal products	56.8	20.8	22.5	100.0
7. Stone, clay, & glass	58.4	19.6	22.0	100.0
8. Iron & steel	58.3	29.6	12.1	100.0
9. Nonferrous metals & metal products	83.4	2.7	13.9	100.0
10. Nonelectrical machinery	24.2	71.3	4.5	100.0
11. Electrical machinery	25.8	66.9	7.3	100.0
12. Transport equipment	7.8	90.9	1.3	100.0
13. Miscellaneous manufacturing	20.3	77.5	2.2	100.0
14. Banking & insurance	42.4	52.8	4.8	100.0
15. Transportation & communications	44.2	48.2	7.6	100.0
16. Services	0.0	99.9	0.0	100.0
Average	45.4	47.1	7.5	100.0

Note: Figures in this table show the degree by which the value of domestic production in the oligopolistic sector of each industry is induced by the total final demands in the competitive sector, the oligopolistic sector, and the public utility and public works sector, respectively.

and public works sector, but it does not reciprocate in inducing growth in the other sectors. In other words, it is a closed system to a considerable extent. The oligopoly system, a frequently used term, perhaps vaguely connotes such a meaning.

Earlier, on the basis of the 1955 input-output table divided between large and small firms I. Sakura and T. Nakamura (16) reported an interesting finding that "though an increase in final demands for small firms considerably affects large firms, an increase in final demands for large firms is mainly circulated within large firms with little effect on small firms." Their finding agrees precisely with what we have found, and this represents one of the characteristics of the Japanese market structure.

Integration and Concentration Ratios

Generally speaking, when a firm can expect better cost performance or more profits through an increased market share by opening a new factory or a sales office than by using the existing marketing system, it normally seeks horizontal, vertical, or conglomerate expansion, as shown in Figure 1, through the expansion of its own facilities or integration through acquisitions of or mergers with other firms. By taking this broad sense of the word integration, we observe that this sort of integration determines and changes the concentration ratio in any market. Let me present a preliminary statistical review of how integration and the market structure are related to each other in Japan's industrial organization.

We have already seen in Table 5 the position of highly concentrated oligopolistic industries in Japanese industry as a whole. As for principal markets in each industry, the Fair Trade Commission continues to survey concentration ratios in them. The FTC survey refers to products specified in detail in close correspondence to the legal concept of relevant market and does not cover all products of any industry. This may give an impression that the survey is partial and lacks in comprehensiveness. However, a comparison with our 450-

industry input-output table divided into the oligopolistic and the nonoligopolistic sectors reveals that almost all products not included in the FTC survey come from competitive markets with a very large number of firms. In what follows, therefore, I rely primarily on the FTC time series (1955-1972) of concentration ratios by industry.

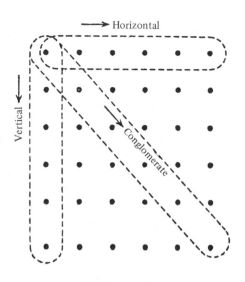

Figure 1

Then, what significance does the concentration ratio in a given industry have as a statistical indicator? True, the number of firms and their size distribution in a given market provide useful information to indicate basic features of its market structure. But the concentration ratio is nothing more than an element of the market structure. In many instances, competition is intense in a highly concentrated market if the demand is growing rapidly in this market and new entry is relatively easy. Therefore, the concentration ratio should not be overevaluated as an index of the market structure. Moreover, the concentration ratio encounters many technical difficulties in statistical measurement. For instance, the concept of industry or product in official statistics involves statistical compromises. Industry and product classifications often disagree with markets as defined in economics. Besides, when imports compete with domestic products, the concentration ratio refers to concentration in sales including imports. But, usually, the concentration ratio in domestic production is employed in its place.

Technical difficulties involved in measuring the concentration ratio have been made well known by the celebrated article of M. A. Adelman. Adelman himself later noted that "a single concentration ratio tells us little about a given industry at a given time, but much may be learned from analysis of groups of industries over time.... So the close attention to industry detail is bound together with broad comparisons in time and space." (17)

There are a large number of studies on the changes in concentration in U.S. industry. (18) Here, let me review a long-term analysis covering 100 years by A. D. Chandler, a well-known authority on business history. (19) Though his statistical treatment somewhat lacks in rigor, he as a business historian offers a quite suggestive study. He classifies industries into three groups by long-term trend of concentration.

Group A comprises industries of low concentration, including major industry groups (at the 2-digit level of industrial classification) of leather products, printing and publishing, lumber and wood products, furniture, and apparel; they include very few 4-digit industries that can be classified to be oligopolistic (see note 13). Also, their concentration ratios showed almost no upward long-term trend since 1909. Group B comprises industries with moderate concentration, including major industry groups of textile, paper and paper products, metal products, nonelectrical machinery, and food processing; at the 4-digit level of industrial classification, one quarter to one half of industries are oligopolistic. In this group, concentration tended to increase to some extent since 1940. Group C consists of typical oligopolistic industries, including major industry groups of stone, clay and glass, chemicals, petroleum products, rubber products, primary metals, electrical machinery, transport equipment, precision instruments, and tobacco. In Group C, the level of concentration tends to correspond to technological characteristics of individual industries. The trend of concentration is affected largely by individual firms' attempts at diversification. There are not a few instances in which concentration was in fact lowered while large firms trying diversification competed to invade one another's markets. It is Group C that held the reins of economic development. This group's business behavior exerts a decisive influence upon the performance of industry in general because its industries employ the majority of research and development personnel.

In Japan, concentration statistics are available on a continuous basis only since 1955. However, even this limited data for a decade and a half points to patterns of change roughly similar to those observed in the United States. The detailed data underlying our Table 3 show that industries in Group A consisting of leather products, printing and publishing, lumber and wood products, furniture, and apparel are all competitive with the exception of the daily newspaper industry that is classified as oligopolistic. No upward trend in concentration is detected with respect to product items such as textbooks by the Fair Trade Commission. In Group B, textiles, paper and paper products, metal products, nonelectrical machinery, and food processing all have an oligopoly share of about 20%, except for textile, as shown in Table 3. Among its industries, one can note a slightly upward trend in concentration in a number of oligopolistic markets such as liquefied pulp, cast-iron roll, drill, ham and sausage, edible milk, and soy sauce or a trend reversal to the upward direction since around 1965 in staple fiber yarns, newsprint, power cultivators and so on. In Group C, chemicals, primary metals, electrical machinery, and transport equipment have been leading industries in the economic growth of postwar Japan just as in the United States. While the concentration ratio is relatively high in these industries because of their technological structure (mainly due to economies of scale in production), concentration tended to decline in quite a few of them under rapid industrial growth. (20)

It is often believed that capitalist economy is destined to move toward monopolization or that concentration tends to rise inevitably due to characteristics of modern technology. It is true that such a tendency exists in some specific markets of a country at a given time. However, a tendency more or less common to all advanced economies is that "industry concentration has remained so stable for so long, through stronger and weaker antitrust enforcement; through war, depression and boom." (21)

However, this holds only as a general observation on the average market structure of industry as a whole. It does not mean that the structure of any specific market is stable. In the latter, the market shares of individual firms constantly vary, either overtly or covertly, through existing firms' competition for market shares, absorption and mergers, or new firms' entry. Basically speaking, however, the concentration ratio neither rises nor falls markedly, except for extraordinary cases, because the force working to intensify concentration such as advantages of mass production based on large-scale technology and marketing is balanced by the force of reducing concentration through creation of market demand suited to new firms and medium and small old firms.

Analysis of the Growth of Firms by Size

Changing the viewpoint, let us take a look at the behavior of firms, which determines the market structure and concentration. In particular, let us probe an important and closely related problem, namely, how the groups of large firms and small firms or of firms classified by size grew, respectively. Many people may have an off-hand impression that large firms as a group have enjoyed a higher growth rate. However, this is not the case. The foreign literature carries many studies of the growth of firms by size, which has established a statistical, probabilistic proposition called Gibrat's Law or the hypothesis of proportionate growth, namely, the growth rate of a firm is unrelated to its initial size and, therefore, the probability of growth is the same between a large firm and a small firm. This proposition has been empirically verified by many studies (22) of British and American firms, following the famous article by P. E. Hart and S. J. Prais. It is verified with respect to Japanese firms, too, by Masao Baba (23) and others. Moreover, these empirical studies demonstrated that small firms tended to grow faster, particularly in Japan and to a modest extent in foreign countries.

Table 6 below is presented to reconfirm this fact. This table

Table 6

Growth Rates and Profit Rates of Firms by Size

	Annual growth rate of sales			Profit rate on total capital[a]		
	Small firms[b]	Medium firms[c]	Large firms[d]	Small firms[b]	Medium firms[c]	Large firms[d]
1961	22.8	20.0	21.7	8.3	7.4	6.6
62	10.0	8.9	7.9	6.0	5.3	4.7
63	14.8	16.6	16.5	5.9	5.2	5.2
64	16.2	15.1	16.3	5.1	3.9	4.6
65	7.5	6.8	6.0	4.1	3.1	3.6
66	16.2	16.0	16.7	5.3	4.3	4.9
67	21.2	20.0	20.2	6.9	5.2	6.0
68	16.7	17.0	16.7	7.6	5.9	5.8
69	17.9	19.4	22.1	7.7	6.5	6.3
1970	18.5	17.5	16.1	7.0	5.7	5.4
71	6.4	5.8	5.4	5.1	3.7	3.6
72	11.8	13.1	11.6	5.7	4.4	4.3
73	34.2	36.6	28.7	10.0	7.3	6.1
74	19.9	25.8	22.9	6.9	4.1	3.7
Average	16.7	17.0	16.3	6.5	5.1	5.0

Notes: a) Total capital = liabilities + net worth.
  b) Small firms = 50-299 employees.
  c) Medium firms = 300-999 employees.
  d) Large firms = 1,000 or more employees.
  Source: Bank of Japan, Kigyo Kibobetsu Keiei Bunseki
[Financial Statements of Firms by Size].

compares the annual growth rates of small, medium, and large firms on the basis of financial statements of firms collected by the Bank of Japan. It is clear that the growth rate tended to be less in large firms. (24)
  In addition, in order to be more specific about the growth of

firms by size and to supplement this overall fact of ours,
Table 7 gives a transition matrix of firms by size from 1967
to 1970. Matrices since 1960 are all roughly of the same type
as this one, namely, upward shifts of a considerable number of
small and medium firms. Reading the table horizontally, we
find that in the 50-99 size class, in 1967, 69.7% of firms remained in the same class in 1970, but 17.6% moved upward into
the 100-199 size class, 0.6% into one class further up, and so
on. About 30% of small firms (except for those in the 10-29
size class) changed size classes. This proportion reached
nearly 40% in the largest size class, 200-299, of small enterprises. The upward movement is similarly strong among
medium-sized firms with employees from 300 to 999, but tends
to be lower among large firms with employees more than
1,000. (25)

As we explained earlier, in the process of the postwar economic growth, large oligopolistic firms grew up through introducing innovations of large-scale technology which enabled
them to enjoy advantages of mass production and mass marketing. They gave the driving force of rapid growth, thereby
expanding industrial fields subject to large-scale production.
On the other hand, however, the process of rapid growth, accompanied by changes in the industrial structure, diversified
consumer demands and helped to create a great many opportunities for different kinds of goods to be produced in small
lots by small firms, thereby giving rise to the new types of
distribution and services. Such opportunities created favorable conditions for the growth and development of firms of
various sizes, including small firms. These led to the aforementioned growth dynamics of Japanese firms.

As is well known, the dual structure has been emphasized in
the analysis of the industrial structure of Japan. (26) Special attention is given to the factor markets in labor and capital and
emphasis is placed on differentials in wages and cost of capital between large and small firms. It is true that these differentials existed among firms of different sizes, but it is also
true that they have tended to decrease gradually in the growth

Table 7

Size Distribution of Firms and Their Interclass Transitions

1967 \ 1970	1-9 persons	10-29 persons	30-49 persons	50-99 persons	100-199 persons	200-299 persons	300-499 persons	500-999 persons	1,000-4,999 persons	5,000-9,999 persons	10,000 persons and above	No. of firms 1970	%
10- 29 persons	0.034	0.823	0.130	0.013	0.000							4,579	36.0
30- 49 persons	0.001	0.159	0.646	0.183	0.011	0.000						2,226	17.5
50- 99 persons		0.007	0.110	0.697	0.176	0.006	0.002	0.001	0.001			1,856	14.6
100- 199 persons			0.003	0.090	0.710	0.167	0.024	0.004	0.001			1,273	10.0
200- 299 persons					0.103	0.607	0.271	0.018	0.001			717	5.6
300- 499 persons		0.001			0.004	0.092	0.673	0.228	0.001	0.001		855	6.7
500- 999 persons							0.075	0.768	0.158			641	5.0
1,000-4,999 persons								0.055	0.909	0.036		471	3.7
5,000-9,999 persons										0.891	0.109	55	0.4
10,000 and above										0.027	0.973	37	0.3
No. of firms 1967	156	4,138	2,242	1,874	1,334	740	852	732	532	68	42	12,710	100.0
%	1.2	32.6	17.6	14.7	10.5	5.8	6.7	5.8	4.2	0.5	0.3	100.0	

Source: Chusho Kigyo Kinyu Koko Geppo [Smaller Business Finance Corporation, Monthly Bulletin].

process of Japanese firms. It is for this reason that we have
not singled out this particular aspect alone.

Along the lines of the dual structure, however, we must note
the fact that there are, and will be, many industries whose
market structure is of the bimodal type according to the FTC
classification. This type refers to an industry with 40 to 200
firms, with the 4-firm concentration ratio high and with the
rest of firms very small. Examples are ham and sausage,
powdered milk, butter, soy sauce, synthetic dyes, tires and
tubes, rubber-sole shoes, springs, and power loom industries.
In these industries, a very few large firms deal with the national market via their mass advertising and powerful sales
networks, and all other peripheral firms sell in local markets
or transact with specific clienteles. The two groups may differ in the nature of equipment or in the mode of production.
In other words, these industries have the dual structure. (27)

It goes without saying that the coexistence of modern and
premodern firms is inevitable in any country in the process
of rapid industrialization, and that the presence of large firms
dealing with the national market and small firms specializing
in local and regional markets is a common phenomenon in any
country. However, it is peculiar to Japan that there are relatively many markets of this kind, with interfirm wage differentials. Despite these influences of history, it is also true
that, in many industries, large firms and small firms are moving toward equal footing, giving full play to their respective
specialties in technology, management, and distribution in
their respective markets. We should draw attention to the
process of their transformation and the multistoried structure
among firms of different sizes, as well as probing related policy problems.

Determinants of Changes in Market Structure

Through these changes and vicissitudes of firms, the concentration ratio in a market also changes subject to various
factors which determine market characteristics. Quantitative

studies of this subject in the United States and elsewhere have
made it clear that there are, generally speaking, two important
variables that affect the concentration ratio. They are the
growth rate of an industry and the expenditures of advertising
and other sales promotion. The growth rate of an industry
often functions to decrease the concentration ratio, because a
high growth rate gives birth to new fields of demand which invite firms to challenge, while creating new types of demand
available to small firms. On the other hand, the expenditures
of advertising and other sales promotion activities normally
function to raise the concentration ratio, because large firms
hold extreme advantages in sales promotion including heavy
television advertising. Generally speaking, this raises the
concentration ratio in an industry which allows not only real
product differentiation in price, quality and performance but
also imaginary differentiation under the influence of advertising.

Needless to say, in addition to these two factors, the concentration ratio is determined by a host of other factors including
economies of scale, barriers to entry, and the extent of the
market. However, the aforementioned two variables are the
ones that determine changes in the concentration ratio. This
point has been revealed by empirical studies of Gort, Mueller
and Hamm, and others in the U.S. (28) and has been similarly
confirmed by econometric studies of concentration in Japan. (29)

However, this proposition seems to raise an important problem in connection with our studies of concentration in Japanese
industry. It concerns the evaluation of the trend of moderately
rising concentration in Japan after 1970. (30) As we already
noted, our long-term review of postwar Japanese industry as
a whole gives no indication of any significant trend of monopolization or concentration in Japan. On the contrary, concentration has tended to decline in the leading industries. With 1970
as a turning point, however, a subtle change has occurred in
this connection, and concentration has begun turning slightly upward. At the present moment at least, this tendency deserves
no serious attention. But we must keep in mind that basic
changes could occur in the Japanese economy which would affect

the two important variables, <u>viz.</u> the growth rate of the industries would generally decline, and advertising and other sales
promotion activities would increase their weight in the interfirm competition, thus increasing the possibility of pressing
concentration upward. At the same time, the decline of the
growth rate would lead to interfirm cooperation and coordination, particularly in the markets of producer goods and capital
goods and to the control of distribution channels, especially in
the markets of consumer goods. When these factors reinforce
one another, it is quite possible that monopolistic elements
would increase in the market structure.

On the other hand, however, the successful conversion of the
industrial structure may give rise to new fields of demand,
creating urbanization-oriented or welfare-oriented firms, and
will lead to changing market shares in old fields due to development of new technology and new marketing methods, thus
opening up Schumpeterian new combinations to undermine
monopolistic restraints.

The market structure of Japanese industry, as represented
by concentration, is now at a crossroads. To explore the direction of its future is the task of this book. Before beginning
this exploration, however, we must continue to review the basic facts involved.

"Loose Combinations" of Firms

So far, we have reviewed the market structure of the Japanese economy as a whole, paid particular attention to changes
in concentration, presented a systematic statistic examination
of Japanese industrial organization, with an emphasis placed
on business behaviors. These would suffice as an outline of
industrial organization if every firm were specialized in one
market and sold its products only on this market. However,
as Figure 1 showed earlier, many firms today are engaged in
many markets, with an aggressive expansion directed not only
horizontally but also vertically and conglomerately, backed up
by appropriate allocation of resources within their own orga-

nizations. Then, to grasp and understand the relationship between markets and firms (31) in an analysis of industrial organization is a complicated problem. We are now going to examine this type of a problem. We shall attempt to clarify their
relationship in the light of diversified behaviors of firms. Before that, let us discuss the "loose combinations" of firms.

Firms may be able to act as if they were a unified organization through forming a loose combination called cartel; in this
event, individual firms need not try to expand market shares
or to monopolize markets through internal expansion or mergers.
A firm may also use outside distribution channels as if they
were its own when these channels are placed under a single
control; it need not form its sales network or open branch
stores. Multilateral business groupings may realize the same
effect as cartels do. A gray area like this can exist between
firms and markets. "Loose combinations" are a close substi-
tute for "solid combinations" by integration. What provides the
institutional setup for such a "loose combination" of firms is
an important aspect of the market structure.

Cartel

By a cartel, the participating firms exercise concerted action
or common policy concerning only the agreed-on matters, while
maintaining their individual sovereignty as independent and
equal partners. In most cases, the participants of a cartel are
either sellers or buyers in the same market. This is, therefore, a "horizontal" combination.

Tables 8 and 9 show cartels organized in various industries
in Japan as officially investigated by the Fair Trade Commission.

The lower panel of Table 8 shows that cartels were organized
more often in the markets of producer goods. In these markets, it is easier to organize cartels because goods can be
standardized in quality and specifications as product differentiation has less scope. Also in these markets, there is a strong
incentive to organize cartels, because competition is limited

Table 8

Illegal Cartels by Firm Size and Type of Goods

	1965	66	67	68	69	70	71	72	73	Total
Products of large firms		2	1	3	4	6	13	11	33	73
Products of small firms	3	2	1	5	2	8	4	3	14	42
Producer goods	1	4	2	4	4	11	14	14	41	95
Consumer goods	2	0	0	4	2	3	3	0	6	20

Note: A product of large firms is the item, more than 50% of whose shipments is accounted for by firms with equity more than 50 million yen. Products of small firms are all others.

Source: K. Sanekata, M. Uekusa, and J. Atsutani, "Cartel no Tetteiteki Kenkyu" [A Thorough Study of Cartels], Chuo Koron Keiei Mondai, Autumn Issue, 1975.

in advertising and other sales promotion measures and depends mainly on prices. As these goods are mainly produced by large firms, illegal cartels are relatively frequent in the field of their products. Table 9 shows illegal cartels by year and by concentration ratio. Note that illegal cartels increased in recent years in the high concentration markets.

In addition to these cartels that are officially investigated, it is alleged that there are numerous black-market or underground cartels. There are also a number of illegal cartels which have been informally reviewed by the Fair Trade Commission. There is no statistical information on them. Apart from these illegal cartels violating the Antimonopoly Law, however, there are those officially exempted from this Law or semiofficially authorized under the administrative guidance. When the Japanese economy is said to be cartel-prone, it refers to the fact that cartels, including the exempted cartels, are prevalent in Japanese industry in general.

After listing the product items under exempted cartels

Table 9

Illegal Cartels by Concentration (Manufacturing)

4-firm concentration (1969)	1965	66	67	68	69	70	71	72	73	Total
80-100%			1		1		1	5	5	13
70-79							2	1	1	4
60-69									1	1
50-59		1			1		1	1	9	13
40-49		1			1		2	2	1	7
30-39						1		1	3	5
20-29						1			4	5
0-19	1	1		2	2	1	1	1	3	12
Total	1	3	1	2	5	3	7	11	27	60

Note: Of 115 cases of illegal cartels in manufacturing (1965-1973), the table classifies 60 cases, for which the concentration ratio is available, by 4-firm concentration ratio in 1969 (MITI, Seisan Shuchudo Shiryo [Concentration in Production], 1972).
Source: See Table 8.

in one way or another, Table 10 shows the importance of officially exempted cartels in various manufacturing industries by computing the ratios of shipments of cartel products to total shipments in the respective industries to which these cartels belong. (The figures for 1960 are due to the Fair Trade Commission, and those for 1970 are due to the present author.) It should be noted that though, generally speaking, exempted cartel shares somewhat declined (see also Figure 2), they were still high in textile, apparel, and lumber and wood products.

In nonmanufacturing industries, price agreements are in effect through professional associations in barbershops, beauty shops, and restaurants on the basis of the "Law concerning Adjustments to the Operation of Environmental Sanitation Related Business." The "Law concerning the Maintenance of the

Table 10

Importance of Exempted Cartels (percent of shipments)

Industry	1960	1970
Food products	34.2	17.9
Textile products	78.1	69.1
Apparel & other textile goods	64.8	67.0
Lumber & wood products	9.8	74.2
Furniture & fixtures	5.7	—
Pulp, paper & paper products	27.4	8.5
Publishing & printing	47.0	—
Chemicals	22.6	22.7
Rubber products	13.2	42.7
Leather & leather products	7.4	13.4
Stone, clay and glass	41.2	17.6
Iron & steel	34.5	58.8
Nonferrous metals	50.8	29.9
Metal products	7.0	19.9
Nonelectrical machinery	15.5	27.5
Electrical machinery	8.3	26.3
Transport equipment	1.9	31.9
Precision instruments	25.8	55.6
Other manufactured goods	6.7	6.5
Total (manufacturing)	28.0	30.7

Note: The legal grounds justifying the exemption of cartels from the Antimonopoly Law and the numbers of exempted cartels are as follows:

	1960	1970
Antirecession cartels	4	0
Rationalization cartels	9	10
Medium and Small Enterprises Organization Law	370	469
Provisional Measures Laws	10	22
Liquor Tax Law	9	7
Export-Import Transactions Law	172	218
Others	21	160
Total	595	886

Cartels' shares are overstated in a few instances in the table because cartels are assumed to apply nationwide even though they apply to a certain region or a group of regions only.

Sources: For 1960, see Yoshida, ed., Nihon no Cartel [Cartels in Japan] [Tokyo: Toyo Keizai Shimpo Sha, 1964], p. 172, and for 1970, see the annual report of the Fair Trade Commission.

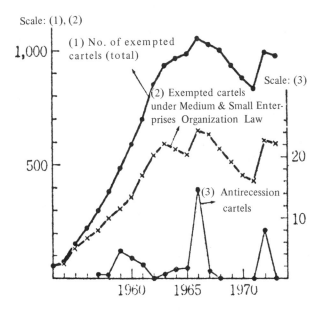

Figure 2. Status of cartelization in Japanese industrial structure.

Liquor Tax and the Liquor Business Association" places the retailing of liquor under a license system which controls its retail prices.

Concerning investment in plant and equipment and interest rates which affect the foundation of the national economy, a de facto cartel on investments is officially recognized on the basis of the earlier-stated agreement between the MITI and the Fair Trade Commission, "Concerning the Promotion of Structural Improvements in the Industries and the Operation of the Antimonopoly Law," and a de facto agreement on interest rates exists in the Japanese banking system under the "Provisional Interest Rates Adjustment Law." We repeat our emphasis that the presence of the quasi-cartel framework has greatly affected the competitive mechanism in Japanese industries. (32)

Control of Distribution Channels

Normally, it is advantageous for a manufacturer to utilize services by wholesalers and retailers through common distribution channels in the market. However, in case available services in the market are not trustworthy with respect to sales methods, quality maintenance, post-purchase services, and the like, or in case it seems more efficient for the manufacturer to manage distribution by his own managerial resources, the manufacturer carries on forward integration by opening sales stores and branch stores. Short of forward integration, the manufacturer may attempt to keep control over distribution channels in one form or another and to achieve a loose form of integration.

Forms of integration are the exclusive sales store system, territory system, discrimination (rebates in accordance with shares, progressive rebates), commissioned sales system, and so on. All of these are managerial forms for the sake of improving enterprise and distribution performances through cost reduction by rationalization, sales promotion, improved post-purchase services, etc., as well as powerful means of controlling the market. Placing sales stores under the manufacturer's control enables him to improve marketing and post-purchase services for his products, to rationalize deliveries of goods, and to adapt his production planning quickly to changes in demand; it, therefore, proves to be an effective form of transaction, especially, at the stage of initial mass production or of new entry into the market, insofar as no element of direct restraint is involved in transactions. Once this control becomes permanent and sales dealers become subservient to the producer, however, they are prevented from introducing new ideas or innovations, thus creating disadvantages to the producer himself.

Distribution plays two important roles: one is to convey manufacturers' information to consumers, and the other is to feed back consumers' needs to manufacturers. However, sales stores under a manufacturer's control often fail to perform the second task well. In this respect, specialty traders dealing with many manufacturers in a specialized group of goods can act more efficiently in many cases. On the other hand, large retail stores ask manufacturers to produce their private brand goods or to plan production in accordance with their sales schedule. In other words, retailers place manufacturers under their control. In this vertical interfirm relationship, there arises a diversity of systems of distribution from production to consumption, depending on industries and stages of development, and competition takes place among these systems.

It is by no means easy to get statistical data on this kind of control of distribution. Table 11 presents a statistical summary on the basis of the MITI's survey of commerce, just to give the reader the order of magnitude. In the wholesale trade, many (30-34%) wholesalers with 50 or more employees are controlled by manufacturers. They in turn control retailers (12-17%). This sort of control is prominent in machinery and equipment, minerals and metals, chemicals, pharmaceuticals and toiletries.

It is also interesting to analyze how this kind of control over distribution corresponds with concentration ratios and other structural market characteristics and to ascertain how it affects distribution margins. To the best of my knowledge, however, there are no comprehensive statistics available on distribution margins. So, keeping in mind the incompleteness of data, we compute the distribution margin rates as the ratios of wholesale and retail margins respectively to the value of production at purchaser prices, as recorded in the input-output table. When we correlate them with production concentration ratios, we find the retail margin rate to be higher to some extent as the concentration ratio is higher in those industries with active sales promotion. (33)

In connection with the general setup of distribution, it must also be noted that the presence formerly of the Department Store Law and currently of the Large Retail Store Law has substantially limited new market entry by large retail stores which should be the bearers of innovations in distribution. The Department Store Law of 1956 was enacted with a view to pro-

Table 11

Control of Distribution (percent)

No. of regular employees	Controlled by				Controlling				
	None	Manufacturers	Wholesalers	Total	None	Manufacturers	Wholesalers	Retailers	Total
Wholesalers									
by size of employment									
1- 4 persons	86	8	8	100	94	2	3	3	100
5- 19	77	15	11	100	90	4	4	4	100
20- 49	69	24	10	100	83	6	5	8	100
50- 99	62	32	9	100	76	7	7	12	100
100-299	61	34	9	100	69	11	10	15	100
300-	64	30	9	100	59	18	19	17	100
Total	79	13	10	100	90	3	4	4	100
300 or more employees									
by type of goods handled									
General merchandise	80	15	10	100	35	50	50	35	100
Textile	78	14	11	100	69	17	17	3	100
Apparel and accessories	88	10	1	100	60	31	4	7	100
Farm, livestock, and fishery products	69	10	22	100	61	10	14	25	100
Food and beverages	81	15	4	100	58	15	38	12	100
Drugs, toiletries & toilet goods	74	25	3	100	63	7	25	14	100
Chemicals and allied products	70	30	11	100	63	26	22	4	100
Minerals and metals	45	49	9	100	51	18	25	28	100
Machinery and equipment	34	57	15	100	54	15	18	24	100
Building materials	78	17	6	100	72	11	17	6	100
Furniture and house furnishings	100	—		100	64	27	9	9	100
Others	76	22	8	100	76	14	8	5	100

Note: Components do not necessarily add up to 100 due to overlaps in controls.

Source: Small and Medium Enterprise Agency and MITI, Shogyo Jittai Chosa Hokokusho [Third Report on the Survey of Commerce], 1975. Preliminary report on wholesale trade, table 2, "Control of Firms."

tecting medium and small retail stores from the marketing power of department stores. According to this law, the application by any department store company for opening its new store or expansion of its existing store needed approval by the MITI which, prior to approval, referred the application to the Department Store Council; however, this Council further referred it to the regional Commerce Relations Adjustment Council concerned, which normally strongly reflected the view of the local Chamber of Commerce and Industry representing the interests of local retailers. In other words, this law functioned strongly to limit the opening of new department stores or expansion of existing stores. In 1973, this law was revised into the current Large Retail Store Law, including not only department stores but also supermarket chains, changing the approval system into a report system subject to prior examination. Since there was no change to the important role of the regional Commerce Relations Adjustment Council, however, it has remained frequently to block new entry. This system will possibly become a restraint to innovations in distribution.

Interfirm Grouping

In addition to these horizontal and vertical "loose combinations," firms also organize themselves into groups involving conglomerate interfirm relations in order to exchange information, to transact in capital, and to interchange personnel. This gives rise to the problem of business groups. We shall analyze the function of the business group as an information exchange club and shall determine its position in industrial organization in later chapters of the book. At this point, it suffices to clarify a statistical fact on business groupings.

It is already known that the concentration ratio which has been used as an indicator of the market structure is subject to considerable change when recomputed by firms taking into account respective business groups by virtue of stock ownership. In particular, the top-firm concentration ratio is increased considerably in many instances. Table 12 compares the pro-

Table 12

The Top-Firm Shares with and without Firms Affiliated with the Top Firm Through Stock Ownership
(Chemicals, Primary Metals, and Machinery, 1972)

Market	The top-firm share	The top-firm share including firms affiliated with the top firm[a]	Market	The top-firm share	The top-firm share including firms affiliated with the top firm[a]
1. Titanium oxide	46.2	52.2	13. Bearing steel	49.5	71.4
2. Synthetic phenol	65.7	78.4	14. Stainless steel	18.9	47.3
3. Synthetic rubber	49.9	53.0	15. High tension steel	46.7	50.1
4. Pig iron	43.1	46.2	16. Free cutting steel	25.1	55.6
5. Crude steel	34.0	38.1	17. Special cold strip	23.2	35.5
6. Heavy rail	75.4	83.5	18. Cast iron pipe	55.1	61.9
7. Steel plate	35.3	36.6	19. PC cable	31.8	41.1
8. Steel sheet	42.6	52.5	20. Electrolytic copper	25.5	36.3
9. Broad hoop iron	47.7	53.7	21. Zinc	28.4	40.4
10. Cold broad hoop iron	43.3	52.3	22. Telephone	25.7	48.4
11. Galvanized sheet	39.8	59.3	23. Stereo equipment	27.9	42.3
12. Spring steel	30.4	48.8			

a) The share of the top firm plus firms, more than 10% of whose stock is owned by the top firm.

Source: Based on preliminary findings of a project on business groups conducted by the present author and his associates at the Japan Economic Data Development Center.

duction share of the top firm in selected markets in chemicals, primary metals, and machinery with the share of the top firm plus its affiliated firms, namely, those more than 10% of whose stocks are held by the top firm.

It is obvious from the table that the top-firm share is raised substantially by this adjustment in many of the markets listed in the table. In particular, observe that the share of the Nippon Steel Corporation, the top firm in the primary metal industry, rises uniformly in all iron and steel products. This is of important significance in determining market control to be examined later in the book. We may add that about 10 markets in the three industries covered in the table can be regarded as oligopolistic according to the classifications of the Fair Trade Commission because the 3-firm concentration ratio exceeds 60% when affiliated firms are added.

Needless to say, it is not possible to identify group affiliations from stock ownership alone. We must make a detailed factual examination to determine what sort of interfirm relationships are actually formed. It may be misleading as well to think that any company is controlled by another company that holds its corporate stock. While we do not pursue this problem any further at this point, it seems that these facts indicate that interfirm relationships are undeniably an element of the market structure.

Diversification of Firms

A firm grows and develops on the strength of its own strategy by making use of loose combinations with other firms, and bearing in mind its horizontal, vertical, and conglomerate growth possibilities. Let us call the firm's development in the vertical and conglomerate directions "diversification," which is a popular term nowadays. To give a more accurate definition, according to Gort (1962), a study which is often quoted in the literature on this subject, the diversification of a firm is an increase in the diversity of markets supplied by a firm, namely, the expansion of a firm into diverse markets quite different from its principal market.

The diversification of a firm is a matter of its strategy which determines the direction of its growth as far as the firm is concerned. From the viewpoint of industrial organization, however, it is new entry of firms into one another's markets. In other words, the diversification of a firm, particularly when it is large, causes an impact of great significance on the market structure. When a firm diversifies itself to many markets, it is a new entry into each of these markets and contributes to promoting competition therein. Sooner or later, however, the firm will develop into a mammoth conglomerate. The more this type of firm appears, the greater general or aggregate concentration will become. In this sense, the diversification of firms is an important point of contact between firms and markets, enabling us to have a clue in analyzing the multilateral market structure.

In the United States, Gort (34) demonstrated that the diversification of large firms was primarily through expansion into high-growth markets on the strength of their research and development efforts, which often took the form of new entry into high-concentration markets, thereby promoting competition in general.

Let us now summarize major findings of our own empirical study of the diversification of Japanese firms. (35)

The degree of diversification of a firm may be measured statistically by a number of indicators such as the number of new products added to the menu of its products, the ratio of the sales of its principal business line to its total sales (the primary specialization ratio), or the ratio of diversification which is 1 minus this primary specialization ratio, and the Bailey index of the distribution of a firm's products. These indicators reveal the following features. (36)

(1) As for changes in the diversification over time all indicators show that all (124) principal firms tended to become more diversified. For instance, the number of products on the 2-digit level of industry classification increased from 3.24 in 1963 to 3.46 in 1972 per firm. During the same period, the total number of products increased by 52. (According to Gort,

Table 13

The Average Diversification Ratio of 124 Principal Firms

Industry classification	1963	'64	'65	'66	'67	'68	'69	'70	'71	'72
At the 4-digit level	0.489	0.486	0.484	0.479	0.482	0.481	0.483	0.485	0.484	0.492
At the 3-digit level	0.400	0.399	0.393	0.393	0.399	0.401	0.405	0.414	0.410	0.420
At the 2-digit level	0.266	0.260	0.254	0.251	0.254	0.254	0.257	0.259	0.263	0.273

Source: K. Imai, A. Goto, and K. Ishiguro, "Kigyo no Tayoka ni Kansuru Jissho Bunseki" [An Empirical Study of Diversification], The Japan Economic Data Development Center, 1975.

the number of products of 111 major American firms increased on an average by 48 from 1929 to 1939, 43 from 1939 to 1950, and 108 from 1950 to 1955.)

Table 13 shows the diversification ratio (1 minus the primary specialization ratio) of the 124 principal Japanese firms from 1963 to 1972, which tended to rise at each of the 2-, 3-, and 4-digit levels.

(The estimates by Gort give changes in the diversification ratio of the 111 American firms from 31.0% in 1947 to 36.0% in 1954 at the 4-digit level.)

(2) As for differences in the diversification by industry (Table 14), the diversification ratio at the 2-digit product level is low in all crude-material industries such as primary metals, clay, stone and glass, petroleum and coal products, and pulp and paper. Moreover, the ratio tended to decline in many of them over time, indicating that the firms specialized mostly in their own industries. In contrast, the diversification ratio was relatively high and tended to rise over time in chemicals, machinery, and precision instruments.

A comparison of the diversification ratio as the 2-digit and 4-digit product levels enables us to clarify whether diversification has taken place at the periphery of firms' primary business or has moved to less related fields. One can note that

Table 14

The Diversification Ratio by Industry

Industry	2-digit level	4-digit level
1. Primary metals	0.161	0.441
2. Electrical machinery	0.437	0.594
3. Transport equipment	0.221	0.352
4. General chemicals	0.430	0.628
5. Other chemicals	0.282	0.599
6. Textile	0.206	0.595
7. Stone, clay, and glass	0.136	0.205
8. Nonferrous metals	0.251	0.447
9. Machinery	0.506	0.574
10. Food products	0.138	0.428
11. Petroleum & coal products	0.134	0.655
12. Rubber products	0.152	0.208
13. Precision instruments	0.468	0.613
14. Pulp & paper	0.171	0.442
15. Miscellaneous	0.267	0.472
16. Total	0.273	0.492

Source: See Table 13.

the low diversification ratio in stone, clay, and glass and rubber products both at the 2-digit and the 4-digit level indicates that firms in these industries are specialized in relatively narrow fields. On the other hand, in primary metals and textile industries, the diversification ratio is low at the 2-digit level and high at the 4-digit level. This implies that firms in these industries are diversified in the periphery of their principal business fields.

In addition, Table 15 which is the matrix of diversification, indicates that a great many firms diversified themselves into machinery and chemicals, followed by electrical machinery, transport equipment, and others and services. This

Table 15

Diversification Matrix (Trend of Diversification in 124 Major Firms, 1972)

Product \ Industry	Food manufacturing	Textile	Paper & pulp	General chemicals	Other chemicals	Petroleum & coal products	Rubber products	Stone, clay, and glass	Primary metals	Nonferrous metals	Nonelectrical machinery	Electrical machinery	Transport equipment	Precision instruments	Other manufacturing	Total
No. of firms	13	8	5	12	6	6	3	5	10	11	8	15	16	3	3	124
1. Food products	28	2	1		1											32
2. Textile products		8		2												10
3. Apparel & other textile goods		2														2
4. Lumber & wood products			5													5
5. Furniture & fixtures																0
6. Pulp, paper and related products			5		2							2				9
7. Publishing, printing & related products															2	2
8. Chemical industry products	1	11	2	24	10	1	1	1	2	7	1				2	63
9. Petroleum & coal products				2		6				2						10

Industry	1	2	3	4	5	6	7	8	9	10	11	12	13	14	15	Total
10. Rubber products						3										3
11. Leather & fur products																0
12. Stone and clay products		1		5	1	1		9	10		1		1			18
13. Primary metals				3			1	1	10	2			1			22
14. Nonferrous metals		1		5				1		19						26
15. Metal products				4	2	2			4	1	2	5	5			15
16. Nonelectrical machinery				4	1	2	1	1	9		30	2	24	3		78
17. Electrical machinery			1							3		39				43
18. Transport equipment									2	1	8	4	24	1	2	42
19. Precision instruments			1						1		1	3		7	1	13
20. Ordnance										1						1
21. Others & services	6	2	1	3	2	5	1		1	11	3	3	3	2	2	39
Total	35	27	14	48	18	16	6	12	29	46	48	56	58	11	9	433
Average per firm	2.7	3.4	2.8	4.0	3.0	2.7	2.0	2.4	2.9	4.2	6.0	3.7	3.6	3.7	3.0	3.5

Note: Entries in the table represent the numbers of products of sample firms (124 companies) in each of the industries listed at the top of the table.

Source: See Table 13.

pattern of diversification agrees well with Gort's finding that firms tended to diversify into those fields that achieved high growth via technical progress.

(3) Following the Harvard Business Policy Research Group, we have classified business diversification into 4 types, namely, (i) Single Business, (ii) Dominant Business, (iii) Related Business, and (iv) Unrelated Business; our 124 Japanese firms in 1972 comprised (i) 2.4%, (ii) 22.6%, (iii) 33.1%, and (iv) 41.9%. As our classification of (iii) and (iv) is based on the 2-digit product level, no exact comparison with the American composition is possible. However, the latter for 500 major firms in 1970 was (i) 6%, (ii) 14%, (iii) 60% and (iv) 20%.

Business performances of firms by type of diversification reveal that those of type (i), Single Business, are the worst both in terms of the profit rate and the growth rate, while those of type (ii), Dominant Business, are good in both indicators. This preliminary finding of our agrees roughly with the findings of the Harvard Group, thus attesting to the effectiveness of this classification and signifying the importance of diversification strategy to firms.

These trends in the diversification of major Japanese firms are suggestive of the problem of industrial organization in the following context. The fact that diversification does not progress but rather retrogresses in crude-material industries and in industries such as transport equipment indicates the difficulty of structural conversion, should such a trend continue; firms in these industries continue to seek profits without leaving their principal business fields despite their stagnant demand. Since firms in these industries attempt to strengthen vertical combination through placing their orders of parts with their affiliated companies and increasing their holding of stocks of affiliated firms, they are strongly directed to becoming "stagnant oligopoly." However, if these firms opt for diversifying their operations into new areas such as housing and urban development by utilizing their technical know-how, marketing, and other managerial resources, there will be possibilities for their contribution to competition in these new areas and for weakening their tendency toward monopolization in their principal business areas.

One may generalize from these observations that the direction of diversification in Japan from now on holds an important key to determine the performance of industrial organization in Japan. If the diversification of firms proceeds on the basis of their monopoly position in their principal business markets and their financial capability, it will lead them to conglomerate-type enterprises, thus strengthening the evils of monopoly. What may come out of this situation will be unfavorable to the future of Japanese industrial organization. On the other hand, if diversification leads to new entry into one another's markets or monopolistic markets, it will function to promote competition by weakening the market control of existing firms. If inter-firm affiliations develop beyond the territorial borders of the existing business groups or with technically advanced firms seeking new combination with other firms, it will also contribute to expediting competition, thus leading to the formation of flexible industrial organization in Japan. In this respect, too, Japanese industrial organization stands at a crossroads.

Notes

1) Though 325 corporations were designated for investigation under the Economic Deconcentration Law, only those listed above were ultimately designated for dissolution after many twists and turns of discussions and negotiations. On this process, see E. M. Hadley, Antitrust in Japan (Princeton: Princeton University Press, 1970). See also M. Uekusa, "Kigyo Bunkatsu no Kenkyu" [A Study of Enterprise Dissolution], Business Review, March 1976 for a new finding in this connection.

2) Hadley, op. cit., p. 109 and p. 120.

3) Production concentration ratios of major industrial products in 1937 were as follows:

Pig Iron	Ships	Caustic Soda	Rayon Yarn
3 Major firms	Mitsui & Mitsubishi	Mitsui, Mitsubishi & Sumitomo	Top 4 firms
94.0%	50.7%	63.0%	45.4%

Ammonium Sulfate	Cement	Pulp	Paper
Mitsui, Mitsubishi & Sumitomo	Asano, Mitsui & Mitsubishi	Former Oji	Former Oji
49.0%	63.0%	49.3%	71.7%

Source: Japan Statistics Research Institute, ed., Nihon Keizai Tokei Shu [Economic Statistics of Japan] (Tokyo: Nihon Hyoron Sha, 1968).

4) The zaibatsu did not maintain large stock ownership in even their core companies, e.g., 16% for Mitsui (Holding Company and Mitsui Family) in the Mitsui Trust Bank, 23.1% for Mitsubishi (ditto) in the Mitsubishi Heavy Industries, and 13.1% for Sumitomo (ditto) in the Nippon Electric Company (all at the time of dissolution). Holding Company Liquidation Commission, Nihon Zaibatsu to Sono Kaitai [Japan's Zaibatsu and Their Dissolution], 1951, pp. 93-125.

5) Hadley, op. cit., pp. 390-391.

6) For instance, MITI formally adopted a policy of curbing excessive investment in the petrochemical industry both as regards machinery imports and technology imports. See MITI, ed., Tsusho Sangyo Gyosei Shihanseiki no Ayumi [A Quarter-Century History of MITI Administration] (Tokyo: Tsusho Sangyo Chosakai, 1975), p. 162.

7) Among the cartels exempted from the Antimonopoly Law from 1952 to 1963 had been 10 cases under the Provisional Machinery Industry Development Measures Law (enforced in June 1957), 3 cases under the Provisional Textile Industry

Equipment Law (October 1956), 1 case under the Provisional
Silk Industry Equipment Law (May 1957), 1 case under the Provisional Law concerning Measures for Rationalization of the
Coal Mining Industry (September 1956), 1 case under the Provisional Law concerning Measures for Rationalization of the
Ammonium Sulfate Industry and Adjustment to Ammonium Sulfate Exports (September 1954), and 11 cases under the Law
concerning Development of Exports of Marine Products (December 1954), see N. Yoshida, ed., Nihon no Cartel [Cartels
in Japan] (Tokyo: Toyo Keizai Shimposha, 1964).

8) See Y. Okudaira, "Gyoseiken to Keizai" [Administrative
Power and Economy], Iwanami Commentaries on Gendai Ho
[Contemporary Law], vol. 7, 1966, pp. 387-388.

9) According to the Industrial Structure Investigation Committee's recommendation, "Needless to say, the Japanese economy basically permits enterprises to act freely, while regarding their ideas and ingenuity as creating the driving force of
the economy," and "It seems necessary to further raise the
level of recognition of the role and effects of the Antimonopoly
Law." However, what it actually emphasized was a "formula
for coordination" as follows: (1) A "coordination panel" may
be organized with representatives of the industries, banking
interests, neutral groups, and the government participating to
express and discuss their opinions and to make decisions on
an equal footing. (2) The coordination panel is expected to
decide on "the future mode of the specific industry concerned
and its targets (in production, exports, investment, and so on)
and then to determine the orientation that the industry ought to
follow. (3) If it becomes necessary to break down the total
quota established by the coordination panel to the level of the
individual firms involved, "consultations may as well be held
among such individual firms," though, first of all, each of them
is expected to follow the agreement voluntarily. See Industrial
Structure Investigation Committee, ed., Nihon no Sangyo Kozo
[The Industrial Structure of Japan], Vol. 1, (Tokyo: Tsusho
Sangyo Kenkyu Sha, 1964), pp. 82-88.

10) It goes without saying that as is obvious from the actual operation of the Antimonopoly Law since its revision in 1953, the fact that the revision opened the door for authorization of antirecession cartels and rationalization cartels marked an important change in the rule governing the framework of industrial organization. As long as antirecession cartels can be authorized whenever a recession occurs, the prohibition of cartels under the Antimonopoly Law would eventually lose its significance.

11) H. Morikawa called this aspiration "in-the-community individualism." See H. Morikawa, "Kigyosha Katsudo no Nihonteki Etosu" [The Japanese-Type Ethos of Entrepreneurship], M. Sumiya, ed., Nihonjin no Keizai Kodo [Economic Behaviors of the Japanese], Vol. 2 (Tokyo: Keizai Shimpo Sha, 1969).

12) E.g., see M. Nicholson, Oligopoly and Conflict — A Dynamic Approach (Liverpool: Liverpool University Press, 1972).

13) Two input-output tables were prepared, one for the narrow definition and the other for the broad definition of oligopoly. The narrow definition deems industries with the 3-firm concentration ratio above 60% as being oligopolistic (a definition adopted by the Fair Trade Commission). The broad definition extends to industries with the 6 or less firm concentration ratio above 50% or with the 12 or less firm concentration ratio above 75%. The latter is taken to enable us to compare our result with the one prepared by A. D. Chandler, who reviewed changes in the oligopoly position in the United States over one hundred years (A. D. Chandler, "The Structure of American Industry in the Twentieth Century: A Historical Overview," Business History Review, Autumn 1969). Our data tapes are available at the Computation Center of Hitotsubashi University.

14) The oligopoly share seems to have been close to 30% in the United States, too. See below.

A. D. Chandler's Estimate of the Oligopoly Share in Product Value

%

1909	1919	1929	1939	1947	1958	1963
16	18	21	28	26	25	27

Source: Chandler, op. cit., pp. 283-289.

G. Nutter's Estimate of the Share of Industries, with the 4-company Concentration Ratio above 50%, in Total Value Added of Manufacturing

%

1947	1954	1958	1963	1966
24.4	29.9	30.2	33.1	28.6

Source: G. W. Nutter, The Extent of Enterprise Monopoly in the United States, 1889-1939, (Chicago: The University of Chicago Press, 1951), pp. 35-48.

15) The degree of dependence on final demands is computed basically by using the following matrices:

$$
\begin{bmatrix} X_1 \\ \vdots \\ X_{25} \\ X_{43} \\ \vdots \\ X_{50} \end{bmatrix}
\begin{matrix} \text{Competitive} \\ \\ \\ \text{Oligopolistic} \\ \\ \text{Public utility} \\ \text{Public works} \end{matrix}
= \left| 1 - A + M \right|^{-1}
\begin{pmatrix} F_1 & 0 & 0 \\ \vdots & & \\ F_{25} & & \\ 0 & F_{26} & 0 \\ & \vdots & \\ & F_{43} & \\ 0 & 0 & F_{44} \\ & & \vdots \\ & & F_{50} \end{pmatrix}
$$

Competitive sector   Oligopolistic sector   Public sector

where X is the value of domestic production, A the input co-efficient matrix, M the import coefficient matrix, and F the final demand total. X consists of three rows, each showing the dependence on final demands in one sector.

16) I. Sakura and T. Nakamura, "Sangyo Renkan no Kigyo Kibo Betsu Bunseki" [Analysis of Interindustry Relations by Enterprise Size] Keizai Kenkyu, October 1960.

17) M. A. Adelman, "The Two Faces of Economic Concentration," in D. Bell and I. Kristol, eds., Capitalism Today (New York: Basic Books, 1971), p. 120.

18) J. M. Blair, Economic Concentration (New York: Harcourt Brace Jovanovich, 1972), Chap. 1, presents an excellent survey of these studies.

19) Chandler, op. cit.

20) As for Group C, the falling tendency of concentration is illustrated below with respect to a few products.

3-Firm Concentration Ratio

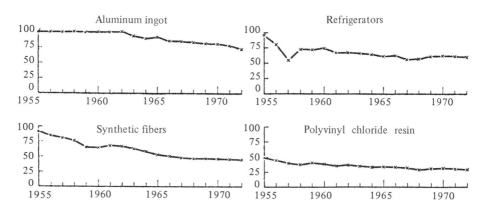

21) Adelman, op. cit., p. 125.

22) For a concise survey, see my "Kigyo no Seicho ni Tsuite" [On the Growth of Firms], Keizai Kenkyu, January 1966. For an analysis of the probabilistic growth process of Japanese firms, see my "The Growth of Firms in the Japanese Manufacturing Industries," Hitotsubashi Journal of Commerce and Management (November 1966), (paper presented at the First Far Eastern Meeting of the Econometric Society) and

my "Kigyo Seicho no Kakuritsu Katei" [Probabilistic Process
of the Growth of Firms] in Yamada, Emi, and Mizoguchi, eds.,
Nihon Keizai no Kozo Hendo to Yosoku [Structural Changes and
Projections of the Japanese Economy] (Tokyo: Shunju Sha,
1969).

23) M. Baba, Handokusen no Keizaigaku [Economics of Anti-
monopoly] (Tokyo: Chikuma Shobo, 1974), Chapter II.

24) The Bank of Japan sums up sales of firms each year in
each of the three size classes as defined in Table 6. Our growth
rates are computed from them. Therefore, firms in each class
vary from year to year. If we wish to prove the statement in
the text more exactly, we have to compute growth rates for
fixed panels of firms in each size class from one year to the
next.

25) Since Table 7 is based on a sample survey, the size distribution of all manufacturing firms is obtained from the Census
of Manufactures in the table below and illustrated as a Lorenz
curve for the sake of checking the authenticity of Table 7.

Size Distribution of Manufacturing Firms: 1970

Size by equity (¥ million)	Number of firms (%)	Value of shipments (%)
Less than 1	22.3	1.9
1-2	24.5	3.3
2-5	25.6	6.2
5-10	12.0	5.5
10-50	12.6	16.3
50-100	1.4	5.4
100-1,000	1.5	14.5
1,000-10,000	0.4	21.4
More than 10,000	0.1	25.5
Total	100.0	100.0

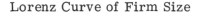

Lorenz Curve of Firm Size

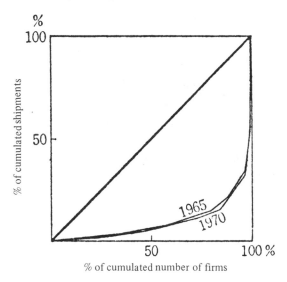

% of cumulated number of firms

26) For a survey of the dual-structure theory, see H. Kawaguchi, M. Shinohara, K. Nagasu, K. Miyazawa, and M. Ito, Nihon Keizai no Kiso Kozo [The Basic Structure of the Japanese Economy] (Tokyo: Shunju Sha, 1962).

27) The Fair Trade Commission Secretariat, ed., Nihon no Sangyo Shuchu [Industrial Concentration in Japan] (Tokyo: Toyo Keizai Shimpo Sha, 1969), p. 41.

28) M. Gort, "Analysis of Stability and Change in Market Shares," Journal of Political Economy, February 1963; W. E. Mueller and L. G. Hamm, "Trends in Industrial Market Concentration, 1947-1970," Review of Economics and Statistics, November 1974.

29) The table below shows the results of a regression analysis of the available data of 136 product items. The dependent variable is changes (in percentage points) in the 3-firm concentration ratio from 1959 to 1970; the explanatory variables are the initial concentration ratio, the market size, the growth rate, and the degree of product differentiation (represented by 2 dummy variables).

It is clear that concentration tends to decline when the growth

Independent variable / Dependent variable	Concentration at the beginning (1959)	Market size (1970)	Growth rate (1970/1959)	Degree of product differentiation: A-High, B-Moderately high (A) (B)	Constant term	$\bar{R}$
Changes in concentration (1959-1970)	−0.284 (−5.65)	0.002 (1.47)	−0.041 (−1.93)	6.449 2.967 (1.64) (0.51)	12.728	0.49

(t-ratios in parentheses).

rate is high and to rise when the degree of product differentiation is high.

30) The table below indicates that the 3-firm concentration ratio began to rise in 1970.

3-Firm Concentration Ratios

	1965	1968	1970	1972
Index (Simple average)	100.0	100.3	102.9	104.1
(Weighted average)[a]	100.0	103.1	109.8	112.1

a) Weighted by value of production.

Note: The index covers 170 manufacturing industries (including coal mining) surveyed by the FTC. They account for 62.2% of the value of total manufacturing production in 1972.

Source: Fair Trade Commission Secretariat.

31) In this connection, see my "Soshiki to Shijo" [Organization and Market], Soshiki Kagaku, 9 (Winter 1975).

32) The fact that fixed investment adjustments give rise to peculiar investment cycles and interfere with the smooth balancing of demand and supply can be verified by the regression

analysis given below. The dependent variable, the excess capacity (measured by the inventory stock of finished goods/ shipments), is regressed on the explanatory variables given below for a sample of 136 markets, yielding the following result:

Independent variable ⟍ Dependent variable	Market Size, 1970	Growth rate, 1970/1959	Concentration ratio, 1970	Investment adjustment dummy	Constant term	$\bar{R}$
Excess capacity, 1970 (Inventory Shipments)	−0.0002	−0.00005	0.00015	0.0147	0.0494	0.36
	(−4.73)	(−0.10)	(1.14)	(2.26)		

(t-values in parentheses.)

The table shows that industries tend to have more excess capacity as they are more concentrated, and as they are subject to investment adjustments.

33) The Retail Margin Rates and the Concentration Ratio (1970)

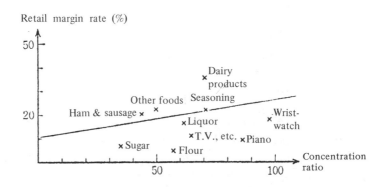

Notes: The retail margin rate is the ratio of retail margins to the value of domestic production as reported in the 1970 input-output table. The concentration ratio is the 3-firm concentration ratio published by the Fair Trade Commission. (In some cases, the concentration ratios are averaged in order to correspond with product coverages.)

34) M. Gort, Diversification and Integration in American Industry (Princeton: Princeton University Press, 1962).

35) K. Imai, A. Goto, and K. Ishiguro, "Kigyo no Tayoka ni Kansuru Jissho Bunseki [An Empirical Study of Diversification], Japan Economic Data Development Center, 1975.

36) Covered by these indicators are 124 principal firms in Japan which appear in the lists of the top 100 firms either by size of equity or by total sales. The selection is made among them so as to have at least three firms in every industry. Statistical indicators of diversification were prepared from the data, estimated by ourselves from various sources, on values of sales by products of individual companies from 1963 to 1972.

II.

INDUSTRY STUDIES

5

THE AUTOMOBILE INDUSTRY
OF JAPAN

Hiroya Ueno and Hiromichi Muto*

I. Attractions and Evils of Automobiles

Symbol of the Economic Power of a Nation

The first automobile in the world was made by N. J. Cugnot
(1725-1804), a Frenchman, some 200 years ago in 1769. This
three-wheel steam-engined vehicle, however, ran into a brick
wall at a speed of 3.5 kilometers per hour and broke down. As
compared with current passenger cars, it was indeed a primitive
vehicle. Yet it was undoubtedly an automobile in that it was an
engine-loaded wheeled vehicle which could turn into a mobile
criminal weapon as soon as it had been driven in the wrong way.
In fact, the main features of this primitive vehicle fit what the
Japanese Road Traffic Law defines as "cars with prime movers,
except prime-mover attached bicycles, which can be driven
without the railway or cableway." This might lead one to wonder

*Hiroya Ueno and Hiromichi Muto, "Jidosha." In Hisao Kumagai,
ed., Nihon no Sangyo Soshiki [Industrial Organization in Japan],
Vol. I (Tokyo: Chuo Koron Sha, 1973), pp. 119-181. Translated
and published by permission of the authors and publisher. Translated by Hitokatsu Ogasawara.

This translation originally appeared in Japanese Economic
Studies, III (Fall 1974), 3-90 (55-88 omitted in this reprint).

if there had been any substantial technical progress in automobiles during the past two centuries.

Yet nobody can deny the fact that remarkable progress has been achieved in automobiles. In 1885 G. Daimler and K. Benz made a gasoline engine car. Following the invention of the tubed tire in 1888, many structural and exterior changes in the automobile have been made in this century, including three-step transmission, self-starter, four-wheel brakes, and automatic transmission. People who were attracted to automobiles both in the fields of manufacturing and driving increased rapidly. A great many enterprises, as if in a gold rush, entered into and disappeared from the automobile markets of their countries.

However, more important is the fact that the automobiles not only attracted individuals and enterprises but were also extremely valuable to the national economy for the following reasons:

1) In an advanced country, the automobile industry has large weights in production and employment, and the automobile stock is expected to rise faster than the income level (in other words, it has a strong advantage in terms of income elasticity). Thus by establishing an automobile industry within its economy, a country adds new and substantive industrial activity that contributes to its economic growth.

2) Since the automobile industry depends on many other industries, its development will be accompanied by the expansion of related industries and their technical improvement.

3) As an export trade, the automobile industry has a high foreign exchange earning capacity.

4) The diffusion of automobiles helps improve the transportation capacity in the national economy, facilitates the efficient use of production factors, and thus leads to the modernization of other industries.

As point 4 needs no further elaboration, we shall now analyze why development of the automobile industry is attractive to a country in the light of points 1 to 3.

Table 1 compares Japan, the United States, and the United Kingdom as to the relative position of the automobile industry in the manufacturing sector in 1955. At that time the Japanese

Table 1

Position of the Automobile Industry in the
Manufacturing Sector, 1955*

	Value added		Persons engaged		Per capita value added	
	(million yen)	As % of all manufacturing	(thousands)	As % of all manufacturing	(thousand yen)	As multiple of all manufacturing
Japan	64,397	3.1	128	2.3	503	1.19
U.S.	3,391,920	7.2	832	4.9	4,076	1.45
	(52.7)	(2.3)	(6.5)	(2.1)	(2.1)	(1.2)
U.K.	806,400	11.9	917	11.9	879	1.02
	(12.5)	(3.8)	(7.2)	(5.2)	(1.7)	(0.9)

*Figures in parentheses represent levels relative to Japan.
Sources: Ministry of International Trade and Industry (MITI),
Census of Manufactures; Department of Commerce (U.S.), Sta-
tistical Abstract of the United States; Central Statistical Office,
(U.K.), Annual Abstract of Statistics.

automobile industry was by far the smallest, being only one-
half of the American level and one-quarter of the British level
both in terms of value added and employment. Yet the Japanese
automobile industry had value added per person engaged or
value-added productivity as high as 1.2 times that of total manufacturing. Domestically speaking, it was one of the high-
productivity industries, though its productivity was only one-
eighth of the U.S. level.

The income elasticity of the automobile stock was 1.31 in 8
advanced countries and 1.03 in 26 less-advanced countries,

thus indicating that a rise in the income level induces a more than proportionate increase in automobiles. In other words, the automobile industry is a growth industry which can contribute a great deal to the development of a national economy.

As is well known, the expansion of the automobile industry has impacts on other industries, inducing the growth of such related industries as iron and steel, nonferrous metals, machine tools, tires, glass, and automobile parts. Visitors to an up-to-date automobile assembly plant which boasts a monthly output of 20,000 automobiles may get the impression that with its production lines being something like the assembly of parts into plastic toy cars, anybody who has access to the parts he needs should be able to make automobiles very simply. Despite this impression, it is by no means easy to manufacture automobiles, covering single-handed the entire processes from raw materials to final products. An automobile when completed requires more than 10,000 parts, each of which should be guaranteed of high quality and should meet the market requirements of durability and economy. Therefore, one must think that what supports the growth of the automobile industry is really the growth of these related industries. This is why the automobile industry, being supported by many industries, is said to reflect the economic power of a country.

Propagation Effects of the Automobile Industry

The propagation effects of the automobile industry are most conspicuous in the United States. Table 2 shows the percentages of raw materials used in the automobile industry. In the United States, already before World War II, the automobile industry consumed one-quarter of the steel, one-fifth of the copper and aluminum, and 80% of the rubber. In contrast, in Japan in 1955 these percentages were much lower, namely 2.4% for ordinary steel, 25.2% for aluminum, and 23.3% for rubber, due obviously to the limited scale of the automobile industry in Japan at the time. Nevertheless, it was already clear that the automobile industry had to be supported by many other industries.

Table 2

Percentages of Raw Materials Consumed
in Automobile Production

United States (1935)		Japan (1955)	
1. Steel	24.8	1. Steel	
a. Bar steel	40.1	a. Ordinary steel	2.4
b. Sheet steel	42.5		
c. Hoop	57.1		
2. Malleable cast iron	54.0	2. Malleable cast iron	23.2
3. Copper and copper alloy	20.0	3. Copper	—
4. Lead	36.8	4. Lead	—
5. Aluminum	20.0	5. Aluminum (die cast)	25.2
6. Rubber	80.0	6. Rubber	23.2

Sources:
    U.S.: AMA, Automobile Facts and Figures, 1937;
    Japan: MITI, Waga Kuni Jidosha Kogyo no Shorai [The future of our automobile industry]; MITI, Hitetsu Kinzoku Seihin Tokei Nempo [Annual abstract of nonferrous metals statistics]; MITI, Gomu Tokei Nempo [Annual abstract of rubber statistics].

    According to the 1955 input-output tables, an increase of 100 million yen in demand for the automobile industry creates total demand of 280 million yen. In the 35-sector table, the input coefficient for the automobile industry is 1.258, ranking below 1.413 for cast, forged, and rolled steel, but above shipbuilding, rolling stock, and electrical machinery.
    As for its export potential, automobiles exported in 1955 were only 0.3% of total manufactured exports in the case of Japan. The ratio was far behind West Germany's 8.8%, Italy's

7.0%, the United States' 4.7%, and Sweden's 2.4%. Also, as to the commodity structure of exports, while products of heavy and chemical industries were relatively important in other industrial nations, 40% of Japanese exports were textiles and apparel. However, there was an ample reason for placing great expectations on the export potential of the Japanese automobile industry in view of the increasing weights of heavy and chemical industries in total world exports, as evidenced in the case of West Germany, which exported more automobiles than textiles and clothing.

In May 1955 the Ministry of International Trade and Industry (MITI) announced a "General Plan for Fostering Popular Cars." Its objective was, "by means of positively fostering the small passenger car industry as a new industry, to expedite the expansion of related industries, expansion of employment, and enhancement of the technical level, thus preparing the ground for the small passenger car industry to develop as an export industry and raising the national living standard through the popularization of passenger cars at home." This clearly represented the MITI intention to foster and protect the automobile industry as an important strategic industry from the viewpoint of national interests. We can see why MITI was attracted to the automobile industry. However, the automobile's attraction has since led MITI to step up protection for the automobile industry almost to an excessive degree.

The "Antimotorization" Mood

Although automobiles were given full play in postwar Japanese industrial development, we now see the rise of a reaction to them.

That is, based on suspicions about the utility of automobiles and concern about their problems, an "antimotorization" mood is currently spreading among the public. The origins of the "antimotorization" movement and the popular sympathy with it can be ascribed to: (1) drastic increases in traffic accidents as automobiles were popularized; (2) discovery of a large number of defective cars and their suspect safety; (3) intensified air pollution due to car exhaust gas. However, what lies behind these questions is the public realization that the government's industrial policy, based on its preference for the interests of automobile users and manufacturers, its mass-production-first principle, and its export-oriented mentality, has actually run counter to the people's health and welfare.

Table 3

Pedestrian Mortality in Automobile Accidents
and Per Car Population*

Country	Pedestrian mortality per 10,000 cars	Per car population
U.S.	4.9 persons	2.3 persons
U.K.	5.0	4.3
France	6.3	3.6
West Germany	9.2	4.7
Italy	4.8	5.9
Netherlands	4.7	5.7
Norway	4.1	5.0
Japan 1965	4.3	12.4
1966	4.9	10.6
1967	4.7	8.9
1968	5.1	7.5
1969	5.8	6.3
1970	5.7	5.6
1971	5.5	5.0

*1968 for all countries except Japan.
Source: Economic Planning Agency, Kokumin Seikatsu Hakusho [White paper on national life], 1972.

Table 3 compares pedestrian mortality in automobile accidents per 10,000 cars in Japan since 1965 and in other countries in 1968. In the year 1968 the Japanese pedestrian mortality of 5.1 persons was next to West Germany and France. When the population per automobile is taken into account, we must say that pedestrians in Japan were exposed to greater risks than those in France. The mortality in Japan rose to 5.5 persons in 1971. In other words, more than 10,000 pedestrians were to become the victims of about 20 million "mobile criminal weapons." What is more, the danger of automobiles involves even drivers. An investigation on the problem of defective cars, which was initially brought up by the New York Times in June 1969, revealed that there were 1,298,000 unrepaired cars among a total of 2,456,000 defective cars. In other words, one out of every 10 of 13.4 million registered cars at that time was structurally defective in one way or another; the automobile was not only a mobile criminal weapon for pedestrians but also a "moving coffin" for its driver.

According to the Tokyo metropolitan government's 1970 survey of "The Images of People, Automobiles, and Highways," 41% of those polled returned "negative" impressions about increasing automobiles against 25.9% noting their "contribution to industrial and economic development" and 17.3% favoring their "contribution to convenience and comfort in life," thus indicating that automobiles are no longer an attraction but have become a nuisance to people.

As for air pollution, as shown in Table 4, an Environment Agency survey indicates that automobiles contribute most to each of three air pollutants, carbon monoxide (CO), hydrocarbons (HC), and nitrogen oxide (NOx). Automobiles account for as much as 90% of the total of carbon monoxide discharges, more than half of hydrocarbon discharges, and more than one-third of nitrogen oxide discharges. They are precisely the "arch-culprit" of air pollution. In this connection the evening editions of major newspapers on July 17, 1972, carried the Tokyo metropolitan government's full-page ad calling for equipping automobiles with exhaust-gas reduction devices to reduce photochemical smog in Tokyo. Following this press campaign, the antimotorization movement has rapidly spread. Under the mounting public pressure the Technical Committee on Automo-

Table 4

Sources of Air Pollution*

Pollution sources		1970		1975 (estimate)	
		(tons)	%	(tons)	%
Carbon monoxide	1. Automobile	943,500	(93.0)	1,082,200	(85.2)
	2. Solid waste	63,800	(6.3)	179,000	(14.1)
	3. Commerce and household	4,400	(0.4)	6,900	(0.5)
Hydrocarbons	1. Automobile	231,800	(57.3)	231,800	(51.2)
	2. Organic solvent	101,800	(25.1)	120,900	(26.7)
	3. Petroleum industry	59,800	(14.8)	77,600	(17.2)
Nitrogen oxide	1. Automobile	173,000	(39.0)	277,000	(41.1)
	2. Industry	137,600	(31.0)	233,100	(34.6)
	3. Power generation	95,400	(21.5)	102,800	(15.2)

*Based on a survey covering the metropolitan area of Tokyo and three neighboring prefectures (Kanagawa, Saitama, and Chiba).

Source: Environment Agency, as reported in Nihon Keizai Shimbun, October 4, 1972.

bile Pollution of the Air Pollution Group of the Central Public
Nuisance Deliberation Council published on August 18, 1972, an
interim report, including a recommendation for the enactment
of a "Japanese-style Muskie Act," thus compelling the automobile industry to prepare antipollution measures by the end of
1975.

In this article we apply the theory of industrial organization
to analyze and assess the attractions of automobiles as one of
the mainstays of the postwar economic development, the contribution of MITI's industrial policy to the development of the
automobile industry, the automobile industry's strategy, and its
subsequent achievements and failures.

II. MITI's Protection Policy

Thoroughgoing Protection

The government, at its cabinet meeting on September 13, 1949,
made a decision on "Matters Concerning Industrial Rationalization," which set up the guidelines for building a desirable industrial structure in the future. However, opinions had still been
split even within government quarters at that time as to where
the automobile industry should be placed in the prospective industrial structure.

One side was represented by Mr. Ichimada, then governor
of the Bank of Japan, who claimed, "Since Japan should develop
its foreign trade on the basis of the international division of
labor, efforts to develop the automobile industry will be futile." (1) In his view of international specialization the automobile industry had no significant position in the Japanese
economy. On the other hand, MITI sought to "foster" the automobile industry on the grounds that "since development of the
automobile industry to a high level will lead to the modernization of the machinery industry and, consequently, all other industries, it is desirable to concentrate all possible efforts on
raising its productivity and international competitiveness so

that it can catch up with other advanced countries and can contribute to the growth of our national economy." (2)

Though these contradicting views were based on different
principles — the former was based on the theory of "comparative advantages," and the latter sought "infant industry protection" — they were alike in recognizing that the Japanese automobile industry at that time was far behind those of advanced
industrial nations. And, eventually, the great attractions of
automobiles helped the supporters of the automobile industry
win the controversy. The automobile industry was thus placed
under strong government protection as one of the strategic industries, including synthetic fibers, petrochemicals, and electronics.

Generally speaking, infant industry protection is carried out
by some means such as import restrictions, protective tariffs,
and subsidies. However, in addition to these the Japanese
government adjusted excise taxes, foreign exchange control,
and the special depreciation system to the advantage of domestically made automobiles, including even car bodies, parts, and
accessories.

These measures can be classified into (a) protective measures
to curb the inflow of foreign-made automobiles, and (b) support
measures to strengthen the international competitiveness of the
automobile industry.

The protective measures include the following four:

1) protective tariff rates;

2) the excise tax, providing more advantages for Japanese
automobiles;

3) import restriction through the operation of foreign exchange allocation;

4) control of foreign capital investment.

As shown in Tables 5 and 6, tariffs and excise taxes gave
the most favorable protection to small passenger cars. The
fixed tariff rate on imported passenger cars was 10% higher
than the 30% rate on trucks and parts; moreover, the GATT
rate of 35% was not applicable to small passenger cars with
wheelbase below 254 cm (which covers all Japanese-made small

Table 5

Automobile Import Tariff Rates (May 31, 1960)

		Fixed rate	GATT rates
Automobile	passenger car	40%	35% (with wheelbase above 254 cm) 30% (with wheelbase below 254 cm)
	truck	30%	27% (with wheelbase above 254 cm and loading capacity above 18 tons)
Automobile parts		30%	30%

Source: MITI, Nihon no Jidosha Kogyo [Japanese automobile industry] , 1960-61 edition.

Table 6

Excise Tax Rates on Automobiles (April 21, 1959)

High-class passenger cars	50%	(with wheelbase above 305 cm or cylinder capacity above 4,000 cc)
Medium-sized passenger cars	30%	(with wheelbase above 245 cm and below 305 cm or cylinder capacity above 1,500 cc and below 4,000 cc)
Small passenger cars	15%	(with wheelbase below 245 cm and cylinder capacity below 1,500 cc)

Source: MITI, Nihon no Jidosha Kogyo [Japanese automobile industry], 1960-61 edition.

passenger cars with cylinder capacity below 1,500 cc, the limit later extending to 1,900 cc when the cutoff point was raised to wheelbase over 270 cm. The excise tax rate on small passenger cars was a favorable 15%, against 30 to 50% on medium-sized and large passenger cars, which were mostly of foreign make.

In addition, another barrier was provided against importing foreign automobiles in the guise of the foreign exchange allocation system, which was strengthened even more when the overall import restriction policy was adopted during the 1954 recession in order to cope with the threatening inflow of small passenger cars from Europe, which had broken through the 40% tariff barrier in 1952 and 1953. For instance, the amount of foreign exchange allocations for automobile imports had been reduced to $610,000 in 1954 and $920,000 in 1955, from $13,740,000 in 1953, thus bringing down imported foreign automobiles to 370 and 545 from 5,900. Although the annual foreign exchange allocations for automobile parts had been increased at the same time, this was due to the importation of knock-down assembly parts on the basis of the technical cooperation agreements between Nissan Motors and Austin (December 1952), Isuzu and Rootes, Hino and Renaults (March 1953), and Shin Mitsubishi (which later became Mitsubishi Heavy Industries) and Willys Jeep (September 1953). However, these imports ceased as of 1957, when all parts started to be produced at home.

As regards foreign automobile capital investment in Japan, strict restrictions had been exercised. The problem came to be debated only when Japan joined the OECD in 1965.

Low-Interest Financing and Encouragement
of Related Industries

Support measures adopted by the government are:
1) loans at low interest rates from public financial institutions;
2) government subsidies;
3) special depreciation;
4) exemption of import duties on necessary machinery and equipment;

5) authorization for essential technology imports.

Of particular importance among these were the Japan Development Bank loans, which had amounted to the total of 1.5 billion yen, or nearly 10% of the total investment of 16.26 billion yen in the manufacturing facilities of medium- and small-sized passenger cars during the 1951-1955 period. Following the inclusion of the automobile parts industry in the seventeen industries to be promoted under the "Law Concerning Provisional Measures for Development of the Machinery Industry," which was enacted in June 1956, fund allocations for the automobile parts industry were authorized through the Development Bank's financing of primary automobile parts makers and the Small Business Finance Corporation's financing of secondary parts makers. A comparison of actual plant and equipment investment and loans approved by the public financial institutions shows that Development Bank loans were, on average, 13.6% of fixed investment in the automobile parts industry, even reaching as high as 30% from 1957 to 1959 and 1964 to 1965, when passenger car imports were liberalized.

The law mentioned above was enacted with a five-year time limit in order to rationalize production systems, modernize equipment, encourage exports, develop technology, and secure raw materials supplies in specially designated industries, which do not include the automobile industry itself. However, the amendments to this law in 1961 and 1966 extended the designation to automobile parts, machine tools for automobiles, internal combustion engines, and industrial-use vehicles. The primary objective for the rationalization of the automobile parts industry under this law was to lower the prices of automobile parts; simplification of parts, specialization, mass production, and coordinated research and development were intended to contribute indirectly to lowering automobile production costs. For instance, the Machinery Industry Development Plan of 1961 estimated that parts worth 100,000 to 150,000 yen used for a medium or small car were to be reduced in cost by 25,000 to 30,000 yen by the end of 1963.

As regards the government subsidies, the government dis-

bursed a total of 369 million yen of subsidies and commissions
for the Automobile Technology Association, the Japan Small
Automobile Industry Association, and other organizations from
1951 to 1959, from its appropriations for promotion of the machine industry (which were derived from proceeds of bicycle
races).

Concerning the special depreciation system, the government
authorized a depreciation by one-half in the first year after
acquisition for those machines that were designated for rationalization by the Special Taxation Measures Law and an annual
50% extra addition to the authorized depreciation ratio for
selected essential machines during a three-year period. The
system has been in effect for the automobile industry since
1951 and for the automobile parts industry since 1956, under
Article 6 of the Enterprise Rationalization Expedition Law. As
a result, the automobile industry spent 11.85 billion yen, or
18.4% of total investments of 64.36 billion yen in the 1951-1959
period for purchases of machines designated by the law.

The exemption of import duties on essential machines and
tools was provided as exceptions to the Tariff Law (1954) and
the Provisional Tariff Measures Law (1960) for those machines
deemed indispensable in automobile production in Japan and not
manufactured in Japan, including many kinds of machines for
automobile manufacture and machine tools. As for technology
imports, a total of 155 cases (type A only) were officially authorized, not only for automobile manufacturers but also for
automobile parts makers during the period from 1951 to 1968.

Increasing Pressure for
Import Liberalization

These protective and support measures helped the automobile
industry to grow beyond the infant-industry stage. Along with
this, foreign countries gradually stepped up their pressure on
Japan to liberalize imports and capital investment, and MITI
also started changing its position. Accordingly, the government
liberalized bus and truck imports in April 1961 and passenger

car imports in October 1965 on its judgments that they had reached the internationally competitive level.

Later, in June 1967, through the Kennedy Round negotiations Japan announced that it would reduce import duties on large passenger cars (from 35% to 17.5%), small passenger cars (40% to 30%), and buses and trucks (30% to 15%) by 1972. Following the Japan-U.S. automobile negotiations, in August 1968 the government decided on the following measures:

1) Japan would annually expand the import quota of automobile engines until its complete removal in early 1972;

2) Japan would favorably accept applications for establishing joint-venture knock-down assembly companies;

3) Japan would reduce the tariff rate on large passenger cars to 17.5% beginning in April 1969.

However, since this import liberalization policy failed to achieve its goals because of monopoly pricing policy (to be explained later), the U.S. government and automobile industry further increased pressure on Japan. Finally, in October 1969 the Japanese government announced its full program as follows:

1) capital investment in the automobile industry would be liberalized beginning October 1971;

2) the measure and date would also apply to the automobile parts industry and automobile sales services;

3) in this capital liberalization these industries would be treated as Category I industries (joint-venture enterprises with foreign capital share below 50% and under specific qualifications for automatic approval).

Yet in the meantime, MITI's policy had still been highly protective. For instance, in order to secure efficient mass production through interenterprise links and merger, MITI provided a quota in the Development Bank loans under its selective financing system, beginning with 1963, which enabled it to secure a total of 3 billion yen for the petrochemical and automobile industries in 1963, 6 billion yen for them and the special-steel industry in 1964, 4 billion yen each in 1966 and 1967 for Nissan Motors to cover its merger with Prince Motors, and 1 billion yen each for Hino Motors in 1967 and Daihatsu Automobile

Industry in 1968 to cover the Toyota-Hino and the Toyota-Daihatsu mergers.

However, we must note that such a protection and support policy covered not only the automobile industry but also all other growth industries, such as petrochemicals and electronics. In other words, the government protected and supported the automobile industry only as a part of its overall industrial policy. Therefore, we may have to make some allowances in our evaluation of the government's strong protection of the automobile industry.

Nevertheless, we should note that in return for its protection of the automobile industry, MITI used all available opportunities and measures to intervene in its free-enterprise system. A typical example is MITI's "Popular Car Plan" of 1955, which aimed at "concentrating, in one company, production of an exportable subcompact passenger car," which is (1) a four-passenger car, (2) priced at 250,000 yen, (3) with a cylinder capacity from 350 to 500 cc, (4) with a weight of 400 kg, and (5) with a maximum speed of 100 km per hour. Though this program ended up as a desk plan, its objectives have been well incorporated into MITI's subsequent policies, such as preferential taxes for mini 4-wheel cars, selective financing, and encouragement of production concentration by reorganizing automobile manufacturers into two groups.

III. Development of the Automobile Industry

Expansion by 200 Times in Twenty-two Years

In 1949 the SCAP authorized the Japanese automobile industry to reopen its full-scale operation. The outbreak of the Korean War in 1950 was an unexpected boon that catapulted the industry into a growth orbit. In 1951, when the war came to a truce, production of four-wheel automobiles had reached 100,000 a year — nearly twice as much as the prewar peak record.

Since then, thanks to the government's protection, production has kept on expanding to 1 million in 1963, 2 million in 1966, 3 million in 1967, and 5 million in 1970. During the twenty-two years from 1949 to 1971, Japanese automobile production registered a spectacular increase – as much as 200 times for all cars and 3,475 times for passenger cars (see Figure 1). In 1971 Japan was the second largest automobile producer in the world – the third in passenger cars next to the United States and West Germany and the first in bus and truck production.

This rapid increase in automobile production was due mostly to the rapid progress of motorization at home; expansion of exports added a new field only after 1964. The progress of motorization can be vividly seen in increases in the stock of three-wheel and four-wheel automobiles, which exceeded 1 million in 1956, 5 million in 1964, and 10 million in 1969. In other words, the increase in the last three years was well over that in the preceding eight years. As of the end of 1971, Japan held 19.86 million four-wheel automobiles (including 10.57 million passenger cars), or 189 (105 passenger cars) per 1,000 population, thus almost matching the European level.

This remarkable development was accompanied by equally rapid changes in the pattern of demand for automobiles. First of all, production was initially heavily concentrated on buses, trucks, and other commercial vehicles. As much as 70% of total automobile production was in this category. However, this ratio started to decline after 1962, reaching 50% in 1968 and 36% in 1971, against 64% for passenger cars.

Secondly, as seen from Figure 1, three-wheel vans at first took the lead in truck production, but small four-wheel trucks took their place since 1958. However, while ordinary trucks had been keeping up their relatively steady increase, the stock of small trucks had shown a gradual decrease in its annual average growth rate from 41.6% (1956-1960) to 31.9% (1961-1965) and to 15.1% (1966-1971). The stock of light four-wheel trucks had also marked a slowdown in growth from 106.7% (1961-1965) to 14.1% (1966-1971).

Thirdly, passenger cars took the leading role of motorization

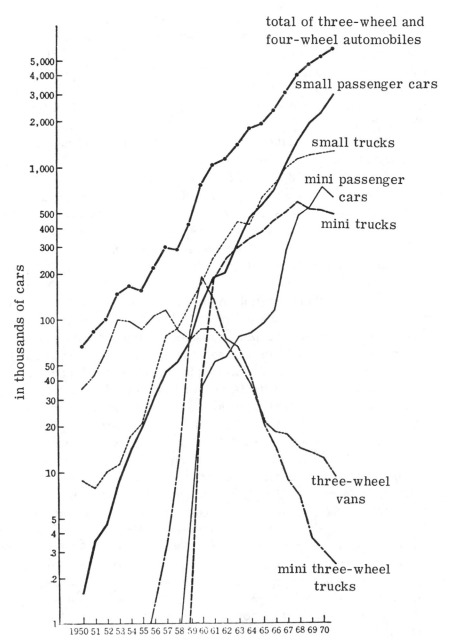

Figure 1. Postwar growth in automobile production.

in 1961 and recorded a tremendous speed of diffusion in the next ten years, as can be readily seen from the high rate of growth in the stock of passenger cars — 24.4% in 1956-1960, 36.7% in 1961-1965, and 30.1% in 1966-1971. This high growth was maintained by household demand. We note that, by type of buyers, passenger cars for private use increased from 0.9% in 1955 to 50.6% in 1970 as percentage of total sales, while those bought by the transportation industry (mainly for taxi and hired car services) decreased from 81.4% to 5.8%.

Fourthly, this rapid rise in personal demand altered the type of passenger cars most in demand, which was four-wheel mini cars of the 360-cc class in 1958-1963, popular cars in the 1,000-cc class in the early part of 1963-1968, and small cars in the 1,500-cc class since then. However, four-wheel mini cars still maintain a solid position with a share of 25.5% as of 1971, partly because of their relatively low maintenance cost, but also possibly because of their low automobile tax (one-quarter of larger cars) and a loophole in the automobile inspection system.

The reasons for such rapid progress in motorization were a rise in the individual income level, the decline of automobile prices, and improvements in the highway network. Among these the income level is most decisive in relation to the diffusion of automobiles. An international comparison shows that the pace of automobile diffusion tends to speed up when per capita national income reaches the $500 level and to slow down when it reaches the $1,300 level, thus giving rise to an S-shaped curve. For this, see Figure 2, which shows the patterns of automobile diffusion in Japan, the U.S., Canada, the U.K., and West Germany from 1955 to 1970. In this connection one should note the trends of automobile prices in these countries. Both the nominal and relative prices in highly developed countries (the U.S., Canada) tended upward; the nominal price remained stationary and the relative automobile price continued to decline in medium-income countries (West Germany, the U.K.); both the nominal and relative prices tended downward in take-off countries (Japan).

Differences in income levels and prices have an appreciable

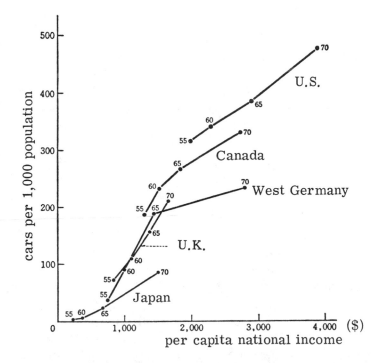

Figure 2. Passenger car diffusion patterns.

influence on stocks of passenger cars held in various countries.
However, even if there is a desired level for the stock of passenger cars in a country corresponding to its given per capita
income and automobile price levels, it is not necessarily attained instantaneously. There are some delays in time. An
econometric model based on these assumptions has revealed the
influences of income and price on the stock of passenger cars
as presented in Table 7. We notice a declining tendency in the
income and price elasticities of the desired automobile stock as
the automobile stock becomes relatively higher. This implies
that the less developed a country is, the stronger influence a
rise in income and a fall in relative price have upon its demand
for the stock of automobiles.

Thus the rapid progress of motorization in Japan was, on the
one hand, due to the rise in the per capita income level and, on

Table 7

Comparison of Income and Price Elasticities by Country

	Income elasticity	Price elasticity
U.S.	1.583	-0.0054
Canada	1.557	-0.0442
West Germany	1.098	-0.0928
U.K.	2.718	-0.2762
Japan	3.246	-0.4253

the other, automobile price decreases associated with economies
of scale through the expansion of automobile production. In
other words, the high economic growth policy resulted in the
spectacular sequence of a rise in per capita income → an increase in automobile demand → greater mass production →
reduced production cost → reduced automobile prices → increased demand for automobiles. In this process MITI's thoroughgoing protection has played a great role in tying increases
in automobile demand completely to the expansion of domestic
production of automobiles.

Arrival at the International Standard

Automobile imports were liberalized for the first time in
October 1965. By that time the top-level Japanese automobile
manufacturers had already been able to compete with U.S. and
European automobile manufacturers in productive efficiency
and performance capability of passenger cars. Moreover, Japan
had been ready to begin full-scale exportation of small passenger cars abroad.

A managing director in charge of technical affairs at a top-
level automobile company said, "I think that it was in 1965 that
the Japanese automobile industry reached the international
standard both in the scale of mass production of passenger cars
and their performance." In other words, the import restrictions

on automobiles were lifted only after enough time was earned
by the Japanese automobile industry to prepare for trade liberalization. In this sense, MITI's protectionist policy was a success.

We thus note that while the number of imported foreign automobiles remained 15,000 to 20,000 a year after the import liberalization, Japanese automobile exports grew spectacularly —
namely, in ten years from 1961 to 1971, passenger car exports
increased by 113 times, from 11,500 to 1,300,000, and commercial vehicle exports by 12 times, from 44,500 to 480,000.
Their annual average growth rates were 60.6% and 27.7%, respectively. The shares of exports in total production were
34.9% and 22.9%, respectively. While the former ratio for passenger car exports was somewhat less than some European
ratios (62.4% – West Germany, 47.6% – France, 37.3% – U.K.,
36.1% – Italy), we can consider it to be quite comparable to
the European standard in view of the fact that European exports
contain intraregional trade within the European Community and
the European Free Trade Association areas that amounts to
one-quarter to one-half of their total. In addition, the increase
in Japanese automobile exports has been not only in terms of
quantity but also has been associated with changes in direction
of trade toward North America and Europe. In particular,
Japan's passenger car exports to the United States were 654,000
in 1971, which was 50.3% of Japan's total exports of passenger
cars, 6.7% of car sales in the United States (9,729,000), and
44.6% of U.S. imports of foreign passenger cars (1,466,000).

During this period Japanese passenger cars have been improved remarkably both in performance and price, and they are
currently roughly equal to competitive foreign passenger cars.
For instance, there is little difference between compact cars
in the 1,000- and 2,000-cc class produced by the Big Three
(General Motors, Ford, and Chrysler) and major Japanese producers. Japanese cars are believed to be superior to American
counterparts in the class below 1,500 cc in cylinder capacity.

This remarkable leap forward of the automobile industry in
Japan has also meant a rise in its position among Japanese

industries. Table 8 shows that the automobile industry increased
its value-added share in all manufacturing from 1.7% in 1955 to
3.5% in 1969, and its employment share from 0.8% to 1.4%.

Table 8

Changes in Position of Major Industries in Japan

Industry	Value added		Persons engaged	
	1955	1969	1955	1969
	%	%	%	%
Automobile and accessories	3.1	6.6	2.3	4.9
Automobile manufacturing	1.7	3.5	0.8	1.4
Textiles	13.6	6.2	19.2	11.2
Chemicals	13.8	10.6	6.6	4.3
Iron and steel	8.1	7.0	5.0	4.7
General machinery	6.3	11.2	6.9	9.7
Electrical machinery	5.3	11.5	4.2	11.1
Total manufacturing	100.0	100.0	100.0	100.0
	(2,099)*	(20,551)*	(5,517)**	(11,412)**

*Value added (in billions of yen).
**The number of persons engaged in production (in thousands).
Source: MITI, Census of Manufactures.

The rise of the automobile industry's position in the industrial
spectrum has led to higher dependence of other industries on it.
In 1967 consumption of ordinary steel, the automobile industry
accounted for 9%, following the construction industry (48%) and
the shipbuilding industry (10%). It was the largest consumer of
polished plate glass and rubber, using about 50% of each. As an
export industry the automobile industry has also achieved outstanding growth, with automobile exports increasing from 0.3%
($6,355,000) of total exports in 1955 to 9.9% ($2.37 billion) in

1971, following iron and steel (14.7%) and textiles (11.5%).

Thus the hope entertained fifteen years ago for the automobile industry as a champion of the economy of Japan has been eminently realized.

IV. Competition and Industrial Reorganization

Low Barriers of Entry

The automobile market is often described as an oligopoly with product differentiation. Economies of scale in the fields of production, sales, advertising, and consumers' popular support all give overwhelming advantages to large enterprises, thus making the automobile industry highly liable to become an oligopoly industry.

Therefore, it is highly probable that any country would find itself with a strongly oligopolistic market for its automobile industry by the time it has become fully competitive in the world market.

The Fair Trade Commission's "static" classification of industries by the number of enterprises and the concentration ratio characterizes passenger cars and trucks (both excluding those of mini size) the "quasi-oligopoly" type (to which newsprint and wire rod also belong), mini passenger cars and mini trucks as the "high-level oligopoly" type, and buses as the "moderate concentration" type. (3) In this scheme four-wheel automobiles as a whole would be classified as the "quasi-oligopoly" type, since there were eleven automobile manufacturers with the one-firm concentration ratio of 34.0% and the four-firm concentration ratio of 79.2% in 1971.

However, this static approach is not adequate enough to analyze dynamic changes in the automobile industry, which has experienced rapid changes in market structure and production structure: More appropriate concentration indicators are necessary for this purpose. Let us first inspect entry and exit of firms by type of manufacturers of passenger cars in Figure 3. There

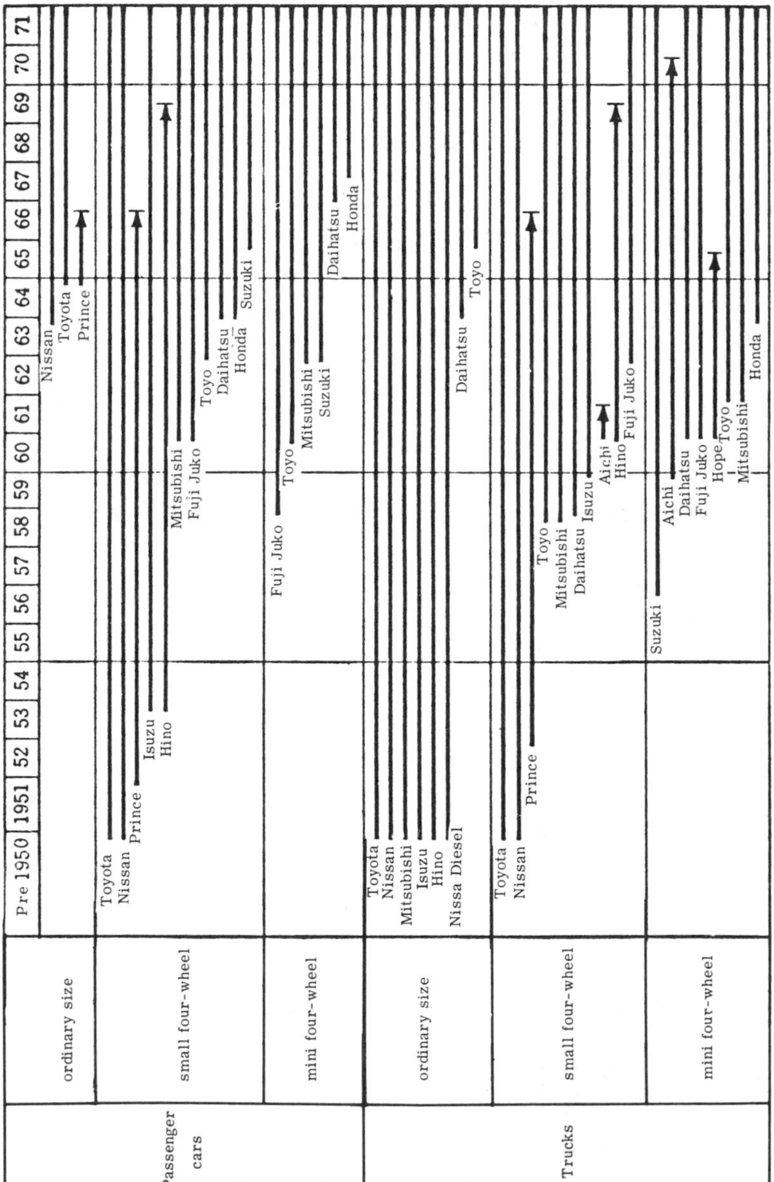

Figure 3. Entries and exits by types of car.

Source: Prepared from Japan Automobile Industry Association, <u>Jidosha Tokei Nempo</u> [Automobile statistics yearbook].

were only five in 1958; the rapid increase in demand induced
new entries, the number of manufacturers rising to eleven in
1965 and nine today. There were nine truck manufacturers in
1958; the number rose to thirteen in the peak year of 1961 and
is currently eleven. These figures indicate that the automobile
industry has been attractive and that barriers of entry were
relatively low.

Generally speaking, barriers of entry are the relative advantages of existing firms over potential entrants or the cost that
potential entrants must bear in entering the market and that
enterprises already in the market do not face. It covers, for
instance, the absolute costs related to patents or to raw materials monopoly, differentiation due to brands, good will, patented
designs, and economies of scale in production, sales, and advertising. Barriers of entry are comparatively low when a potential entrant can expect some profits after paying for these
costs.

We can surmise that barriers of entry were not so high in
the automobile industry, judging from the fact that a sizable
number of firms entered the market. But the fact that the new
entrants were limited to three-wheel vehicle and motorcycle
manufacturers suggests that they were more or less exempt
from the absolute-cost barrier of entry as regards production
technology and raw material availability, and that they were
also able to overcome the economies-of-scale barrier of entry
because of the rapidly increasing demand. Our conjecture is
corroborated by the Japan Economic Research Council's report
that the new entrants in the passenger car market faced the
foremost difficulty in organizing their sales networks and then
in procuring necessary funds.

The Rising Shares of the Top Two
Automobile Manufacturers

Table 9 shows changes in the production shares of individual
automobile manufacturers over seven years from 1965 to 1971.
Both Toyota and Nissan increased their shares, the former from

166

Table 9

Automobile Manufacturer's Production and Shares*

	1965	1967	1969	1971
Toyota	477,600 (25.5)	832,100 (26.4)	1,471,200 (31.5)	1,955,000 (33.6)
Hino	51,000 (2.7)	32,700 (1.0)	39,400 (0.8)	48,900 (0.8)
Daihatsu	148,200 (7.9)	255,500 (7.2)	264,300 (5.7)	311,800 (5.4)
Suzuki	42,000 (2.2)	115,600 (3.7)	238,100 (5.1)	267,400 (4.6)
Nissan	436,700 (23.3)	726,100 (23.1)	1,148,700 (24.6)	1,591,500 (27.4)
Nissan Diesel	5,000 (0.3)	11,100 (0.4)	18,200 (0.4)	22,100 (0.4)
Aichi Machinery	33,600 (1.8)	42,600 (1.4)	22,000 (0.5)	—
Fuji Heavy Industry	91,500 (4.9)	173,100 (5.5)	187,400 (4.0)	184,400 (3.2)
Isuzu	98,100 (5.2)	132,800 (4.2)	155,200 (3.3)	135,700 (2.3)
Toyo Kogyo	274,400 (14.6)	388,300 (12.3)	428,200 (9.2)	501,100 (8.6)
Mitsubishi	165,000 (8.8)	317,400 (10.1)	337,300 (7.2)	484,200 (8.3)
Honda	52,500 (2.8)	149,300 (4.7)	364,900 (7.8)	308,600 (5.3)
Total	1,875,600	3,146,600	4,674,900	5,810,800

*Figures in parentheses are shares (%).

25.5% in 1965 to 33.6% in 1971, and the latter from 23.3% to 27.4%; this combined share grew from 48.8 to 61.0%. On the other hand, other companies saw their shares declining — e.g., Toyo Kogyo, from 14.6 to 8.6%, Mitsubishi, from 8.8 to 8.3%, and Isuzu, from 5.2 to 2.3% — with the exception of Honda and Suzuki, which increased their shares from 2.8 to 5.3% and from 2.2 to 4.6%, respectively, owing to their success in increasing their mini car sales through their unique sales systems. The slowdown of the growth of internal demand for passenger cars in 1969 definitely affected the balance of power among automobile manufacturers to the advantage of Toyota and Nissan in strengthening their oligopoly position, while it dealt a heavy blow to such medium-sized manufacturers as Toyo Kogyo, Mitsubishi, and Isuzu.

Next we compute the Herfindahl concentration index in order to show a better picture of changes in concentration on the basis of the number of firms and market shares. (4) Figure 4 shows changes in concentration in the automobile industry from 1955 to 1971 as measured by the Herfindahl index. We note the following three points:

1) In general, concentration is higher in passenger cars than in buses and trucks;

2) Concentration declined remarkably from the end of 1957 to 1961;

3) Concentration showed a gradual decrease in the first half of the sixties and a gradual increase in the latter half of the decade.

As a general trend, since 1960, when new entities virtually ceased, concentration has been stable and even shown recently an upward trend. Still, the automobile industry is more competitive in Japan (with 0.2117 in 1971) than in the U.S. (0.3413) and West Germany (0.2390) in 1970. To sum up, insofar as the number of automobile manufacturers and their market shares are concerned, the Japanese automobile industry is still less concentrated than those in the United States and West Germany and, therefore, can be considered as a competitive oligopoly.

Nevertheless, this judgment underestimates the degree of oligopolization or reorganization in the automobile industry.

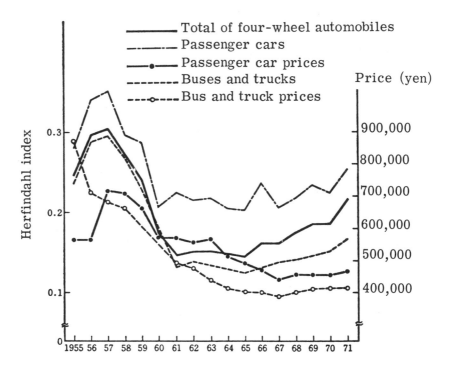

Figure 4. Changes in concentration (Herfindahl index)
and in prices.

For not all of the eleven automobile manufacturers are completely independent of each other. As a matter of fact, business
tie-ups and stock holdings resulted in consolidating business
groupings. In both passenger car and commercial-vehicle markets, effective competition is limited to six — namely, the
Toyota group (Toyota, Hino, Daihatsu, and Toyota-oriented
Suzuki), the Nissan group (Nissan, Fuji Heavy Industries,
Nissan Diesel, and Aichi Machinery), Toyo Kogyo, Mitsubishi
Heavy Industries, Isuzu, and Honda.

The Toyota and Nissan groups were organized in 1966, when
Nissan and Prince were merged, followed by a series of business tie-ups between Toyota and Hino, Toyota and Daihatsu,
and Nissan and Fuji Heavy Industries. More recently we have
witnessed some indications of reorganization of the automobile

industry in the tie-up of Mitsubishi and Chrysler through the founding of a joint-venture company, in that between Nissan and Isuzu (unsuccessful, with Isuzu later joining hands with General Motors), and in Ford's (unsuccessful) offer to Toyo Kogyo to hold the latter's shares. The Toyota and Nissan groups resulted in a substantial increase in the Toyota group share from 38.39% in 1955 to 44.4% in 1971 and in a very small increase from 30.3% to 31.0%, the two groups together accounting for 75.4% in 1971.

If each group is counted as a single enterprise, the Herfindahl index of concentration in Japanese automobile industry rises to 0.3334 in passenger cars and 0.2781 in buses and trucks, much above the West German level and comparable to the American level. Obviously, then, the Japanese automobile industry is a high-level oligopoly.

Indications of Administered Pricing

Figure 4 also shows changes in passenger car and commercial vehicle prices. Automobile prices fell by a fair degree in the late fifties, when concentration also rapidly declined; price declines slowed down in the late sixties, when concentration started to gradually increase. After 1968 prices tended to rise, indicating that the rise in concentration leads to price rigidity or price stability on a higher level. Tables 10 and 11 illustrate price competition in the Japanese and U.S. automobile markets. Common to the two cases is the presence of price leadership with General Motors and either Toyota or Nissan playing the role of the price leaders. However, Japanese and American price decisions differ most conspicuously in that American auto makers are more collusive in raising prices, while the Japanese producers are relatively competitive. Almost all the competitive price reductions in Japan originated in either a price leader's unilateral price markdowns or the announcement of a new model car at the unchanged prices (effective price reductions due to quality improvements). The major exception was Toyo Kogyo's announcement of a price rise for

Table 10

Price Competition in the Small Passenger Car Market*

	1963		1964		1967
Date	Maker and Brand	Date	Maker and Brand	Date	Maker and Brand
September 18	Nissan: Bluebird (model change) (12,000–18,000)	May 30	Toyota: Crown (40,000) Corona (35,000) Publica (10,000)	August 15	Nissan: New Bluebird model on sale
September 20	Toyota: Crown (40,000–50,000) Corona (50,000–65,000)	June 1	Nissan: Cedric (40,000) Bluebird (20,000–26,000)	September 25	Toyota: Corona (10,000–50,000)
September 21	Nissan: Cedric (30,000–50,000)	June 1	Prince: Gloria (30,000–40,000)	September 30	Mitsubishi: Colt 1500 (34,000) Colt 1100 (23,000) Colt 1000F (15,000–18,000) Colt 800 (15,000)
September 23	Prince: Skyline (40,000–60,000)	June 2	Isuzu: Bellel (30,000–40,000) Hillman (30,000) Bellel (20,000–25,000)	October 2	Toyo: Luce (20,000–30,000) Familia Coupe (50,000)
September 28	Isuzu: Bellel (18,000–60,000) Hillman (30,000–50,000)	June 3	Mitsubishi: Colt 1000 (10,000–20,000) Colt 600 (10,000)	October 19	Isuzu: Bellet 1500 (30,000) Bellet 1300 (25,000–35,000)
September 30	Hino: Contessa (37,000)	June 23	Fuji: Subaru 450 (10,000) Subaru 360 (10,000)		
October 9	Shin Mitsubishi: Colt 1000 (20,000)				

*Figures in parentheses are price reductions (in yen).
Source: Nihon Keizai Shimbun, various issues.

Table 11

Auto Price Increases in the United States

	1967		1968		1969
Date	Maker and Price Rise	Date	Maker and Price Rise	Date	Maker and Price Rise
September 11	Chrysler ($133 – 4.6%)	September 16	Chrysler ($84 – 2.9%)	September 11	General Motors ($119 – 3.9%)
September 18	General Motors ($110 – 3.6%)	September 23	General Motors ($49 – 1.5%)	September 17	Ford ($103 – 3.6%)
September 20	Ford ($114 – 3.9%)	September 25	Ford ($47 – 1.6%)	September 18	Chrysler ($107 – 3.5%)
September 25	Chrysler ($101 – 3.5%)	September 26	Chrysler ($52 – 1.8%)	September 24	AMC ($81 – 3.5%)
September 25	AMC ($87 – 3.8%)	September 27	AMC ($43 – 1.5%)		

Source: Nihon Keizai Shimbun, various issues.

Luce in September 1968 after it was equipped with new safety devices. It took six months for other manufacturers to follow suit; in the meantime, Luce's market share decreased from 4.5% in the first half of 1968 to 3.4% in the latter half of the year. In this respect we must note the following two points:

1) Insofar as safety device-equipped cars are concerned, all manufacturers added cost increments to their prices without trying to cover the cost additions by raising productivity.

2) In September 1968, when Toyota announced price cutbacks on improved Coronas and offered the new model of Mark II on sale, Nissan alone announced price markdowns to compete with Toyota, while others remained unresponsive.

The fact that automobile manufacturers have begun avoiding intense price competition is a significant point in conjecturing about the future of price competition.

Progress of Product Differentiation

Generally speaking, competition in a differentiated oligopoly is more intense in the nonprice fields, such as product efficiency, new product developments, model changes, advertising, and sales activities, than in prices. Therefore, weakened price competition will lead automobile manufacturers to intensify their nonprice competition.

The automobile industry is a representative industry in that product differentiation is fairly advanced. Broadly speaking, product differentiation is classified into (1) differentiation embodied in products themselves and (2) differentiation in marketing channels. The former includes differentiation in types, styles, and performance of cars, and the latter includes differentiation in guarantees, advertising, selling, and service. Both are identical in their effect of reducing the price elasticity of demand. This is why product differentiation is an important element determining market structure. Auto manufacturers not only can let mental and physical diversities of an automobile correspond to diversities of consumers' preferences, but also the limited frequency of purchase makes users unable to

judge a car's merits and demerits within a short period. All
these factors induce automobile manufacturers to rely less on
price cuts and more on product differentiation as a factor in
nonprice competition in order to increase demand.

Differentiation embodied in products includes differences in
types, models, and styles, such as two-door, four-door, station-
wagon, and sports bodies; differences in performance, such as
cylinder capacity; and image differences, such as deluxe,
special, and standard models. Combinations of these differences led to 590 varieties of passenger cars in Japan as of
1972. What is important in this competition through product
differentiation is how automobile manufacturers choose their
ranges of specialization by type of cars; for instance, in the
case of passenger cars, how they distribute their products over
a variety of sizes, ranging from ordinary-sized passenger cars
with cylinder capacity over 2,000 cc to mini cars with cylinder
capacity less than 360 cc.

Table 12 compares brands of passenger cars produced by
each automobile manufacturer as of February 1972. We note
that Toyota and Nissan produce, respectively, seventeen and
nineteen brands of passenger cars above and including popular
cars, while Toyo Kogyo and Mitsubishi, respectively, produce
thirteen and five brands of medium-sized and smaller cars.
Isuzu is specialized in six brands of medium-sized cars. Honda
and Fuji Juko produce, respectively, four and three brands of
small and mini cars, while Daihatsu is specialized in three
brands of popular and mini cars, and Suzuki produces only
one brand of mini car.

As regards differentiation embodied in products, we must
also note dynamic differentiation, that is, model changes. This
deserves special mention because a change of a model discrim-
inates not only against other models produced both by its own
manufacturer and other manufacturers alike, but even against
preceding models of itself. The model-change competition is
the most intense in the small car (with cylinder capacity between 1,201 and 1,500 cc) market, and this competition has
grown in intensity since 1965, when new entries ceased.

Table 12

Passenger Car Brands of Each Automobile Manufacturer, October 1972

	Ordinary car above 2,001 cc	Medium-sized car 1,501-2,000 cc	Small-sized car 1,201-1,500 cc	Popular car 361-1,200 cc	Mini car below 360 cc
Toyota	Century Crown 2600	Crown 2000 Corona Mark II 2000 Mark II 1700 Corona 1700 Corona 1600 Celica 1600 Carina 1600	Celica 1400 Carina Sprinter 1400 Corolla 1400	Sprinter 1200 Corolla 1200 Publica 1200 Publica 1000	
Nissan	President Cedric 2600 Gloria 2600 Fairlady 240Z	Cedric 2000 Gloria 2000 Fairlady Z Laurel 2000 Laurel 1800 Skyline 2000 Skyline 1800 Bluebird 1800 Bluebird 1600	Skyline 1500 Bluebird 1400 Sunny 1400	Sunny 1200 Cherry 1200 Cherry 1000	
Mitsubishi		Debonaire Executive Colt Gallant 16L	Colt Gallant 14L	Gallant Coupe	Minica

175

Toyo Kogyo	Luce 1800 Luce Rotary	Luce 1500 Capella 1600 Capella Rotary Savanna Grand Familia 1500 Grand Familia 1300	Familia Prest Rotary Familia Prest 1300 Familia Prest 1000 Cosmos Sports	Shanti
Isuzu	Isuzu 117, 1800 Isuzu 117, 1600 Florian 1800 Florian 1600 Bellet 1800 Bellet 1600			
Daihatsu			Consorte 1200 Consorte 1000	Fellow Max
Honda		Honda 77		Honda N III Honda Z Honda Life
Fuji		Subaru Leone 1400 Subaru 1300		Subaru R-2
Suzuki				Fronte

Source: Prepared from Jidosha Kogyo Shinko Kai [Automobile industry development association], Jidosha Guidebook [Automobile guidebook], Vol. 19.

Figure 5 shows that both Corona and Bluebird have undergone model changes almost every year, if minor changes are counted, coming very close to annual model changes in the American market.

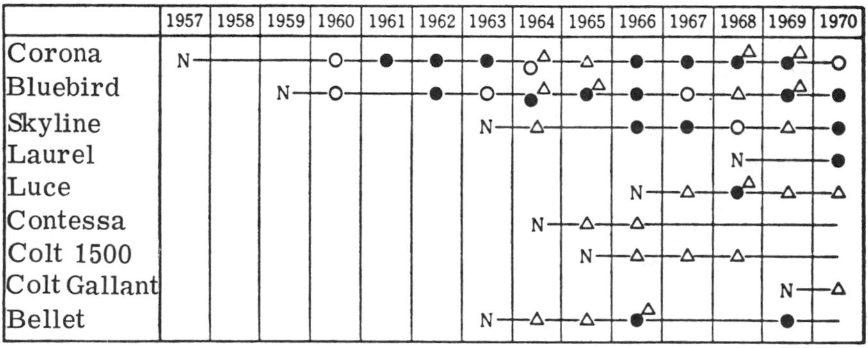

	1957	1958	1959	1960	1961	1962	1963	1964	1965	1966	1967	1968	1969	1970
Corona	N		o		●	●	●	o△	△	●	●	●△	●△	o
Bluebird			N	o		●	o	●△	●△	●	o	△	●△	●
Skyline							N	△		●	●	o	△	●
Laurel												N		●
Luce									N	△	●△	△		△
Contessa								N	△	△				
Colt 1500									N	△	△	△		
Colt Gallant													N	△
Bellet							N	△	△	●△			●	

N — new entry; o — major model change; ● — minor model change; △ — addition of new model.

Figure 5. Model changes in small-sized passenger cars.

As to differentiation in the sales field, the most important factor is the sales and service network. We should note in the Japanese sales system that most sales and service stations are incorporated into the networks of automobile manufacturers.

When a consumer is deciding on which car to buy, he finds a strong attraction in the network of an automobile manufacturer for marketing, supplies of parts, and postpurchase servicing that covers the entire country and is always available to him. Should cars be equivalent in performance and price, he will choose the car of a producer with a well-organized network of services. As a matter of fact, the Toyota and Nissan cars are not necessarily superior to nor cheaper than others.

Table 13 compares the sales systems of major automobile manufacturers. The fact that they clearly reflect differences in market shares suggests that market-share differentials must be due to differences in sales capacity.

As new products and model changes have been introduced

Table 13

Sales Systems of Major Automobile Manufacturers*

	Toyota	Nissan	Toyo Kogyo	Mitsubishi	Isuzu	Fuji Juko	Daihatsu	Honda
Dealers (number of stores)	237	266	84	142	78	51	69	218
Capital (in billion yen)	15.9	18.2	2.4	6.6	5.3	1.5	2.0	
Employees	71,547	64,392	30,170	27,703	20,025	7,963	11,072	40,000–50,000
Salesmen	17,716	18,231	9,025	7,725	4,574	2,152	3,062	
Company sales stations	1,937	1,402	824	807	436	196	257	
Subdealers	76	579	943	1,874	85	271	554	
Service garages (designated)	1,800	2,353	1,308	1,684	772	442	266	
Market share (%)**	26.9	24.0	11.3	8.8	3.6	4.4	6.4	7.8

*As of the end of 1968.

**As of 1969.

Sources: Based on reports of the Toyota Automobile Sales Company, except for Honda, which is based on data published by the Honda Motor Company (we have adjusted Honda figures for comparability).

more actively, advertising competition has also become intense.
The total of advertising expenditures by Toyota (Toyota Motor
Co. and Toyota Automobile Sales Co.), Nissan, Toyo Kogyo,
Isuzu, and Honda increased from 4.2 billion yen in 1961 to 12.1
billion yen in 1965, and to 27.1 billion yen in 1970, or 6.5 times
in nine years. Advertising expenditures in 1970 (in billion yen)
were 10.97 by Nissan, 10.51 by Toyota, 3.89 by Honda, 3.28 by
Toyo Kogyo, and 1.46 by Isuzu. Here again, Toyota and Nissan
are by far the largest.

As we have seen, nonprice competition is more intense than
price competition in the automobile industry. The balance of
power among enterprises is determined by these several factors combined together, the results of which are typically reflected in market shares and earnings.

We can make clear the oligopolistic control by Toyota and
Nissan by examining their market shares by type and size of
cars. Of the total passenger car production of about 3.72 million in 1971, Toyota's share was 37.7% (a 3.8% increase from
1965), and Nissan's was 29.6% (a 1.5% decrease), their total
being 67.3%.

It is said that one who dominates the market of principal
passenger cars rules the automobile industry. In 1971 Toyota
and Nissan together had a share of 78.3% in popular cars and
of more than 80% in small and larger passenger cars. Concentration proceeded at a rapid pace, and the two companies have
become dominant in the passenger car market (see Table 14).

On the other hand, no single automobile manufacturer holds
a predominant share in the market of four-wheel mini cars,
although Honda has expanded its share and replaced Toyo
Kogyo, which fell back in this market (see Figure 6).

As regards trucks, the share of the two top manufacturers
declined to below Mitsubishi's 36.9%, Isuzu's 27.8%, and Hino's
17.2% in the ordinary-sized truck market, while they still
maintain a share about two-thirds of the market of small
trucks. Market shares are much closer to one another
in the mini truck market than in the mini car market
(see Figure 6).

Table 14

Total Market Shares of Toyota and Nissan
by Type and Size of Cars

Type	Size	1960	1965	1970	1971
Passenger cars	Medium-sized and above	69.0	83.9	98.9	99.2
	Small-sized	86.5	74.3	80.1	80.0
	Popular car	—	39.0	74.2	78.3
Trucks	Ordinary-sized	33.2	13.9	4.0	3.7
	Small-sized	73.4	64.1	72.7	72.7
Buses		14.0	32.4	54.7	42.6

Source: Toyota Automobile Sales Company, Sharyo Tokei
[Statistics on motor vehicles].

Thus, broadly speaking, both Toyota and Nissan succeeded
in achieving high concentration in production of automobiles
with cylinder capacity between 1,000 and 2,000 cc (passenger
cars except mini cars, small trucks, and mini buses), which
have engines and parts more in common than other types
and sizes of automobiles, while the other manufacturers are
competing for market shares in the markets of ordinary-sized
trucks, big buses, and four-wheeled mini cars, which the big
two are not primarily interested in.

V. Market Performance — Differences in Earnings and Excess Profits

Changes in Earning Differences

Intent on its path of rapid growth so far, the Japanese
automobile industry has just entered the stage of maturity.
This means that the Japanese automobile industry formed a
growth-oriented, competitive oligopoly under the government's

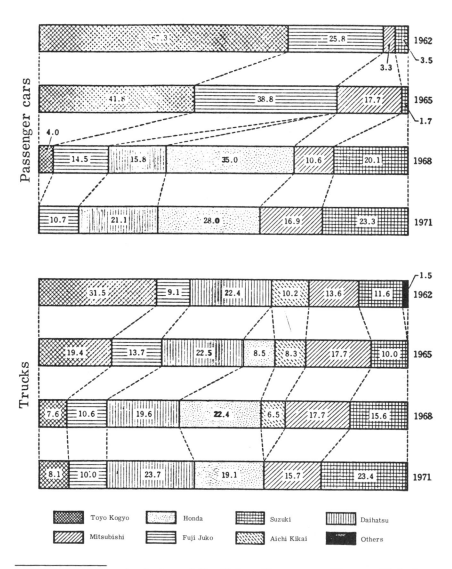

Source: Toyota Automobile Sales Company, Sharyo Tokei [Statistics on motor vehicles].

Figure 6. Market shares in four-wheel mini cars.

strong protection. Its market has been quite competitive, even though automobile enterprises have recently begun avoiding price competition and have been moving toward nonprice competition in model changes, advertising, and sales promotion.

Unlike in the United States and Western Europe, the progress of the reorganization and concentration in the automobile industry in Japan was not due to a market slump or recession. It took place in accordance with the requirements of MITI's plan for discontinuing industrial protection so that the automobile manufacturers could prepare for the U.S. Big Three's anticipated advances into the Japanese market following the liberalization of imports and foreign capital investment.

Still, it can be said that, even without the fear of foreign giants entering the Japanese market or without MITI's guidance, the reorganization and concentration of the Japanese automobile industry ought to have been realized through fair market competition, as long as they reflect the balance of power among domestic competitors in the domestic market and the capitalist principle of the survival of the fittest.

A great many changes have taken place in the automobile industry through its competition and reorganization. In this respect we must examine what these changes have meant to the national economic welfare. In other words, we must evaluate the automobile industry's performance in the light of industrial organization theory. The conventional criteria of industrial performance for the sake of the national economy are (1) productive efficiency, (2) excess profits, (3) excess capacity, (4) sales cost relative to production, and (5) technical progress.

Among these five, we need not question (3) and (4) in the Japanese automobile industry. We shall discuss (5) in the next section. We shall concentrate on (1) and (2) in this section.

As regards production efficiency, it is closely related to whether the industry has followed the path of natural selection through fair competition and achieved the optimum scale of production. At the same time, it is closely associated with whether leading enterprises enjoyed excess profits or not.

Figure 7 shows changes in the ratio of (pretax) profits to
sales since 1955. We may note that Toyota and Nissan both
maintained a profit ratio much above the weaker companies,
Isuzu and Toyo Kogyo. In particular, Toyota's 1955-1970 average profit ratio of 11.3% is 5 percentage points higher than
Isuzu's. Toyo Kogyo obtained a profit ratio as high at Toyota's
for a few years following 1961 when it entered the four-wheel
mini car market, but suffered from its rapid decline after its
withdrawal from this market. Daihatsu's profit ratio also had
begun increasing with its participation in the four-wheel mini
truck market, was sustained at a high level while sales of small

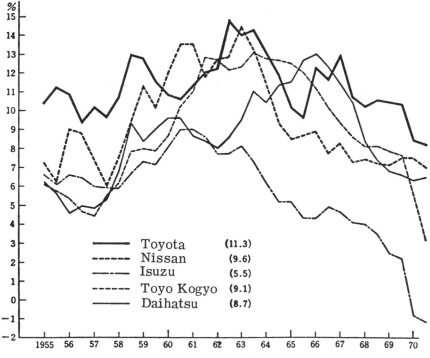

Figure 7. Changes in major manufacturers'
profits-to-sales ratios.*

---

*Figures in parentheses are the average for the entire
period.

trucks and popular cars were growing smoothly, but tended to decline as their growth slowed down. These developments indicate that the more products there are in which an automaker competes with Toyota and Nissan, the less earnings it is likely to get.

Differentials in the profits-to-sales ratio are equal to differences in unit production cost if all enterprises set identical prices under price leadership. Therefore, we shall now conduct cost analysis in order to find the factors responsible for earnings differences.

The Optimum Number Is Six Brands, Huge Excess Profits

Cost analysis of automobile production (5) requires that the product mix be the same among manufacturers. However, in reality we observe considerable differences in product composition. Since Toyota, Nissan, and Prince are relatively similar in this regard, we shall confine our cost analysis to these three companies. Differences in product composition are adjusted by using unit steel consumption. (6)

Table 15

Marginal Costs of Three Companies

Company	Marginal cost curve	Average number of cars produced (A)	Marginal cost corresponding to (A)
		(cars)	(yen)
Toyota	MC = 306.3 - 0.00738 × (cars produced)	214,400	304,700
Nissan	MC = 363.0 - 0.240 × (cars produced)	158,800	324,900
Prince	MC = 515.4 - 3.645 × (cars produced)	27,400	415,500

Table 15 shows the marginal cost functions estimated by regressing total cost of production on the (adjusted) number of cars produced. (7) This table indicates that the slope of the marginal cost curve is the least for Toyota and the largest for Prince. The marginal cost corresponding to the average number of automobiles produced a year during the sample period (from the first half of 1955 to the latter half of 1966) is 305,000 yen for Toyota, 325,000 yen for Nissan, and 416,000 yen for Prince, thus indicating that Prince is far behind. The corresponding average cost, derived from the total cost curve, is 305,000 yen tor Toyota, 344,000 yen for Nissan, and 482,000 yen for Prince.

Figure 8 shows short-run marginal and average cost curves, as well as points corresponding to the average number of automobiles produced. It should be noted that the curves connecting these points of the three companies are roughly long-run average and marginal cost curves of passenger cars. This indicates that average cost declines by 10,500 yen for an increase of each 10,000 cars from Prince (37,000) to Nissan (159,000) and by only 6,900 yen for each 10,000 cars from Nissan to Toyota. As a whole, they are similar to the Silberston curves. (8)

As regards estimates of the optimum scale of production, there are some differences among researchers, namely, Romney (annual production of 180,000 to 220,000 cars on one shift), Bain (at a minimum 300,000 a year, cost continuing to decrease up to 600,000 cars a year), and Maxey-Silberston (100,000 cars in the assemblying process, 500,000 in the machinery process, and 1,000,000 in the pressing process). However, as is obvious from the cases of the Big Three, the actual optimum output level is believed to be around 200,000 cars a year. This figure represents economies of scale not only in production but also in distribution; this is because around 200,000 cars in one brand must be sold a year if economies of scale are to be achieved in sales — that is, if an adequate number of dealers is to be maintained in the sales network. As of the end of 1969, there were only six brands of cars that passed this test — Toyota's Corona (400,000), Toyota's Corolla

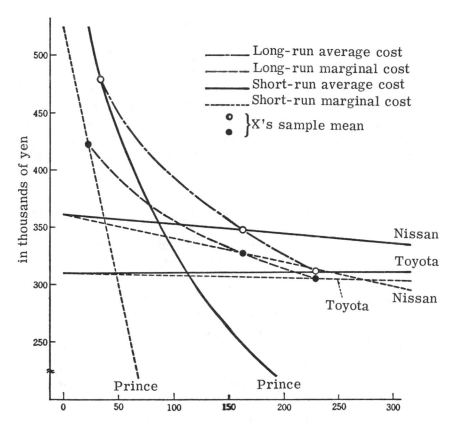

Figure 8. Cost curves of three companies
(Toyota, Nissan, Prince).

(400,000), Nissan's Bluebird (250,000), Nissan's Sunny (180,000),
Honda's N360 (250,000), and Toyo Kogyo's Familia (190,000).
Since 1970, when a number of new brands were introduced suc-
cessively, only four of the above, namely, Corolla, Corona,
Sunny, and Bluebird, were successful in maintaining production
above the 200,000 car level. Although the number of passenger
cars produced in 1971 indicated that the number of brands that
could achieve efficient production would be thirteen to fourteen,
there were actually more than thirty brands (by taking one
series for one brand) of cars on the market, thus indicating

that product differentiation had gone beyond a necessary level.

The question of excess profits is tantamount to that of fair prices. Table 16 shows changes in automobile prices in 1960-1965 and in 1965-1970. All automobile prices tended to decline, while the average wholesale price index and the consumer-durable price index were both slightly on the increase. In particular, reflecting intense competition, the prices of mini passenger cars declined by 3.9%, and those of mini trucks by 2.5% in 1965-1970.

Table 13

Changes in Automobile Prices (annual average)

	1960-1965	1965-1970
Wholesale price index (total)	+0.4%	+2.2%
Auto price { small passenger car	-3.0*	-1.6
mini passenger car	-2.3	-3.9
small truck	-0.1	-0.6
mini truck	-1.8	-2.5
Consumer-durable price index	-0.2	+0.3

*Small passenger cars include ordinary-sized passenger cars in 1960-1965.

Source: Bank of Japan, Wholesale Price Index Annual.

Despite these price reductions, the automobile industry managed to maintain a rather high profit ratio as compared to other industries (see Figure 9). It was also insensitive to business cycles. One then supposes that automobile prices must have contained sizable excess profits.

Based on the full-cost principle, we derived a price-markup equation in the automobile industry during the 1955-1966 period as follows:

$$P_A = 39.307 + 0.309 C_p + 0.7 P_{A,-1} - 0.988 r$$

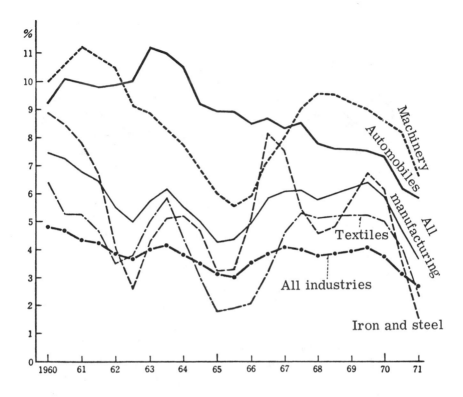

Source: Bank of Japan, Shuyo Kigyo Keiei Bunseki
[Analysis of financial statements of main industrial cor-
porations].

Figure 9.   The (pretax) profits-to-sales ratios of
principal industries.

where P_A is the average wholesale price (in thousands of yen)
of all automobiles (passenger cars, buses, and trucks); C_p is
unit prime cost (labor cost and raw material cost, in thousands
of yen); and r is the share of mini four-wheel automobiles.

From this equation we estimate the average markup to be
37.1% (after adjusting prime cost for the part for non-automo-
bile cost). This is obviously very high and suggests that the
automobile manufacturers have continued to earn large excess
profits.

Reviewing 1959-1963 price competition at the automobile
market, Toyota states in its company history (9): "Price competition reflects a business philosophy that 'live and let live' is
essential to business success. At the same time, it is also
true that automobile industry executives had a common un-
easiness about a storm in the 'hot house,' so that they could
prepare well for forthcoming relentless competition with foreign manufacturers." This seems to be an honest confession.

The Mechanism of High Imported Car Prices

One may think of automobile imports as a factor keeping
excess profits in check. But they have not played the expected
role for the following reasons.

As one of the measures to protect the domestic automobile
industry, automobile imports were placed under government
control in 1954; foreign car imports had been authorized only
to hired taxi services and news organizations, so that less than
1,000 foreign cars were imported every year until 1959. Subsequent to the relaxation of import restrictions (1960) and the
liberalization of automobile imports (1965), auto imports gradually increased. Nevertheless, imported foreign automobiles
as of 1971 were a little over 20,000, or less than 1% of all
registered cars. The main reason why auto imports have not
grown even after the import liberalization is their high retail
price in Japan. For instance, while popular cars with cylinder
capacity of the 1,000-cc level in Japan are priced at around
500,000 yen (for the deluxe grade), the retail prices of foreign
equivalents are 50 to 100% higher — a Volkswagen 1200 was
sold at 756,000 yen, a Renault R10 at 1,180,000 yen, and a Fiat
128 at 1,295,000 yen. U.S. cars with much larger cylinder
capacity are sold at higher than 4 million yen. Two factors
are responsible for these high imported car prices: (1) in
addition to protective tariff rates, higher excise tax rates
were imposed on imported foreign cars than Japanese-made
cars; (2) imported car dealers maintain high margin rates.

We see in Table 17 the cost structure of imported cars.
The net prices of both U.S. and European cars, including freight
costs, insurance premiums, tariffs, excise taxes, and dealers'

Table 17

Cost Structure of Imported Car Prices

(1,000 yen and percent)*

		FOB price	Freight	Insurance	Tariffs	Excise	Charges	Net price	List** price	Margin rate (%)
U.S. car	A	2,285 (100.0)	295 (12.9)	39 (1.7)	460 (20.1)	1,236 (54.0)	426 (18.7)	4,741 (207.4)	7,260 (317.7)	53.1
	B	1,182 (100.0)	199.5 (16.9)	23 (1.9)	246.8 (20.9)	662.4 (56.0)	288 (24.3)	2,601.5 (220.0)	3,995 (338.0)	53.6
	C	1,047.8 (100.0)	199.7 (19.0)	16.9 (1.6)	222 (22.2)	596.3 (56.8)	252.9 (24.1)	2,340 (223.7)	3,240 (309.2)	38.5
European car	A	894.9 (100.0)	113.4 (12.7)	15.8 (1.8)	179.2 (20.0)	360 (40.2)	353.2 (39.5)	1,916.5 (214.2)	2,570 (287.2)	34.1
	B	616 (100.0)	104 (16.9)	4.3 (0.7)	260.5 (42.4)	147.8 (24.0)	208 (33.8)	1,341.3 (218.0)	1,780 (289.0)	32.7
	C	283.9 (100.0)	59.2 (20.9)	2.7 (1.0)	124.9 (44.0)	70.8 (24.9)	30.8 (10.8)	572.3 (201.6)	698 (245.9)	22.0

*Figures in parentheses are relative to FOB prices = 100.
**List prices in this table (as of 1970) are those of brands that seem to correspond to given specifications.

service charges, are nearly twice as much as their FOB prices.
For instance, the net price for U.S. car A is 4,741,000 yen,
against its FOB price of 2,285,000 yen. Still, its list price for
the consumer is 7,260,000 yen with a difference of as much as
2,519,000 yen, or 53% over its net price, which can be considered a dealer's margin. The dealer margin rates range between 33% and 53%, except 22% for European car C, which is
the lowest of all. Since Japanese-made car dealers' margin
rates are said to be around 25%, and the dealers' margin in
the United States is from 22 to 26%, the margin rates for imported car dealers in Japan are certainly high.

There were fifty-one imported car dealers in Japan as of
February 1970, and all of them were members of the Japan
Automobile Importers Association, which was founded "to establish orderly and cooperative marketing in import transactions so as to promote the development of the automobile import business." The association acts as an agent for clearing
customs office procedures on behalf of automobile importers.
Moreover, each dealer maintains a contract with a specific
foreign automobile manufacturer to deal only in the designated
brand(s) within a specified sales territory. Thus dealers are
subject to foreign automobile manufacturers' control, on the
one hand, and are bound to mutual cooperation among themselves on the other. (10) Roughly half of the imported car market is controlled by Yanase, Kintetsu Motors, Toho Motors,
and New Empire Motors; and the rest is shared by forty-seven
import car dealers, each of which can therefore sell an average of 220 cars a year. Needless to say, this implies that their
average sales cost is much higher than that of the four major
importers. It is not hard to imagine that the mutual coordination of import car dealers resulted in maintaining high margin
rates to make marginal dealers survive.

The unreasonably high imported car prices under the government's protectionist policy and import dealers' coordination
restricted domestic demand for imported cars to special consumer groups, forestalled natural selection of dealers through
competition, and indirectly discouraged efforts to lower domestic automobile prices.

6

IRON AND STEEL

Ken'ichi Imai*

1. The Iron and Steel Industry at a Turning Point

The Light and Dark Sides of the Winner

The first showing of Cinerama in Japan was in early 1955. This new type of film, titled This Is Cinerama, introduced in documentary style some main features of a number of countries. The part on Japan, represented as usual by Mount Fuji and geisha girls, was too repulsive to me. But the United States was shown in the last segment as a country of iron and steel, which somehow stuck in my memory. A sharp, wide-angle picture of a rust-covered iron bridge under construction conveyed the image of the United States as an industrial super-state. The image of a steel-framed bridge as a symbol of America

*Ken'ichi Imai, "Tekko." In Hisao Kumagai, ed., Nihon no Sangyo Soshiki [Industrial Organization of Japan], Vol. II (Tokyo: Chuo Koron Sha, 1973), pp. 1-58. Reprinted in English by permission of the author and publisher. Translated by Hirokatsu Ogasawara.

This translation originally appeared in Japanese Economic Studies, III (Winter 1974-75), 3-67 (55-67 omitted from this reprint). An updated revision of the paper appears in the author's book, Gendai Sangyo Soshiki [Japan's Industrial Organization] (Tokyo: Iwanami Shoten, 1976), chapter 4, 127-181.

overwhelmed me, perhaps, because as a graduate student I was
thinking of specializing in industrial economics. At the same time,
it overlapped with the image of "frail" Japanese industry.

But Japan's iron and steel industry was then already set to
begin its giant steps. The Ministry of International Trade and
Industry (MITI) and major steel corporations had compiled a
five-year development plan for 1955-1960; they had also been
contemplating a long-term, twenty-year plan extending to 1975,
involving construction of up-to-date steel mills. In this long-
term plan, the 1975 target for Japan's steel output was set at
25,190,000 tons. To avoid misunderstanding, I note that
25,190,000 tons in 1975 is not a misprint. The actual steel output in 1972 was nearly 100,000,000 tons and is expected to reach
120,000,000 to 150,000,000 tons in 1975 — five times as much
as the plan target.

Thus, in less than twenty years, Japan and the United States
have reversed their positions in steel production. While steel
industries in the United States have been on the decline, Japan
today monopolizes the most up-to-date blast furnaces in the
world, and covers the entire Japanese archipelago with its
annual steel output of 100 million tons, leaving rust-covered
steel frames all over the country. Another Cinerama must
show Japan as a country of iron and steel.

Yet, we now find contradictory assessments of the steel industry's growth and development in Japan. While some quarters view the current Japanese steel industry as the blossom
and fruit of the postwar industrial development policy that particularly emphasized heavy and chemical industries, and as the
symbol of Japan's economic power, there are others who regard it as a symbol of distortion produced by the high-growth
policy, the archculprit of environmental pollution, and a representative example of the collusion between the government and
big business.

These contradictory assessments, however, may have arisen
because each group has seen only one side of the coin. As in
everything, one must examine both sides. This need is partic-

ularly acute in the case of the iron and steel industry, because the front and the back of its coin confront problems of completely different natures. Contradictions are found in the organizational nature of the industry itself. Let me first cite a few instances in this connection to introduce the problems at issue in the industrial organization of steel production.

Problems of the Steel Industry

The steel industry is often referred to as the citadel of monopoly capital. To be sure, it is in our terminology a typical and highly concentrated oligopoly with big business at its core. Generally speaking, a monopolistic industry yields excess profits in the long run, reflecting the control of its industrial organization. As for the Japanese steel industry, there seems to be no doubt that it has earned excess profit in some periods, but at other times small producers and wholesalers often go bankrupt, leading economic journals to start speculating even about "the crisis of the Nippon Steel Corporation." During such periods, the evils of monopoly are quite alien to the industry. In other words, the industry is quite sensitive to the ups and downs of business cycles. Is this universally true of the steel industry anywhere, or is it peculiar only to Japan?

The evils of monopoly arise from restriction in market competition. Instances of restricted competition under a cartel, either overt or covert, or by tacit agreements are not rare in the Japanese steel industry. It is also true, however, that the Japanese steel industry at times enters into violent competition. Steel industry sources claim that excessive competition is its normal market condition. Strong competition may also occur in fixed investment while competition in prices and production is restricted under a cartel. In other words, the Japanese steel industry has a dual structure in that its competition is too little on one side and too much on the other. How does this contradiction arise?

Table 1

Comparison of Profit Rates of the Steel Industry and of
Manufacturing as a Whole
(Profits after taxes on total capital, in %)

	Steel	All manufacturing
1960 I*	6.3	4.8
II**	5.5	4.6
1961 I	4.8	4.2
II	3.9	3.8
1962 I	1.8	2.9
II	1.0	2.6
1963 I	2.2	3.0
II	2.9	3.6
1964 I	2.4	3.0
II	2.2	2.7
1965 I	1.3	2.2
II	1.4	2.3
1966 I	2.8	2.8
II	5.5	3.7
1967 I	5.1	4.1
II	4.4	6.0
1968 I	3.4	5.6
II	3.4	3.9
1969 I	3.5	4.1
II	4.6	4.4
1970 I	3.8	4.0
II	2.1	3.1

Source: Bank of Japan, Shuyo Kigyo Keiei Bunseki [Financial
Statements of Principal Enterprises].
    *First half.
    **Second half.

The steel industry at times organizes cooperative effort, as it did in 1972 in a campaign to raise steel prices, while at other times it finds itself in a complete schism. Though this is a common characteristic of cartels in general and of many oligopolistic industries, the Japanese steel industry exhibited extreme swings in the postwar period. Almost every year, newspapers report on the "steel industry's voluntary adjustment in hard sailing." Still fresh in everyone's memory is the so-called Sumitomo Kinzoku case, which was carried almost daily by newspapers and magazines. What is the cause of the Japanese steel industry's contradictory behavior as manifested in its swings between collusion and intense competition?

The iron and steel industry takes many forms of industrial organization in the capitalist world. Free enterprise is the basic form in Japan and the United States, while Britain has adopted a public corporation system, and the European Community nations more or less promote steelmakers' reorganization. As my analysis below will make clear, a strong tendency toward monopoly is inherent in the steel industry. Therefore, steel industry policy and antitrust policy often clash in a free-enterprise economy like Japan or the United States. This is why mergers of steel firms often become a controversial issue in these countries. However, antitrust measures are not the only weapon against monopolization. For instance, planning may be introduced in a broader perspective, or monopolies may be legalized just as are public corporations and other public utilities, with certain measures taken to keep the evils of monopoly under control. The Japanese government's steel policy has been confused under the influence of these mutually inconsistent ideas. What injuries have been done to the steel industry by this confusion? Can we not straighten out these muddled policy concepts?

Analytical Points of View

I have introduced a few main problems of the organization of the steel industries and how to analyze them. To be more specific, I want to examine all aspects of the functioning of the market system in the steel industry and of its distortions due to the industrial policy of the Japanese government.

To use the metaphor of a physician's diagnosis, Japan's steel industry is a giant that has been raised under peculiar circumstances, and has some abnormally developed organs that make its blood circulation sluggish and its metabolism malfunctioning. It is not particularly sick, yet something is wrong with its body.

The physician must make a comprehensive examination of the patient's circulatory system instead of making separate diagnoses of individual organs of his body. This is why I have decided to focus in this article on the functioning of the market system, which is the basic issue in the theory of industrial organization. I wish to probe thoroughly the question of why Japan's steel industry has come to have a peculiar constitution. I believe that an adequate treatment for this deformity will suggest itself during the course of this analysis.

2. The Market Structure of the Steel Industry — Oligopoly and Competition

Classification of Steelmakers by Production Process

Let me first review the main features of the market structure of the steel industry. Its production processes can provide a good starting point. Among the raw materials necessary for iron- and steelmaking — such as iron ores, coal, scrap steel, manganese ores, and limestone — the Japanese steel industry relies heavily on imports for iron ores and coal. Therefore, the iron and steel industry in Japan excludes iron-ore mining, unlike in the United States. The iron and steel production processes consist of the following three stages: (a) the ironmaking process for the manufacture of pig iron by heating iron ores, cokes, and limestone in a blast furnace; (b) the steelmaking process for the manufacture of steel ingots from pig iron in either an open-hearth furnace, a converter, or an electric furnace; (c) the rolling process by which final products are produced from steel ingots.

Steel enterprises can be classified into three categories according to the degree of integration of these three production processes.

The "integrated" firm carries out all three processes. Included in this category of ikkan, or integrated, steelmakers are the Big Five, namely, the Nippon Steel Corporation, Nippon Kokan, Kawasaki Steel, Sumitomo Metal Industries, and Kobe Steel, as well as a few smaller ones, Nisshin Seiko, Nakayama Steel, and Osaka Steel Manufacturing Company.

The "semi-integrated" firm owns no ironmaking facilities but buys pig iron for steelmaking and rolling. Semi-integrated firms are subdivided into "open-hearth furnace steelmakers" and "electric furnace steelmakers" in Japan. The former group contains eight firms, including Tokyo Seitetsu, Topy Industries, Japan Steelworks, Otani Heavy Industrial Company, and Aichi Steelworks. Sixty-odd enterprises, including Daido Steel, Hitachi Metals, Nippon Yakin Kogyo, Mitsubishi Steel Manufacturing, and Sanyo Special Steel belong to the second subgroup.

The "nonintegrated" firm purchases semifinished products such as billets, blooms, and sheet bars for rolling, and is called a "nonintegrated rolling mill." Larger firms in this group are Toyo Kohan, Yodogawa Steelworks, Daido Kohan, Amagasaki Seihan, and Daitetsu Steel. There are about 170 smaller mills in this category.

The steel production processes end with shipments of rolled steel. However, these are still semifinished goods as far as consumers are concerned. These steel materials are processed into secondary steel products (such as wire, line, and galvanized sheets), machines, ships, and automobiles. There are quite a few steelmakers which manufacture these products.

This kind of integration over several processing stages is known as "vertical integration" in the theory of industrial organization. It is subclassified into "backward integration" and "forward integration" depending on whether the integration is extended backward or forward from the core of the firm. In the steel industry, backward integration combines mining and transport of iron ores, while forward integration extends into production of industrial machines and ships. Many integrated steelmakers in Japan go into not only machine building and shipbuilding but even housing construction, urban planning, and civil engineering. Foward integration is noted in the United States, where U.S. Steel already has expanded its activities into industries related to cement, chemicals, bridge construction, building construction, maritime transport, dockyards, and railways; more recently, Armco has diversified into machinery, shipbuilding, and aircraft leasing, and Youngstown Sheet and Tube into leasing of rolling stock and shipyards, and insurance and banking.

Oligopoly Without Product Differentiation

In view of the steel industry's broad range of business activities, I shall deal mainly with the integrated steelmakers and examine their production activities from pig iron to crude steel, with particular emphasis on their investment behavior, production adjustment, and pricing decisions. These firms are the part and parcel of the industry, and are the key to the problems under study.

The semi-integrated and nonintegrated companies are called the "competitive fringe" vis-à-vis the integrated steel corporations that form the oligopolistic core. Though this fringe exerts important influences on the performance of the industry, it usually follows whatever the core does. Therefore, we shall refer to the periphery only insofar as is necessary in order to understand the behavior of the core.

With this particular focus, let us examine the industry. What are the characteristics of its market structure? By market structure we mean more or less permanent "anatomical" characteristics of the market of a specific commodity in a given locality.

Table 2

Concentration Ratios in the Steel Industry — Market Shares of Major Steel Corporations*

Japan		United States		Federal Republic of Germany		France	
Nippon Steel	36.0%	U.S. Steel	23.9%	ATH AG	27.2%	Wendel-Sidélor	34.4%
Nippon Kokan	13.8	Bethlehem Steel	15.7	Hoesch	14.8	USINOR	33.7
Sumitomo Metal	12.0	Republic Steel	7.3	Krupp	9.3		
Kawasaki Steel	11.8	National Steel	6.4	Mannesmann	8.6		
Kobe Steel	5.2	Armco Steel	6.0	Klöckner	7.6		
Subtotal	78.8		59.3		67.5		68.1
All integrated steelmakers	83.5		89.8		92.6		82.7

*Share equals each steelmaker's output of crude steel as a proportion of total national output.
Sources: For Japan, Nihon no Tekkogyo to Tosha [The Japanese Steel Industry and Our Company] , Sumitomo Metal Industries, Ltd., October 1971; for foreign enterprises, annual company reports and IISI data.

Main indicators in this analysis are seller concentration (production concentration), buyer concentration, barriers to new entry, and degree of product differentiation. Of particular importance among these in the iron and steel industry is seller concentration. The steel industry is a typical example of oligopoly without product differentiation. Product differentiation is the differentiation of an enterprise's products from those of other firms through real differences in efficiency, quality, design, and packaging or through advertising, rebates and other sales promotion activities.

For rolled steel, the chief product of the industry, product differentiation is very limited; small price differences are enough to overturn any variation in quality. This is in sharp contrast to other industries with strong product differentiation, such as electrical household appliances and automobiles.

The concentration ratio is the most important parameter of the market structure in an oligopolistic industry without product differentiation, and provides the basic framework determining the industry's market behavior toward cartels and mergers.

Economics of Large Scale

Before analyzing the importance of the concentration ratio in the steel industry, I must explain why this industry tends toward oligopoly with as few as ten major firms dominating its market.

Basically speaking, economies of large scale of integrated steelmakers play a decisive role in the steel industry. Economies of large scale are decreases in the unit cost of production, or in long-run average cost, with increases in plant or firm size. While it is difficult to estimate economies of scale exactly, Figure 1 gives a rough idea of such economies for integrated steelmakers.

This figure shows the long-run average and marginal cost curves per unit of crude steel. It was constructed by Charles Rowley (1) and is based on studies of cost curves and economies

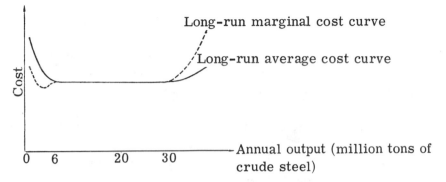

Fig. 1. Economies of scale in the steel industry. (Based
on C. K. Rowley, Steel and Public Policy, [New York:
McGraw-Hill, 1971], p. 57.)

of scale by J. Bain, G. Stigler, W. G. Shepherd, and L. Weiss.
These curves reflect economies of scale not only in a single
plant but also in multiple plants.

According to this figure, the average cost of production of
crude steel is at a minimum for an annual output of 6 million tons,
which is the minimum optimal size of a steel mill. This level
of production corresponds to the capacity of the Kimitsu Mill
of the Nippon Steel Corporation, which was often referred to
as the most advanced steel mill in the world. Though there are
many problems in the concept of economies of scale which must
be cleared before definite conclusions are drawn, the conjecture
that a plant of the size of the Kimitsu Mill is the minimum optimal scale seems to correspond to what is generally believed
by Japanese steelmakers.

This observation implies that any integrated steelmaker must
be of at least this minimum optimal size to compete successfully in the market. Since some 400 billion yen have already
been invested in the Kimitsu Mill, any enterprise wishing to
enter the industry must be large enough to command this much
capital. A small enterprise with less than a billion yen of funds
cannot hope to join the market unless it has an epoch-making

new invention; small quality improvements or new marketing techniques are not enough for entry. Thus, the situation differs from that in industries such as electrical household appliances, food processing, and services, into which new firms can enter if they develop some minor new ideas or innovative sales methods.

The Japanese crude steel market is currently about 90 million tons; given that the minimum optimal mill size is a capacity of 6 million tons annually, it takes only a simple calculation to see that a steelmaker must be as large as one-sixteenth of the market in all respects in order to be able to participate effectively in market competition. That is to say, in addition to its mastery of up-to-date technology and technical know-how, the enterprise must be able to secure one-sixteenth of the raw materials, labor force, sales network, and funds which the industry as a whole currently needs. Economies of scale require this minimum capacity for an integrated steelmaker. In other words, the Japanese steel market can accommodate at most only sixteen integrated steelmakers. While not a monopoly, this number is too small to permit firms to pay little attention to rivals; that is, the industry is controlled by a few firms or, in short, subject to oligopoly control.

Thus, economies of scale are the basic cause for oligopolization of the industry, but not so large as to eliminate competition entirely. When economies of scale are too large, only one or two enterprises survive competition, and the industry thus becomes a "natural monopoly" as in railroads and electric power. The steel industry does not have a market structure that allows "natural monopoly." The cost curves in Figure 1 essentially agree with the U-shaped cost curves found in textbooks on price theory, except that the former are somewhat longer at the bottom. The demand curve for steel is also properly downward sloped, though its price elasticity is small. Thus, there is no reason why the steel market is not suitable for free play of the price mechanism.

In discussions on industrial policy, one often meets the assertion that the price mechanism cannot fully function in a process industry such as iron and steel. This is not theoretically correct. I shall demonstrate this point in what follows.

Rivalry for Concentration

The fact that the steel oligopoly "lacks product differentiation" is associated with the following features of its market structure and market behavior. First of all, with no product differentiation, enterprises compete less in sales promotion activities, such as advertising, model changes, and postpurchase servicing, and more in prices. With little product differentiation, customers can buy from any supplier. A small price differential is enough to induce them to shift their purchases to lower-priced sellers immediately. This intensifies price competition in the market.

On the other hand, the absence of product differentiation indicates the ease of standardizing qualities and specifications and paves the way for price cartels or collusive price leadership. The market structure is thus prone to cartels. The steel price structure is such that extra charges are added for changes in quality, size, and quantity, making price adjustments easy. This provides the technical base for formation of a cartel.

While the U.S. and European steel industries use detailed extra-price tables, the Japanese steel industry still follows the prewar price structure formulated by the now defunct "Nittetsu" Steel Company. Yet, it is much easier in the steel industry to establish a price agreement on its many products than in other industries with full product differentiation such as automobiles and electrical household appliances.

The fact that the steel industry has little product differentiation promotes intense price competition, on the one hand, and induces cartel formation against free competition, on the other.

This means that minor changes in the market structure or industrial policy tend to have a great impact on the steel market, which swings between competition and monopoly. It also means that steelmakers are strongly tempted to raise their concentration and to form a collusive market structure. The main focus of industrial policy is to prevent or eliminate this tendency. Thus, the concentration ratio becomes the key issue in the steel market.

The Steel Industry's Propensity Toward Merger

This tendency toward a less competitive market structure is most typically expressed in mergers, which are almost the sole means to increase concentration in the steel industry. In the United States, expansion in market shares or concentration ratios has been accomplished exclusively by mergers; no single U.S. firm has expanded its market share by more than 4% in this century without resorting to mergers. Though the Kawasaki Steel Corporation and Sumitomo Metal Industries have remarkably expanded their market shares in the postwar Japanese steel industry, the increases are only 4.6% and 4.0%, respectively. The recent birth of the Nippon Steel Corporation through the merger of the Yawata Steelworks and the Fuji Iron and Steel Corporation has caused a definite change in the steel market structure. Though their merger was a controversial issue for many reasons, the basic problem from the viewpoint of the theory of industrial organization was that it was a large-scale merger in an industry in which concentration ratio is the most strategic parameter.

Other Barriers to Entry

We have outlined the central problems of the steel market structure. We shall now briefly discuss other barriers to entry.
Generally speaking, there are four barriers to entry, namely: (1) the barrier of economies of scale; (2) the barrier of product differentiation; (3) the barrier of absolute cost advantage; and (4) the barrier of capital requirement. Joe Bain concludes that in the steel industry the first type of barrier is a little high, the second is insignificant, and the third and fourth are remarkably high. Since I have already touched upon the first

and second barriers, here I shall examine the third and fourth
types. This barrier refers to the cost advantage that existing
firms have over new entrants. It is due to their control of raw materials, production technology, and so on. Bain believes that
this barrier is particularly high in the U.S. steel industry,
mainly because existing firms have already integrated iron-ore
mining, and any new entrants can hardly find a reasonable access to iron ores.

Access to supplies of iron ores or other raw materials raises
no problem in Japan, however, for since the war Japanese steel
mills have imported iron ores from any markets abroad. As
for production technology, Japanese steel production is based
on foreign technologies acquired from other nations — for example, blast-furnace technology from the United States and West
Germany, converter technology from Austria, and strip-mill
technology from the United States. Therefore, the acquisition of
new technology was not a substantial barrier either. Of course,
not every firm can master advanced technology since it requires careful preparations, as seen in the case of Sumitomo
Metal Industries, which had absorbed the Ogura Steelworks in
order to acquire pig-iron technology before it entered the market. However, I think that the technological barrier has not been
a decisive element for a steelmaker capable of achieving the
minimum optimal scale.

Since the barrier of capital requirement stems from the
largeness of the minimum optimal scale, barriers to entry
are almost entirely due to economies of scale. It is true that
new entry is difficult below the minimum optimal scale, but
there seems to have been no particular barrier to entry into the
steel market of a firm above this size if it carefully prepared
its plan. As I have noted earlier, economies of scale are not too
large to be incompatible with competition in the Japanese steel
industry. Hence, neither are barriers to entry so high as to
restrict competition substantially.

In addition, in the postwar Japanese steel market, latecomers
had a singular advantage in realizing economies of scale because their fixed investment embodied more up-to-date tech-

niques. Thus, except in the case of a few products that we shall
examine later, they have been able to enter the markets of
steel products monopolized by older steelmakers and help to
make them competitive (see Figure 2 and Table 3).

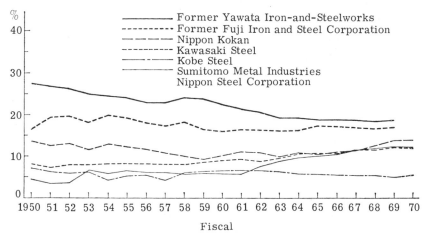

Fig. 2. Market shares of major steelmakers in crude steel.
(Ministry of International Trade and Industry,
Census of Manufacturers.)

3. Market Behavior (1) — Plant and Equipment Investment Adjustments

A Cartel in Plant and Equipment Investment

Under the given market structure, an enterprise purchases
raw materials, determines production and prices for its products, and makes investment decisions. These are what theory
of industrial organization calls market behaviors.

Of these, plant and equipment investment is of particular importance in the steel industry. Formally speaking, such investment may be regarded as a purchase of raw materials with
long durability. However, a decision on the timing and scale of
investment is especially important for a steel firm which requires a scale as large as one-sixteenth of the market, because
its investment decision effectively determines its subsequent pro-

Table 3

Market Shares of Major Steelmakers in Main Steel Products,
1967 (in %)

	I	II	III	IV	V	Sub-total	Nat'l total
Pig iron	43.7	15.9	14.2	13.3	7.2	94.2	100
Crude steel	35.7	13.7	11.5	12.0	5.5	78.7	100
Ordinary hot rolled steel	37.0	14.3	12.8	11.1	3.8	79.1	100
Of which: Bars, section steel	20.0	4.5	6.8	3.7	4.8	39.8	100
Wire rods	36.6	—	3.6	10.7	24.2	75.1	100
Thick and medium plates	37.9	19.9	17.2	10.8	4.9	90.9	100
Sheets	46.4	18.4	15.9	12.6	—	93.3	100
Special hot rolled steel	13.1	3.9	5.5	16.9	14.5	53.9	100
Cold rolled sheets	41.5	15.6	14.6	5.7	—	77.4	100
Tin plates	52.1	9.8	7.9	—	—	69.8	100
Galvanized sheets	35.1	6.5	5.8	4.8	—	52.2	100
Ordinary steel tubes	20.5	22.0	6.8	23.8	1.1	74.1	100
Special steel tubes	5.3	20.8	—	53.4	5.5	84.9	100

I — Nippon Steel; II — Nippon Kokan; III — Kawasaki; IV — Sumitomo; V — Kobe Steel.

Source: Iron and Steel Federation, Tekko Kojo Seisan Jisseki [Production Statistics of Steel Mills].

duction and pricing decisions and, hence, its market behavior.

In the free market, an enterprise makes its investment decisions competitively and rationally at its own risk. It is not so in the Japanese steel industry. A Japanese steelmaker is bound by "voluntary" adjustments, or cartel action on plant and equipment investment and is subject to intervention by government authorities (MITI).

There are pro and con opinions on voluntary investment ad-

justment. Among steelmakers themselves, we find the Nippon
Steel Corporation representing the former view by emphasizing
the inevitability of such adjustment measures, and the Sumitomo
Metal Industries representing the latter view with its advocacy of
liberalization. As for methods of voluntary adjustment, differences of opinion are found in this area as well; some groups
call for adjustments based on market shares, while others support the so-called step-up formula or the "unit" share formula.
Among economists, we find one group asserting that cartelization or investment planning is inevitable in the steel industry
because of its market structure, while another group insists
that voluntary investment adjustments are the root of the organizational ills of the industry.

It is by no means easy to resolve these differences. However,
a careful examination of these conflicting views will at least
make clear the controversial issues. Therefore, we shall first
review the process of voluntary investment adjustment, clarify
the controversy related to it, and then present our own view.
This examination will reveal various clues that will help us to
understand the organization of the steel industry.

How Voluntary Investment Adjustment
Was Brought About

Full-scale investment in the postwar Japanese steel industry
started with the "First Modernization Program" (1951-55),
which was based on the "Report on the Modernization of the
Steel Industry" adopted in February 1952 by the MITI's Industrial Rationalization Council. This government program provided for the appropriation of Development Bank loans and officially specified even small items of investment in plant and
equipment.

Unlike the first one, the "Second Modernization Program"
(1955-60) was not an official program, but the MITI assumed
leadership over the steelmakers concerned and adjusted their
differences by taking advantage of its authority to contact the
World Bank and its influence on the Export-Import Bank's fund

appropriations. Up to this stage, the steel industry's investment in plant and equipment had been under the direct control of the MITI, though the force of this control varied from time to time.

In contrast, post-1961 investment programs, including construction of new steel mills such as Yawata's Kimitsu Plant, Fuji's Oita Plant, Kawasaki's Mizushima Plant, Sumitomo's Kajima Plant, and Kobe Steel's Kakogawa Plant, all of which are major current bases of steel production, had been planned by the enterprises themselves; the only role of the MITI's Industrial Structure Council was to accept their individual investment plans for statistical purposes. The MITI had obviously retreated from center stage. Representatives of the steelmakers met together every year to mutually adjust their own investment plans. This was what they called "voluntary adjustment."

What, then, is this "voluntary adjustment"? Is it not a cartel? Is not the consultation on voluntary investment adjustment among the steelmakers a cartel action? If so, then why was their voluntary investment adjustment given quasi-official approval, when the Antimonopoly Law prohibits cartels?

Some assert that, while "adjustment of production" is a cartel action, "adjustment of investment" is not. This is a preposterous argument. Article 2 of the Antimonopoly Law clearly stipulates "unfair trade restrictions" as "... mutually binding business activities by restricting quantity, techniques, products, facilities, or trading partners. ..." In other words, any concerted decision with other entrepreneurs on either the quantity of production, techniques, or facilities constitutes an unfair restriction of trade. The Antimonopoly Law does not discriminate between production adjustment and investment adjustment. In view of this, why is the adjustment in plant and equipment investment given semiofficial recognition?

The key to this question lies in the "Memorandum on the Operation of the Antimonopoly Law with Respect to the Promotion of Structural Improvements in the Industries" which was exchanged between the MITI and the Fair Trade Commission (November 1966). The points of this memorandum concerning

voluntary adjustment are: (1) The act of compiling demand forecasts for a specific trade sector and preparing criteria for investment activities with a view to providing a basis for each
enterprise to make an independent judgment on its investment activities does not infringe the Antimonopoly Law. (2) The act of consultation among entrepreneurs to limit each enterprise's investment does not infringe the Antimonopoly Law insofar as their
consultation does not substantially affect the current or forthcoming supply and demand relationships.

As is obvious to any careful reader, the Fair Trade Commission in no way says in this memorandum that investment
adjustment is permissible under the Antimonopoly Law but recognizes the "exchange of information" to the extent that it does
not substantially restrict market competition. While it is not
clear how explicitly aware the Fair Trade Commission was, it was
on the right track in its attempt to regard investment adjustment as
a problem of "information exchange." (2)

Opinion is divided as to whether such information exchange
promotes or suppresses competition, particularly in the case
of price information. However, no one will object to the necessity for a certain amount of information exchange in investment
decisions.

Prior to making its investment decisions, an enterprise must
obtain a certain amount of information about prospects for the
market, prices, profit rates, and investment plans of rivals.
The gathering of information on these matters will help protect
enterprises from acting on insufficient or unfounded information. The passage in point (1) of the memorandum, ". . . providing a basis for each enterprise to make an independent judgment on its investment activities . . . does not infringe the Antimonopoly Law," should be interpreted as pointing to and recognizing the necessity of this sort of information exchange.

The question in this connection, however, is whether the exchange of information beyond a reasonable degree through "consultation among entrepreneurs to limit each enterprise's investment" can be justified. Is such information exceptionally
necessary in the steel industry?

Discussions on Excessive Investment

There are discussions with some variances in nuance supporting the necessity of voluntary investment adjustment in the steel
industry. In short, these discussions are based on a fear of excessive investment. They claim that when demand forecasts are more
or less precise, excess investment will ensue if each enterprise
makes its own investment plan without exchanging information.

A hypothetical example may make the point clear. When demand for steel increases at an annual rate of 10%, what will be
the pattern of investment behavior in the steel industry, if it
consists of ten integrated steelmakers, each operating a single
mill of the minimum optimal size?

If all the steelmakers simultaneously start investment to add
one mill each, the steel industry's capacity will be doubled, thus
obviously causing a temporary excess of capacity. In such a
case, investment can exactly match demand increases in the industry as a whole only when the firms take turns in investment
from year to year. But there is no market mechanism that will
make the firms take turns. Therefore, the argument goes, the
enterprises must exchange information and consult with one another to adjust their investment plans and schedules.

The first half of this argument is reasonable. Because the
minimum optimal size is large in the steel industry relative to
its market size, the danger of excess capacity always exists if
the enterprises start investing all at once. But it does not follow readily that voluntary adjustment to investment is therefore
necessary. Why? The answer can be found by a careful study
of the cases that do not lead to excess capacity.

Before it makes an investment decision, an enterprise must
face various uncertainties — for instance, whether demand for
steel will definitely increase, how demand will vary if it fluctuates, and which will be the leading item among plates, sheets,
tubes, section steels, and bars.

Different assessments of these uncertainties make one firm
bullish and another bearish in their investment plans. One enterprise may formulate a first-term construction plan that calls

for completing a rolling mill that can turn out a large variety of steel products, while another may plan to complete such a mill gradually over the first to third terms, cautiously adding new rolling facilities as demand prospects become more certain.

Even an optimistic enterprise, however, may not be able to undertake planned investment at once. For instance, it might be unable to raise the required funds due to its worsened liquidity position. Or it might become unable to secure necessary engineers and workers.

More important is the uncertainty about rivals' behavior. Oligopolistic enterprises must guess what others are going to do. Just as in chess, there is no end to such speculation. If the players are both masters, they might both be able to read through the game to the end. E. H. Chamberlin, who initiated the theory of monopolistic competition, asserted that oligopolistic enterprises could make such thorough-going projections of rivals' behavior and, consequently, would arrive at the monopoly equilibrium.

However, as actual history indicates, oligopolistic enterprises often misread their rivals' actions and commit errors. They then adjust their next steps to correct earlier mistakes. Their investment behavior is also highly unstable because of uncertainties about the actions of rivals. If all oligopolists could read through one another's hands, there should be no need for consultations for voluntary adjustment of investment.

Thus, even if all enterprises prepared investment plans independently and simultaneously to meet definite increases in market demand, they do not necessarily undertake investment projects of the same scale at the same time because, generally speaking, uncertain information and imperfect factor markets lead to natural time lags in investment responses. (3)

Paradox of Artificial Intervention

It is presumable that such time lags do not arise in some cases. During the high growth of postwar Japan, increases in demand for iron and steel were predicted with a high degree of

Enterprise	Plant	1951	52	53	54	55	56	57	58	59	60	61	62	63	64	65	66	67	68	69	70	71	72	73	74	75
Yawata	Yawata										No 1	No 2	No 3													
	Tobata																No 1		No 2		No 3	No 4				
	Sakai																			No 1	No 2	No 3				
	Kimitsu																			No 1						
Fuji	Hirohata										No 3		No 4													
	Muroran																			No 4						
	Kamaishi														No 1											
	Nagoya																No 2			No 3						
	Oita																				No 1					
Nippon Kokan	Kawasaki									No 2																
	Tsurumi																									
	Mizue											No 2		No 1												
	Fukuyama																No 1		No 2	No 3	No 4		No 5			
	Ogishima																							No 1		
Kawasaki	Chiba				No 1					No 2		No 3	No 4			No 5		No 1		No 2	No 3		No 4			
	Mizushima																		No 1			No 2				
Sumitomo	Kokura			Merger																						
	Wakayama											No 1		No 3			No 4	No 5		No 1		No 2				
	Kajima																									
Kobe	Amagasaki					Equity acquisition		No 2																		
	Nadahama									No 1		No 2			Merger		No 3			No 1	No 2					
	Kakogawa																									
Nakayama Osaka Seiko Nisshin Yahagi	Funamachi				No 1			No 2				No 1		No 1						No 2						
	Nishijima												No 1				No 2			No 2						
	Kure																									
	Nagoya																									

Fig. 3. Blast furnace construction. (Iron and Steel Federation, Tekko Tokei Yoran [Iron and Steel Statistical Handbook]; Tekko Journal [Iron and Steel Journal], Tekko Nenkan [Iron and Steel Yearbook]; Gendai Nihon Sangyo Hattatsushi, IV, Tekko [Contemporary History of Japanese Industrial Development, Vol. IV, Iron and Steel].)

accuracy. There were no strong limitations on the capital market to operate against the steel industry's investment. Under such circumstances, it is quite possible that all enterprises start investment at the same time, thereby creating temporary excess capacity. In such an event, what will be the effects of voluntary adjustment among the enterprises concerned when they make public their investment plans and exchange information? Will this prevent the creation of excess capacity. The answer is clearly No.

By assembling their independent investment plans for open discussion, the enterprises can learn about differences in their individual market forecasts as well as the main features and preconditions of their rivals' investment plans. In other words, the process of voluntary adjustment allows each enterprise to eliminate uncertainties. Therefore, if no agreement is reached on voluntary adjustment, the reduction in uncertainties due to the exchange of information will help to stimulate investment and lead to creation of excess capacity.

The situation referred to in point (2) of the memorandum exchanged between the MITI and the Fair Trade Commission when it states "...insofar as their consultation does not substantially affect the current or forthcoming supply and demand relationships," is exactly this case where the exchange of information does not lead to voluntary adjustment but, on the contrary, brings about excess capacity.

In order to bind enterprise investment plans by going beyond voluntary adjustment, some rules for setting up investment quotas are necessary. However, the Fair Trade Commission will raise an objection to such an action, since it will substantially affect the current and forthcoming supply and demand relationships. But let us disregard this point for the time being. Will such rules help prevent excess capacity? The answer is again No.

Investment quotas directly involve the interests of individual enterprises. An enterprise which has had a large share in the past may ask that more weight be given to its past performance, while another which has recently expanded its share may call

for using the current market shares, and another which has
large sales relative to its capacity will demand consideration
for sales volume. Some compromises are necessary for agree-
ing on the rules of allocation. In the bargaining process, enterprises with larger production capacity tend to have more say
because they have more "fighting reserves" than others and
can advance their negotiating position by intimidating other
companies through price cuts if the others insist on greater
quotas.

Small firms such as the earlier Kawasaki Steel or Sumitomo
Metals, when their market shares are only a few percentage
points, do not exert strong influence on the market even if they
try to disrupt the market in order to express their dissatisfaction with their investment quotas. However, a firm will have a
strong voice when its share exceeds 10% of the market. Therefore, in the allocation of investment quotas, production capacity
gains in importance. If individual firms want to avoid market
disruptions, they have to acknowledge the status quo and maintain the present market shares. Therefore, once investment
quotas are determined, each enterprise will opt for expanding
its production capacity even beyond the limit of its sales capacity in order to use such a fait accompli to strengthen its
position at the next negotiations on investment.

Thus, by imposing quotas, investment adjustment may, contrary to its initial intention, invite the creation of potential excess capacity, even though the adjustment can tentatively suc-
ceed in balancing demand and supply at the market level.

In this way, no matter what its form may be, voluntary investment adjustment with the express purpose of avoiding excess
capacity will rather increase it. And, once production capacity
is definitely in excess, it becomes imperative to adjust production in order to avert price markdowns. The "curtailment
of production" under the advice of the MITI and "voluntary production cutback" have been enforced off and on in the Japanese
steel industry. The antidepression cartel on crude steel, in
force until a while ago, is also an instance of this production
adjustment. However, such a production adjustment or cartel

also induces expansion of output capacity because it is a collusive action to prevent price reductions or to mark up prices.
The elimination of price competition results in nonprice competition, but the very limited product differentiation in the steel
industry makes sales promotion activities such as advertising
and quality improvements ineffective means of competition.

In commodities such as steel which are bought by large customers, the key to sales is suppliers' business ties with customers. The effective nonprice factor that establishes such ties
with customers is productive capacity itself. When steel production is in excess, the market is a buyers' market; consumers
can purchase from any supplier. Marketing then does not help
to solidify ties with specific suppliers. However, when the supply is tight on a sellers' market, prompt delivery of products of
particular specifications needed by buyers at prices agreeable
to both buyers and sellers is a very effective marketing strategy
that helps suppliers to strengthen ties with customers. In other
words, a supplier that finds itself short of supply capacity in a
business boom tends to lose its customers to rivals, and thus to
have its market share reduced. The prevention of price competition in an oligopolistic market with no product differentiation
results in competition through capacity. The postwar steel industry repeated the sequence of investment adjustment to production adjustment. Though this was an attempt to match supply
increases to demand increases, it resulted in the creation of excess supply, contrary to its intention.

Whenever excess capacity becomes too great, all enterprises
suddenly stop their investment; when business conditions improve, they once again repeat the same sequence. Therefore,
investment adjustment builds in a unique rhythm in investment
cycles in the steel industry.

It is often argued that investment cannot be left to the free
decision of the enterprises because excess capacity is created
even when so much adjustment is being made. This logic is
topsy-turvy. Excess capacity is created because the sequence
of investment adjustment to production adjustment is practiced.

The Rhythm of Investment under
Voluntary Adjustment

Let us look at some facts. Up to 1960, steel firms basically
accepted the total volume of investment set annually by the
MITI. Though there were minor variations from year to year,
this was a kind of quota system.

As we have explained, with the investment quota system in
force and price competition absent, enterprises compete with
one another in expansion of capacity. The interfirm competition
thus centers around investment in plant and equipment. Immediately after the drastic cutback of investment in the recession
in 1954, the "Jimmu Boom"* of 1955 and 1956 swept over the
economy, and steel enterprises found themselves extremely
short of supply capacity. This experience must have convinced
steel producers of the disadvantages of insufficient production
capacity and induced them to accelerate investment. For
instance, in the voluntary investment adjustment for 1960,
the MITI asked steel producers to submit their plans for 1962
and 1965 and tabulated their returns. The results turned out to
be very bullish. While the Japan Iron and Steel Federation
estimated the industry output of crude steel at 26,540,000 tons
in 1965 — or about 50% higher than the 1959 total — the MITI
figure for planned output of all enterprises was more than
39,000,000 tons for the same year. One firm submitted a plan
to triple its output by that year.

This resulted in the first voluntary investment adjustment,
the main point at issue then being Kawasaki Steel's strong opposition to the draft plan that based adjustments on market
shares since 1951. Kawasaki Steel called for bringing together
individual investment plans and introducing adjustments by
product items and by types of rolling facilities — the so-called
step-up formula.

---

*The boom was so remarkable that it was named after the first
emperor of Japan — Trans.

Yoshihiro Inayama,* who chaired the meeting, withdrew his pet "market share" formula; an agreement was reached to restrict adjustment to the construction projects scheduled to begin in 1960. The final adjustment plan approved the construction of Yawata's Tobata Plant, Fuji's Muroran Plant, and Kobe Steel's Nadahama Plant. Of course, Kawasaki Steel was reluctant to accept this final plan for the following interesting reason: Not to mention the projects for the first two corporations, the plan gave approval to Kobe Steel for construction of the Nadahama Plant but disqualified Kawasaki's Chiba plant, which Kawasaki could not accept. Kawasaki was unwilling to step back because Kobe Steel's new mill would affect subsequent voluntary adjustments. Though Kawasaki yielded to Inayama's persuasion, it has since held a sort of grudge against him.

However, an odd event — though in fact not so odd as it may have appeared — took place only fifteen days after this voluntary investment adjustment plan on blast furnaces had been agreed upon: A number of open-hearth-furnace steelmakers announced their blast furnace construction plans one after another, and major integrated steelmakers expressed support for these plans. This is a typical case supporting the proposition that investment adjustment under a cartel tends to destabilize investment.

Investment adjustment under a cartel can bind only its members; it cannot prevent new entrants from investing unless restrictions are placed against outsiders. Open-hearth-furnace steelmakers were such new entrants; they had asked major steelmakers to sell them pig iron at cheaper rates, but they met deaf ears and sometimes even found their purchase orders cut back. These experiences made them realize correctly the advantage of entering the pig-iron market, in which voluntary adjustment restricted investment.

On the other hand, integrated steelmakers who were bound by

_____

*Then president of the Yawata Iron- and Steelworks and currently president of the Nippon Steel Corporation — Trans.

voluntary investment adjustment and unable to construct blast
furnaces wanted smaller firms that were under their control to
construct blast furnaces. This fact clearly proves that the voluntary investment adjustment is nothing but a cartel action by
which senior firms such as Yawata, Fuji, and Nippon Kokan intended to prevent junior firms from expanding.

In December 1960, the MITI, on its own initiative, made a
peculiar decision in authorizing Nippon Kokan, Kawasaki Steel,
and Nisshin Steelworks to construct new blast furnaces to meet
rising demand for iron and steel, as evidenced by steady increases in pig-iron imports. If this decision was due to the
growing demand for steel, making productive capacity short,
enterprises could have revived their suspended investment
plans without such an authorization. According to the explanation of the MITI, "although such additional investment should
have been subject to voluntary investment adjustment, it had to
resort to this expediency because not all enterprises concerned
were ready yet with their long-term investment plans."

This development inspired all enterprises to prepare aggressive long-term investment plans. When investment adjustment for 1961 was under discussion, ten blast furnaces (including
those of open-hearth-furnace steelmakers) were initially planned.

Subsequently, Yawata drew up an aggressive long-term plan
extending to 1970, while Fuji did not feel ready to set up a long-
term plan and was also cautious in its current investment.
Sumitomo maintained a reasonable view: "Voluntary investment
adjustment which becomes hung up on mere methodology, as in
1960, is meaningless; there are doubts as to the need for such
adjustment. In fact, there is no reason to worry because financing and technology do not allow firms to pursue indiscriminate expansion." This is exactly the situation which gives rise
to natural time lags, as we noted earlier.

Integrated steelmakers thus differed very much in their attitudes toward investment. Nonetheless, when the MITI asked
them in January 1961 to submit their investment plans for the
period up to 1965, it received proposals for as many as nineteen

new blast furnaces. It should be obvious to the reader that investment adjustment actually leads to creation of excess capacity. Witness also that major steelmakers had already decided
to leave the investment adjustment for 1961 to the MITI's discretion, and the MITI itself had emphasized the necessity of
limiting investment because of its belief that the planned investment in hot and cold strip mills, converters, and oversize
rolling facilities would be excessive. But, surprisingly, the
MITI suddenly announced a change in policy to flexible investment adjustment, "because it had learned that hot strip mills
and converters require a year to reach standard capacity because of their large size."

Even without investment adjustment, limitations in financing
and technology, as noted by Sumitomo, or delays in reaching the
standard capacity, as the MITI allegedly discovered, would have
given rise to natural time lags in investment responses, thus
making it easier for the steelmakers to react spontaneously to
increasing demand.

It is known both theoretically and empirically that investment
adjustment leads to a unique rhythm in investment cycles. The
Japanese steel industry is no exception. If the Japanese steel
industry is more depressed at times during recessions than are
other industries, it is due to this unique rhythm created by repeated investment adjustments.

4. Market Behavior (2) — Price Formation

Price Volatility

The essence of industrial organization lies in whether it is
capable of determining product prices at a (socially) optimal
level or not. When product differentiation is limited, product
designs or postpurchase services are not very important to
industrial organization. The decisive factor is whether product
prices are high or low.

Intense price competition often occurs in the steel industry because product prices can be used as a strategic weapon in market competition. On the other hand, collusive pricing may also predominate because limited product differentiation facilitates agreements on product qualities and prices. In other words, the steel industry sometimes forms very low prices and at other times maintains high quasi-monopoly prices.

There are two factors in the steel industry which make price changes volatile. First of all, demand for steel fluctuates a great deal during business cycles. This is because demand for steel is influenced very much by total investment in the economy. It is something unavoidable in the steel industry. Second, the steel industry is a "fixed cost" industry in which fixed cost is a relatively large proportion of total cost. This requires the steel industry always to maintain a high rate of capacity utilization. Conventional argument puts very strong emphasis on this supply factor of the process industry; some economists go as far as to claim that the market mechanism does not function in such an industry because the industry cannot reduce its capacity use under the burden of fixed cost.

It is true that wages are quasi-fixed in Japan because employment cannot be adjusted by layoffs as in the United States. But fixed cost covering interest payments, depreciation charges, and wages and salaries is above 25% of total cost in the steel industry, a ratio comparable to that in the chemical and paper and pulp industries. The price mechanism is unable to function fully to adjust demand and supply only when the ratio of fixed cost to total cost exceeds 50%, as in transportation and electric power. In the steel industry, the relative importance of fixed cost contributes merely to a greater volatility in price changes than in other industries.

Therefore, it is necessary to note the phase of the business cycle in checking steel prices. In other words, one must view prices through two lenses — one when looking at a boom and the other when looking at a slump. One is likely to misjudge price data if they are viewed through only one lens. One may be told that steel prices are too low in a recession, but this may be only an optical illusion.

Are Prices Stable? — Comparison with the U.S. Steel Industry

I shall next examine in detail how steel prices are formed in Japan and then explain how wrong the Japanese steel pricing policy is in terms of economic theory.

To begin with, let us get a sharp focus on the problem through a couple of graphic illustrations. Figure 4 shows thick plate prices since 1955. Though it is by no means easy to get accurate statistics of steel prices, we rely here on the Bank of Japan's wholesale price indexes, which are believed to reflect actual prices fairly correctly. The figure also shows the Economic Planning Agency's diffusion index that gives business cycle references. As is obvious from the figure, steel prices represented by plate prices fluctuate with business cycles along a somewhat downward trend.

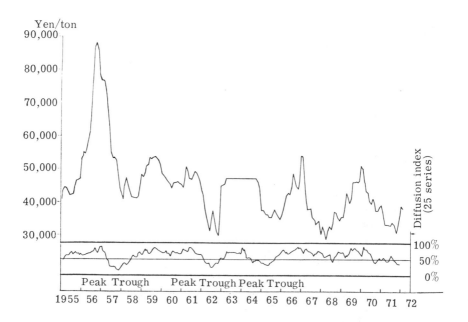

Fig. 4. Fluctuations of thick plate prices (soft steel, grade 1).
(Bank of Japan; Economic Planning Agency.)

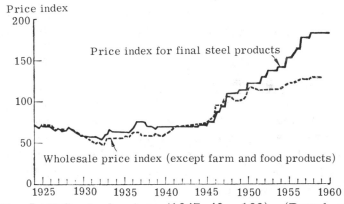

Fig. 5. U.S. steel prices (1947-49 = 100). (Based on
L. W. Weiss, Economics and American Industry (New York,
John Wiley and Sons, 1967), p. 308.

A striking contrast is provided by U.S. steel prices, as shown
in Figure 5, which covers a thirty-five-year period from 1925
to 1960; this longer time span is used to reveal the nature of the
problem. Note that U.S. steel prices fluctuated with business
cycles until 1940 but showed steady rises step by step since
then. In other words, steel prices were downwardly rigid,
merely halting their rises in a recession and then jumping in
the next boom, which then determined the new floor of prices.
This figure clearly describes the pathological conditions of
American steel prices, thus indicating that industrial organization itself is defective. Movements of Japanese steel prices
point to much better performances for Japan's steel industry.

Yet, there are many Japanese steel industry sources who believe that Japanese steel prices are pathological and insist that
they should be stabilized by all means. They are bent on advertising through the mass media how sick steel prices are.
The MITI in its postwar steel pricing policy also continued to
seek stabilizing steel prices through the "openly quoted price"
system.

Both the MITI and the steel industry continued untiring efforts to stabilize steel prices, but they failed. Why? Should
they have succeeded, would not the mechanism of steel price

formation in Japan have followed the American price mechanism? We shall consider these questions in light of both fact and theory.

A Cartel Under the Name of "Openly Quoted Price" System

There are more than ten varieties of steel pricing systems. Let us note three of them here — tatene (sales-quotation system), kohan kakaku* (openly quoted price system), and shichu kakaku (market sales price system). We shall see how they were developed historically.

Up to July 1950, steel prices were under government control. After the official price system was abolished, steel prices were left free until January 1955, when Yawata, Fuji, and Nippon Kokan revived the "sales-quotation" system, under which all steelmakers "accept orders at the quoted prices instead of determining, case by case, special contract and special delivery prices." In other words, this was a kind of monopoly pricing by the Big Three. This system had to be suspended frequently, however, because it stopped functioning when prices were unstable.

In the meantime, the MITI, in an effort to authorize the steel industry's voluntary cartel as an exception to the Antimonopoly Law, planned to submit a draft bill on "Iron and Steel Demand and Supply" to the Diet, published a position paper on the stabilization of iron and steel prices, and took a number of policy measures, one of which was the kokai hanbai seido (openly quoted price system), or kohan for short, that was enforced in June 1958.

This system works as follows: (1) Member companies decide on monthly production and sales pursuant to the MITI's production guidelines, and report them to the MITI; (2) they also report and announce sales prices; (3) they start sales at the same time at certain designated locations in accordance with their predetermined sales and prices as reported to the

---

*Abbreviation for kokai hanbai kakaku — Trans.

MITI; (4) any surplus is to be purchased by wholesale dealers. In other words, this system is a virtual cartel in which the MITI, by its administrative guidance, determines the volume of steel output.

The actual operation of this system also demonstrates that it was a cartel. Inayama, then Executive Director of the Yawata Iron- and Steelworks, who had taken leadership in adopting this system, commented as follows: "The kohan system is the second best, next to pricing agreements, which the Antimonopoly Law prohibits" (Tekkokai [Iron and Steel Industry], July 1958).

The Fair Trade Commission, which would subsequently make repeated requests to the MITI to abolish the system, approved it initially under very loose conditions: (1) that it would be placed under the guidance of the MITI; (2) that it would not be used for profiteering; and (3) that fair competition would be continued while excessive competition would be avoided.

Such an inconsistent attitude is now inconceivable, but it was comprehensible at that time in view of the balance of power between the commission and the MITI. It is also understandable that the steel industry, which inaugurated the kohan system as a counterrecession measure, hated to submit a formal application to organize an antidepression cartel, which required the industry to make public detailed data on production costs, and attempted instead to organize a virtual cartel outside the jurisdiction of the Antimonopoly Law. But the kohan system continued into the next boom, when the steel industry even raised prices by 2,000 to 3,000 yen per ton in April 1959 by restricting production.

Though the MITI insisted then that the steel industry should first lift its production control before announcing the price increases, the industry continued the control on grounds that competition would become intolerable without it and claimed that the price rises were intended to cover losses suffered on some items sold below cost.

This is obviously restraint of trade by a cartel. Yet, to our surprise, the steel industry openly continued the kohan system even in the boom under the extraordinary name of a counter-

boom cartel! The argument for it was that the kohan system
was necessary to curb large price rises. We can understand the
situation if the industry insisted on a cartel for price stabilization.
But, as a matter of fact, the industry seems to have attempted
to justify a cartel by employing whatever reasons available.

The Fair Trade Commission finally expressed its disapproval
of such a counterboom cartel and more than once urged the MITI
to review the kohan system. To this, the MITI answered that
"the system should continue as a long-term measure for steel
price stabilization." After these exchanges, the Fair Trade
Commission conceded to its continuation on condition that "the
MITI exercise its guidance over production and prices only at
times of significant fluctuations." However, what does it mean
that the kohan system should continue with the MITI's guidance
on production control in order to curb large price rises?

To be sure, this policy seems at first sight to have achieved
some results; for example, in April 1961, when the prices for
medium-size section steel rose over 50,000 yen per ton from
their kohan prices of 39,000 to 41,000 yen per ton, the MITI in-
structed the steel industry to increase production quotas for this
product, thus leveling down its prices four or five months later.
This instance has often been cited as a success of the kohan
system. But it really proves that production control was in
force, for the steelmakers did not increase production without
the MITI's instruction, in spite of the supply shortage that had
caused extreme price rises. Without the kohan system, supply
would have increased automatically and prices would have set-
tled at a fair level. In fact, in response to the MITI's instruction, eighteen steelmakers issued a joint statement declaring
that they would "do their best to increase production, though an
immediate large-scale increase is difficult because the production plans on medium-size section steel for April have already
been decided." They must have had supply capacity, and yet
they needed several months to catch up with increasing demand.
This is evidence that the kohan system functioned to control
production. It is not an example of the success of the system,

but proof that it was a de facto cartel.

As a cartel often perishes due to a conflict of interests among its members, this kohan cartel, too, was doomed to collapse. From 1960 on, when major steelmakers began lowering actual prices by offering rebates and nonmembers of the cartel continued to increase their market shares, the kohan prices gradually became unenforceable.

In the meantime, leading steelmakers strived to maintain the kohan system, claiming that "its destruction spells doom for the steel industry." The MITI also offered its assistance by asking steelmakers to abide by the system and organizing a policing committee. In spite of these efforts, the system gradually lost its force and turned into a price-reporting system.

Finally, in December 1962, six integrated steelmakers announced floor sales prices, calling them "effective prices." The Fair Trade Commission also published its official view that these prices were to be considered as the base prices, which ought not to be maintained by collusive actions.

The Logic of the Prior Price Notification System

From the viewpoint of the theory of industrial organization or antitrust policy, the kohan system cannot be accepted insofar as it plays the role of a cartel. It is another thing when it merely serves the function of a price notification scheme. There are quite a few scholars who approve such a system as the American system of openly quoted prices or the British price notification scheme.

Logically speaking, the price notification system is a system for the exchange of price information. The theory of industrial organization can support such an information exchange system provided that it does not restrict competition. Therefore, let us first examine the effect of such information exchange on prices in the market.

In this connection, it is important to distinguish between prior and posterior price notification. In almost all competitive markets, prices determined by individual enterprises on their own discretion are made public later on, whether notifications are obligatory or not. Such practices do not restrict competition.

The question is whether the prior notification system can be permitted. Economists who support it (for example, G. B. Richardson) (4) argue as follows: Short-run price competition must be distinguished from long-run competition. Long-run competition reflects the efficiencies of individual enterprises and should be encouraged; short-run competition is merely a temporary tactic and should be discouraged. To maintain normal supply, some degree of excess capacity is necessary; intense short-run competition tends to induce oversupply from excess capacity and results in earnings squeezes, thus eliminating capacity surplus. In order to avoid such short-run competition, the exchange of price information is necessary. Therefore, prior price notification should be permitted.

The same view has persisted in the Japanese quarters which support the kohan system of steel prices. Quite a few economists also support this view. However, in my opinion, such thinking reflects insufficient understanding of the essence of competition. I shall summarize my own argument here and then amplify it later at different places in this paper.

First of all, one must question whether an effective distinction can be made between short-run and long-run competition. However, for the sake of argument, let us accept this distinction. We must then observe that short-run competition is a necessary condition for long-run competition; any reduction in the former will lead to a decline in the latter.

Take, for instance, the case of Kawasaki Steel and Sumitomo Metal Industries at the earlier stage of the postwar steel industry when they adopted a strategy of installing advanced facilities so that they could lower product prices and expand their market shares. This obviously belongs to the category of long-run competition. But what would have followed if a prior price notification system had been in force as a means of reducing short-run competition, so that competing firms would have been notified of their planned price reductions in advance? Competing enterprises would themselves have lowered prices to avoid losing customers. If all actions are known beforehand, there will be no inducement to initiate aggressive price competition. Under such circumstances, even innovating firms will attempt to maintain stable equilibrium as before and remain content with increased earnings due to cost reductions. Thus, reduced short-run competition necessarily implies reduced long-run competition.

In price negotiations, a corporation manager will have to resolve his position case by case. At one time, he will offer a cheap price to expand his corporation's share in the market. At another time, he will keep prices as they have been and end up losing customers. Thus, he is always in competition under uncertain circumstances. This is short-run competition, but a manager's decision is based on the totality of short-range and long-range information, conveyed to him as instructions from higher above, through discussions at management meetings, or in other ways, all of which reflect the corporation's investment plan, feasibility of technical innovations, or assessment of future demand. While they may seem indirect, long-run factors can affect an enterprise's decision making only in this way. In other words, short-run competition is not devoid of long-term considerations. There are no other forms of long-run competition; long-run competition per se is nothing but an illusion of top business leaders out of touch with reality.

When price uncertainties are reduced, competition declines. Oligopolistic enterprises cannot indiscriminately raise prices due to uncertainties involving the loss of some of their customers. If adequate information exchange eliminates such uncertainties, the enterprises will opt for the safest course of action, namely, raising prices in unison; this also will entail reduced competition in investment and technical innovation, which is induced by and gives support to price competition. This is why price competition is the pivot of all kinds of competition; it is price uncertainties that give rise to such competition. Without such uncertainties there will be no profits in the true sense of the word, and private enterprises in the capitalist economy will lose their raison d'être.

Therefore, we cannot support the exchange of price information in a form as strong as the kohan system, even when it does not involve cartel actions such as production restriction. Granted that it is necessary to stabilize steel prices, this should be achieved by some other means. The kohan system kills the price mechanism.

Economics of Price Stabilization

Let us consider why stable steel prices are necessary. Are they desirable for the operation of the Japanese economy as the steel industry claims? Do stabilized steel prices really contribute to more efficient resource allocation in the economy?

It is difficult to conduct a full analysis of the effects of price stabilization upon resource allocation or economic welfare. The answer is not readily available. Even in a very simple case, it depends on the size of price elasticity, inventory cost due to stabilized prices, and other conditions; moreover, influences of future markets, speculations, etc., and their feedback on the price mechanism have to be taken into consideration. All these factors make a clear-cut answer difficult to obtain; all we can do is to pass a comprehensive judgment, case by case.

We shall now examine the case of Japanese steel prices.

Let us begin with an extreme case: Demand for steel clearly differs during booms and during slumps, which alternate in a systematic fashion. The production facilities are constructed to provide adequate supply to meet peak demand, which inevitably leads to excess capacity during slumps.

What is the most desirable form of price formation in this case from the viewpoint of resource allocation? What should be theoretically the best pricing?

The answer is obvious: Determine the price equal to marginal cost at <u>each</u> moment. Price theory shows that this is the price that results in the optimal allocation of resources. In other words, the price should be equated to the marginal cost required to supply peak demand in a boom and to the marginal cost to supply an additional unit in a slump. Since facilities are designed to meet peak demand, the fixed cost of investment is incorporated into the marginal cost in a boom, thus reducing the marginal cost in a slump to the variable cost. Such price formation results in high boom prices and low slump prices.

This type of price formation is known as peak-load pricing in a market where demand varies seasonally or hourly. Examples are peak and off-peak rates for electric power and winter discounts in railroad fares. From the standpoint of economic welfare, this type of rate structure is also desirable in public utilities with periodic variations in demand.

In private enterprises, too, this pricing system may apply, for instance, to rentals of summer houses; since a summer house is built for summer usage, its fixed cost is recouped in its summer rent, while its off-season rent is heavily discounted. The owner can earn more by differentiating rents by season than by adopting a uniform year-round rent; such a practice is also more desirable from the standpoint of resource allocation.

Because of the need to stabilize supply of basic materials, the primary objective of fixed investment in the postwar steel industry was to maintain capacity surplus so as to avert supply shortage at peak demand. Imports could have been used to adjust supply, but the MITI, in keeping with its postwar industrial policy, wanted to maintain domestic supply potential at all times. Then, the equality of price and marginal cost permits the price in a boom to be higher than that in a slump.

Needless to say, it is necessary to prevent prices from rising far above the marginal cost, but any efforts to keep them stable below the marginal cost will distort resource allocation. In theory, it is not unusual that, during a slump, steel prices should be lowered to the marginal cost under excess capacity, namely, to the level that is sufficient to cover the variable cost.

This is merely an extreme case, presented here only as a model to straighten out our own thinking. This type of pricing can be applied without change to private enterprises such as summer-house rental. However, in the case of steel, the periodicity of demand is not perfectly systematic like seasonal demand, since it is subject to the somewhat irregular waves of business cycles. Therefore, there is no guarantee that losses during a slump can be fully covered by profits during a boom. Moreover, since a cycle lasts as long as two to three years, it may be difficult for a firm to put up with deficits for a few quarters at a stretch. Indeed, such a pricing policy may push an otherwise efficient enterprise into bankruptcy due to financial hardships, causing dumping and other market disruptions. It may also lead to abnormal price rises during a boom because of heavy speculative activities. Therefore, some measures are necessary to prevent extreme price fluctuations.

It is only in this sense that price stabilization in the steel market is desirable for the national economy. However, its purpose is not to stabilize prices at a certain fixed base but to curb abnormal price rises in a boom and to hold back drastic price falls in a slump.

This interpretation of steel price stabilization indicates that a special scheme such as the kohan system is, in fact, unnecessary. Inventory stocks can fulfill the required function equally well. In many industries, prices do not fluctuate as much as textbooks might suggest because inventories of finished products work as a buffer stock between fluctuations in production and prices, thereby helping prices to stabilize.

In the steel industry, wholesale dealers buy steel products while they are cheap and store them in their warehouses until they can be sold at higher prices for a good profit. They earn speculative profits and at the same time contribute to the stabilization of steel prices.

There are some steel wholesale dealers who engaged in speculations that resulted in market disruptions, but there are also

a number of dealers, such as the Hanwa Kogyo Company, who
earned substantial profits through their inventory policy
and contributed at the same time to stabilizing steel prices.
Had there been no kohan system and no specially designated wholesalers, wholesalers would have been able to enter the
market at will and make use of the free market mechanism;
then, the survival of the fittest would have followed and dealers
who correctly anticipated price developments would have gained
power. Their inventory operations then would have stabilized
steel prices in a normal manner.

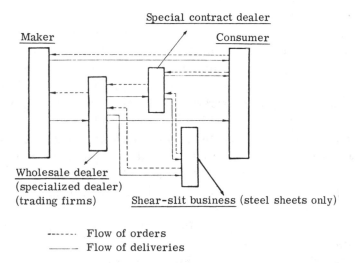

        ------- Flow of orders
        ─────── Flow of deliveries

Fig. 6. Distribution routes of ordinary rolled steel. (Tatsuji
Ohki, Tekko no Ryutsu Kiko [Distribution Network of Steel],
            Japan Steel Structure Association.)

As for "tied sales" transactions with the automobile and shipbuilding industries, which go through without the intervention of
wholesalers, suppliers and customers can stabilize prices by
concluding long-term contracts if they so desire.

The Consequence of the Principle of Cost plus
Fair Return

My argument should have made it clear that the steel industry is wrong in its leading principle of stabilizing prices at the level of "cost plus fair return." Essentially, this is equivalent to administered prices, which will lead to stabilization of prices at a much higher level, as seen in Figure 5 showing American price formation.

This may offend steel people, who will promptly retort that they are trying to stabilize steel prices at a low level. It is probably true that they intend to stabilize prices at a low level rather than at a high level. But let me point this out. Though I am not particularly in favor of the view that private enterprises are "born evil," I must conclude that, no matter what their intention may be, their guiding principle of cost plus fair return will inevitably push up prices. I shall now explain why.

Cost plus fair return can be accepted only in price formation by public utilities — electric power, and the like — which are obligated to provide services for all customers and are subject to a strict review of their cost accounting. But even in such public utilities, it has recently been proved theoretically and empirically that the formula of cost plus fair return results in many kinds of waste that are now dubbed as X-inefficiency.

How is cost to be computed in the steel industry to realize cost plus fair return?

Rises in iron-ore and coal prices are obvious increases in cost. Cost rises when wages are increased or even when political donations and contributions are made. Cost also increases to offset losses in the business subsidiary of an enterprise. The steel industry is notorious in defending its pricing policy. We noted earlier that it justified price increases while production was cut back under the antiboom cartel on a pretext of paying for items sold below cost in the past. The industry will not hesitate in the slightest to cover its losses in subsidiary business by regarding them as cost increases. This is impossible in public utilities. For instance, a private railway company whose subsidiary department store experiences deficits will never be permitted to include such losses in its railway fare computations.

Wages are obviously a component of cost, but wage increases are left to the negotiations between labor and management. Major steel firms pay comparatively high wages. Considerable pay increases were agreed upon in the spring labor offensive in recent years, though steel companies continued to complain about their management difficulties to justify their antidepression cartel.

M. A. Adelman, who analyzed American steel prices, concluded that steel prices are wage-push prices based on labor-management collusion rather than administered prices. The principle of cost plus fair return will justify raising prices to pay for wage increases when the wage-increase system of the American type is incorporated.

Let us take another look at Figure 5. Successive increases in steel prices in the United States are due to the "cost plus target return" pricing of U.S. Steel, which acted as the leader for other steel corporations. The fundamental cause of American steel price hikes is the cost push based on wage increases; they have not resulted in monopoly profits. Therefore, no matter what emphasis steel managers may place on "fair return," in contrast to "high return," steel prices will continue spiraling upward if there is no check on cost under the cost-plus-fair-return formula.

The cost is not the only danger spot. Is there any guarantee that fair return will be kept down to an appropriate level once prices have been raised? True, steel industry leaders issue public statements that they will check price rises whenever steel prices rise drastically; they are no doubt aware of the need for maintaining profits at a fair level. However, the "fair" level itself is a very vague concept. The profit rate may creep upward in the wake of slow steel price spirals and yet be justified as fair return. (This is evident from the steel price rises after the formation of an antidepression cartel in 1972.) How can this kind of a situation be prevented?

In the market economy, such creeping increases in cost and profits can be curbed by the pressure of competition. Interfirm competition eliminates wasteful cost and excessive profits. Though competition is not a panacea, once competitive forces are gone, prices are sure to start creeping upward in an oligopolistic market.

Some may object and propose the counterargument that the Japanese steel industry is still subject to intense competition and that prices are comparatively low. I agree with this and admit it at the time of this writing (early 1972).

However, what I have been driving at is the following: the Japanese steel market is characterized by its frequent swings from one extreme to the other — from intense competition to collusion. Even a minor change in the market structure can cause these swings. The presence of fairly intense competition now must therefore be due to the effects of voluntary investment adjustment that has created excess capacity, contrary to its objective of collusion, and of the kohan system that worked as a destabilizer, though it was intended to stabilize prices.

The Nippon Steel Corporation and Tacit Collusion

Next, I shall consider what market structure will arise after this phase is dealt with.

The normal market mechanism seems to be returning quickly to the steel industry. The kohan system is virtually gone. Voluntary investment adjustment will be soon abolished. Even if it is in force, it will be substantially deprived of its influence. In other words, with interventions gone, the steel market will recover its normal market mechanism. Then, what problems will arise? How will steel prices be formed?

One thing is certain: given oligopoly without product differentiation, the steel market will keep on swinging between competition and monopoly. Even the normal market mechanism can by no means guarantee free competition. Tacit collusion among oligopolistic firms will favor monopoly. They will reach a tacit understanding among themselves by guessing what each other's behavior will be and establish joint action without consultations or agreements.

In the merger of Yawata and Fuji, what economists feared most was that it might create a market structure amenable to such covert collusion, which would give rise to price leadership of the American style. Were they alarmists? We shall now examine this question by looking at recent events.

The kohan system virtually collapsed in December 1962 when the Big Ten adopted the "floor sales price" system, Yawata announced its sales prices, and the others followed suit. Since then, what can be regarded as price leadership seems to have been established by Yawata. However, tacit collusion was not always being practiced.

A typical example of noncollusion is the so-called Sumitomo case in 1965. When Yawata tried to exercise its leadership by cutting crude steel production and raising steel prices, Sumitomo Metal Industries resolutely opposed it because of its discontent with the assigned quota. The MITI intervened in the dispute, threatening Sumitomo by hinting at a cut in its coal quota.

When the Yawata-Fuji merger was being debated publicly, supporters of the merger cited the Sumitomo case to argue that the presence of such militant firms as Sumitomo and Kawasaki would prevent tacit collusion after the merger.

Though it is premature to make a definite judgment from the two years' experience since the merger, we can note a subtle change in Sumitomo's attitude over time, with some shift toward collusion, at least up to now. For instance, take the case of crude steel production cutback in October 1970. On the nineteenth of the month, the Nippon Steel Corporation made a public announcement of a 10% cut in its crude steel production, and its president Yoshihiro Inayama issued a statement that similar action by the other steel corporations would be most desirable for the steel industry. Four days later, October 23, Nippon Kokan also announced a 10% production cut beginning in November. Sumitomo clarified its attitude by announcing that "the steel industry's joint action in production cutback at the current stage is contrary to the Antimonopoly Law; however, we shall start cutting crude steel production if the market situation grows worse and oversupply develops." But only five days after this statement, Sumitomo announced its decision to make a 10% production cut.

Why did Sumitomo decide on its production cut so soon? During the five days, had Sumitomo found any evidence of a seriously aggravated market? Sumitomo explained that, though there was no indication of excess inventory in its own distribution channels, it had decided to cut down its production in order to cooperate in revitalizing the steel market, since the steel industry as a whole seemed to be in a state of oversupply.

It is obvious that during the five days, Sumitomo had obtained no new information about sudden aggravation of the market. Furthermore, one does not expect a sudden change in a global judgment on the market situation in general. Sumitomo's decision could have been reasonable if it had been made on the basis of its own information and judgment of the aggravated market situation at that time. However, since there seemed to have been no such information, Sumitomo cannot defend itself even if it were accused of issuing the earlier statement as a coverup for its predetermined position of collusion.

The next day, October 28, Kawasaki followed suit by announcing a 10% production cut, thus completing the circle by joining the other three of the four major steelmakers in the production cutback.

Needless to say, tacit collusion or cartel can be easily established when cost and demand conditions do not differ much and when there is no decisive conflict of interests among firms. The case noted above happened to be one such instance. Under different circumstances, Sumitomo and Kawasaki might act otherwise.

As we shall note later, however, with the establishment of in-

vestment planning, major steelmakers have been finding less
and less disagreement of interests. In such circumstances,
tacit collusion can be long-lasting. As a matter of fact, major
steelmakers are now (1972) cooperating closely to raise steel
prices. Apart from this, the case of October 1970 is a good example indicating that the presence of militant enterprises has
nothing to do with the competitiveness of the market.

5. Market Behavior (3) — Merger

The True Purpose of the Yawata-Fuji Merger

It should be clear that what is important about the industrial
organization of steel is to keep its market structure as competitive as possible after economies of scale are achieved. Without
this competitiveness, the presence of militant firms is not
enough to keep the market away from collusion.

As was noted earlier, integrated steelmakers inevitably tend
to become highly concentrated oligopolies because of economies
of scale. The absence of product differentiation may lead to
intense competition in some instances and to cartel and other tacit
collusion in others because of the ease of agreements on qualities and prices of products. At the same time, a steelmaker
cannot expect to realize a substantial expansion of its market
share by developing new products or employing special marketing strategies. Therefore, in the steel industry merger becomes the outstanding strategic tool as well as the key to maintaining competitiveness in terms of industrial organization and
antitrust policy. This is why mergers in the steel industry provoke clamorous debates everywhere — in the United States,
Europe, and Japan alike. Economists are also very persistent
in examining steel mergers for the same reason.

I have no intention of assessing here the Yawata-Fuji merger
that took place some three years ago, as I may have some other
opportunity to do so. Besides, I cannot devote more space to
this merger than it deserves in an article dealing with the in-

dustrial organization of steel as a whole. However, the discussion above must have made clear what the true motive for the Yawata-Fuji merger was.

Recall the sequence of voluntary investment adjustment to kohan system to price leadership. The steel industry wants to organize a cartel no matter what its form may be. At first, steelmakers collaborated with the MITI to evade the Antimonopoly Law itself. Having discovered the difficulty of such collaboration, and fearful of possible bureaucratic control, they turned to voluntary investment adjustment and the kohan system as two mainstays of a virtual cartel to adjust investment and control both production and prices.

However, since this cartel was always subject to disintegration due to conflicting interests among its members, the collusion could not work to the fullest extent. On the contrary, it could even be rather harmful. The last recourse was covert agreements under price leadership. But as is obvious from the Sumitomo case, tacit agreement could not give full play in the absence of strong leadership. Immediately after the Sumitomo case, Shigeo Nagano, then President of the Fuji Iron and Steel Corporation, suggested a large-scale merger in the steel industry, stating that collusion cannot be effective unless major firms are consolidated into two or three enterprises. Such a sense of crisis was responsible for the Yawata-Fuji merger. The internal circumstances of Yawata and Fuji as regards their investment plans and financial positions at that time were merely a supporting condition for their merger.

The professed objective of this merger was to strengthen "international competitiveness" and "technological development capacity." It is now evident that these were nothing but convenient subterfuges to justify the merger. Within only two years after the merger, the Nippon Steel Corporation developed its "international competitiveness" beyond a necessary level to the point where Japanese-U.S. relations may be brought to another crisis similar to that which developed over textiles at one time. How much effort has been devoted to "technological

development"? Newspapers report that the Nippon Steel Corporation abandoned its R&D work on the use of soft bituminous
coal in coke ovens, while Sumitomo Metal Industries has recently succeeded in developing that technology. The principle
of cost plus fair return provides no inducement to search for
more efficient use of coal, even if the merger may have improved R&D capability. The slogans for the merger were nothing but illusions and myths.

Monopoly in the Legal Sense and the Economic Sense

Why, then, did the Fair Trade Commission authorize the
Yawata-Fuji merger? Setting aside fine details, I shall limit
my discussion to one point that concerns the main theme of this
article.

The answer to the above question is, in short, that the Fair
Trade Commission lacked a correct understanding of what the
market structure is in the economic sense. In its statement on
"Application of the Law and Rationale" to this merger, the Fair
Trade Commission explained that the passage, "in cases where
it results in a substantial restraint of competition in a specific
field of trade," in Article 15 of the Antimonopoly Law refers to
"a case where the said merger results in converting the market structure into a less competitive one and leading a specific
enterprise toward attaining a dominant position in the market."
Then, the statement defined the "dominant position in the
market" as follows: "a case in which an enterprise monopolizes
the market or attains power to influence to some degree, at its
will and at its liberty, price, quality, quantity, and other market
conditions, thus limiting its competitors' independent business
activities."

In the theory of industrial organization, a situation such as
"attaining power to influence to some degree, at its will and at
its liberty, price, quality, quantity, and other market conditions"
is exactly tantamount to the control of market. In this sense,
therefore, the clause "thus limiting its competitors' independent

business activities" is totally superfluous. However, the Fair Trade Commission interpreted the "substantial restraint of competition" in terms of "limiting its competitors' independent business activities," and consequently regarded as a major issue in judging the state of competition in a specific field of trade the question of whether or not competitors and new participants "can be assessed as an effective checking force." In this approach, although the commission recognized that, insofar as the existing market structure was left intact, the merger would substantially restrict competition in the trading fields of rails, tin plates, pig iron for casting, and sheet piles, it maintained that the merger would not restrict competition if, to take the case of rails as an example, Nippon Kokan should participate in producing rails and become a "competitor with effective checking force." Thus, the way was open for the merger.

As long as the presence of "competitors with effective checking force" is made a criterion of primary importance, a merger between the second- and the third-ranking corporations or between the third and fifth against the first can be considered not to restrict competition but rather to intensify it. Such a view is based on a misunderstanding of the market structure and competition.

The economic concept of "competition" concerns the state of the market and has nothing to do with the rivalry between two enterprises. With fewer independent enterprises, the possibility increases for their eventual collusion even if competition may be practiced for a while. (5)

It is not very meaningful to define the presence of militantly competitive enterprises as competition. The conventional view that the presence of Sumitomo and Kawasaki maintains competition in the industry was shown to be wrong. Neither can we accept the view that competition is not restricted in the four trading fields which the Fair Trade Commission questioned until the last moment in the Yawata-Fuji merger. Figure 7 shows the excellent stability of prices of the four items, in contrast with other strongly fluctuating steel prices.

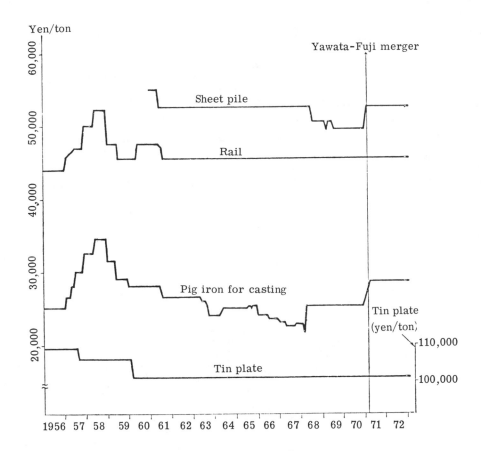

Fig. 7. Price trends of four controversial items (based on
the Bank of Japan wholesale prices indexes).

Notes

1) Charles K. Rowley, Steel and Public Policy (New York:
McGraw-Hill, 1971).

2) For analytical reviews of this question, see D. P. O'Brien
and D. Swann, Information Agreements, Competition and Efficiency (London: Macmillan, 1968), and K. Imai, "Kigyo Kodo
to Joho Kokan — Tekkogyo no Setsubi Toshi to Kakaku Keisei o
Megutte" [Business Behavior and Information Exchange — on
Fixed Investment and Price Formation in the Steel Industry],

Business Review, Vol. 20, No. 2 (1972).

3) For a theoretical analysis of this question, see F. M. Sherer, Industrial Market Structure and Economic Performance, (Chicago: Rand McNally, 1971), pp. 318-323.

4) G. B. Richardson, "Price Notification Schemes," Oxford Economic Papers, Vol. 19 (1967), pp. 359-369.

5) On this point, see K. Imai, H. Uzawa, R. Komiya, T. Negishi, and Y. Murakami, Kakaku Rion, III [Price Theory, III], (Tokyo: Iwanami Shoten), pp. 279-281.

III.

BIG BUSINESS
AND
BUSINESS GROUPS

7

THE ESTABLISHMENT OF
THE BIG BUSINESS SYSTEM

Tadao Kiyonari and Hideichiro Nakamura*

1. The Nagasu-Komiya Controversy: Its Implications

The Nagasu Thesis on the Age of Big Business

The development of big business in the process of rapid economic growth of Japan in the late fifties and the early sixties
was truly spectacular. In manufacturing industries, in particular, big business accomplished very rapid capital accumulation
by adopting technological innovations based on imported technology and succeeded in strengthening its international competitive power. Coinciding with this continued expansion of the
business scale, there developed in Japan a theory of big business in the form of State Monopoly Capitalism under the strong
influence of Marxian economics. Read widely as a clear and
enlightening piece of popular writing, among others, is the Nihon
Keizai Nyumon [Introduction to the Japanese Economy] (1) au-

*Tadao Kiyonari and Hideichiro Nakamura, "Daikigyo Taisei
no Kakuritsu," Chapter 16 of T. Iida et al., Gendai Nihon Keizai
Shi — Sengo Sanjunen no Ayumi [Contemporary Economic History of Japan: Progress in the Three Postwar Decades]
(Tokyo: Chikuma Shobo, 1976), Vol. II, pp. 5-37. Translated
by Jun Uramatsu Smith.

This translation originally appeared in Japanese Economic
Studies, VI (Fall 1977), 3-40.

thored by Kazuji Nagasu* and published in 1960. A distinctive
feature of this book is its simple and clear-cut exposition,
which is worth being introduced right here.

Nagasu's thesis may be summarized in a sentence thus:
"Both growth and modernization are realities, and a dual split
of economic life into light and shade is another reality; these
two aspects must be looked at not as disjointed entities but as
parts of a whole." Nagasu, unlike his contemporary Marxists
who, deeply immersed in dogma, were reluctant to acknowledge
Japan's economic development, was frank enough to recognize
realities as realities.

To quote: "The Japanese economy has a tenacious vitality ... as evidenced by its internationally extraordinary growth
rate after the war.... Especially remarkable is manufacturing,
the hub of modern industry. By 1959 its production quadrupled
over the prewar level. Beware that this expansion is not mere
increases in volume and in economic scale but accompanied by
a great deal of change in quality and substance."

He goes on: "Japan ranks the seventh or eighth in total national income among forty or so capitalist nations. In industrial
production, it is abreast with France and Italy, just behind the
United States, the United Kingdom, and West Germany. One
can count among Japanese firms a few of the world's Big
Business, for example, Yawata Steel, Fuji Steel, Hitachi,
and Toshiba, each of which has annual sales easily surpass-
ing 100 billion yen. In short, Japan is a top-ranking economic power. At least it can be ranked in the middle of
the top."

Nagasu notes that, in 1959, Fortune magazine ranked five
Japanese firms among the top hundred in the capitalist world
outside of the United States. (See Table 1.) So many lesser
firms followed the five: Nippon Oil, Tokyo Electric Power,
Toyo Rayon, Shin Mitsubishi Heavy Industries, Sumitomo Metal

---

*Kazuji Nagasu is a well-known economic writer, formerly
professor of economics at Yokohama National University, and
currently governor of Kanagawa Prefecture. — K. S.

Industries, and Matsushita Electric Industrial, just to cite a few. "Two to three hundred companies — 1,500 at most — are the Big Business that holds the reins of the Japanese economy. Without them, it doesn't function."

Table 1

Japanese Firms Included in the Top 100 Companies in 1959

Rank	Firm	Sales ($ mn)
24	Hitachi	580
28	Yawata Steel	554
38	Toshiba	480
53	Fuji Steel	398
79	Nippon Kokan	297

Source: Fortune Magazine.
Note: Capitalist countries other than the United States.

The Control by Big Business: Requirements

It cannot be asserted that the control by Big Business has been established merely because Big Business has developed. Nagasu therefore makes the following points:

(1) Japanese industry is broadly divided into two main groups: a key industrial sector controlled by a few large oligopolies with advanced technology and a secondary processing sector crowded by a mass of small and tiny enterprises with underdeveloped technology. The latter very often provides processed materials to or subcontracts to the former. This way, the two complement each other. That is, they are the top and the bottom of the dual structure. Economic power is much more concentrated in Big Business than the production concentration ratios indicate.

(2) Large corporations have joined hands to form groups. They have formed something like ten giant interest groups,

which divide and conquer the Japanese economy while competing against each other.

(3) These groups have the power not only to control the economy but also to exert great influence upon Japan's politics and foreign policy, either alone or together through business associations like the Federation of Economic Organizations, the Japan Federation of Employers' Association, the Japan Committee for Economic Development, or the Japan Chamber of Commerce and Industry.

(4) These big businesses and their groups are indeed the most powerful and fundamental elements that give rise to diverse political and economic phenomena in contemporary Japanese society. Not a single soul can live outside of their influence.

(5) The leading or ruling class that influences Japan's economy and society has about one million members or about 3% of the working population of 40 million. It is this 3%, the power elite, that controls the remaining 97% of workers.

Thus, Nagasu concludes that there was the Big Business Establishment in Japan already by 1960. Needless to say, the Establishment is not ipso facto evil. What matters is its performance. On this, Nagasu argues as follows:

(1) Business groups are always groupings of private capital and combinations for the sake of private profits. They compete and fight violently, one against the other, each for the expansion of its own capital and power. There is no room for sweet, sentimental do-goodism for the sake of society or the nation.

(2) Big business has concentrated control over the Japanese economy in its own hands and is exploiting a huge number of small businesses.

(3) Big business is exploiting workers, particularly those in small businesses.

(4) Big business is manipulating consumers and dehumanizing them.

(5) Big business is exercising political power against the interests of the people.

Thus, Nagasu judges the performance of big business as extremely poor. But he does not see the Big Business Establishment as a permanent system. He notes: "No well ordered pyramid control of the prewar type has been established in the modern zaibatsu. It is unstable and fluid. It is precisely for those reasons that competition cannot help becoming all the more fierce." He goes on: "This struggle is only among the giants, however. For some time after the war, the nouveaux riches could come out of small businesses. But now there is scarcely any room for newcomers. The elimination contest is already over. Runners in the finals are a very few giants." In short, he believes that the Big Business Establishment is virtually complete and is to be increasingly strengthened. In this view, one can note the logical prototype of the "one-set" principle, developed subsequently by Yoshikazu Miyazaki, on the control mechanism of business groupings.

The Komiya Thesis on "Monopoly Capital" as an Illusion

Ryutaro Komiya attempted to bring the thesis of Monopoly Capitalism propounded by Nagasu and others to a critical examination in a paper entitled "Dokusen Shihon to Shotoku Saibumpai Seisaku" [Monopoly Capital and Income Redistribution Policy] (2). He argues as follows:

(1) It is hard to support the contention that in contemporary Japan all big businesses are monopolists or oligopolists as a general rule and realize profit rates higher than small businesses do. A piece of counterevidence is net profit rates of small businesses above those of large businesses (rates of profits over net worth).

(2) The share of property income in distributed national income is substantially lower in the postwar period than in the prewar period. It is also much lower than in the United States, the United Kingdom, and elsewhere.

(3) The power elite that controls Japan consists typically of managers, whose interests are not too closely tied to property

income. A situation like this almost certainly exists in socialist society as well.

(4) There are all sorts of conflicts of interest within the
group itself generally called the working class. It is difficult
to conclude that the capitalist-worker confrontation is the basic
one in contemporary Japan.

(5) The most inequitable aspect of Japan's income distribution
today is managers' and workers' pay in big business which is markedly higher than all others'. The basic measure to cope with it
is to dissolve the dual structure of industry and to spread education.

(6) The most effective short-term income redistribution
policy is to expand social security and to raise direct taxation
on incomes, inheritances, and the like. Little is expected of
the income redistributive effect from the antimonopoly policy.

Komiya notes the ambiguity in the concept of Monopoly Capital and makes a point that Marxian economists fail to analyze
the market performance of big business. He also observes that
the low share of property income implies that "the simple no-
tion that the people's economic life would be very much bettered
by the redistribution of enormous monopoly profits Monopoly
Capital extracts from the people is nothing short of a sheer
fantasy."

He then goes on to make a number of specific assertations
such as follows: The ruling class of Japan today is typically
made of managers and not capitalists; the majority of Japanese
managers originate from the middle class with little inherited
properties; there are no quantum jumps in the control hierarchy
within Big Business as well as between large and small enterprises; it is almost meaningless to claim that a mere handful
of twenty to thirty thousand persons control the Japanese economy and exploit the rest of the people; it is doubtful that Monopoly Capital controls Japan and that the capital-labor confrontation is the most fundamental antagonism in Japan today economically and socially; the antimonopoly policy in Japan is
aimed chiefly at raising the overall economic efficiency through
improving industrial organization; the income redistribution

policy has, after all, no other recourse than direct taxation including personal income taxes and estate taxes as well as social security.

As this outline suggests, Komiya believes that Big Business has not necessarily performed poorly. At the same time, however, he views Big Business as a privileged class and calls for eliminating the wage differentials between big and small businesses.

2. Characteristics of Postwar Big Business

The Zaibatsu Revived?

The Nagasu-Komiya controversy over Japan's Big Business Establishment calls our attention to the need to start afresh empirically, completely free of the conventional wisdom on Monopoly Capital or Interest Groups, if we wish to understand modern features of Big Business. Hideichiro Nakamura came to grips with this problem in a paper entitled "Nihon Big Business no Katoteki Seikaku" [The Transitional Character of Japanese Big Business]. (3)

Nakamura brings group financing to a critical review because it is invariably cited as evidence of banks' control of businesses. In Japan's postwar recovery process, Big Business depended more and more on bank loans, while banks responded by seeking credit from the Bank of Japan. Banks and Big Business came to be more deeply tied together in the 1951 slump in reaction to the Korean War boom and in the 1954 recession. Thus, quite a few insisted that financial capital had established its control by way of group financing. But the truth was that no single bank was able to meet financial needs of Big Business in its giant investment projects incorporating technological innovations. Risk was too large, too. Thus, banks had to collaborate with the Japan Development Bank, the Long-Term Credit Bank, and other city banks to form consortia.

Moreover, to make themselves stronger, banks were forced to lend actively to growing enterprises outside their own groups.

A concrete piece of its evidence is the fact that businesses depend for only 20% of their borrowings on their respective main group banks (see Table 2).

Table 2

Percentage of Loans of Zaibatsu-Affiliated Firms
from Leading Banks

	1953	1954	1955	1956	1957	1958	1959	1960
Mitsubishi affiliates (41)a	21.9	20.7	19.5	20.2	23.8	23.2	21.6	20.9
Mitsui affiliates (37)	21.9	21.9	20.6	20.1	24.2	19.2	17.1	16.2
Sumitomo affiliates (25)	24.4	26.9	21.3	15.9	22.7	21.0	18.2	18.2
Fuji affiliates (31)	20.4	22.9	25.7	22.7	27.7	26.4	23.1	22.3
Daiichi affiliates (36)	24.7	24.7	20.4	18.9	22.9	19.9	17.5	15.4
Sanwa affiliates (21)	25.5	28.0	24.8	23.4	25.6	27.9	26.1	23.0

a) Number of firms.
Note: Prepared from the Economic Planning Agency, Jiyuka to Kigyo Keiretsu [Liberalization and Business Groups], pp. 10-11; and the Economic Development Association, Nempo — Keiretsu no Kenkyu (1961) [Annual Report on Keiretsu, 1961 ed.], p. 24.

It is true that, on the one hand, group financing has been formed. But, on the other hand, the arrangement is not so exclusive. While group financing has functioned as a mechanism for concentrating finances to Big Business, it has never been able to restrict individual members of Big Business as to how to behave. Then, how should we evaluate the zaibatsu revival, which is supposed to have occurred as evidenced by the rebuild-

ing of the trading companies of Mitsui and Mitsubishi, the interlocking ownership of corporate stocks of zaibatsu affiliates, the
revived meetings of company presidents, the joint ventures in
petrochemicals and atomic power, and so on?

True, the Big Three, Mitsui, Mitsubishi, and Sumitomo, are
reborn as enterprise groups in pursuit of common interests.
But they differ from their former self, i.e., centralized industrial combines with the head companies at the core and member
firms as de facto operation divisions. Now, they are federations of major corporations, financial institutions, and general
trading companies, whose members are on their own, that is,
"not companies for the sake of the group but the group for the
sake of companies" (President Hosai Hyuga [presently, Chairman of the Board] of the Sumitomo Metal Industries). (4) The
presidents' club is formed by major member companies of each
group in order to adjust their common interests to a certain
extent, but it is not the decision-making body of the group. The
zaibatsu revival is not a simple revival of the prewar type of
centralized power.

Postwar Industrial Groups

Besides the former zaibatsu groups, industrial groups of a
new type have developed in heavy and chemical industries. They
center around large non-zaibatsu firms like Yawata, Fuji, and
Hitachi, firms that have gotten out of the zaibatsu since the war
like Toshiba and Toyota, or firms like Matsushita that have
rapidly grown since the war. All of them have been engaged in
growth industries, thereby contributing to changes in industrial
structure, and have become giant companies through rapid capital expansion. These new groups are not tied to any special
banking interests and have the power to select which banks they
go to and how much to borrow in raising funds. They rely very
much on the Long-Term Credit Bank and foreign-affiliated financial institutions. They can also finance by themselves. Not
only do they maintain autonomy vis-à-vis financial institutions
and zaibatsu interest groups, but also form their own groups

through diversification into a number of related fields in which they keep managerial control over a great many "affiliates."

The formation of these two types of groups has led to the forging of financial affiliations between large corporations other than them and large city banks as well, giving birth to the third type of groups led by banks like Fuji, Daiichi, Sanwa, and others. This type, however, has a weaker link among member firms and is inferior in scale and concentration of power to the former two.

Thus, despite the development of Big Business, the zaibatsu revival in the exact sense of the phrase has not occurred, and business groups differ a great deal in character among themselves. A direct cause for this is the prohibition of holding companies like the prewar zaibatsu head companies under the Anti-Trust Act, as well as the prevention of strong financing affiliations from being formed for the reasons noted above. But a more important role is played by technological innovations which promoted the development of heavy and chemical industries and the sophistication of the industrial structure, thereby making industrial organizations more competitive.

Technological innovations based on imported technology destroyed technological monopolies and facilitated new entrants and late starters to challenge the old, well-established firms. In addition, many industries had been at the stage where economies of scale could yield large returns, that is, the stage at which sharp cost reduction could be expected from scale expansion through aggressive investment. This prompted firms to compete in investment.

Early starters were able to realize high profit rates for the time being, with typical cases in synthetic textiles and plastics, but their profits were forced to drop quickly by the invasion of newcomers. Market concentration ratios tended to decline until the late sixties. This made prices less rigid and even giant firms lacked the power to administer prices. In other words, the Japanese system of big business was characterized as a competitive oligopoly system.

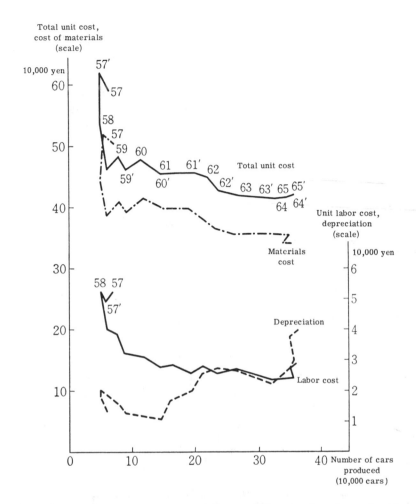

Figure 1. Unit cost of automobile and the scale of production:
auto maker (company A). (Kogin Chosa Geppo [Monthly Survey
of the Industrial Bank of Japan], January 1967, p. 68.)
Note: The figure shows that this leading auto manufacturer established the mass production system by 1960 and attained the
minimum optimum scale by 1965, and achieved a cost reduction
capable of withstanding international competition. Although
they are not shown, Toyota and Nissan achieved the annual level
of 700,000 cars by 1967, bringing them to the same level as
Volkswagen (West Germany).

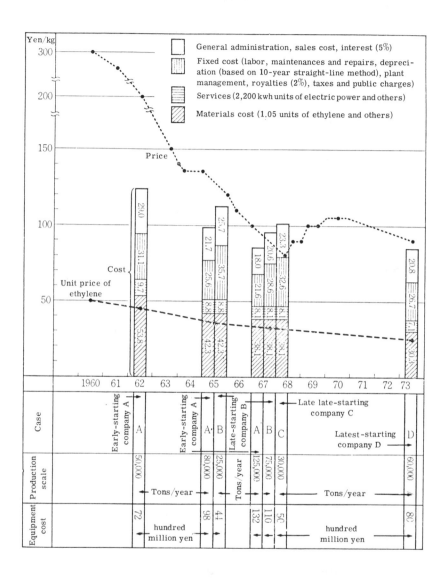

Figure 2. Changes in the estimated cost and prices of high-pressure method polyethylene of early- and late-starting makers. (Prepared by M. Nishio from H. Nakamura, T. Masamura, and T. Yamashita, Gendai no Kagaku Kogyo [The Modern Chemical Industry] [Tokyo: Toyo Keizai Shimpo Sha, 1966], p. 170.) Note: This figure shows that early-starting makers realized a high profit rate, which induced other makers to participate; it also shows that early-starters, despite a decrease in the profit rate, still realized a relatively lucrative profit rate through a rapid increase in scale.

Coexistence of Monopoly and Competition

The emergence of this kind of industrial organization may be attributed to the dissolution of the zaibatsu. But, on the other hand, this industrial structure itself plays a part in preventing the revival of zaibatsu-type industrial groups. New groups were formed by giant firms in heavy and chemical industries, outside of the former zaibatsu groups. Inter-group competition increased. Autonomy of member firms was emphasized in the former zaibatsu groups. Financial institutions' control of business was restricted. And even intra-group competition arose and new industrial affiliations were formed outside the framework of existing groups.

The advantages of the zaibatsu-type consolidation are found in promoting the power to raise capital, in adopting preferential purchases and sales and enforcing discriminatory prices among member firms whenever possible, and in expanding into new industries. But even these did not become factors in limiting competition severely during the 1960s when competition was intense. Those groups based in heavy and chemical industries often expanded into small-scale industries technologically related to themselves, but this, too, did not eliminate competition in them.

As of 1962, Nakamura stressed along these lines the transitional character of postwar business groups and called attention to "the coexistence of monopoly and competition in large-scale industries and its contradictions." Subsequently, however, he arrived at a view that this transitional character itself is the modern characteristic of postwar business groups, as we shall see later.

3. Thesis of the "One-Set" Principle

Financial Affiliations and the One-Set Principle

In the fall of 1962, a paper by Yoshikazu Miyazaki, which was highly rated at the time as a new thesis of Big Business,

"Kato Kyoso no Ronri to Genjitsu — Keiretsu Shihai Kiko no
Kaimei" [The Logic and Realism of Excessive Competition —
The Mechanism of Business Groupings] (5), was published.
The paper carefully pursues the formation of industrial groups
and, then, asks why competition became excessively intensified
among big businesses despite the formation of such powerful
industrial groups. He offers an explanation that this was a phenomenon that came into being as a result of industrial groups,
restricted by financial affiliations, each trying to acquire a
complete set of rising enterprises in every industry. This thesis is popularly known as the one-set principle. Miyazaki develops his thesis in order to provide a mutually consistent theory on seemingly contradictory phenomena of capital concentration on the one hand and the decline in production concentration ratios in individual industries on the other. While the thesis is ingenious, to be sure, it has as an explanation of reality
left many questions unanswered. (6)
    The first question is concerned with the concept of keiretsu
or business groupings mentioned here. Miyazaki regards a
business group as a monolithic body of financial institutions and
enterprises. But Japan's postwar industrial groups cannot be
accounted for by financial ties alone. For there are many kinds
of industrial groups as we saw earlier. As we recognize their
existence (so does Miyazaki later), the one-set principle itself
no longer holds. (7)
    Second, Miyazaki contends that the indirect financing meth-
od (7a) in the special form of bank-based groupings was established at this time, but as Shigeki Koyama points out, the decade
centering at 1960 was a period when indirect financing itself
was "shaken for the first time"; "the greater the growth and
earning capacity of a company was, the more of its funds was
raised via capital increase"; "the main bank's share in its borrowings declined noticeably"; and "it was stagnating firms that
had strong ties with banks and it was they that depended increasingly more on group banks." "This relative decline in
borrowings from group banks by growing firms ... resulted
from the competition among city banks to increase their market

shares, especially directed to growing firms." It may be that "banks' credit supply behavior in favor of growing firms' and enterprises' investment behavior taking advantage thereof were combined together to bring about this intense inter-firm competition." (8) In other words, excessive competition may be explained not because financial ties were established but because these ties became fluid.

Third, it is an erroneous simplification to presume that industrial groups behaved in accordance with the one-set principle in allocating investment to new developing industries. For this, witness the intra-group competition that often developed among chemical companies within the same group when the group decided to form a petrochemical complex, as well as the collaboration of firms of different groups that resulted from this competition. This phenomenon of intra-group competition indicates the lack of power in the management of the group bank to intervene with member firms' strategy and to pursuade them to change their plans in order to avoid overlapping investment and the lack of authority and responsibility in the presidents' club of the group to force member firms to revise their business strategies of vital importance.

The Appearance of Independent Big Businesses

Fourth, Miyazaki tends to neglect the remarkable development of big businesses with independence, especially prominent after the war. He assigns these firms either to various bank-centered groups or to keiretsu. But a number of studies by other researchers all contradict this.

For instance, the Honda Motor is considered as a member of the Mitsubishi group by Miyazaki. But Akira Sakaguchi states that Honda maintains a financial link with the Mitsubishi Bank only because this tie was formed at "the time when Honda was still groping in the dark despite its potential of growth" and that, today, it is still maintained because of Honda's business policy to respect its "debt of gratitude," "although Honda is perfectly capable of borrowing from as many banks as it likes, just as everybody else normally does." "There is neither technical interchange nor tie-up" in this relationship between Honda and Mitsubishi, and "Honda itself has no intention whatsoever to depend on the Mitsubishi group." (9)

Similarly, Sakaguchi points out that the Isetan department store, which is considered to be another member of the Mitsubishi group, maintains a tie with Mitsubishi Bank because the company believes as a managerial principle in limiting its borrowing to a single influencial bank and that it chose the bank as a "business strategy on an equal footing with the bank." (10)

As for SONY, alleged by Miyazaki to be a member of the Mitsui group, Akira Kubota states that its relationship with Mitsui Bank is due to personal ties with the former bank president Junshiro Mandai and that "SONY has never dreamed of itself as a Mitsui-affiliate even though it considers Mitsui to be its correspondent bank." (11)

Further, with regard to the Sumitomo group, Ken'ichi Suzuki points out that, through its improving financial power and the aggressive strategy of banking operations, the group placed a number of influential autonomous firms, such as Matsushita Electric Industrial, Idemitsu Kosan, Toyo Kogyo, Bridgestone Tire, Asahi Chemical Industry, Takeda Chemical Industries, Kubota Ltd., Sanyo Electric, and Komatsu Ltd., under its sphere of influence. And he goes on to show that the latter have a larger turnover than Sumitomo's direct affiliates. Furthermore, for their relationship with the Sumitomo group, Suzuki has this to say, for example: "Matsushita Electric, during the late forties and early fifties, owed its survival to the backing of Sumitomo Bank and took on many officers from the bank, but it was not under the control of the bank. Rather, it blended them into the business philosophy of Konosuke Matsushita. It went on to acquire the power of a very important industrial trust. Now Matsushita is the biggest customer of Sumitomo Bank, a complete reversal in the position." (12)

While independent large companies and industrial groups are related in many different ways, the basic feature is in the interdependence between group banks, on the one hand, which strive for managerial growth and stability, diversified risks, and improved earnings, and businesses, on the other hand, which seek to secure stable sources of funds with strong financial backing in order to maintain their competitiveness. In this, banks' say with enterprises goes only up to the point of protecting their lendings.

Transformation of the Big Business System

To pigeonhole postwar business groups, as the one-set principle does, according to financial links by assuming the existence of business groups of financial capital that were formed through the collusion of industrial and banking powers, is, in effect, to treat all different types of groups alike. This procedure gives little attention to new groups that arose in heavy and chemical industries. It regards the competition among Big Businesses as exclusively inter-group competition. It loses sight of the fact that the rapid economic growth, while broadening the scope of groups, gave rise to intra-group competition, making groups more fluid and that independent big businesses came to be developed.

Our examination of the big business system of postwar Japan seems to convince us that the soft character of its groups and the competitive nature of big business are peculiar contemporary traits rather than mere transitional phenomena. Indeed, it is for this very reason that these industrial groups are able to take the hegemony of the Japanese economy. Thus, it seems to us that the analytical model that claims that the rapid growth of capitalism goes over the sequence from monopolistic enterprises to Konzern formation, to the dominance by financial capital, and finally to State Monopoly Capitalism, is no longer valid in today's level of productive power and new market conditions. It must be reexamined.

For instance, (1) the enormous expansion of the scale of a production unit in materials-producing industries has made it impossible for any single group to restrict its market to only its member firms, unlike the prewar Konzern (12a) in heavy

and chemical industries. (2) The development and popularization that new types of materials achieved as mass-produced
substitutes because of successive innovations in materials prevent large materials-supplying firms from controlling fabricat-
ing firms at subsequent stages of production. (3) Moreover,
big producers of consumer durables are more oriented to mass
production and mass sales and tend to lean more heavily on the
social division of labor rather than move into the production of
materials and parts themselves. (4) Big producers of consumer
goods attempt to control the marketing channels all the way to
the final consumers, in order to achieve product differentiation.
But it is difficult to consolidate and control retail trades except
for a few of durable consumer goods. One factor responsible for
the difficulty is the formation of supermarket chains as a countervailing power. (5) With the rapid industrialization, chains of manufacturing processes are extended through more roundabout production and cut across industries. Specialized firms are formed
at their points of contact, but they can grow only if they do not
belong to any of the groups.

Soft Groups

Under these circumstances, contemporary big business groups
have less power to organize themselves into self-sufficient
markets for themselves alone. Rather, it seems that they can
strengthen their existence by turning themselves into soft
groups with elements of fluidity around them.

Nonetheless, a great many still decry the buildup of financial
capital or the revival of the zaibatsu. This is because bank-
affiliated groupings are more solid in Japan than in other advanced countries. This came about from the Finance Ministry's
banking policy which maintained a low-interest policy to promote industry and supported indirect financing as the main-
stay of the capital market. With this system, for businesses
to ensure priority loans from banks and for banks to keep stable
borrowers (depositors) and to increase the proportion of deposits that stay with them by organizing interdependent firms into

Table 3

Relative Shares of Six Large Industrial Groups in Equity and Total Assets of All Industry (end of March 1974)

Classification		Mitsu-bishi	Mitsui	Sumi-tomo	Fuyo	Sub-total	Daiichi-Kangyo Bank	Sanwa	Total
Firms whose presidents are members of the presidents' club	Number of firms	27	22	16	29	94	57	36	175
	Share of equity (%)	4.4	3.0	2.5	4.8	14.7	3.4	5.0	21.9
	Share of total assets (%)	4.4	3.3	3.4	4.1	15.2	4.0	4.1	22.9
Plus companies with stockholding over 50% to 100%	Number of firms	399	486	260	606	1,751	674	842	3,095
	Share of equity (%)	5.2	3.7	2.9	5.8	17.6	4.1	6.0	26.1
	Share of total assets (%)	4.8	3.7	3.6	4.7	16.8	4.4	4.8	25.3
Plus companies with stockholding over 25% to 50%	Number of firms	1,070	975	578	1,206	3,829	1,180	1,548	6,302
	Share of equity (%)	7.0	4.7	4.3	6.8	22.8	5.2	7.2	33.5
	Share of total assets (%)	5.4	4.1	4.0	5.2	18.7	4.9	5.2	28.2
Plus companies with stockholding over 10% to 25%	Number of firms	1,460	1,367	781	1,581	5,189	1,623	2,003	8,476
	Share of equity (%)	8.3	6.6	5.0	8.1	28.0	6.5	9.0	41.0
	Share of total assets (%)	5.9	4.7	4.3	5.6	20.5	5.4	5.8	30.9

Source: Fair Trade Commission, Sogo Shosha ni Kansuru Dai Nikai Chosa Hokoku [Second Survey of General Trading Companies], January 1975.

Notes: (1) All member firms of the presidents' club are included. Adjustment is made in the total column for 2 firms that belong to 2 groups at the same time. (2) Affiliate companies exclude those of financial institutions and firms with equity less than ¥1 billion, which are members of the presidents' club. Also excluded are affiliates of affiliates. No adjustments are made for duplication of affiliate companies. (3) Equities and total assets for all industry are based on figures given in the Corporate Enterprise Statistics for nonfinancial corporations and in the Bank of Japan Monthly Bulletin for financial corporations, but exclude those for public utilities (electric power and gas). (4) The Big Four zaibatsu (Mitsui, Mitsubishi, Sumitomo, and Yasuda) had a direct and indirect control over 544 companies or 24.5% of all business capital at the end of the war. These can be broadly compared with the subtotal for the 4 groups (Mitsubishi, Mitsui, Sumitomo, and Fuyo) in the table. But, as stated in the text, there is a fundamental break between the prewar zaibatsu groups and the postwar business groups.

a group, businesses found it profitable to borrow from banks for most of their funds, and both of them found it to their mutual advantage to deepen their exclusive tieup. (The liberalization of interest rates and the diversification of the capital market, namely, fund raising through issuing shares and bonds, cannot help weakening bank-based groupings.)

4. Establishment of Managerial Capitalism

"Third-Rate Business Directors"

The series of postwar reforms like the zaibatsu dissolution, the deconcentration of economic power, and the purge of business executives responsible for the war and the subsequent economic growth brought about the collapse of the owners' control of Big Businesses. For the zaibatsu families, forced as a part of the zaibatsu dissolution to dispose of their stocks, lost their controlling interest in many large corporations; the other wealthy, too, lost their assets owing to the postwar inflation, the property taxation and the land expropriation of the land reform, and fell away from large stock ownership; and few large individual stockholders appeared because individuals could not build up their assets fast enough to catch up with corporations' successive large capital increases under rapid business growth.

And this process was, at the same time, a process by which a new body of executives came to the fore as business administrators. As old business executives had been purged, the management of Big Business was passed on almost completely to men at the junior executive level. Though they were called, derogatively, "third-rate directors*," they were well suited to the new postwar era by reason of their youth and competence

---

*Santo Juyaku (third-rate directors) is the title of a best-selling comic novel in the late fifties by popular novelist Keita Genji, which described the tribulations of rising business executives in the postwar turmoil. — K. S.

as professional managers, and they played a vital role as persons charged with a managerial revolution in promoting industrial growth.

The leadership of this professional managerial class in big business went on to establish itself with the weakened owner control of business and the wide dispersion of stock ownership. According to a survey by Tadashi Mito, 66% of Japan's top 200 companies (excluding financial corporations) as of 1956 lacked either individual controlling stockholders or institutional stockholders and were managerially controlled. (13) In other words, Japan's Big Business system accomplished a separation of ownership and management more thorough than that of Western Europe and quite comparable to the United States.

It may be noted, though, from Table 4, that firms under managerial control decreased to 60% between 1956 and 1966 and those under minority-owner control climbed from 32% to 38%. The latter, however (as Mito observes), include two totally different types, namely, those controlled by institutions (corporation-owned) and those controlled by their founders. Of these two, the first signifies an increase in corporate stockholdings, that is, a rise in the reciprocity of share ownership by large corporations (e.g., company A owns stocks of company B, and company B owns those of A). But this is not an indicator of the phenomenon, collapse of managerial control = unification of corporate ownership and control, as emphasized by Yoshikazu Miyazaki later. (14) On the contrary, it is indicative of further progression in managerial control. The reason is this: the reciprocity of stock ownership by big corporations makes one another stable shareholders so that their managerial control is made more autocratic. (It is more accurate to see a business group as strengthening, rather than restricting, the autocratic power of the management of firms in the group.) As a general rule the appointment of the company president in a large corporation is not made through consultation among corporate shareholders, except in the case of crises of near bankruptcy. It is usual that the present management with representative power, especially the president, select his own successor.

Table 4

Changes in Control Types by Shares of Stock
Ownership in the Top 200 Companies

	1936		1956		1966	
	Number	Share (%)	Number	Share (%)	Number	Share (%)
Complete-owner control	12	6.0	0	0	0	0
Majority-owner control	13	6.5	4	2.0	4	2.0
Minority-owner control	93	46.5	64	32.0	76	38.9
Managerial control	82	41.0	132	66.0	120	60.0
Total	200	100.0	200	100.0	200	100.0

Source: Mito, Masaki, and Haruyama, op. cit., p. 35.

Notes: Complete-owner control is complete or virtually complete stock ownership by an individual or a few associates, majority-owner control is stock ownership of more than 50% by an individual. In both cases, stockholders maintain control. Minority-owner control holds when a large shareholder with 10-50% ownership maintains control via small stockholders' surrender of voting rights. Managerial control holds when there are no large stockholders with more than 10% ownership.

Of the second type of minority control, i.e., those controlled by founders, typical of which are SONY and Honda, the founders' control is maintained by their entrepreneurial spirit and managerial ability that made their firms grow into big businesses and not by their ownership. This should be clear from the fact that they themselves are minority stockholders.

Managerial Tyranny

The establishment of managerial capitalism deprived vulgar

Marxist economists of the basis for their insistence that the evils of capitalism are rooted in private ownership and control. (Of course, owner-controlled capitalism still exists in small enterprises. But when they grow, they have to open their stocks to the public and their owner control must shift to managerial control. If owner control persists, it is because of owners' managerial talent.) Adherents to the Marxist formula thereupon try to deny managerial capitalism itself or to discover the roots of private ownership in it. This forces them to turn their back on reality.

But managerial capitalism that has deprived Marxian theorists of their ground for criticizing capitalism is not so free of shortcomings. Managerial capitalism owes its existence to the following: In an industrial society that is based on and developed from the free private enterprise system, the fund-raising machinery of big business has been put on the market, and its stocks have been dispersed among many persons; private ownership of business has turned into mere financial claims; even if stocks are concentrated into a few individual or corporate investors, the management will exercise its power to eliminate the concentration into any individuals or corporations which may aim at the control. Save for a few exceptions, stockholders' ownership right has been transformed into something formal that will never be put to use.

Managers of big business therefore have the authority to determine how to employ managerial resources that have been accumulated in the business and have the de facto ownership through their exercise of the control power. Consequently, managerial capitalism in general enables the management without ownership to make use of autocratic power through stripping stockholders of their rights and to treat big business as if it were their own private property. (15)

This is the root cause for the criticism of big business that burst forth in the 1970s when, having attained the economic level of advanced nations, strains of the industry-first economic policy surfaced all at once in the form of pollution, environmental destruction, the lagging social security, the galloping inflation, and so on, and the sense of unity among business, the people, and the community began to be greatly disturbed.

The reform of this kind of managerial capitalism, rather than coming through any changes in its ownership in form only (16), needs to reflect well in the conduct of business the will and needs of the public and to accomplish management based on social consensus. To that end, a flexible social system of control and check that leads to such an administrative structure must be established.

5. Economic Concentration and Business Mobility

Concentration of Capital

How did economic concentration in big business from the mid-fifties through the mid-sixties progress? Capital concentration in the top 100 large corporations clearly rose during that period, but shows a decline afterward with 1964 as a peak. This is because a considerable increase in small corporate enterprises since the mid-sixties contributed to lowering concentration (see Table 5). It is true, nevertheless, that concentration in big business rose consistently until then. But this rise in concentration does not immediately imply that Big Business strengthened its control over the economy. In fact, the production concentration ratio of largest firms did not necessarily increase in individual industries. On the contrary, it fell in many industries.

Next, let us look at the size distribution of corporations. Table 6 shows changes in the distribution by equity size according to the Annual Report on Corporate Enterprise Statistics of the Ministry of Finance. Though the time series is not strictly comparable over time, the table suffices to indicate the general trend. We see that small corporate enterprises tended to increase in number, thereby contributing to the increase of corporate enterprises as a whole. However, the rate of increase is greater the larger the business size. From 1956 to 1963 the number of enterprises increased 2.3 times in the size class of

Table 5

Changes in Concentration Ratios of 100 Top Firms

Year	Capital concentration ratio (%)	Total-assets concentration ratio (%)	Operating-profit concentration ratio (%)	Total number of corporations
1953	32.1	—	—	261,423
1958	35.3	—	—	417,738
1963	39.3	—	—	464,519
1964	39.4	27.7	28.7	479,973
1965	37.4	26.8	26.9	515,502
1966	36.7	25.5	27.1	558,016
1967	35.5	25.3	25.8	586,315

Source: Annual Report of The Fair Trade Commission, 1970 edition.

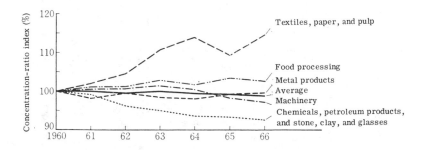

Figure 3. Changes in concentration-ratio index (3-firm concentration ratio, 1960 = 100): 1960-66. (Fair Trade Commission, ed., Nihon no Sangyo Shuchu, Showa 38-41 nen [Japan's Industrial Concentration, 1963-66], 1969. As quoted in K. Imai et al., Kakaku Riron [Price Theory], III [Iwanami Shoten, 1972], p. 118.)

Table 6

Changes in Number of Corporations by Equity Size (all industry)

Year	¥5 mn and less	¥5-10 mn	¥10-50 mn	¥50-100 mn	¥100-1,000 mn	¥1,000 mn and more	Total
1956	348,308 (96.2)	6,068 (1.7)	5,573 (1.5)	856 (0.2)	1,145 (0.3)		361,950 (100.0)
1957	372,573 (95.5)	7,609 (2.0)	7,415 (1.9)	971 (0.2)	1,387 (0.4)		389,955 (100.0)
1958	396,432 (94.9)	10,789 (2.6)	7,958 (1.9)	1,003 (0.2)	1,556 (0.4)		417,738 (100.0)
1959	413,858 (94.4)	12,543 (2.9)	8,924 (2.0)	1,226 (0.3)	1,705 (0.4)		438,256 (100.0)
1960	468,105 (94.1)	15,819 (3.2)	9,901 (2.0)	1,240 (0.2)	1,726 (0.3)	415 (0.1)	497,206 (100.0)
1961	449,101 (93.3)	18,638 (3.9)	9,206 (1.9)	1,705 (0.4)	2,190 (0.5)	537 (0.1)	481,377 (100.0)
1962	416,348 (92.4)	18,054 (4.0)	10,903 (2.4)	2,242 (0.5)	2,599 (0.6)	638 (0.1)	450,784 (100.0)
1963	425,081 (91.5)	20,491 (4.4)	12,946 (2.8)	2,289 (0.5)	2,999 (0.6)	713 (0.2)	464,519 (100.0)

Source: Ministry of Finance, Hojin Kigyo Tokei Nempo [Annual Report of Corporate Enterprise Statistics].

Note: Excludes corporations that are out of operations or of unknown whereabouts. Percentages in parentheses.

10 million to 50 million yen of equity, 2.7 times in the class of 50 million to 100 million yen, and 3.2 times in the class with 100 million yen and more of equity. While large corporations grew in size remarkably, to be sure, their number also increased. The growth was extensive from the bottom to the top, and the increase in the number of big businesses indicates the growth of small into large enterprises as a real fact, even though Table 6 merely shows the size distribution at given points of time.

Shifts of Business over Size: How Did Business Grow?

Tables 7 (a) and (b) show shifts of small businesses between size classes. They reveal conspicuous upward shifts in every size, but particularly noticeable is the medium size of 200 to 499 employees. Though upward shifts are less pronounced between December 1961 and August 1963, the said medium size class is still relatively more mobile upward. In any case, it is clear that business growth is not at all an exceptional phenomenon. Moreover, business growth must have been more pronounced than the tables show if the rise in labor productivity during this period is taken into account, because the firm size is measured in these tables by the number of employees.

Table 8 shows shifts of somewhat larger firms among equity sizes. It should be apparent how striking business growth was between 1955 and 1965. Of the businesses with equity between 100 million to 1 billion yen in 1965, 88% had equities less than 100 million yen in 1955, 64% below 40 million yen, and 27% less than 10 million yen. Medium-sized enterprises thus grew conspicuously within a short span of time into the lower top echelon of the business population.

Likewise, Table 9 shows business growth between 1955 and 1970. Of those businesses whose equities exceeded 1 billion yen as of 1970, 17.2% were not yet established in 1955 and 6.4% had equities under ¥ 10 million. Thus, about one quarter is accounted for by those which did not exist or were small fifteen years ago.

Table 7(a)

Size Shifts of Manufacturing Firms (%)

Size, December 1959 (employees) / Size, August 1961 (employees)	1-9	10-29	30-49	50-99	100-199	200-299	300-499	500-999	1,000 and more
10- 29	12.4	74.5	10.8	2.1	0.2	—	—	—	—
30- 49	0.9	10.7	59.5	27.3	1.3	0.2	0.9	—	—
50- 99	1.0	2.1	12.4	63.9	19.2	1.2	0.2	—	—
100-199	0.3	0.5	1.2	8.1	65.0	21.0	3.7	0.2	—
200-299	—	0.2	0.6	0.9	9.2	58.7	28.6	1.8	—
300-499	0.1	0.4	0.4	0.4	2.9	10.1	54.1	29.6	2.0
500-999	—	—	—	0.6	0.9	1.2	7.8	67.3	22.2
1,000 and more	—	—	—	—	—	—	0.5	5.1	94.4

Table 7(b)

Size Shifts of Manufacturing Firms (%)

Size, December 1961 (employees) / Size, August 1963 (employees)	1-9	10-29	30-49	50-99	100-199	200-299	300-499	500-999	1,000-4,999	5,000-9,999	10,000 and more
10- 29	11.6	73.3	13.2	1.7	0.2	—	—	—	—	—	—
30- 49	0.2	13.8	63.2	22.0	0.8	—	—	—	—	—	—
50- 99	0.3	1.1	8.5	74.7	14.4	1.0	—	—	—	—	—
100- 199	0.1	0.1	0.7	10.2	73.2	13.9	1.8	—	—	—	—
200- 299	—	—	0.2	1.9	13.0	63.5	20.1	1.3	—	—	—
300- 499	—	—	—	0.1	2.2	13.0	62.6	22.0	0.1	—	—
500- 999	—	—	—	—	0.2	0.7	7.8	78.0	13.3	—	—
1,000-4,999	—	—	—	—	—	0.9	0.3	4.3	89.9	4.6	—
5,000-9,999	—	—	—	—	—	—	—	—	5.9	78.4	15.7
10,000 and more	—	—	—	—	—	—	—	—	—	3.7	96.3

Source: Small Business Finance Corporation.

Note: Table (a) shows the size distribution of firms as of August 1961, with each size class set at 100 at the end of 1959; Table (b) shows the size distribution of firms as of August 1963 with each size class set at 100 at the end of 1961.

Table 8

Shifts of Firms by Equity Size (1955-65) (¥100 mn)

1965 \ 1955	Un-known	Less than 0.01	0.01	0.02	0.04	0.08	0.1	0.2	0.4	0.8	1-	2-	4-	8-	10-	20-	40-	80-	Total
Less than 0.04	37	30	20	37	14	5	24	11	2	1									181
0.4-	87	33	23	82	66	6	121	101	53	5	1		1						579
1-	56	17	17	55	45	6	82	87	75	6	17		1						464
2-	24	4	8	24	11	1	34	53	49	14	24	15	1						262
4-	21	1	2	4	11	2	18	36	39	11	27	14	5						192
8-	4		1	1	3		1	4	6	1	8	7	3	1	1				35
10-	15			2			3	5	15	12	41	28	15	3	3				143
20-	3							3	5		10	23	33	3	10	3			93
40-	5										4	6	15	4	19	3			56
80-												1	2	2	3	2	1		10
100-	3												1	1	14	17	12	2	50

Source: H. Nakamura, Chuken Kigyo Ron, 2nd ed., pp. 212-13.

Table 9

Growth of Firms by Equity Size (non-financial corporations)

1955 \ 1970	1-2.9 ¥ bn	3-4.9 ¥ bn	5-9.9 ¥ bn	10-29.9 ¥ bn	30-49.9 ¥ bn	50-99.9 ¥ bn	100 and more ¥ bn	Total
Less than 10 ¥ mn	61	4	3					68 (6.4)
10- 50 ¥ mn	110	10	3					123 (11.6)
50- 100 ¥ mn	80	10	1	1				92 (8.7)
100- 300 ¥ mn	181	40	16	5				242 (22.8)
300- 500 ¥ mn	45	31	31	9				116 (10.9)
500-1,000 mn	31	20	30	14	2			97 (9.1)
1- 3 ¥ bn	8	18	24	43	10			103 (9.7)
3- 5 ¥ bn		2	2	7	5	4	1	21 (2.0)
5- 10 ¥ bn				2	4	5	4	15 (1.4)
10 and more ¥ bn						1	1	2 (0.2)
Unknown		1						1 (0.1)
Not in existence	123	35	14	11				183 (1.2)
Total	639	171	124	92	21	10	6	1,063 (100.0)

Source: K. Takizawa, Kodo Seicho to Kigyo Seicho [Rapid Economic Growth and Business Growth].
Note: Percentages in parentheses.

The Growth of Minor Enterprises

The growth of big business was conspicuous as shown above, but the growth of small business, too, was brisk and some of them attained the status of large enterprises. The rapid growth of the Japanese economy was by no means solely for big business. The active entry of new enterprises and the business growth at every front were indeed the characteristics of the late fifties and early sixties.

It goes without saying that what enabled these small businesses to grow was their high profit rates. This point is made clear in Table 10. The ratio of operating profits over total capital is higher in minor enterprises than in large enterprises. The differences are about 1 to 4% between firms with equities below 10 million yen and with equities over 1 billion yen. The data simply do not prove the anticipated phenomenon of the profit rate declining from large to small firms. On the contrary, the relation is reversed.

Moreover, we cannot forget the important point that the profit rates in this table are no more than the mean values at various size classes. The profit rates tend to be distributed

Table 10

Ratio of Operating Profits to Total Capital in
Manufacturing Corporations (%)

Year Equity	1960	1961	1962	1963
Less than ¥ 10 mn	11.2	13.4	11.5	9.3
¥ 10- 50 mn	10.7	10.2	8.9	9.2
¥ 50- 100 mn	10.0	10.1	8.0	7.7
¥ 100-1,000 mn	10.6	9.1	9.9	8.0
¥ 1 bn and more	10.2	8.6	7.2	7.5
Average	10.5	9.6	8.1	7.9

Source: See Table 6.

closely around the mean in the case of large enterprises, but
are scattered widely around it in the case of small enterprises.
Consequently, while there are not a few small firms with low
rates of return or with operating losses, there are also quite a
few small firms with rates of return far outstripping those of
large enterprises. Some small businesses are capable of growth.
The Marxist economic formula that all small businesses, ex-
ploited by monopoly capital, cannot grow at all is invalid. After
all, we must recognize the correctness of the Komiya thesis.

6. Emergence of Leading Medium-Sized Enterprises

Thesis of Leading Medium-Sized Enterprises

From our statistical examination, we think it necessary to
call our attention to Nagasu's view that "no well-ordered pyramid control of the prewar type has been established in the modern zaibatsu; it is unstable and fluid." In regarding the situation as fluid, Nagasu was already breaking away from the for-
malism of those days. However, he anticipated that the fluid
situation would soon turn into the fixed control by Big Business.
    In contrast, we judge that the situation became increasingly
more fluid under the influence of rapid economic growth. Rather
than regarding this simple-mindedly as a buildup of the big
business system or of the dual structure, we should conclude
that a pluralistic socioeconomic structure was formed.
    The growth of big business was truly diverse, for the growth
of nongroup large enterprises, too, was remarkable, and leading
medium-sized enterprises made their appearance and some of
them grew into large enterprises. Furthermore, as we have
already seen, the autonomous growth of small business, too,
was not an exceptional phenomenon. And it is here that a new
view based on these facts comes on the scene. This is the thesis of chuken kigyo or "leading medium-sized enterprises,"
first proposed by Hideichiro Nakamura in his book Chuken Kigyo Ron [Essays on Leading Medium-Sized Enterprises] (17),
published in 1964. Let us review its significance below.

Distinctive Features of Leading Medium-Sized Enterprises

Nakamura defines leading medium-sized enterprises as "a third group of enterprises that has not yet become big business but is already beyond the limits of small business," with the following basic characteristics:

(1) A leading medium-sized enterprise is not an offspring or subsidiary company of a giant or quasi-giant corporation. It is independent not only in terms of capital but also in having its own power to make decisions on its basic policy. It is not merely an enterprise which has exceeded the scale of small business.

(2) A leading medium-sized enterprise is one that has attained the scale at which funds can be raised publicly through the securities market. In this sense, it can be distinguished from small business when its stocks are listed in the Second Stock Market.

(3) It is distinguished, however, from big business in that, while able to mobilize public capital in the form of equities, it is still unable to do so in a full measure and has to remain more like a private and family business. But it also differs qualitatively from small business in that it has introduced modern management techniques as its scale is enlarged.

(4) It is in possession of market conditions that differ from those of small business. Many of its products originate from the technology and designs developed by itself, and they are successfully mass produced when necessary. It has high shares in its respective product markets and tends to be monopolistic. It is not dependent on particular buyers, and has enough power to cope with the monopsony of big business. It often has a high rate of profits on total assets.

The foregoing is of course an ideal type only. There is a large variety in existence.

Enterprises of this type mushroomed into existence and expanded rapidly because of the sudden and rapid quantitative expansion and the qualitative changes of markets in response to the high economic growth and structural changes of industry.

Many of these firms appeared and developed in old, previously narrow, markets which experienced abrupt expansion or in new markets as the social division of labor became diversified when the industrial structure became highly advanced. This trend is in common with the growth of minor enterprises so that the development of leading medium-sized enterprises is not an isolated phenomenon but one closely related to it. In other words, the few minor enterprises that adapted themselves to dynamic market changes during the advancement of the industrial structure were blessed by rapid market expansion, enlarged their scale in answer to it, and secured a monopolistic character either through a high market share or innovation, and grew into leading enterprises under consideration here.

Leading Medium-Sized Enterprises Take Root

How many of these enterprises were there? One convenient number is that of those firms listed in the second division of the Stock Market but with no affiliation with any of business groups. As shown in Table 11, we count 383 of them in 1963, a number which is not too large. The number is perhaps no more than 500 even when unlisted enterprises are included. But there already was a large reserve army, so to speak, of minor enterprises capable of growth. As a result, the number of leading medium-sized enterprises increased steadily thereafter.

Thus did these enterprises come into being as a group of a different type between the mid-fifties and mid-sixties and take root and become established after the mid-sixties. By the late sixties they started to be differentiated into those which were keeping up growth and those which stabilized into maturity, while many others continued to appear on the scene. By then, they were spread over many sizes, a few even growing into big business. Many more industries came to be covered. Despite criticism on the part of Marxist economics and despite the crisis experienced by these enterprises in the late sixties, they have apparently come to stay in Japan's industrial society.

Table 11

Companies Listed Nationwide in Second Stock Market, Classified by Type — Independent (I) and Affiliated (A) (1963)

	Less than ¥100 mn	¥100- 200 mn	¥200- 400 mn	¥400- 600 mn	¥600- 800 mn	¥800- 1,000 mn	¥1 bn and over	Total
Mining A		2		1				3
Mining I		3						3
Construction A	1	1	5	3	2	1	2	15
Construction I		10	21	5	4	1	6	47
Manufacturing A	1	47	105	45	19	6	17	240
Manufacturing I	1	99	108	61	14	4	6	293
Wholesale and retail trade A		2	7	6	1	2	2	20
Wholesale and retail trade I		9	7	8	6		2	32
Services A		6	2					8
Services I		1	3	1			3	8
Total A	2	58	119	55	22	9	21	286
Total I	1	122	139	75	24	5	17	383
Ratio of affiliated to independent companies (%) A	66.7	32.2	46.1	42.3	47.8	64.3	55.3	42.8
Ratio of affiliated to independent companies (%) I	33.3	67.8	53.9	57.7	52.2	35.7	44.7	57.2
Total number of firms	3	180	258	130	46	14	38	669

Source: H. Nakamura, Chuken Kigyo Ron, p. 17.

Needless to say, Nakamura proposed his thesis not only on behalf of management theory. He had a more broad perspective, viz.: "By analyzing the socioeconomic conditions that gave birth to these leading medium-sized enterprises, we wish to show, albeit from a limited aspect, the dynamic growth process of Japanese capitalism in the decade at the level of individual businesses and individual industries and point out its specific characters in the light of modern capitalism." It was the process of the vigorous economic growth that shaped the conditions for the birth of these firms. In this, Nakamura's critical view was: "We must evaluate autonomous business behavior that actively adapts to new conditions as well as the part accomplished by entrepreneurs in it. Moreover, an inquiry into the limits to which the innovative actions of entrepreneurs can go beyond the confines of individual businesses and change the economic system and social environment seems necessary." He turned his attention to the role of the innovator as the one in charge of evolutionary modern capitalism.

Nakamura, thus, dug up precisely those viewpoints that had been missing in the theory of Big Business control, the theory of monopolistic exploitation, and the fatalism of the dual structure. In order to revolutionize reality, he rejected a mechanical application of nomology and groped for new possibilities by deepening the perception of reality. Therefore, our evaluation of Nakamura's thesis should neither be limited to its analysis of leading medium-sized enterprises nor dwarfed to the academic level of theory of imperfect competition or of oligopoly. Rather, it should be evaluated as a forward-looking, critical theory of the big business system.

Notes

1) Kazuji Nagasu, Nihon Keizai Nyumon [Introduction to the Japanese Economy] (Tokyo: Kobun Sha, 1960).

2) Ryutaro Komiya, "Dokusen Shihon to Shotoku Saibumpai Seisaku" [Monopoly Capital and Income Redistribution Policy], Seikai, March 1961.

3) Published in Keizai Bunseki Kenkyu Kai, Nihon Keizai Bunseki [Analysis of the Japanese Economy], No. 14 (Tokyo: Shiseido, 1962). This paper contains corrections and revisions though there is no fundamental change from the one presented here.

4) "Kigyo Seicho Conference — Sumitomo Kinzoku Kogyo" [Business Growth Conference — Sumitomo Metal Industries], Nihon Keizai Kenkyu Center Geppo [Monthly Bulletin of the Japan Economic Research Center], No. 5 (1964).

5) "Kato kyoso no Ronri to Genjitsu — Keiretsu Shihai Kiko no Kaimei," the Mainichi Economist, special issue, Fall 1962; reprinted in Y. Miyazaki, Sengo Nihon no Keizai Kiko [Economic Mechanism of Postwar Japan] (Tokyo: Shinhyoron Sha, 1966).

6) In regard to the one-set principle, the following critiques are worthy of note: S. Sugioka, "Kigyo Shudan no Haaku ni Tsuite" [Comprehending Industrial Groupings], Nihon Keizai Bunseki, No. 17 (1963). ————, "Kato Kyoso no Mechanism — Miyazaki 'One-Set' Riron e no Gimon" [Mechanism of Excessive Competition — Questions regarding Miyazaki's "One-Set" Theory], Economist, February 23, 1965. S. Koyama, "Kodo Seicho no Kin'yuteki Joken" [Financial Conditions for Rapid Economic Growth], Keikicho Keizai Geppo [Monthly Report of the Economic Planning Agency], July 1964. ————, "Kigyo kan Kyoso to Kin'yu" [Interfirm Competition and Finance], published in H. Kanamori, ed., Keizai Seicho to Kigyo Keiei [Economic Growth and Business Management] (1966). K. Suzuki, " 'Sengo Nihon no Dokusenka Keiko' ni tsuite — Miyazaki Yoshikazu Kyoju no Shosetsu ni taisuru Gimon" [On The Trend Toward Monopolization in Postwar Japan — Questions regarding Professor Yoshikazu Miyazaki's Views], Riron Keizaigaku, February 1963. For the writers' own views, see "Nihon gata Kasen Taisei to Sangyo Seisaku" [Japanese Type Oligopolistic Structure and Industrial Policy], Senshu University Institute of Social Sciences, ed., Nihon Shihon Shugi Kozo no Kenkyu [Studies of the Structure of Japanese Capitalism] (Tokyo: Mirai Sha, 1968). The text is mainly based on this monograph.

7) See Sugioka, op. cit.

7a) When firms are engaged in "direct financing" their funds are raised by new issues of equities and bonds and in "indirect financing" when they borrow from financial institutions.

8) See Koyama, op cit.

9) A. Sakaguchi, Mitsubishi (Tokyo: Nikkei Shinsho, 1966), pp. 160-163.

10) Sakaguchi, op. cit., pp. 163-164.

11) A. Kubota, Mitsui (Tokyo: Nikkei Shinsho, 1966), pp. 127-132.

12) K. Suzuki, Sumitomo (Tokyo: Nikkei Shinsho, 1966), pp. 158, 113-114.

12a) A Konzern is a pyramid of centralized business concentration spanning over a number of industries (including finances). A holding company is located on the top. Prewar Mitsui and Mitsubishi are typical examples.

13) T. Mito, H. Masaki, H. Haruyama, Daikigyo ni okeru Shoyu to Shihai [Ownership and Control in Big Business] (Tokyo: Mirai Sha, 1973), pp. 36-41.

14) See Y. Miyazaki, Kasen — Gendai no Keizai Kiko [Oligopoly — Contemporary Economic Structure] (Tokyo: Iwanami Shinsho, 1977), pp. 66-69. For an evaluation of reciprocal shareholdings by corporations, see T. Nishiyama, Gendai Kigyo no Shihai Kozo — Kabushiki Kaisha Seido no Hokai [Management Structure of Modern Business — Collapse of the Joint-Stock Corporation System] (Tokyo: Yuhikaku, 1975), pp. 243-245.

15) A detailed explanation of this problem is available in T. Masamura, Jiyu Kigyo Taisei no Shorai [The Future of the Free Enterprise System] (Tokyo: Diamond Sha, 1975), Chapter 2.

16) The reason is that even if private enterprise is converted to public enterprise, there will be not the slightest change in the tyranny of the managerial power; also, even though state ownership under socialism is indeed public ownership in form, it merely strengthens the managerial power (de facto ownership) held by the dictatorship and the bureaucracy and weakens the public control of business far below the level in a market economy.

17) H. Nakamura, Chuken Kigyo Ron [Essays on Leading Medium-Sized Enterprises] (Tokyo: Toyo Keizai Shimpo Sha, 1964).

8

THE JAPANESE-TYPE STRUCTURE OF BIG BUSINESS

Yoshikazu Miyazaki*

I. Recent Topics

"Hedoro"

"Business belongs not to individuals but to shareholders. It borrows enormous amounts from financial institutions for equipment investment but at the same time receives protests for decreased production from labor unions. Therefore we want to take countermeasures while considering the survival of business."

So stated President Ryōei Saitō of the Daishōwa Paper Manufacturing Company in his testimony on September 9, 1970, before the Lower House Special Committee on Industrial Pollution Policy for a discussion of pollution of Tagono-Ura Harbor by "hedoro" or sludge.

President Saitō, while apologizing for the trouble his company had caused by the sludge problem at the Special Committee that

*Yoshikazu Miyazaki, "Big Business no Nihonteki Kozo." Sekai, January 1971. Copyright by Yoshikazu Miyazaki. Magazine rights in the English language are arranged with Iwanami Shoten, Publishers, Tokyo. Translated by Thomas W. Cleaver.

This translation originally appeared in Japanese Economic Studies, II (Fall 1973), 3-61. See also the author's book, Kasen [Oligopoly] (Tokyo: Iwanami Shoten, 1972), chapter 1, 1-73.

day, at the same time appealed to "the business standpoint," repeating: "In Fuji City there are 6,800 employees of the company and 70,000 family members and related persons. Half the 180,000 population of Fuji City holds feelings of great anxiety about the Tago Harbor problem. I want to ask for understanding and sympathy in your dealing with the pollution problem." The statement presented in the opening paragraph, which vividly expresses the "business point of view," was made by a business executive in his personal capacity.

In his statement, however, we cannot find even the limited sense of responsibility toward pollution that forced the government to delete the sentence "harmony with the healthy development of the economy" in its revision of the basic law on pollution policy.

We are warned by Galbraith that people's amazement at Japan's growth toward the position of the world's top industrial country would soon be replaced by doubt about Japan's capability to survive. Even at this point in time when they have been indicted for the "crime" (because it is too mild to call it pollution) of flushing untreated industrial drainage, these executives still assert the sovereignty of business over a pollution policy for the sake of people. It seems that by begging for "understanding and sympathy," they hold on to the position that a certain degree of pollution is a necessary evil for the survival of their business. As they try harder to justify pollution for business' sake, we cannot help but perceive the private, antisocial, and antihuman character of business.

For whom does business really exist? What, to us as citizens, is the significance of big business, which has accumulated vast amounts during the high-growth period? More than anything else the pollution problem has made us as common people ask these questions and realize once more the private character of business.

The Chisso Shareholders' Meeting

Is it really true that "business belongs not to individuals but

to shareholders" as the president of the Daishōwa Paper Manufacturing Company asserted? It is well known that the principle of tripartite separation of powers applies to a corporation.
The board of directors is responsible for the administration,
the controller for the judiciary, and the shareholders' meeting
for the legislature.

If the shareholders' meeting is a legislative body comparable
with the Diet, then there must be extensive debates in it on the
corporate management policy. Regretfully, however, a Japanese shareholders' meeting is almost without exception far
from the ideal; it is common knowledge that it is no more than
a parody. When the president, as chairman, proposes deliberation on the annual income statement, a "meeting man" springs
up right away, receives the acknowledgement of the chair, and
calls for "omitting the reading of figures and going immediately
to the controller's report." Then his henchmen second the motion in unison, giving "no objection." All proposals on the
agenda are approved smoothly one after another, and the meeting is adjourned in ten minutes. Shareholders at large have no
way to speak. This is because the company official in charge
of the shareholders' meeting wants to end it as quickly as possible by any means available, including employing these aggressive meeting men who can steer the meeting as they wish. Thus
the shareholders' meeting is in name only.

In this sort of widely accepted convention, the Chisso Corporation opened its forty-second regular shareholders' meeting
at 11:00 a.m., January 28, 1970. In this shareholders' meeting,
the curtain was opened by faint sounds of ringing bells and a
chorus of a Buddhist pilgrim song by shareholders in white
sedge hats and white pilgrims' attire. This strange scene made
a strong impression on many people. This was a remarkable
event as shareholders' meetings go. Sufferers of the Minamata
Disease confronted their assailants, demanding an apology from
the president of the company by thrusting mortuary tablets held
in their hands at him.

The corporate system is very handy for corporations. They
collect necessary funds from as many people as possible.

However, when a stockholder wants to withdraw his principal, he does not withdraw funds directly from his company but finds another investor in the stock exchange, and collects by selling his shares to that person. Shareholders change, but the corporation does not pay them back. It is not obligated at all to repay funds once collected. Thus, insofar as the shareholder is considered as an investor, not a lender of funds, he is an owner of the company. The shareholders' meeting must be the company's highest decision-making body. At least, this is so in theory.

However, as already mentioned, the shareholders' meeting has no meat and flesh in any Japanese corporation. Management leadership is as solid as a rock. The "Association to Indict Minamata Disease" presented a frontal attack to it by promulgating its "single-share" campaign.

Here, the shareholder appeared on the scene not as a mere investor who is only concerned with dividends, but as an inquisitor for the pollution that big business has led to. Those who make accusations about pollution want to present companies with various demands, but up to now their voices have not carried very far. Company heads and local residents are too far apart. They have had the ingenious idea of using the shareholders' meeting as a legal means for protesting directly to the company president. This revelation is epochal. It may possibly revive the shareholders' meeting, long lapsing in utter paralysis, to act as the highest corporate decision-making body, which enables small shareholders and area residents to go directly to the corporate management. Subsequent examples include the shareholders' antiwar movement, sponsored by the Vietnam Peace Association, directed at the Mitsubishi Heavy Industries, and the single-share campaign of the Committee of One Thousand, opposing pollution by the Nippon Steel Pipe Company.

However, up to now, things have not gone beyond exploring possibilities. At the forty-second Chisso shareholders' meeting, as the president started to announce its opening, a single-share shareholder rushed up to the rostrum, shouting: "emergency motions!", but not one of his motions was adopted.

Suddenly a curtain dropped from the ceiling announcing that "the income statement is approved." This took place in only five minutes. Twelve hundred shareholders attended, and even though an amended motion was offered, the Chisso shareholders' meeting ended with neither support nor opposition views being put forth. If it is an outrageous act for the Diet to pass a bill by force, then the Chisso shareholders' meeting is even more outrageous. Can we still say that a business belongs to its shareholders?

Capital Gains by Inflation

As regards inflation, the 1970 Economic White Paper, while discussing the depreciation in savings through price rises, took note that by the same token big business realized enormous capital gains and presented, for the first time, its own estimate by computing the difference between the book value and the replacement cost of fixed assets, namely buildings, machinery, and land for the latest ten years, from the balance sheets of 435 major manufacturing corporations. Their "capital gains" amounted to 1.8 trillion yen. Of this, .92 trillion yen was due to the value of real assets in excess of net worth. At least this .92 trillion yen is "capital gains" arising from the appreciation in value of real assets which big business purchased with funds borrowed from banks and elsewhere. We can assume that financial assets of depositors and other suppliers of funds to big business have depreciated roughly by this amount in the last decade. Thus the White Paper gave official recognition to the fact that price rises benefited big business and harmed depositors. Now that the government has recognized this fact, it remains inequitable unless the government enforces a strong price control policy or corrects the unequal redistribution of wealth from depositors to big business one way or another, e.g., by taxing "capital gains" of big business or allowing depositors to deduct the depreciation of savings from their taxable income. However, the White Paper remains obstinately silent on this point.

The Political Contributions Trial

While it was not as spectacular as the pollution problem, nor did it command as much popular attention as the price problem, a very important event that permits us to gauge the power of big business took place on June 24, 1970.

On that day the Supreme Court acquitted the Yawata Iron and Steel (later merged with the Fuji Iron and Steel into the Shin Nihon Iron and Steel) in a suit, running since 1963, against its political contributions.

In this dispute, a stockholder (Mr. Bensaburo Arita), the plaintiff, charged two defendants, representative directors of the company, with the responsibility for a political donation of 3.5 million yen to the Liberal Democratic Party. In the first trial, the Tokyo District Court passed a decision in April 1963 in complete favor of the plaintiff, taking note that a profit-making company violates the articles of incorporation and its directors infringe their loyalty and duty in making political contributions. However, in the second trial of January 1966, the Tokyo Higher Court overruled the first decision. Standing on a judgment that "A company can perform socially useful acts inasmuch as it is a member of society," it concluded that "a political contribution is no different from a philanthropic donation in public character and is therefore permissible." There was an immediate appeal by the plaintiff, and the question of the legality of a political contribution by a company whose primary objective is profit-making was brought to the Supreme Court.

A complete examination of the Supreme Court decision is not the purpose of the present article. (1) But its verdict includes a recognition that cannot be disregarded in exploring the realities of modern big business. I touch on this point only.

The primary basis for the appellant's appeal is that "A political contribution by a corporation is opposed to the Constitution, which recognizes only the suffrage of citizens who are natural persons; therefore, it is an act which is contrary to the public order and morals of Article 90 of the Civil Code."

However, the Supreme Court's decision refuted this as follows:

> Each article of people's rights and duties set down in Chapter III of the Constitution should be interpreted as applicable to domestic corporations as much as possible. So a company, the same as a citizen who is a natural person, has the freedom to perform political acts, such as supporting, promoting, or opposing specific national or party policies. The donation of political funds is just a link in this freedom; when it is done by a company, <u>even though it influences political trends</u>, there is no legal requirement to treat it differently from donations by citizens who are natural persons...donations to political parties not only by nature <u>do not</u> exert <u>direct</u> influence on individual citizens' rights to vote or otherwise use the franchise, but even when political parties use funds for <u>buying voters</u>, this is nothing more than a pathological, infrequent phenomenon... it is difficult to conclude that it is <u>direct</u> infringement on the free use of the voting right [emphasis mine].

This decision expresses an idea that the company is as much a "social entity" or a member of society as the natural person and, except for the right to vote, it is entitled to possess the same political rights as the citizen does as a natural person. Based on this idea, it gives a complete approval to a company's "freedom" to make political contributions, equating it with natural persons' freedom to give donations to political funds. It not only sees the company as an economic unit independent of natural persons, but takes the view that the company as a political unit is a social entity independent of natural persons and that it is not given the right to vote only because it is a corporation.

Surely, economists distinguish between natural persons and companies and define companies as enormous aggregates of material and human resources not seen in natural persons. (2) This portrays the company as an economic unit which, by means of capital accumulation, mergers and absorptions, realizes continuous expansion and growth utterly impossible to natural persons as homo economicus. It is a theory to explain the reality of a relatively few large companies dominating the economy as a whole. Here, the company is distinguished from homo economicus as an economic unit that has particular interest in oligopolizing the economy.

The Supreme Court is fully aware of the economic power and political influence of corporations (see the italicized portions of the cited decision), and yet attempts to recognize natural persons' political rights in profit-motivated companies. It must be judged a genuinely "dangerous" decision. In the event that huge profit-making companies make full use of their "political rights" and "freedom to donate" that this decision permits them to exercise, they can put pressure on politics on a much grander scale than at present and thereby exert unfathomably bad influences upon democracy.

In fact, in the fall of 1964, when Eisaku Sato, (the late) Ichiro Kono, and Aiichiro Fujiyama were battling fiercely for the chair of premiership upon the retirement of (the late) Prime Minister Ikeda for medical reasons, there was an episode in which Sato boasted in front of two influential leaders of the Liberal Democratic Party, Shōjirō Kawashima and Takeo Miki:

> The financial circles of Tokyo, Osaka, and Nagoya all support me unanimously. It is the will of the whole financial world, nay, the whole nation, that I be selected as Prime Minister (emphasis mine). (Yukio Suzuki, Seiji o Ugokasu Keieisha [Business Leaders Behind Politics], 1965, p. 12.)

This episode suggests that the financial circles make political contributions not only because of "their fear of rising communist power shaking up the capitalist system after the conservative party's election defeat" (3), but that the relative size of their contributions represents how they rank various factions in the conservative party as the financial world as a whole sees them and that business leaders are really in the political saddle and decide among themselves who should be the next premier.

Accordingly, in the mentality of the conservative party, successive prime ministers themselves may have viewed the "support of the financial world" in itself as the "support of the people."
I called the Supreme Court decision a "danger" because I am
afraid that it justifies and rationalizes this sort of Japanese
political climate in a gross contradiction of the ideal of democracy, that is, "of the people, by the people, and for the people."

Indeed, the government and the Diet have for some time, under Article 9 of the Corporate Tax Law and Article 7 of the
Corporate Tax Law Enforcement Regulations, given corporations a special tax privilege of inclusion of donations, up to half
of the sum of 2.5/1000 of equity and 1.5/100 of income, as business losses and exempting them from taxation as business profits. Companies make full use of this privilege in determining
their political contributions. Furthermore, they think that,
within these specified limits, they are free to determine who
should receive how much. In other words, it is no exaggeration
to say that this tax privilege has induced businesses to take
their income due to the government as corporate taxes and to
give it to political parties and their factions as donations. This
sort of a tax privilege does not exist in Britain or America.
The Supreme Court decision gave a legal existence to the tax
privilege which the government and Diet had already allowed
to big business.

Expo 70 Pavilions

Finally, along with the recent topics that we have just discussed, there is one that cannot be disregarded in examining
the activities of big business. We refer to the exhibits at the
World Exposition of 1970.

Along with the foreign exhibits at Osaka's Expo 70 were attractive domestic private pavilions. There were twenty-eight
of these in all, sixteen of which cost more than one billion yen,
as shown in Table 1. Five were "business association" pavilions put up by industrial associations. Ten were "business
group" pavilions exhibited by business groups belonging to the

294

Table 1

Major Domestic Private Pavilions in Expo 70
(with budgets exceeding 1 billion yen)

Exhibition Hall	Theme	Exhibitor	Members (companies)	Budget (billion yen)
Japan Gas Association Hall	"The Laughing World"	Japan Gas Association	201	1
Electric Power Hall	"Mankind and Energy"	Electric Industry Federation	9 (9 groups)	2
Iron and Steel Hall	"Poetry of Iron"	Japan Iron and Steel Federation	53	2
Textile Hall	"Textiles Enrich Human Life"	Japan Textile Hall Cooperative Association	331 (2 groups)	1
Japan Automobile Manufacturers' Association Hall	"The World of Rhythm"	Japan Automobile Manufacturers' Association	15	1.5
5 Industry Association Pavilions: subtotal				7.5
Sumitomo Fairy-Tale Hall	"Beauty, Love and Hope"	Sumitomo Hall Committee	47	1.7
Fuji Group Pavilion	"Message to the 21st Century"	Fuji Group Expo Exhibition Committee	36	2
Mitsui Group Pavilion	"The Garden of Creation"	Mitsui Group Expo Exhibition Committee	32	2

Toshiba IHI Pavilion	"Hope"	Toshiba IHI Group	2	2
Furukawa Pavilion	"Ancient Dreams and Modern Dreams"	Expo Furukawa Pavilion Promotion Committee	31	1
Hitachi Group Building	"Pursuit – Invitation to the Unknown"	Hitachi Group	5	2
Midori Building	"Astrorama"	Midori Association (Sanwa Group)	32	2
Mitsubishi Future Building	"Japanese Nature and the Dream of the Japanese People"	Mitsubishi Expo General Committee	35	2
Ricoh Building	"Ricoh"	Ricoh-Sanai Group	7	1
Matsushita Building	"Tradition and Development"	Matsushita Electric Industrial Company	22	1.2
10 Business Group Pavilions: subtotal				16.9
Life Industry Building	"Each Morning, Each Evening"		72	1
28 Domestic Private Pavilions: grand total				30.722

same lines of capital control. Only the Life Industry Hall was
without the backing of such groups; it was sponsored jointly by
seventy-two independent companies (including Yoshida Industries, Nikka Whiskey, and Kyōwa Bank). Table 1 clearly shows
that business-group pavilions overwhelmed others both in the
number of buildings (36%) and in the budgeted cost (56%). In
this sense, the World's Fair pavilions put Japanese business
groups on parade and presented a display of the existence and
strength of Japanese business groups to the world, and especially to Asia.

Even the Fuji Bank Group and the Midori Building Group
(Sanwa Bank), which heretofore have been regarded as rather
weakly united business groups, maintained their organizational
ties that had been formed in their cooperative exhibition projects in Expo 70. They planned new organizations such as the
Fuyō Marine Development, the Fuyō Information Center, and
the Oriental Information Management Research Institute,
strengthened their connections, and tried to keep themselves
in step at least in setting up new enterprises. Moreover, these
business groups (e.g., Mitsubishi and Mitsui) not only worked
for expansion and reinforcement of business groups but also
started to distribute monthly journals to all employees in
respective groups in order to raise their "family consciousness." In the same view, some of them plan commemorative
events for a group as a whole, such as the Mitsubishi Centen-
ary.

Common to all these topics dealing with big business that we
have discussed is a feeling that big business, as the nucleus of
the Japanese economy, has been strengthening its influences.
Accordingly, in analyzing the postwar Japanese economy, we
must examine its rapid growth not only in terms of the quantitative expansion of GNP but also of the structural characteristics of big business that has steadily strengthened its
power.

II. The Economic Power of Big Business

The Classical Contribution of Berle and Means

The classical work on the economic power of big business is the celebrated study by A. A. Berle and G. C. Means, The Modern Corporation and Private Property (1932). By examining the largest 200 nonfinancial American corporations, ranked by value of assets (total assets less depreciation reserves) at the close of the "Roaring Twenties" (as of January 1, 1930), the authors confirmed that the top 200 big corporations, while only 0.07% of the total number of businesses, controlled about half of total corporate assets. They speculated that the management unit expands in scale as the corporate system is being adopted, thereby inevitably spreading share ownership. The dispersion of share ownership would make it possible to acquire the control of productive assets by holding a minimum of share ownership and eventually to establish "managerial control" with no influential share ownership at all. Accordingly, "ownership of wealth without appreciable control and control of wealth without appreciable ownership appear to be the logical outcome of corporate development." (4) Berle and Means demonstrated that, by 1930, 44% of the top companies had already become subject to managerial control.

As to the Berle and Means thesis of concentration of economic power leading to the dispersion of shares and finally to the establishment of managerial control, there are two opposing viewpoints, one upholding their thesis and the other emphasizing the control by individual owners in denial of the thesis. There are many variants of these points of view.*

---

*For those who support the Berle and Means thesis of managerial control, see, e.g., R. A. Gordon, Business Leadership in the Large Corporation (1945); R. J. Larner, "Ownership and Control in the 200 Largest Non-financial Corporations, 1929 and 1963," American Economic Review (September 1966); J. K. Galbraith, The New Industrial State (1967). For those who

New Facts

I shall not go over these points of view that appeared in the
literature. Instead, I shall begin by first presenting recent
facts on Japanese business. Based on these new facts, I shall
propose a new view.

These facts are obtained from a study of 466 (or 464 as the
case may be) corporations. This sample is derived by excluding a total of 26 (or 28) corporations — 9 government enterprises, 8 special corporations, 8 life insurance companies, and
2 (or 3) companies for which data are not available — out of
492 companies with reproducible tangible assets of 5 billion
yen or more (which is the concept adopted in the National
Wealth Census, defined as the total value of fixed tangible assets [excluding land] and inventories as of the end of the 1966
fiscal year [the latest for which this study has been completed]).
At this point, I may outline the conclusions of the study, which
will be described in detail later. First of all, there are more
corporations owned by (private) corporations than there are individually owned or managerially controlled corporations in
postwar Japan. Consequently, one can notice a pronounced
trend toward concentrated business groupings through the interlocked holding of companies. Furthermore, the dispersion of
shares among shareholders is rare in the case of newly established companies under corporate ownership; there are quite a
few cases of complete or majority control. Accordingly, there
is a trend toward concentration of share ownership by a few
large owners. These facts suggest a new trend, which is not
fully explicable by a number of prevailing views on business
control (e.g., individual ownership control or managerial control).

---

reject the thesis, see, e.g., T.N.E.C., The Distribution of
Ownership in the 200 Largest Non-Financial Corporations
(1940); P. M. Sweezy, The Present as History (1953); V. Perlo,
The Empire of High Finance (1957); P. A. Baran and P. M.
Sweezy, Monopoly Capital (1966). — K. S.

Business units typical of the nineteenth century were those
owned by individuals or a small group of persons. They were
managed by the individuals themselves or by those directly appointed by them. Their management scale was determined by
the size of personal assets of those individual owners. In other
words, their ownership and control were unified in the person
of individuals. But as Berle and Means pointed out, the formation of the corporate system polarized the business ownership
and control unified in individuals into two directions, namely,
the dispersion of ownership to a large number of individuals
and the concentration of control in managers who pledge loyalty
to corporations. The polarization was into "company ownership
without control" and "managerial control without ownership."
Now in the zaibutsu-dissolved Japanese economy, there is a
marked tendency toward the forms of company ownership by
companies and of interlocking ownership among companies.
We can observe in these developments that the ownership and
control, once unified in individuals, are again to be unified in
companies. (5)
     In what follows, I shall verify these trends statistically, and
then analyze their implications in some depth.

The Measurement of Economic Power

     First, we must deal with how to measure the economic power
of big business. Indeed, the influence of Berle and Means is so
deep that the calculation of the top "200 firms" has subsequently
become a magic symbol in any measurement of economic power,
as Galbraith noted. Even for Japanese big business, "200 firms"
measurement is pretty much the rule. (6) In the study to be reported below, I deviate from this practice. Assets are defined
to be reproducible tangible assets (the total of fixed tangible
assets [excluding land], and inventories). All corporations, including government enterprises, special corporations, and private corporations whose asset values were more than 5 billion
yen at the end of the fiscal year 1966, are completely enumerated. There were 492 big businesses as defined here. This

method has an advantage in that it enables us to make a complete coverage of big businesses among those unlisted joint-
stock companies such as foreign-related businesses, joint ventures, subsidiaries, and family companies, as well as life insurance companies, special corporations, and government enterprises. (7)

Unfortunately, it is not possible at the present time to compute the share of these 492 companies in national wealth. This
is because the government's national wealth census is incomplete. Not only is it incomplete, but it seems to be more and
more simplified each time the census is undertaken.

The first national wealth census, conducted at the end of
1955, was a really full-scale survey in both coverage and methodology; its epoch-making report was published in six volumes
easily exceeding 1,000 pages. In the second census, as of the
end of 1960, personal effects of households and weapons held by
the Defense Agency were omitted; its report was a single volume of 475 pages. The third National Wealth Census, as of the
end of 1965, was "limited to the assets of the private business
sector, which is of particular importance in the national economy." Its census report was a slim 109-page pamphlet. This
makes it difficult even to attempt a comparison of the quinquennial national wealth statistics. While Japan's GNP statistics
are as good as those of any other advanced countries, its national wealth statistics are glaringly incomplete. This may be
another manifestation of its GNP-ism.

The only available method to estimate the economic power of
the 492 big businesses with more than 5 billion yen in tangible
assets seems to be to rely on the amounts of paid-in capital.
However, our 492 corporations include 9 government enterprises (such as the Japan Monopoly Corporation, the Japan
National Railways, and the Nippon Telegraph and Telephone
Public Corporation), 8 non-joint-stock special corporations
(such as the Japan Broadcasting Corporation, the Japan Highway Public Corporation, and the Japan Housing Corporation),
and 8 life insurance companies. Since none of these is a joint-
stock corporation, no data on paid-in capital are available for

Table 2

Capital Concentration by Industry for 464 Corporations with
Tangible Assets of More Than 5 Billion Yen
(as of end of 1966)

		Number of companies			Paid-in capital (mn yen)		
	Industry	464 Co. (a)	National total (b)	a/b (%)	464 Co. (c)	National total (d)	c/d (%)
Heavy and chemical industry	Primary metals	32	31,538	0.10	601,470	940,875	63.9
	Machinery	63	32,688	0.19	750,513	1,195,024	62.8
	Chemicals	83	7,425	1.12	519,284	688,233	75.5
	Subtotal	178	71,651	0.25	1,871,267	2,824,132	66.3
Tertiary industry	Wholesale and retail trade	32	287,919	0.01	196,415	977,714	20.1
	Finances	18	155	11.60	292,500	498,681	58.7
	Real estate and warehousing	5	25,159	0.02	33,567	196,293	17.1
	Land transportation	18	19,055	0.09	165,276	427,952	38.6
	Marine transportation	18	2,756	0.65	90,418	142,408	63.5
	Electricity and gas	18	152	11.84	719,173	679,917	105.8
	Others	15	59,553	0.03	105,283	285,820	36.8
	Subtotal	124	394,749	0.03	1,602,632	3,208,795	49.9
Others	Agriculture, forestry and marine products and foodstuffs	32	36,621	0.09	161,308	335,720	48.0
	Mining	18	3,694	0.49	134,886	197,812	68.2
	Textile products	20	20,961	0.10	80,742	208,417	38.7
	Paper and pulp	22	5,918	0.37	69,783	119,801	58.2
	Glass, cement and ceramics	12	9,168	0.13	88,230	186,487	47.2
	Others	58	131,576	0.04	269,188	691,936	38.9
	Subtotal	162	207,938	0.08	804,137	1,740,173	46.2
	Total	464	674,338	0.07	4,278,036	7,773,100	55.0

Note: Compiled from the 1966 Business Group Table. Out of the 492 big businesses with tangible assets of more than 5 billion yen, a total of 28 companies (9 government enterprises, 8 nonjoint-stock special corporations, 8 life insurance companies, and 3 companies for which data were unavailable) are excluded. National totals are from the Ministry of Finance Annual Corporate Enterprise Statistics (1966) and Monthly Statistics of Public Finance and Banking.

them. In addition, the volume of paid-in capital is unknown for
Suntory and two other family-owned companies. Having excluded these 28 companies, we come to a total of 464 companies. Table 2 classifies these companies by industry and lists
the number of companies (column [a]) and the amounts of paid-
in capital (column [c]). Of the 464 companies, the table reveals
that 178 companies belong to heavy and chemical industries
with total paid-in capital of 1.8713 trillion yen; 124 to tertiary
industries with total paid-in capital of 1.6026 trillion yen; and
162 to other industries with total paid-in capital of .8041 trillion
yen. The table also presents the national totals of joint-stock
companies — total number in column (b) and total paid-in capital in column (d). The percentages of our 464 companies in the
nationwide totals are shown in column a/b (the number of companies) and in column c/d (total paid-in capital).

High Concentration of Capital

The table clearly reveals that the 464 companies are only
0.07% of the national total in number but account for 55%
of the national total of paid-in capital; in particular, in
heavy and chemical industries, the 178 companies own 66.3%
of the national total of paid-in capital. (The percentage reported in the c/d column for electricity and gas exceeds 100.
This must be due to an error in the national total of paid-in
capital compiled by the Ministry of Finance.)

As already mentioned, the Berle and Means estimates dis-
closed that in the U.S. as of January 1, 1930, the top 200 big
business, numerically merely 0.07% of all companies,
owned 49.2% of total corporate assets. Similarly, Table 2
discloses that in Japan at the end of the fiscal year 1966,
the 464 big business, again only 0.07% of all companies,
controlled 55% of the national total of paid-in capital. The
postwar Japanese economy seems to have had a higher degree of capital concentration than the U.S.

To sum up, it is clear that big businesses with tangible assets of more than 5 billion yen have a leading role in Japanese

industry, especially in heavy and chemical industries. In what follows I shall narrow the focus on these 464 companies and try to clarify their structural characteristics.

III. The Structure of Capital

Japanese Characteristics of the Capital Structure

Before analyzing the 464 giant Japanese corporations, it is convenient here to consider, in general terms, salient features of the capital structure in postwar Japan.

The best-known feature is that, in the postwar period, Japanese businesses have very heavily relied on borrowings in their finances. This is the so-called indirect financing method. In this way, Japanese firms grossly violate the well-known principle of corporate finance that equity should not be less than debt (the 50% rule of the equity-asset ratio). They also continue overborrowing in wholesale disregard of the principle that liquid assets should be twice as much as liquid liabilities (the 200% rule of the liquidity ratio).

In addition to indirect financing and overborrowing, another recent notable feature is that private ownership of corporate shares has fallen below 50%, and consequently share ownership by corporations is now above one half. Moreover, among corporate shareholders, financial institutions are becoming more important. Thus the proportion of corporate shares has been reduced in individuals' financial assets, while the percentage of shares held by financial institutions has increased. This shift of ownership from individual to corporate shareowners, particularly financial institutions, is worth noting.

From Individual to Corporate Shareowners

Let us verify these features statistically. We reverse the order and examine first the distribution of share ownership in Table 3, which compares the shareholder distribution quinquennially in 1950, 1955, 1960, 1965, and 1970. We readily note the

Table 3

Distribution Status of Shares by Ownership, percent
(end of year)

		1950	1955	1960	1965	1970
Government and public institutions		3.2	0.4	0.2	0.2	0.3
Corporations	Financial institutions	12.6	19.5	23.1	25.6	} 32.3
	Investment trusts	–	4.1	7.5	5.1	
	Securities companies	11.9	7.9	3.7	6.1	1.2
	Other domestic corporations	11.0	13.2	17.8	17.3	23.1
	Foreign corporations	–	1.5	1.1	1.6	3.0
	Subtotal	35.5	46.2	53.2	55.7	59.6
Individuals	Individuals and others	61.3	53.1	46.3	43.9	39.9
	Foreigners	–	0.3	0.3	0.2	0.2
	Subtotal	61.3	53.4	46.6	44.1	40.1
Total		100.0	100.0	100.0	100.0	100.0

Note: Survey of listed companies in the first section of stock exchanges.

Source: Ministry of Finance, Share Distribution Status Survey (the 1970 data due to a survey by the national securities exchange).

following four points:

1) Since the Securities Democratization Movement, initiated under the leadership of the Securities Democratization Committee in November 1947, had released to the general public the large number of shares gathered into the hands of the Holding Company Liquidation Committee upon the dissolution of the zaibatsu, share ownership by individuals exceeded 60%.

However, this proportion continued to decline year after year, and by about 1955 fell below 50%. It fell still further after the 1965 disorder in the securities market and was below 40% by 1970.

2) On the other hand, share ownership by corporations gradually rose. It exceeded 50% at about 1957 and was nearly 60% in 1970.

3) Among corporate shareholders, financial institutions are especially prominent. Their share ownership increased year after year, reaching 32.3% by 1970. The next largest shareowners are domestic nonfinancial corporations. Their proportion remained unchanged at 17-18% from 1960 to 1965, but subsequently surged to 23.1% in 1970. Shareholding by foreign corporations was no more than 3.0% as of 1970, but exhibited a very noticeable upward trend. Among these changes, we may note sharp declines in the shareholding by investment trusts and securities companies, which were once large owners. These declines were obviously due to the 1965 disorder in the securities market.

4) Financial institutions' ownership of 32.3% in 1970 is broken down as follows: banks and trust banks (including investment trusts but excluding mutual banks) — 15.4%; life insurance companies — 11.1%; non-life insurance companies — 4.0%; and other financial institutions — 1.8%.*

Indirect Financing

Next, let us verify the Japanese-type characteristics of business financing. Even though stock ownership has shifted greatly from individuals to corporations, this is nothing but a shift in ownership of equities, which are merely one of many sources of funds. Besides, as Table 5 shows, Japanese firms raised only 3.8% of their funds by stock issues in 1968. We also note

---

*A subsection reviewing American institutional investors (containing Table 4) is excluded from the present translation at the author's suggestion. — K. S.

Table 5

International Comparison of Sources of Business Funds,
the Equity-Asset Ratio and the Liquidity Ratio (percent)

		Japan (1968)	U.S. (1968)	U.K. (1967)	W. Germany (1967)
Sources of Business Funds	Retained earnings	6.4	21.3	10.5	11.1
	Depreciation allowances	21.2	42.8	27.7	67.4
	Equity	3.8	− 0.8	12.1	5.7
	Bonds	4.5	12.5	19.5	3.6
	Borrowings	34.8	12.8	1.9	10.6
	Others	29.3	11.4	28.3	1.6
Equity-asset ratio		20.8	56.2	53.1	45.0
Liquidity ratio		108.36	214.02	156.35	125.12

Note: Trade credits are included in "others."
Source: Bank of Japan, Comparative International Statistics.

that the corresponding ratio was only 12.1% for the U.K. in
which the ratio was the highest. In other words, new equity issues are no longer a major method of business finance in advanced countries. We must look at more important methods of
financing that have replaced it. According to Table 5, these
methods are depreciation allowances and retained earnings in
the U.S., the U.K., and West Germany. In contrast, Japan depends heavily on borrowings, which account for 34.8% of the
total. Thus, while the U.S., the U.K., and West Germany rely
on self-financing based chiefly on internal accumulation, Japan
alone depends on indirect financing. In this, as already mentioned, the basic feature of the postwar Japanese capital structure is brought out in vivid relief.

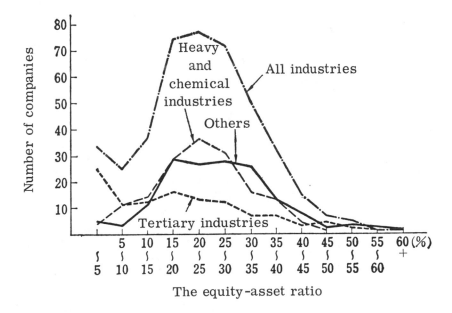

Heavy
and
chemical
industries

All industries

Others

Tertiary industries

The equity-asset ratio

Fig. 1. Distribution by the equity-asset ratio.

This basic characteristic appears also in the phenomenally
low ratios of equity to assets and of liquid assets to liquid liabilities in Japanese firms. While American, British, and West
German firms almost always obey the 50% rule of the equity-
asset ratio, the Japanese ratio, according to Table 5, is not only
as low as 20.8% but also tends to fall. As this ratio, 20.8%, is
an average value for Japanese business as a whole, it may not
necessarily be representative of Japanese business behavior.
Figure 1 shows graphically the distribution, by this ratio, of the
429 companies for which data are available among our 492 big
businesses with physical assets of more than 5 billion yen. For
all businesses, we see that the largest number of firms have the
equity-asset ratio in the range between 20 and 25%. The distribution is almost normal. The same regularity applies a fortiori
to heavy and chemical industries. The distribution for tertiary
industries has a peak lower than the average in the range between 15 and 20%. On the other hand, the distribution for other

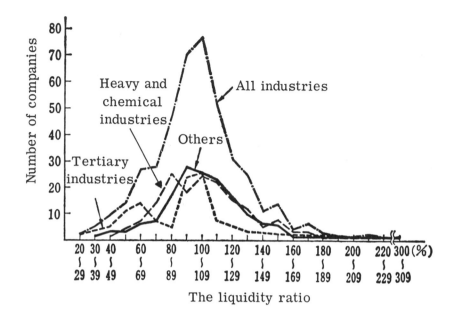

Fig. 2. Distribution by the ratio of liquid
assets to liquid liabilities.

industries has a flat top from 15 to 35%. Of the 429 companies
only 15 have the equity-asset ratio above 45%.

It is thus clear that a large number of Japanese big businesses use the equity-asset ratio of 20-25% as the rule of
thumb in raising business funds.

The bottom row of Table 5 shows that American firms observe the 200% liquidity-ratio rule. The Japanese liquidity
ratio is 108%, only half of the U.S. level. It is also lower than
the British and West German ratios. Figure 2 presents a graph
of the distribution of the 429 companies by the liquidity ratio.
For the entire sample, we see again that the largest number of
companies fall between 100 and 109%, with the distribution almost normal around this range as a peak. In the present case,
it is the tertiary-industry distribution that has the same peak
as the entire sample. The distribution for other industries has
a slightly lower peak at 90-99%. That for heavy and chemical

industries is bimodal with two peaks at 80-89% and 100-109%. Only 18 of the 429 companies have the liquidity ratio exceeding 160%.

It is thus clear that most Japanese big businesses use the liquidity ratio of 100-109% as the rule in raising funds.

The Economic Meaning of the Equity-Asset and Liquidity Ratios

In order to clarify the characteristics of the capital structure in postwar Japan, we must understand the economic significance of the 50% rule of the equity-asset ratio and the 200% rule of the liquidity ratio. In general, sources of funds for investment available to firms are: (1) internal funds (depreciation allowances and retained earnings), (2) borrowings, and (3) equity issues. The three sources are ordered according to the interests to the company.

Internal funds may appear at first sight to be costless and limited only by the amount available. However, it would be strange if the available internal funds are all invested whenever the expected rate of return of investment (Keynes' marginal efficiency of capital) is positive even in a recession. Obviously, firms must consider the opportunity cost of funds. The marginal unit of funds is invested at the sacrifice of profits that could be earned if that unit is invested elsewhere. The cost of funds is then the maximum sacrifice, or the opportunity cost. Alternatively, internal funds may be used to repay outstanding liabilities. Thus the opportunity cost of internal funds is generally regarded as equal to the prevailing market rate of interest.

The second source of funds, borrowings, apparently entails interest payments as monetary cost. In addition, it also incurs the following costs:

1) Fixed-interest debt (including bonds) has a strong cyclical effect on firms' published position of profits and dividends according to whether the rate of return on investment exceeds the interest rate or not. This effect is greater, the more debt firms

owe in relation to their equity.

2) The greater are the debt-equity ratio or the ratio of liquid assets to liquid liabilities, the more conscious both borrowers and lenders become of the risks of default. This appears to lenders as the fear of borrowers' bankruptcy and induces them to intervene in borrowers' business. Borrowers in turn are inconvenienced by restrictions placed by lenders on the freedom of conducting business.

3) In addition, these circumstances will be reflected in the stock prices. This is another kind of cost.

These costs eventually make firms go to the third source of funds, namely new equity issues, in spite of higher financing cost (including the corporation tax burden) than borrowings.

These three kinds of cost, however, are all more or less subjective. They are therefore influenced by types of business and differences in managers' conventional attitudes. As debt gets larger relative to equity, these subjective costs increase more than proportionately. Accordingly, the financial cost of borrowed funds is only slightly higher than the market interest rate up to a certain limit, but tends to increase steeply beyond this limit because of sharp rises in subjective costs. Duesenberry (8), calls this limit "a safe ratio of debt to equity capital." The sharp increases in the cost of debt beyond this limit were once called "the principle of increasing risk" by Kalecki. (9) As a result, there comes a stage where borrowings are replaced by equity issues, which are the most costly method of financing. (10)

The 50% rule of the equity-asset ratio may be taken as a quantitative expression of Duesenberry's "safe ratio of debt to equity capital." Similarly, the 200% rule of the liquidity ratio is another quantitative expression of safety.

In particular, the 200% liquidity ratio rule means that a firm must hold liquid assets, which are about twice as large as liquid liabilities, in order to get cash quickly in the event that it has to meet sudden requests for repayment of liquid liabilities. As long as this rule is observed strictly, creditors need not be disconcerted even in an emergency. In other words, this rule is necessary if a borrowing firm and a lending bank which holds claims on liquid debt of the firm are to avoid intervention and to remain independent of each other.

However, the fact that this rule has been largely disregarded in the postwar Japanese economy, with the liquidity ratio falling to only 100%, means that claimants of liquid debt of firms have to share their fate in emergencies. A debtor's bankruptcy inevitably affects the fortunes of holders of its liquid liabilities. The firm which is a debtor had to get into short-term debt in order to promote high growth, or, alternatively, high growth was made possible only by means of this type of financing. But looked at in another way, firms diligently carried out investment at the expense of their own independence. Once a financial institution makes loans beyond debtors' safe limits, it has virtually decided to share in debtors' fate and there is no alternative but for it to intervene in debtors' business affairs. Thus, the gravitation of firms toward indirect financing inevitably leads to forming a mechanism of financial dependence. To this date, the capital structure of postwar Japan, based on this mechanism, remains unchanged. It is impossible to ignore this point in discussing the characteristics of the postwar Japanese capital structure.

IV. The Forms of Company Ownership and Control

Method of Investigation

Not only are the equity-asset and liquidity ratios conspicuously low and indirect financing the rule, but share ownership by companies reached 60%. Taking note of these characteristics of the postwar Japanese capital structure, I have constructed Table 6 in an attempt to examine the various forms of business ownership and control in the 492 big businesses mentioned earlier.

First, let us explain briefly the method used in compiling this table. As already noted, this study was conducted for 465 giant corporations as of the end of 1966 (fiscal). Thus the

Forms of Ownership and Control in Corporations

Controlling ownership		Shareholding percentage (%)	Majority share-holding control		Minority share-holding control		
			90%+	50-90%	30-50%	10-30%	3-10%
Family			1	2	5	16	11
Family and related company			1	3	6	18	7
Direct control	Company — Single company	Domestic nonfinancial company	8	17	18	4	1
		Bank	0	0	0	5	3
		Life insurance	0	0	0	7	0
		Foreign-related company	4	3	2	1	0
		Subtotal	12	20	20	54	4
	Multiple companies	Domestic nonfinancial company	5	8	2	2	1
		Including financial company	0	7	9	57	17
		Foreign company only	0	1	0	1	0
		Foreign and domestic company	8	6	3	4	0
		Subtotal	13	22	14	64	18
Total			25	42	34	118	22
Managerial control			—	—	—	—	—
Government and local public bodies			1	4	1	3	0
Grand total			28	51	46	155	40
Composition (%)			6.0	11.0	9.9	33.2	8.6

Source: Compiled from the 1966 business group table. A total of 27 companies, 9 government enterprises, 9 non-joint stock special corporations, 8 life insurance companies, and 1 company for which data are unavailable are excluded from the 492 big businesses with tangible assets of 5 billion yen or more. Hence the total number of corporations is 465 in the table.

Note: Shareholding percentages of less than 10% are in principle treated as "managerially controlled" (no controlling interest group), but minority shareholder control

Table 6

with Tangible Assets of 5 Billion Yen or More

— As of the end of 1966 (fiscal) —

Managerial control	Grand total	Composition (%)		Majority shareholding control		Minority shareholding control			Managerial control	Grand total	Composition (%)
				90%+	50-90%	30-50%	10-30%	3-10%			
—	35	7.5		2	4	6	20	12	—	44	9.4
—	35	7.5		1	3	6	22	6	—	38	8.3
—	85	18.4		0	0	0	1	0	—	1	0.2
—	8	1.7		0	0	0	1	0	—	1	0.2
—	7	1.5		0	0	0	7	0	—	7	1.5
—	10	2.2	Ultimate control	5	4	3	2	0	—	14	3.0
—	110	23.8		5	4	3	11	0	—	23	4.9
—	18	3.9		} 3	20	18	73	21	—	135	29.1
—	90	9.2									
—	2	0.4		1	1	—	1	—	—	3	0.6
—	21	4.5		9	6	4	3	0	—	22	4.7
—	131	28.0		13	27	22	77	21	—	160	34.4
—	241	51.8		18	31	25	88	21	—	183	39.3
145	145	31.3		—	—	—	—	—	191	191	41.1
—	9	1.9		1	4	1	3	0	—	9	1.9
145	465	100.0		22	42	38	133	39	191	465	100.0
31.3	100			4.7	9.0	8.2	28.6	8.4	41.1	100	

is recognized in the following cases:
    (1) When family or family-related companies hold more than 3% of the shares.
    (2) When more than 3% of the shares of the company are owned by single companies or multiple companies which have strong relationships with a specific business group, when it maintains an interlocking shareholding relationship, and when it belongs to the presidents' club of the business group or when it sends out directors to other companies.

scope differs from the Berle and Means study in that it is not limited to the top 200 nonfinancial corporations. The magnitude of the economic power of these big businesses and the types of industries to which they belong have already been described in detail in Section II.

The data are mainly from corporations' officially filed statements on negotiable securities, from which the percentages of shares owned by ten largest shareowning individuals, companies, and related companies are computed. Based on these data, I apply classifications by shareholding percentage columnwise and by controlling shareowner rowwise.

To be more specific, I first classify forms of ownership and control into (1) family (ownership and) control (including both single and multiple family control), (2) family and family-related company (ownership and) control, (3) single company (ownership and) control, (4) multiple company (ownership and) control, (5) managerial control (with no controlling interest group), and (6) government or local public-body control. Furthermore, single company (ownership and) control is subdivided into domestic nonfinancial company (ownership and) control, bank (ownership and) control, life insurance company (ownership and) control, and foreign-related company (ownership and) control. Multiple company (ownership and) control is subdivided into multiple domestic nonfinancial (ownership and) control, multiple domestic company — including financial company — (ownership and) control, and multiple company — including foreign-related company — (ownership and) control. In addition to classifying controlling ownership in this way, I apply a broad three-way classification to each type of ownership, namely, majority shareholder control exceeding 50% (and subdivided within this by taking more than 90% as complete control), minority shareholder control of 10 to 50%, and managerial control when the shareholding percentage is below 10%. (Space does not permit me to publish the classification list of the firms here.) In the present study I undertake a breakdown into immediate control and ultimate control, as attempted by Berle and Means. This division is especially important for companies

which fall under company (ownership and) control. Companies
which fall under company control naturally have companies
which control them, but if the controlling companies are themselves under managerial control, then the ultimate control of
the companies in question is classified as managerial control.
When the controlling company is not under managerial control,
but under individual or company control, the company in question ultimately has either pyramid control or an interlocking
shareholding relationship. If the controlling company has foreign connections, I classify it as single foreign-related company
(ownership and) control regardless of its parent company's
ownership and control relationship, and if the controlling company is a life insurance company, it is classified in the single
life insurance company (ownership and) control row.

Results of the Study

Table 6 reads as follows. According to the figures in the direct control rows, the total for family control plus family related company control is 15.0%; company control, 51.8%; managerial control, 31.3%; and government or local public-body con-
trol, 1.9%. Company control is obviously overwhelming. Even
in the figures for ultimate control, company control makes up
39.3%, exceeding the proportion of managerial control. Moreover, majority shareholder control reaches 17.0% of this, complete control accounts for 28 companies or 6.0%. Minority
shareholder control is 51.7%, and managerial control is 31.3%.
In the figures for ultimate control, managerial control rises to
41.1%.

It has already been made clear in Table 3 that share ownership by Japanese corporations reaches 59.6%, of which financial institutions account for 32.3% with banks and trust banks
at 15.4%, life insurance companies at 11.1%, non-life insurance
companies at 4.0%, and other financial institutions at 1.8%. Second, share ownership by nonfinancial domestic companies
reached 23.1%, and that by foreign corporations, 3.0%. Securities companies accounted for a mere 1.2%. These figures surely

indicate the overwhelming importance of the business ownership form in the ownership and control of big business. It must
be noted that these are two sides of the shield.

What is the meaning of the dominance of this company ownership and control form in postwar Japanese big business, also
corroborated by the increase in share ownership by corporations? I shall present a tentative theory in section VI below.

Revival of the Trend Toward Share Concentration

Table 6 makes it clear that the holding-company control of
big businesses, which once disappeared after the dissolution of
the zaibatsu, appear in the company control form row in 25
cases (of these, 12 are single company control, and 13 are multiple company control). These companies are as follows.

Single company control (12 firms): Nippon Petrochemicals,
Tonen Petrochemicals, Yawata Chemical Industries, Hitachi
Chemical Industries, Idemitsu Petrochemicals, Hitachi Home
Electrical Appliance Sales, Toshiba Shoji, Esso Oil, Mobil
Oil, Shell Oil, Showa Electric, and Nippon IBM.

Multiple company control (13 firms): Daikyowa Petrochemicals, Babcock-Hitachi, Mitsubishi Monsanto Chemicals,
Asahi Dow, Nippon Unica (Union Carbide), Nippon Exlan Industries, Mitsubishi Acetate, General Oil Refining, Nippon Oil
Refining, Fuji Sanki Steel Tube, Matsushita Electronic Industries, Kyodo Oil, and Nippon Electronic Industries.

With the exception of such completely foreign-controlled
firms as Esso Oil, Mobil Oil, Shell Oil, and Nippon IBM, these
are all either joint concerns or subsidiary companies newly
born during the process of rapid growth. Thus, in the case of
newly established companies, even after the zaibatsu dissolution there are many with the complete company control form.
This trend cannot be ignored. The previously noted increase
in share ownership by companies and the establishment of subsidiary companies and joint concerns with the complete control

Table 7

Size Distribution of Shareowners and Shares (percent)

Total	1966 698 Firms		1970 798 Firms	
	Number of shareowners 15,797 thou.	Number of shares 79,198 mns	Number of shareowners 16,120 thou.	Number of shares 110,268 mns
Less than 100 shares	6.9	0.0	7.2	0.0
100 - 499 shares	11.4	0.6	10.9	0.4
500 - 999 shares	13.6	1.8	9.7	1.0
1,000 - 4,999 shares	58.9	21.0	58.8	16.8
5,000 - 9,999 shares	6.2	7.6	9.5	8.6
10,000 - 49,999 shares	2.5	8.4	3.3	8.1
50,000 - 99,999 shares	0.2	2.2	0.2	2.3
100,000 - 499,999 shares	0.2	10.3	0.2	7.7
500,000 - 999,999 shares	0.0	5.1	0.1	5.3
1,000,000 - 4,999,999 shares	0.1	17.9	0.1	19.3
More than 5,000,000 shares	0.0	25.1	0.0	30.5

Note: Data refer only to companies listed in the first section of stock exchanges.

Source: National Stock Exchange, Kabushiki Bumpu Jokyo Chōsa [Report on Share Distribution Status].

form explain the recent marked trend toward concentration of shares in the hands of a few large shareowners. For this trend, see Table 7, which shows the size distribution of shareowners and shares held. According to this table, although the number of shareowners only increased by 2% between 1966 and 1970, the number of shares increased by 39% during the same period, and the percentage of shares owned by large shareowners with more than five million shares rose rapidly from 25.1% in 1966 to 30.5% in 1970. This trend is clearly in contradiction with the Berle and Means thesis that share ownership tends to be dispersed as the corporate form becomes more important. There is once again a strong trend toward share concentration, shifting ownership from individuals to corporations.

V. Prewar and Postwar Business Groups

Various Forms of Company Ownership and Control

The forms of ownership and control in postwar Japanese big business were clarified in the preceding section. Compared with the individual ownership form and the managerial control form, the company (ownership and) control form is numerically overwhelming. We have verified that this is the case not only for direct control but also for ultimate control. As previously noted, subsidiary and joint companies, etc., with complete or majority shareholder control are naturally included among companies with the company control form, under ultimate control. In general, in the case of pyramid control in such a parent company-subsidiary company relationship, when we trace the control relationship we ultimately find either family ownership, managerial control, or foreign-related company control. The first is the case of the prewar zaibatsu, the second that of subsidiary companies in new industries in postwar Japan, and the last is, in many cases, that of recent multinational corporations. Recently the multinationalization and conglomeratization of American business has been striking. This is characterized by the new form of company (ownership and) control by companies. In other words, the company control form is spreading on a world scale.

Interlocking Shareholding

However, most of the company control forms under ultimate control in Table 6 are not necessarily this sort of pyramid control, parent company-subsidiary company relationship. Instead, we can see that for the majority of cases there is an interlocking shareholding relationship. I shall illustrate this relationship by taking fifteen big businesses affiliated with the Hakusui Kai, which is the Sumitomo business group presidents' club. Table 8 presents their interlocking shareholding relationship. Each entry shows the number of shares held. As is obvious, diagonal elements are zero; nondiagonal elements are almost all nonzero. (As the Sumitomo Life Insurance Co. is not itself a joint-stock company, it is removed from the rows and appears only in the shareowner column. This is why there is a nonzero value in the diagonal element for it.)

For example, the shareowners of the Sumitomo Bank (and the number of shares held by each) can be found by looking from the top to the bottom of the Sumitomo Bank column. This shows Sumitomo Life Insurance (24,198,000 shares), Sumitomo Coal Mining (1,448,000 shares), Sumitomo Metal Mining (4,592,000 shares), Sumitomo Metal Industries (19,200,000 shares), Sumitomo Electric Industries (10,560,000 shares), Sumitomo Machinery (2,816,000 shares), Nippon Electric (16,000,000 shares), Sumitomo Chemical (20,800,000 shares), Nippon Sheet Glass (14,400,000 shares), Sumitomo Cement (3,200,000 shares), Sumitomo Shoji (12,000,000 shares), and Sumitomo Warehouse (1,408,000 shares). These twelve companies account for 18.3% of all shares of the Sumitomo Bank. The bottom rows show that the corresponding ratio was 52.1% at the time of the zaibatsu dissolution and 10.2% before the take-off of rapid growth (September 1954).

On the other hand, if one wishes to find out of which Sumitomo Business-Group companies the Sumitomo Bank itself is a shareowner, one reads the Sumitomo Bank row from the left to the right. These are the Sumitomo Marine and Fire Insurance (6,300,000 shares), Sumitomo Coal Mining (3,826,000 shares), Sumitomo Metal Mining (5,461,000 shares), Sumitomo Metal Industries (76,709,000 shares), Sumitomo Electric Industries (10,125,000 shares), Sumitomo Machinery (4,575,000 shares), Nippon Electric (35,646,000 shares), Sumitomo Chemicals

Interlocking Shareholding in
(as of September 30, 1968; in 1,000

Shareowner \ Company	Sumitomo Bank	Sumitomo Trust	Sumitomo Marine and Fire Insurance	Sumitomo Coal Mining	Sumitomo Metal Mining	Sumitomo Metal Industries
Sumitomo Life Insurance	24,198	7,500	2,464	1,775	5,971	47,711
Sumitomo Bank	—	—	6,300	3,826	5,461	76,709
Sumitomo Trust	—	—	2,422	1,519	5,564	52,815
Sumitomo Marine and Fire Insurance	—	—	—	1,654	3,164	—
Sumitomo Coal Mining	1,448	1,000	1,080	—	1,079	4,977
Sumitomo Metal Mining	4,592	4,880	1,750	1,365	—	4,907
Sumitomo Metal Industries	19,200	8,000	2,150	2,797	—	—
Sumitomo Electric Industries	10,560	8,000	1,500	—	2,922	2,954
Sumitomo Machinery	2,816	2,000	800	1,056	1,299	3,585
Nippon Electric	16,000	8,000	2,850	3,936	5,286	12,909
Sumitomo Chemical	20,800	8,000	2,000	1,697	2,058	7,203
Nippon Sheet Glass	14,400	5,000	1,400	—	—	3,093
Sumitomo Cement	3,200	2,300	300	—	500	427
Sumitomo Shoji	12,800	5,600	1,500	2,101	8,500	14,870
Sumitomo Warehouse	1,408	4,060	850	—	129	1,990
Total shareholding percentage of 15 Sumitomo companies (%)	18.3	32.2	25.3	32.8	25.0	18.9
Reference — Proportion of intra-group financing as of Sept. 30, 1968 (%)	—	—	—	33.5	42.7	30.7
Reference — Shareholding percentage as of zaibatsu dissolution (%)	52.1	45.0	22.3	—	100	39.7
Reference — Shareholding percentage as of Sept. 1954 (%)	10.2	25.3	14.7	23.7	14.8	18.5

Source: Compiled from Yuka Shoken Hokokusho [Statement on Negotiable Securities], for the period ending in September 1968; reference rows, except the percent-

Table 8

the Sumitomo Business Group
shares; converted at 50-yen par value)

Sumitomo Electric Industries	Sumitomo Machinery	Nippon Electric	Sumitomo Chemical	Nippon Sheet Glass	Sumitomo Cement	Sumitomo Shoji	Sumitomo Warehouse	
19,169	6,110	34,000	46,216	5,597	7,632	7,742	3,600	
10,125	4,575	35,646	29,600	8,782	7,718	16,916	2,500	
8,989	4,920	10,439	19,433	7,758	—	7,013	2,000	
—	3,645	15,840	—	—	—	5,775	2,300	
300	1,040	1,730	1,400	—	10,969	2,600	206	
3,375	2,108	8,000	1,600	—	434	7,219	303	
2,438	2,693	6,208	4,000	—	2,218	11,468	900	
—	2,268	20,920	2,200	750	568	6,638	484	
600	—	640	2,400	600	4,294	1,500	511	
11,550	1,955	—	4,800	960	434	5,790	—	
1,688	3,000	3,840	—	500	2,166	15,016	650	
900	2,738	1,440	1,400	—	1,300	5,775	300	
200	—	300	2,000	500	—	900	—	
2,000	3,000	6,072	8,200	3,060	3,249	—	600	
505	627	1,152	600	225	87	866	—	
22.9	35.8	36.6	18.4	18.0	27.4	42.6	39.9	Overall shareholding proportion 23.7
48.0	39.2	39.3	33.5	56.8	43.8	40.5	65.4	Overall 36.0
38.3	97.2	19.8	31.5	24.3	—	—	99.8	
12.1	18.9	30.1	8.4	5.2	—	42.9	28.1	

age of intra-group financing, reproduced from my Sengo Nihon no Keizai Kiko
[Economic Mechanism of Postwar Japan] (1966), p. 228.

(29,600,000 shares), Nippon Plate Glass (8,782,000 shares), Sumitomo Cement (7,718,000 shares), Sumitomo Shoji (16,916,000 shares), and Sumitomo Warehouse (2,500,000 shares), or twelve companies in all. Symmetry is lost only in the cases of the Sumitomo Life Insurance and the Sumitomo Marine and Fire Insurance companies. Otherwise, entries are completely symmetrical. An almost complete interlocking shareholding relationship is established. This matrix form of company control or interlocking shareholding relationship was not observed before the war and cannot be found in foreign countries. This interlocking business relationship is peculiar to postwar Japanese big business. As already mentioned, it can be thought that a presidents' club (the Hakusui Kai in the case of the Sumitomo business group) has been formed as the human organization at the base of this sort of interdependent relationship of capital. Or perhaps the presidents' club was actually established as a human organization first, and gradually had to strengthen this base by consolidating the interdependent network of capital.

Interlocking Shareholding in Business Groups

There are six representatives of significant business groups having presidents' clubs as the human organizations along with interlocking shareholding relationships. They are the Mitsubishi, Sumitomo, Mitsui, Daiichi (the present Daiichi Kangyō Bank), Fuji, and Sanwa groups. Table 9 shows changes in interlocking shareholding percentages for each of these six groups.

The table clearly shows that each group has been increasing its mutual shareholding percentage. This trend has recently been accelerated. Since 1967 the Sumitomo, Daiichi, and Fuji groups, and since 1968 the Mitsubishi, Mitsui, and Sanwa groups, appear to be escalating their shareholding percentages sharply.

The shareholding percentages in one of the reference rows of Table 8 have already shown this trend for individual members of the Sumitomo business group. It is definitely shown that the shareholding interdependence was extremely high at the time of the zaibatsu dissolution, indicating a strong pyramid form of

Table 9

Changes in Interlocking Shareholding Percentages

Group	1963	1964	1965	1966	1967	1968	1969	1970
Sumitomo	14.26	15.04	15.13	15.60	16.99	18.62	19.71	20.11
Daiichi	10.18	9.44	10.26	10.58	12.62	15.84	15.66	17.19
Fuji	9.85	10.13	10.41	10.74	11.75	13.57	14.83	14.56
Mitsubishi	12.91	13.36	13.93	14.46	15.03	16.35	18.12	19.45
Mitsui	8.27	8.70	9.51	9.83	10.04	11.20	11.93	12.93
Sanwa	6.96	7.78	7.73	8.12	8.96	9.60	9.55	10.18

Note: Percentages of shares held by businesses in each group in the total shares issued by the group as a whole.

Source: Prepared from Keizai Chosa Kyokai (Economic Research Association), ed., Keiretsu no Kenkyū [Study of Business Groups] (1971). Shares held by trust banks are excluded.

company control that peaked at the Sumitomo zaibatsu holding company. Despite the dissolution of the central holding company and the liquidation of zaibatsu family shareholdings, the percentage of shares held by the old zaibatsu business group did not necessarily fall to a negligible level. A cooperative system continued in order to keep up the percentage of shares held by member firms of the group. This is evidenced when the Sumitomo group banded itself together in establishing the Sumitomo Shoji. (This sort of cooperative system was earlier noted in the Mitsui group in 1941 when it defended the Taisho Marine and Fire Insurance Company against an attempt to buy up its shares.) Not only that, but the 1953 revision of the Anti-Trust Law relaxed the limit on the share ownership by financial institutions (banks, mutual banks, trusts, insurance and securities companies) from 5% to 10%, and paved the way for new types of business combinations in the form of interlocking shareholding relationships in place of the prewar form of pyramid control. Thus the shareholding proportion, while registering a large-scale decrease as of September 1954 as compared to the zaibatsu period, still remained at 10%. The Sumitomo Shoji and the Nippon Electric even improved the shareholding proportion.

Percentages of Intra-Group Financing

A reference row of Table 8 shows the percentage of "intra-group financing" as of the end of September 1968. This percentage is the ratio of each company's borrowing from the financial institutions of the group (Sumitomo Bank, Sumitomo Trust, Sumitomo Marine and Fire Insurance, and Sumitomo Life Insurance) to its total borrowing (excluding discounted commercial papers). For the group as a whole, percentage was as high as 36%. It is believed that this type of intra-group financing started in the 1951 recession, which came as a reaction to the Korean War, when the financial institutions in the groups started to make their selective lendings more stringent. This development suggests that intra-group financing preceded interlocking shareholding in strengthening postwar Japanese business groups. Why then did this sort of process take place after the zaibatsu dissolution? Probably the failure in enacting the "Financial Company Law" during the Occupation is closely related to this evolution.

It is widely known that financial institutions were neither designated as holding companies nor included in the decentralization measures when the zaibatsu were dissolved. (However, as already mentioned, Article 11 of the Anti-Trust Law placed a limitation on the percentages of share ownership by companies conducting financial business.) On how this came about, Takeshi Watanabe, the then deputy director of the liaison office of the Ministry of Finance states: "On May 17 (1948) I met with Mr. Chamberlain of the National City Bank and 'hoped that decentralization would not apply to financial institutions.'" (11) Professor Yoshitaro Wakimura, who was a member of the Holding Company Liquidation Committee at the time, also thought that "if only we enact for banks...regulations which have very strict limits on business (such as those on amounts loaned to single companies or the prohibition of bond issues by chartered banks) as in the American banking laws, then it is not necessary for Japanese banks to be divided." (12) However, on July 30 of that year (1948) there was a formal announcement by the Holding Company Liquidation Committee to the effect that there would be no application of concentration prohibition to financial institutions. But the "Financial Company" Law, which had been considered as a prerequisite for this exclusion, has never been enacted except in its draft version. The only innovation along this line was establishing the Bank of Japan Policy Board. Thus there has been no legal "control on the concentrated lending to companies in the same group or heavy lending to single companies." (13)

Formation of Business Groups

Thus the zaibatsu dissolution measures, which placed a fairly strict control on the share ownership of the zaibatsu holding companies, added little control over loans by financial institutions as the Korean War period of economic reconstruction and then that of rapid growth followed. This fact cannot be ignored in explaining the characteristics of the capital structure in postwar Japan. Thus the failure of the "Financial Company" Law and more selective lending to intra-group firms after the Korean War prepared the way for establishing the capital structure of big business in postwar Japan.

This process brought the very low liquidity ratio and equity-assets ratio into being. Via the law of increasing risk, the intervention deepened from loans to investment and finally led to the interlocking holding of shares.

This is why we have to focus our attention on intra-group financing and interlocking shareholding on the capital side and the presidents' club and the assignment of executives to debtor firms on the human side in the process of business-group formation in postwar Japan. If we take note of these sorts of relationships, it is possible to cover a large number of business

Prewar and Postwar Capital Concentration by Industry in the
(National total =

Industry	Group / Year	Mitsui	Mitsubishi	Sumitomo	Yasuda	Big 4 zaibatsu total	National total (1 million yen)	Mitsui
				1937				
Heavy and chemical	Primary metals	1.6	1.4	6.1	—	9.1	912	3.0
	Machinery	3.1	8.1	3.2	0.5	14.9	1,311	7.6
	Chemicals	5.7	2.6	2.8	0.2	11.3	1,389	8.2
	Subtotal	3.8	4.3	3.8	0.2	12.1	3,613	6.5
Tertiary	Wholesale and retail trade	4.3	0.8	—	0.2	5.3	2,920	0.9
	Finance	4.3	7.7	3.6	8.6	24.2	1,640	4.5
	Real estate, Warehousing	2.0	1.9	9.0	3.2	16.1	635	1.7
	Land Transportation	0.6	0.7	3.5	0.6	5.4	1,278	0.8
	Marine Transportation	0.6	15.6	—	—	16.2	476	1.3
	Electricity and gas	0.4	—	0.7	1.9	3.0	2,649	0.8
	Others	—	—	—	—	—	—	—
	Subtotal	2.4	2.5	1.9	2.4	9.2	9,598	1.4
Other	Agriculture, forestry, fisheries, foodstuffs	1.6	2.1	—	—	3.7	718	4.2
	Mining	11.2	7.4	2.3	—	20.9	1,453	12.4
	Textile products	3.8	0.5	2.8	1.2	8.3	1,075	4.5
	Paper and pulp	—	2.3	—	2.6	4.9	346	—
	Glass, cement and ceramics	8.6	11.1	1.8	—	21.5	298	10.2
	Others	1.3	0.8	0.2	—	2.3	554	2.7
	Subtotal	5.6	3.9	1.6	0.5	11.6	4,444	7.4
Total by business group		3.5	3.3	2.2	1.4	10.4	17,655	4.4
Number of companies		48	42	34	34	158		89

Note:
1) Data for 1937, 1941, and 1946 from Holding Company Liquidation Committee,
Nihon no Zaibatsu to sono Kaitai [Japan's Zaibatsu and Their Dissolution]; data for
1955, 1960, and 1966 from my "Sengo Nihon Kigyo Shūdan" [Business Groups in Post-

Table 10

Former Big Four Zaibatsu Business Groups (by paid-in capital)
100; percent)

	1941					1946				
Mitsubishi	Sumitomo	Yasuda	Big 4 zaibatsu total	National total (1 million yen)	Mitsui	Mitsubishi	Sumitomo	Yasuda	Big 4 zaibatsu total	National total (1 million yen)
1.8	7.5	—	12.3	2,449	7.1	4.8	14.4	0.1	26.4	7,632
7.6	3.2	1.3	19.7	3,894	11.7	16.0	8.4	1.4	37.5	3,830
4.2	2.7	0.3	15.4	2,292	19.0	6.3	5.7	0.3	31.3	2,969
5.0	4.3	0.7	16.5	8,635	12.0	11.1	9.4	0.8	33.3	14,431
1.6	—	0.2	2.7	4,570	5.8	5.6	2.1	0.1	13.6	2,724
8.0	3.7	9.0	25.2	1,583	13.9	13.2	5.4	17.2	49.7	1,216
2.2	7.4	4.2	15.5	788	8.2	6.7	2.8	5.0	22.7	600
1.2	—	0.4	2.4	1,657	2.0	1.4	0.1	1.4	4.9	933
22.8	—	1.6	25.7	806	18.1	40.3	0.6	1.8	60.8	992
—	1.2	2.3	4.3	3,193	—	—	0.5	—	0.5	3,826
—	—	—	—	—	—	—	—	—	—	—
3.4	1.2	2.2	8.2	12,596	5.6	7.4	1.6	2.7	17.3	10,290
2.2	—	—	6.4	842	2.0	0.6	0.1	—	2.7	1,183
9.2	1.3	—	22.9	2,635	15.7	8.9	3.6	0.1	28.3	3,071
0.1	—	1.9	6.5	1,352	9.7	0.8	0.2	6.7	17.4	1,289
1.8	—	1.7	3.5	545	0.8	2.0	—	1.7	4.5	535
11.5	2.0	—	23.7	395	20.1	4.7	3.6	—	28.4	315
1.5	1.2	—	5.4	834	4.5	2.3	1.2	1.7	9.7	1,266
5.0	0.8	0.5	13.7	6,604	9.9	4.5	1.8	1.6	17.8	7,659
4.3	2.1	1.3	12.1	27,835	9.5	8.3	5.1	1.6	24.5	32,380
44	36	42	211		212	157	119	56	544	

war Japan] (unpublished). Observations after 1955 are limited to large companies
with tangible assets of more than 5 billion yen.

Industry	Group	Mitsui	Mitsubishi	Sumitomo	Fuji-Yasuda	Former Big 4 zaibatsu total	National total (100 million yen)	Mitsui
Heavy and chemical	Primary metals	1.1	–	6.6	6.6	14.3	754	1.9
	Machinery	1.0	12.6	2.2	2.2	18.0	1,146	1.9
	Chemicals	6.2	6.1	6.0	3.5	21.8	1,070	11.7
	Subtotal	2.9	7.0	4.7	3.8	18.4	2,970	4.1
Tertiary	Wholesale and retail trade	1.2	1.0	0.5	0.7	3.4	2,447	2.4
	Finance	1.7	2.4	2.0	2.3	8.4	1,165	4.1
	Real Estate, Warehousing	–	7.5	–	–	7.5	274	2.1
	Land Transportation	–	2.5	–	1.4	3.9	592	–
	Marine Transportation	8.5	21.7	17.9	–	48.1	424	4.4
	Electricity and gas	–	–	–	–	–	1,110	–
	Others	–	–	–	–	–	459	–
	Subtotal	1.4	2.8	1.7	0.8	6.7	6,470	1.9
Other	Agriculture, forestry, fisheries, foodstuffs	–	2.0	–	–	2.0	623	1.0
	Mining	15.9	13.5	6.6	–	36.0	288	15.1
	Textile products	4.9	1.3	2.2	1.3	9.7	779	–
	Paper and pulp	15.3	5.1	–	–	20.4	308	2.9
	Glass, cement and ceramics	21.1	12.7	–	10.3	44.1	243	16.6
	Others	3.8	–	7.9	0.6	12.3	522	2.2
	Subtotal	7.3	3.9	2.8	1.4	15.4	2,764	4.5
Total by business group		3.1	4.1	2.7	1.6	11.5	12,205	4.1
Number of companies		20	19	13	10	62		24

Notes:
2) National totals of paid-in capital by industry for 1937, 1941, and 1946 from HCLC, op. cit. For 1955, 1960, and 1966, national totals of paid-in capital by industry from Ministry of Finance, Annual Corporate Enterprise Statistics, plus the total for the finance industry, due to the Ministry of Finance.

Japanese Big Business Structure 329

Table 10 (continued)

1960					1966					
Mitsubishi	Sumitomo	Fuji-Yasuda	Former Big 4 zaibatsu total	National total (100 million yen)	Mitsui	Mitsubishi	Sumitomo	Fuji-Yasuda	Former Big 4 zaibatsu total	National total (100 million yen)
0.4	7.5	10.2	20.0	3,862	1.5	0.9	7.3	9.2	18.9	9,409
12.7	5.8	0.6	21.0	4,670	2.1	11.1	6.5	0.6	20.3	11,950
10.6	6.7	5.9	34.9	2,527	16.7	13.9	8.7	3.9	43.2	6,882
7.9	6.6	5.2	23.8	11,058	5.4	8.4	7.3	4.3	25.4	28,241
2.7	2.8	1.1	9.0	4,452	2.4	2.8	3.1	2.0	10.3	9,777
5.1	4.6	5.0	18.8	2,187	3.6	7.1	4.5	6.4	21.6	4,987
8.5	–	–	10.6	608	2.9	13.6	–	0.6	17.1	1,963
2.5	5.8	1.3	9.6	1,829	0.8	8.1	7.8	4.0	20.7	4,280
3.9	1.9	1.9	12.1	1,244	9.2	13.0	3.4	5.2	30.8	1,424
–	–	–	–	2,741	0.4	–	0.4	0.2	1.0	6,799
3.8	1.2	–	5.0	1,062	–	–	–	1.0	1.0	2,858
2.9	2.6	1.5	8.9	14,123	2.1	4.4	2.9	2.6	12.0	32,088
2.3	0.7	3.9	7.9	1,522	1.0	9.1	–	4.1	14.2	3,357
12.2	7.2	–	34.5	802	10.5	9.6	5.9	–	26.0	1,978
2.6	2.9	1.9	7.4	1,171	6.6	11.8	–	1.1	19.5	2,084
3.3	3.1	–	9.3	690	18.9	8.3	5.6	2.0	34.8	1,198
12.5	3.5	6.9	39.5	721	10.7	15.9	8.3	5.6	40.5	1,865
1.6	2.7	–	6.5	2,505	1.4	2.8	4.3	2.8	11.3	6,919
4.3	2.9	1.8	13.5	7,412	5.2	7.6	3.6	2.8	19.2	17,405
4.9	4.0	2.8	15.8	32,593	4.0	6.6	4.7	3.2	18.5	77,731
30	30	18	102		40	56	39	36	171	

3) The reporting dates were April of the year stated for 1937 and 1941; for 1946, the date at which each zaibatsu was designated as a holding company; for 1955, 1960, and 1966, the end of each fiscal year.

groups with strong or weak ties clustered around member firms of the presidents' clubs.

That the business groups themselves are positively aware of these points can be ascertained, for example, in the following statement in the May 1970 issue of the Mitsubishi Group Monthly, which the Mitsubishi Publicity Committee (41 member companies) issues in order to strengthen the family conciousness of Mitsubishi group members: "Compared with the prewar Mitsubishi zaibatsu, the connections within the present Mitsubishi group can be said to be comparatively loose. But there are fairly tight cooperative relationships among member companies in financial and personnel affairs, as well as in material and spiritual aspects. These cooperative relationships, such as mutual shareholding, the exchange of executives and personnel, and the founding of the 'Friday Club' [Mitsubishi presidents' club], show the family consciousness and feeling of affinity among the presently more than 300,000 group employees."

Needless to say, in the postwar Japanese economy the patterns of ties from business to business are not necessarily only a connecting relationship via this financial route. Besides this, there are technical relationships as seen in the combinats, and there are also connecting relationships that flow between productive factors and products and distributional connections via sales companies, wholesalers, and department stores. Even limiting them to capital relationships, the orthodox pyramid form of parent company-subsidiary company control also exists. The Nippon Steel Group, the Kobe Steel Manufacturing Group, the Toyota Group, the Hitachi Group, the Toshiba Group, the Matsushita Group and so on are all this type of business group. However, it is hard to say that these groups are especially new. On the contrary, connecting relationships of the type typically seen among the old zaibatsu business groups after the zaibatsu dissolution have many noteworthy properties as a new form of big business in postwar Japan.

The Economic Power of the Former
Big Four Zaibatsu Business Groups

Table 10 measures the postwar economic power of business groups, in particular the former big four zaibatsu business groups, with the new capital structure which has appeared in postwar Japan. According to this table, the economic power of the former big four zaibatsu business groups declined for a while after the zaibatsu dissolution but since recovered gradually, and by the end of 1966 the combined economic power of the four groups (171 companies) reached 18.5%. This surpassed the 1941 level and approached the 1946 level at the time of the zaibatsu dissolution. To be sure, their economic power at 1946, namely the capital concentration ratio of 24.5%, must be a considerable overstatement much above the normal level because companies under the control of these four zaibatsu groups were enumerated as completely as possible (witness that as many as 544 companies were listed in 1946), while the national total of paid-up capital was at a particularly low level owing to business inactivity just after the war. If this conjecture is correct, the economic power of the former big four zaibatsu groups at the end of 1966 must have almost reached the prewar level.

Comparing the prewar and postwar total capital concentration ratios by business group in the second row from the bottom, the rankings were Mitsui, Mitsubishi, Sumitomo, and Yasuda before the war. In the postwar period, the Mitsubishi replaced the Mitsui. The more recent rankings are Mitsubishi, Sumitomo, Mitsui, and Fuji-Yasuda. This change corresponds perfectly to the change in rankings of the big four business groups in the heavy and chemical industry sector. (14)

VI. Unification of Ownership and Control in Companies
— Who Owns Big Business ?

Capital Structure of Business Groups

We have found that the former big four zaibatsu business

groups had economic power already in 1966 comparable with the prewar level, accounting for 18.5% of the paid-in capital of all joint-stock companies. In order to clarify the capital structure of the former big four zaibatsu business groups, in which such great economic strength is concentrated, let us examine the Sumitomo business group again as a typical example.

First, we will look at the Sumitomo Light Metal Industries, Ltd., a company in the Sumitomo business group. The company is engaged mainly in aluminum and copper-rolling. It was founded in March 1951 as a subsidiary of the Sumitomo Metal Industries, Ltd. Accordingly, the latter, as the parent company, owns 27.5% of total shares of the former. This company's ten largest shareowners are listed in the right-hand column of Table 11.

As is clear therein, shareowners that follow Sumitomo Metals, the parent company, are the Sumitomo business group financial institutions and then the Sumitomo Shoji. Looking next at the ten largest shareowners of the Sumitomo Shoji in the same table, we find that all of them are members of the Sumitomo business group presidents' club (Hakusui Kai). Of course, the Sumitomo Shoji is also a member of the club. (The Sumitomo Light Metals is not a member, being a subsidiary of the Sumitomo Metals, which is a member.) Furthermore, the ten largest shareowners in the Sumitomo Bank, the top shareowner of the Sumitomo Shoji, which are shown in the left-hand column of the table, all belonged, in the broad sense of the term, to the Sumitomo business group. (15)

Note that no individual shareowners appear in the list of the ten largest shareowners of these three Sumitomo group firms. Apparently, ownership and control of big business has shifted from individuals to corporations. We have already affirmed this in our study of 465 big businesses (see Table 6). In addition, Table 11 clearly reveals that each of these Sumitomo group companies is not only directly but also ultimately under the ownership and control of the Sumitomo group. This fact shows that no matter how thoroughly we trace shareownership, it only shifts around within the Sumitomo-group companies.

Table 11

Ten Largest Shareowners in Three Firms of the Sumitomo Business Group,
as of March 31, 1967 (percent)

Sumitomo Bank		Sumitomo Shoji		Sumitomo Light Metals	
Shareowner	Share-holding proportion	Shareowner	Share-holding proportion	Shareowner	Share-holding proportion
Sumitomo Life Insurance	3.13	Sumitomo Bank	8.06	Sumitomo Metal Industries	27.50
Matsushita Electric	2.91	Sumitomo Chemical	7.15	Sumitomo Bank	8.08
Sumitomo Chemical	2.91	Sumitomo Metals	5.46	Sumitomo Trust Bank	6.38
Asahi Chemical	2.23	Sumitomo Life Insurance	3.67	Sumitomo Life Insurance	3.83
Sumitomo Metal Industries	2.23	Sumitomo Metal Mining	3.44	Sumitomo Shoji	3.67
Nippon Electric	2.23	Sumitomo Trust Bank	3.33	Nippon Industrial Bank	1.79
C. Itoh & Co.	2.01	Sumitomo Electric Industries	3.16	Nippon Securities	1.72
Nippon Sheet Glass	2.01	Nippon Electric	2.76	Sumitomo Marine and Fire Insurance	1.67
Kubota Iron	1.97	Sumitomo Marine and Fire Insurance	2.75	Sumitomo Chemical	1.63
Marubeni-Iida Co.	1.96	Nippon Sheet Glass	2.75	Nippon Life Insurance	1.14
10 shareowners total	23.59	10 shareowners total	42.52	10 shareowners total	57.41
Total shares outstanding	448 million	Total shares outstanding	140 million	Total shares outstanding	112 million

Source: Yūka Shoken Hōkokusho [Statement on Negotiable Securities].

In short, interlocking shareholding dominates the Sumitomo group.

Table 8 above also shows this sort of relationship in the form of a matrix of fifteen companies which belong to the presidents' club (Hakusui Kai). In these we can discover the important characteristics of postwar Japanese big business, especially the former zaibatsu business groups.

Interlocking Shareholding and Managerial Control

What is the interlocking shareholding relationship? This is nothing but a relationship in which Company A is an important shareowner in Company B and, at the same time, Company B is an important shareowner in Company A. If this form of in-direct company control is dominant in postwar Japanese big business, then the managerial control is certainly not a valid explanation.

Berle and Means pointed out that the adoption of the corpo-rate system expands the scale of the management unit and in-evitably disperses share ownership, which in turn makes it possible for a minimum share ownership to control productive assets, eventually establishing managerial control, that is, "ownership of wealth without appreciable control, and control of wealth without appreciable ownership" as "the logical out-come of corporate development." So they finally predicted: "It is conceivable — indeed it seems almost essential if the corporate system is to survive — that the 'control' of the great corporations should develop into a purely neutral technocracy, balancing a variety of claims by various groups in the commu-nity and assuming to each a portion of the income stream on the basis of public policy rather than private cupidity." (16) This is representative of the views supporting "managerial control."

Tycoon Capitalism and Managerial Control

The thesis of managerial control is that the technocracy,

completely "neutral" toward the ownership of capital, becomes
the corporate control mechanism. Unlimited dispersion of
share ownership is necessary for this to happen, and Berle and
Means were confident that the trend would continue. In this
case, what Berle and Means had in mind is the extinction of
large individual shareowners. (17)

The typical nineteenth-century enterprise unit was owned by
individuals or a small group of persons; it was managed by
owners themselves or by persons directly appointed by them.
The scale of the enterprise was determined by the personal
wealth of the individuals in direct control. In short, ownership
and control of the enterprise were unified in individuals. Here
the capitalist existed as a literal personification of capital.
Even after the corporate system was established, there were
"tycoon"types of capitalists, for example, the Japanese zaibatsu,
the J. P. Morgan firm, and the Rockefeller family. Baran and
Sweezy argued in their Monopoly Capital thus: These tycoons
did not intend for their funds to be tied for long even to their
own corporations. The majority of corporate assets were other
people's money, and they mobilized this money freely, not for
the profit of others, but for their own. Besides methods such
as embezzlement, fraud, and buying up, their own greatest interests were the capital gains to be realized by buying stocks
cheap and selling them dear. These aims could sometimes be
advanced by setting up companies, and sometimes by driving
them into bankruptcy.

Berle and Means felt that the "tycoon" type of individual
shareowners will disappear as share ownership is dispersed.
Certainly in the Japanese case the Zaibatsu dissolution seems
to have artificially and, in a certain sense, drastically established the conditions for managerial control by dispersing the
shares of the "tycoon" type shareowners. As a matter of fact,
when the storm of official purges blew in the financial world,
"those who graduated from the university curriculum at about
1921 with solid three-year training in the economics depart-
ments of the Imperial Universities or Tokyo Commercial College were left unscathed because they had not yet reached

'purgeable' posts. Generally, those who were purged studied law or political science with no education in economics in universities earlier." This brought an unexpected result of "appointing and promoting competent fiftyish people to the executive positions." It paved the way for managerial control as far as objective human conditions were concerned. (18)

However, the differences between "tycoons" and new managers are that the former rendered the utmost loyalty to themselves and their families, while the latter are attached to organizations (big business) which represent them, and they render loyalty to the organizations. To the former the corporation is merely a means to wealth, but to the latter the pursuit of the company's profit becomes an economic and ethical goal. (19)

The Collapse of Managerial Control

The managerial control by managers, who are "company men dedicated to the progress of the company," is completely "neutral" from ownership of capital if and only if the corporation itself is "neutral" from capital. This is why Berle and Means anticipated the unlimited dispersion of stock ownership. However, the fact is, as we have already verified, that the corporation itself is a shareholder of other companies and is itself also owned by other companies.

By way of an experiment, we may classify the ten largest shareowners of each of the 466 corporations with more than 5 billion yen in tangible assets in 1966. Table 12 shows that corporate shareholding is as much as 92.7% of the total. Moreover, financial institutions account for 54.6%. Thus Japanese corporate shareowners are strongly tied to financial relationships.

The fact that corporations to which managers are expected to be loyal are themselves dominantly owned by other single or multiple company shareowners which are tied together through financial or business group relationships is at variance with the Berle and Means premise. It suggests that companies are by no means "neutral" from private capital. This

Table 12

Breakdown of Ten Largest Shareowners (percent)

Corporate shareowners		92.7
Financial institutions	54.6	
Banks	19.9	
Trusts	10.0	
Life insurance	18.0	
Non-life insurance	6.8	
Securities companies	13.2	
Nonfinancial corporations	23.1	
Government	0.5	
Foreign companies	1.3	
Individual shareowners		7.3
Total		100.0

Note: Corporations with more than five billion yen in tangible assets as of the end of 1966 (fiscal).

Source: Prepared from Yūka Shoken Hōkokusho [Statement on Negotiable Securities].

is not all. The same fact indicates that the more loyalty man-agers have for the company, the more they must show their loyalty to those corporations which are shareowners of the company. What must be noted here is that in the case when, as on the Berle and Means premise, shares of a corporation are dispersed and there are no controlling shareholders — that is, when managerial control in the true sense is established, to the extent that this company is the major shareowner of a subsid-iary company — the managers are not just managers but are "company men" who must also swear loyalty to a company which functions as a shareowner. When the company to which the manager "belongs, and through which he represents him-self" itself owns and controls other companies, how can the

manager be "neutral" from capital, "balancing a variety of
claims by various groups in the community" and acting "on the
basis of public policy rather than private cupidity"? This type
is characteristically observed in a multinational business
which has complete or majority control of foreign subsidiaries
or a conglomerate, a form which is in fashion in America.
There are many cases which prove that these managers are
not afraid of reigning over subsidiary companies as if they
were "tycoon" shareowners. These examples prove that it is
incorrect to think that managerial control is neutral from capital. The case of big European and American business is one
in which accumulations of retained earnings are so large so as
to not only free them from financial institutions but also provide them with surpluses over and above what they need for
their own investment. These surpluses are naturally used to
purchase other businesses. This is worthy of notice as a new
trend of big business.

"Personification of the Corporation" and "Incorporation of Capital"

In an attempt to deny the personification of capital, the managerial control thesis pushed forward "company men" = managers as the personification of the corporation. But the thesis
misses an important fact, namely that the corporation to which
the managers pledge their loyalty, inasmuch as it is a private
entity, will inevitably follow the direction of capital that attempts to own and control other companies as its own retained
earnings are amassed into excess funds, and that the managers
as "company men" have no power to resist it. Berle and Means
saw the dispersion of individual ownership as depersonification
of capital and, on the other hand, assumed the establishment of
managerial control to be the personification of the corporation.
But their logic seems to have completely overlooked the possibility that corporations themselves become shareowners.
    The reality in postwar Japan is that company ownership by
companies is the rule. In other words, capital is progressively

incorporated. At the same time, the corporation is itself per-
sonified (through business leadership by managers who are
"company men" devoted to the progress of the company). To
represent this change somewhat schematically, we can perhaps
say that we have progressed from the unity of ownership and
control in individuals to the unity of ownership and control by
companies passing through an intermediate stage of the dispersion of individual ownership and managerial control. This
trend is also seen in the United States and in England (e.g.,
the rise of institutional investors, of multinational corporations,
and of conglomerates), but is especially conspicuous in Japanese big business after the zaibatsu dissolution.

Problems of Business Leadership

There is a final matter which must be touched upon. This is
the fact that unity of ownership and control by companies is not
inconsistent with business leadership by managers. Rather,
business leadership of "company men" loyal to the company
gives direction, orientation, and coordination to the company.
The company does not exist without them. But, even so, the
company is the master, and the managers only servants. As
Paul Sweezy said, the tycoon commanded his corporation from
above, but the manager is within, and is controlled by the corporation. (20) Moreover, the company aims to maintain im-
mortal life as a going concern, but managers have only a fixed
term of office. They are always ephemeral and, in this sense,
only a group of transients as far as the company is concerned.
Accordingly, there must be power somewhere to hire and fire
these managers. Formally speaking, such power rests with the
shareholders' meeting, but as a matter of fact it is relegated
to a certain person, among the managers, empowered with special authority. This is usually the company president. In Japan,
his authority is particularly strong. When President Makita of
Mitsubishi Heavy Industries died suddenly in 1971, presidential
will-making became a topic of conversation in the financial world.
This famous episode illustrates the president's power vividly.

In the United States, too, it is said that elections to choose officers at shareholders' meetings are really only formalities and the directors are always selected by the top officials. There is strong evidence of this. (21)

In the Japanese case, it is the presidents' club or directors sent out by shareowning corporations who have the authority to hire and fire the president. For example, in the recent Toyo Kogyo presidential succession affair, the statement of President Hotta of the Sumitomo Bank, the major bank of the company, that the bank would have no objection to the promotion of Vice President Matsuda so long as the company itself decided on it served reportedly as a deciding vote in his promotion to the presidency. (22) Thus presidents' clubs have come to be organized not only more or less naturally but also inevitably in the remarkable postwar Japanese big business of interlocking shareholding relationships because the "unity of ownership and control by companies" requires a human organization that serves as an agent in the control function, apart from the everyday business leadership.

The Danger of "Private Corporation Dictatorship"

The coexistence of unity of ownership and control by companies and business leadership by "company men" means that business exists for the sake of its own growth and enrichment. What is portrayed here is the union of private-corporation dictatorship and company bureaucracy. The company is ordinarily thought to belong to its shareholders, employees, consumers, and society (see the earlier statement of the president of the Daishōwa Paper Company). However, the foregoing analysis makes it clear that the company only exists for its own growth and enrichment. This is why the company ignores the shareholders' meeting while respecting the presidents' club and the board of directors. The company also stands firm in the maintenance of oligopoly pricing and does not pass on productivity increases to consumers. Furthermore, it does not consent to employee wage raises without first raising its administered prices and, as seen in the case of the Chisso Corporation, it is eager to shirk corporate responsibility for pollution.

In the opening section I touched on the trial of the Yawata Iron and Steel for its political contributions and pointed out the danger of recognizing the social reality of a company's independence as a political entity apart from natural persons and of permitting it "freedom of political action." However, as is clear in the foregoing analysis, if a company does not belong to its shareholders, employees, consumers, or society, but exists solely for its own growth and enrichment, then the meaning of the Supreme Court decision is important. It seems that we have actually recognized in Japan that government of the people, by the people, and for the people is now becoming government by companies for companies.

On the other hand, the recent rise in Japan of movements of consumers against administered prices, of residents against industrial pollution, of single-share owners who bring these matters to shareowners' meetings, etc., are all intuitive reactions of people who have seen through the basic character of postwar Japanese big business. So long as we are agnostic of any doctrine that proclaims business as fundamentally good, we should regard these movements as feedback movements which, in opposition to private corporate dictatorship, pursue the remaining possibilities of restoring democracy.

Notes

1) See Fusae Ichikawa, "Saikōsai Hanketsu to Seiji Shikin no Jittai" [The Supreme Court Decision and the Realities of Political Contributions], Sekai, October 1970.

2) E. T. Penrose, The Theory of the Growth of the Firm (1959).

3) In the words of Keisuke Idemitsu in Asahi Shimbun, ed., Seitō to Habatsu [Parties and Cliques], 1968, p. 195.

4) Berle and Means, p. 66.

5) What is meant by control here is the holding of the power to select and change managers; it does not mean leadership of

the real management. It is assumed that business leadership, as the supervision, orientation, and coordination of business, is exercised by the top management composed of specialist managers. Accordingly, the unification of ownership and control in companies and business leadership by specialist managers are complementary to each other. That is, a big business in the currently prevalent form is a composite of the ownership and control of wealth by the company itself and the business leadership by managers (or the technostructure) with neither ownership nor control.

6) See, for example, T. Mito and H. Masamoto, "Waga Kuni Dai Kigyō ni okeru Shoyū to Shihai" [Ownership and Control in Japanese Big Business], Soshiki Kagaku [Organizational Science], Fall and Winter issues, 1969.

7) As to why reproducible tangible assets are used, see my "Kigyō Shudanhyō Bunseki no Igi to Hōhō" [Significance and Method of the Analysis of Business-Group Tables], in S. Tsuru, ed., Atarashii Seiji-keizaigaku o Motomete [In Search of a New Political Economy], vol. I (1966).

8) J. S. Duesenberry, Business Cycles and Economic Growth (1958).

9) M. Kalecki, Essays in the Theory of Economic Fluctuations (1939).

10) According to the availability hypothesis of F. Modigliani and M. H. Miller, the capital structure of a business can be explained better by the availability of funds than by the difference between the costs of borrowings and new equity issues. However, in the present study, I rely on the relative cost hypothesis which explains the capital structure by differences in financing costs on the basis of the present corporate tax system.

11) Takeshi Watanabe, Senryōka no Nihon Zaisei Oboegaki [Notes on Japanese Finance Under the Occupation], 1966, p. 140.

12) Yoshio Ando, ed., Shōwa Keizai-shi e no Shōgen [Testimony to Shōwa Economic History], Vol. 2, 1966, p. 192.

13) Ibid., Vol. 2, p. 192.

14) For a detailed comparison of the prewar zaibatsu and

postwar business groups, refer to my Sengo Nihon no Keizai Kikō [Economic Mechanism of Postwar Japan] (1966), Supplement II, "Keiretsu to Zaibatsu no Idō" [Differences Between Groups and Zaibatsu].

15) For the basis for this judgment, refer to my "Kigyō Shūdan-hyō Bunseki no Igi to Hōhō" [Significance and Methods of the Analysis of Business-Group Tables], in S. Tsuru, ed., Atarashii Seiji-keizai-gaku o motomete [In Search of a New Political Economy], Vol. I (1966).

16) Berle and Means, pp. 312-13.

17) For complete "neutrality" not only from ownership of capital but also from borrowings, corporations must repay debt to financial institutions and obtain their own necessary funds by internal retentions of earnings in order to be completely independent of financial institutions. These conditions have already been attained in Europe and America, as is clear in Table 5. However, in the Japanese case, they have not yet materialized.

18) See the statement by Yoshitaro Wakimura in Shōwa Keizaishi e no Shōgen [Testimony to Shōwa Economic History], Final volume, p. 184.

19) See Baran and Sweezy, Monopoly Capital.

20) Ibid.

21) See, e.g., M. Mintz and J. S. Cohen, America, Inc. (1971), p. 41.

22) Mainichi Shimbun, November 26, 1970.

9

THE MEASUREMENT OF INTERFIRM RELATIONSHIPS

Yusaku Futatsugi *

An Approach to Business Group Analysis**

I. Preface

As the Japanese economy is moving toward oligopolistic structure under liberalization of capital, we witness lively discussions about business groups such as Mitsui, Mitsubishi, and Sumitomo. Apart from topical discussions, the analysis of these business groups presents an important problem to economics, since business grouping is a salient feature of Japan's productive structure. We can, of course, count several points which should be studied in connection with business groups,

*Yusaku Futatsugi, "Kigyo kan kankei no sokutei." Kikan Riron Keizagaku (Economic Studies Quarterly), August 1969, pp. 37-49. Translated and reprinted with the permission of the author and the publisher. Translated by Thomas W. Cleaver.

This translation originally appeared in Japanese Economic Studies, II (Fall 1973), 62-89. See the author's book, Nihon no Kigyo Shudan [Japan's Business Groups] (Tokyo: Toyo Keizai Shimpo Sha, 1976).

**This study is based on my report at the 1968 Western Section Meeting of the Japanese Association of Theoretical Economics. In preparing this final version, I have received advice and assistance from many persons. Moreover, I have made some corrections and revisions according to comments by a referee of this journal. I express my heartfelt gratitude to all of them.

such as their earnings based on financial analysis or their role in the circular flows and reproductive structure of the Japanese economy. In this paper, however, we examine business groups by inquiring into what firms belong to which business groups and how they are tied together in forming these groups. In other words, we focus on the associative relationships among firms in our analysis of business groups. We think that this is a basic point that precedes all analysis of business groups.

Broadly speaking, there have been two methods of measuring these interfirm associative relationships. The first of them takes the interlocking share ownership as an indicator. It goes without saying that it is the most orthodox method of analyzing corporations' interdependence relations. Needless to say, the prewar zaibatsu made full use of this type of interfirm share ownership.

However, the rapidity of postwar economic growth, which has centered on investment expansion, is accompanied by a dispro-portionate increase in business debt. Accordingly, it has come to be thought that interfirm relationships can be more accurate-ly measured in terms of debt rather than equity. This is the second method of measuring interfirm relationships. However, this method is defective in that it uses only the relationships between financial institutions and nonfinancial institutions and not those among nonfinancial institutions.

In other words, the first method is orthodox but ignores the realities of interfirm relationships in Japan. On the other hand, the second, although it reflects the realities, lacks an overall viewpoint. In this sense, either method provides only a partial or particular theory and not a general one.

Moreover, these methods are both limited to handling only direct interfirm relationships. They are both powerless in analyzing their indirect aspects. (1)

In investigating interfirm relationships, their indirect as-pects have to be analyzed for the following reasons. Assume that there are three companies, A, B, and C. A has majority ownership of B's shares and B is a majority owner of C. Must we conclude that, in this case, there is no associative relationship between A and C? Further, if C owns shares of A, how should we view the associative relationship among these three companies? It is not possible to answer these kinds of questions unless we go beyond direct interfirm relationships. In particular, the postwar antitrust law not only prohibited the establishment of holding companies but also restricted a financial institution from owning more than 10% of outstanding equity of any single company in order to prevent financial institutions from functioning as de facto holding companies. The result has been the formation of business groups through interlocking ownership of shares by a number of firms, including banks. Consequently, we must consider not only direct but indirect ties in order to understand interfirm relationships. Clearly, the consideration of these indirect relationships will bring out a new viewpoint in the measurement of interfirm relationships.

The purpose of this study is to present a method which will correct the defects of existing methods with regard to the measurement of interfirm relationships, to carry out measurement of interfirm relations, according to this method, and to reveal significant characteristics of Japanese business groups.

II. Method of Measuring Interfirm Relationships

Our measurements are based on balance sheets of individual firms. Interlocking shareholding and lending-borrowing relationships have something in common in that they both reflect interfirm flow-of-funds relationships. It is the balance sheet that shows these capital flow relationships comprehensively.

Here, we focus on the capital plus liabilities accounts of the balance sheet. As is well known, they show sources of each firm's total assets, namely, who owns the equity of the firm. We have a balance equation for the balance sheet of firm i

$$\sum_j X_{ij} + E_i + G_i + D_i = S_i \quad (i = 1,\ldots,n) \tag{1}$$

where X_{ij} is firm i's liabilities and capital owed to firm j, that is, the portion of the total assets of firm i to which firm j holds claims; E_i is the surplus of firm i, G_i is the indebtedness of firm i to domestic individuals, foreigners, etc. (such as shares held by individuals); D_i is the outstanding deposits of financial institutions; S_i is total assets; and n is the total number of firms. D_i is positive for financial institutions and zero for non-financial firms.

The coefficient a_{ij} is defined as

$$a_{ij} = X_{ij}/S_j \quad (i, j = 1, \ldots, n), \tag{2}$$

that is, firm j provides firm i with funds, in one form or another, equal to a fixed proportion a_{ij} of its total assets. We can call this coefficient the interfirm flow-of-funds coefficient. Thus, equation (1) can be expressed in matrix form as

$$AS + E + D + G = S \tag{3}$$

where A is an $n \times n$ square matrix, and the others are all column vectors of nth order. By assuming that E, D, and G are exogenous variables, we can carry on the analysis as follows:

First, based on this equation, we compute

$$(I-A)^{-1} D^k = S^h. \tag{4}$$

D^k is a column vector with zero elements except for the element representing outstanding deposits of bank k. (2) This calculation shows how much of total assets of individual firms emanates from outstanding deposits of bank k after the completion of the infinite sequence starting from the initial flow of funds to nonfinancial firms in the form of bank loans and share ownership and moving to other firms via the flow-of-funds coefficients. This analysis gives an essential viewpoint to the analysis of business groups such as Mitsui and Mitsubishi, which are formed around financial institutions, and to the analysis of influence of government-related financial institutions on nonfinancial firms. In such cases, however, rather than presenting the absolute amount (S^h) of individual firms' assets which depend on D^k, it would be more useful for the purpose at hand to compute its ratio to total assets. Thus,

$$p_{ih} = S_i^h / S_i \tag{5}$$

where S_i^h is the ith element of S^h. We call this coefficient the "total asset dependence coefficient" of firm i on outstanding deposits of bank k.

Similar calculations can be performed for each of the exogenous variables E^m and G^p in place of D^h. These would show how much of the total assets of each firm depends on other firms' surplus and equities held by individuals and foreign firms.

We must take note of coefficients b_{ij} of the inverse matrix $(I-A)^{-1}$. These coefficients show how much of the assets of firm i depends directly and indirectly on each unit of firm j's exogenous variables. Thus these coefficients make the following three analyses possible in investigating general interfirm relationships, except for financial institutions.

The first of these makes clear the degree of linkage between any pair of individual firms. Needless to say, it is necessary to examine individual elements b_{ij} of the inverse matrix. However, the more numerous firms under study are, the more cumbersome it becomes to examine individual entries of the inverse matrix. Therefore, we compute the coefficients

$$b_{ij}^* = b_{ij} + b_{ji} \qquad (6)$$

and investigate the degree of interfirm linkage based on these b_{ij}^*. Clearly, these coefficients b_{ij}^* show the degree of association between firms i and j without regard to direction. Thus, we will call this coefficient the "coefficient of interfirm linkage." Based on these coefficients, we will clarify the relationships between individual firms.

The second and third methods of analysis by using the inverse matrix coefficients demonstrate general interfirm relationships from a more comprehensive point of view by investigating the influence of a certain firm on all other firms and, conversely, the influence it receives from all other firms. These can be found by calculating the column sum of the inverse matrix coefficients

$$B_j = \sum_{i \neq j} b_{ij} \qquad (7)$$

and the row sum

$$\gamma_i = \sum_{j \neq i} b_{ij}. \tag{8}$$

First, the column sum B_j shows how much direct and indirect influences one unit of firm j's exogenous variables has on the total assets of all other firms. In this sense, we can call this coefficient the "influence coefficient" of firm j.

On the other hand, the row sum γ_i shows to what degree one unit of the exogenous variables of all firms other than firm i influences directly and indirectly the total assets of firm i. So, generally speaking, if a certain firm's total assets are large, then its coefficient γ_i also tends to be large. Therefore, it is not adequate to compare directly the γ_i for the purpose of measuring each firm's susceptibility to influence. Here let us divide these coefficients by total assets. Thus,

$$\gamma_i^* = \gamma_i / S_i. \tag{9}$$

We will call this coefficient γ_i^* the "influence susceptibility coefficient."

Thus far we have discussed methods of measuring interfirm relationships, principally on the basis of flows of funds among firms. These methods, however, are defective in that they cannot distinguish between whether interfirm flows of funds are as liquid as interfirm credits or more fixed like interlocking shareholding or long-term loan-debt relationships — in other words, whether they merely reflect interfirm transactions or represent close connections of capital. Since business groups are collections of firms joined by rather tight elements of mutual holding of capital or long-term debt relationships, rather than merely groups of firms tied by transactions, it is necessary to distinguish between the two when analyzing business groups.

This distinction can be taken into account by modifying our methods as follows. First, we divide the X_{ij}, which show direct interfirm relationships, into long-term fixed items Y_{ij} (more specifically, shareholding, long-term debt, etc.) and interfirm credits Z_{ij}. Then, our balance equation, (1), becomes

$$\sum_j Y_{ij} + \sum_j Z_{ij} + E_i + G_i + D_i = S_i \quad (i = 1,\ldots, n). \tag{10}$$

Further, if firm j provides firm i with a fixed proportion, c_{ij}, of its total assets in the form of fixed liabilities and another fixed proportion, h_{ij}, in the form of interfirm credits, we can define the two coefficients $\underline{(3)}$

$$c_{ij} = Y_{ij}/S_j \quad (i, j = 1,\ldots, n) \tag{11}$$

$$h_{ij} = Z_{ij}/S_j \quad (i, j = 1,\ldots, n) \tag{12}$$

It follows, then, that equation (4) becomes

$$(I - C - H)^{-1} D^h = S^h. \tag{13}$$

Considering the propagation process, this equation can be broken down into two equations:

$$(I - H)(I - C - H)^{-1} D^h = MD^h \tag{14}$$

and

$$H(I - C - H)^{-1} D^h = ND^h. \tag{15}$$

The former represents the fixed part and the latter the liquid part (interfirm credit) of each firm's total assets which depend ultimately on outstanding deposits of bank k. Then, the analytical method described up to now on the basis of equation (4) can be used exactly the same way on the basis of equation (14). At the same time, loan-debt relationships arising from current transactions can be analyzed in principle by referring to equation (15); the method so far described can be used in the same form.

However, we must note from an empirical point of view that the method cannot be applied as is. This is because it is impossible to find actual interfirm credit conditions from available data sources. Of the two matrices in our basic equation (10), Y is available, but Z cannot be extracted from existing sources. Thus, for actual calculations, the inverse matrix is not that of equation (14). We have to use

$$(I - C)^{-1} \tag{16}$$

by setting $H = 0$. In this case, a certain discrepancy is created between the two.

This is measured as

$$
\begin{aligned}
(I-H)(I-C-H)^{-1} - (I-C)^{-1} \\
= (I-C)^{-1} CH(I-C-H)^{-1} \\
= (I-C)^{-1} CN.
\end{aligned}
\tag{17}
$$

In other words, the difference between (16) and (14) is equal to $(I-C)^{-1} CN$. Note that (CN) is the part which has become fixed after once becoming liquid in the propagation process; it is transformed into $(I-C)^{-1} CN$ when it propagates itself into the fixed part. But, since matrix H is unknown, we must proceed with the analysis ignoring this gap in the actual calculations. Thus, I must warn the reader that the empirical analysis which follows is only approximate. Even though approximate, the measurement of interfirm relationships seems to be sufficiently meaningful, and general trends can be discerned even when ignoring the gap. (4)

III. Preliminaries for Measurement

In the rest of the paper, we present our measurement of interdependence relationships of major Japanese firms by the method developed in the preceding section.

Let us first enumerate a number of premises adopted in our measurement exercise.

1) Our study covers 112 private nonfinancial firms, with fixed tangible assets of more than 1.5 billion yen as of the end of 1962 (fiscal), which are listed on the Tokyo Stock Exchange First Market. (5) The date of measurements is, in principle, the end of September 1964. (6)

2) As for financial institutions, we aggregate them appropriately into several groups, each of which is treated as if it were a single entity. (7) We call them "financial groups." Below is the list of our financial groups and their members.

Government Financial Group: Japan Development Bank,
Export-Import Bank of Japan, Central Cooperative Bank
of Agriculture and Forestry.

Mitsui Financial Group: Mitsui Bank, Mitsui Trust and Banking, Mitsui Life Insurance Co., Taisho Marine and Fire
Insurance Co.

Mitsubishi Financial Group: Mitsubishi Bank, Mitsubishi
Trust and Banking, Meiji Life Insurance Co., Tokyo Marine and Fire Insurance Co.

Sumitomo Financial Group: Sumitomo Bank, Sumitomo Trust
and Banking, Sumitomo Life Insurance Co., Sumitomo Marine and Fire Insurance Co.

Yasuda Financial Group: Fuji Bank, Yasuda Trust and Banking, Yasuda Life Insurance Co., Yasuda Fire and Marine
Insurance Co.

Daiichi Financial Group: Daiichi Bank, Asahi Life Insurance
Co.,

Sanwa Financial Group: Sanwa Bank, Toyo Trust and Banking, Daido Life Insurance Co.

Long-Term Credit Bank Financial Group: Japan Industrial
Bank, Long-Term Credit Bank, Nippon Fudosan Bank.

Hypothec Bank Financial Group: Hypothec Bank of Japan.

Other Bank Financial Group: Bank of Tokyo, Tokai Bank,
Daiwa Bank, Bank of Kobe, Kyowa Bank, Hokkaido Taku-
shoku Bank.

To be sure, when we follow this procedure, we must prepare
a balance sheet for each of these financial groups, in particular
by deleting lending and borrowing within each group to the extent possible.

3) As for the Y_{ij}, we have obtained data on shareholdings
which show direct interfirm relationships, from the itemized
list of holdings of securities and on borrowings from the itemized list of borrowings in Company Reports on Securities.

4) Outstanding deposits of the financial groups, which are
an exogenous variable in our analysis, apply only to ordinary
banks and, therefore, cannot be found in the balance sheets of

other financial institutions such as trust banks and insurance companies. However, as is clear from the explanation in the previous section, these deposits are meaningful as an exogenous variable only because they are not directly related to flows of funds among firms. Accordingly, cash in trust at trust banks and bonds of long-term credit banks, for example, are exogenous in the same sense and should be dealt with in our analysis as though they played the same role as outstanding deposits of ordinary banks. In the analysis below, outstanding deposits include all of these items.

IV. Results of Measurement

Based on these premises, we have attempted to measure relationships among representative Japanese private firms. In this section, we examine the results of our measurements. For expository convenience, the examination is set out in the following three steps: (1) Relationships between financial groups and nonfinancial firms, (2) Interfirm relationships within business groups, (3) Interdependent relationships among all nonfinancial firms.

1) Relationships Between Financial Groups and Nonfinancial Firms

First of all, we examine what sort of influence each financial group has on the 112 nonfinancial firms under study here. To do this, we focus on the p_{ih} of equation (5) above, that is, the "total asset dependence coefficient" of each firm on outstanding deposits of each financial group. Table 1 shows these values; Table 2, based on these, lists for each financial group the firms for which the total asset dependence coefficients meet certain standards. Table 3 shows as percentage assets of individual firms included in Table 2 (of the aggregate assets of the 112 nonfinancial firms) and the influence coefficients (8) of each financial group on nonfinancial firms.

These tables enable us to note the following characteristics

Table 1

Total Asset Dependence Coefficients

%

No.	Firm*	Government	Mitsui	Mitsubishi	Sumitomo	Yasuda	Daiichi	Sanwa	Long-Term Credit Bank	Hypothec Bank	Other
1.	Kyokuyo Hogei	3.14	2.67	4.64	0.61	0.93	0.15	0.37	4.02	—	15.42
2.	Nippon Suisan	2.26	0.06	0.83	1.50	5.36	0.69	5.17	9.17	3.55	0.55
3.	Taiyo Fishery	2.31	1.47	3.18	0.77	1.56	0.55	0.87	6.56	2.22	0.69
4.	Mitsui Mining	11.15	7.95	—	0.10	—	—	0.07	5.22	2.41	2.65
5.	Mitsubishi Mining	12.28	—	8.22	0.02	0.01	—	—	4.78	—	0.02
6.	Hokkaido Colliery & Steamship	9.11	4.03	0.06	0.03	0.04	—	0.18	3.63	—	1.94
7.	Teikoku Oil	3.47	2.74	0.63	0.28	1.15	0.52	0.85	15.54	0.04	0.40
8.	Kajima Corp.	0.04	1.46	0.96	4.49	0.28	0.47	0.53	0.79	—	1.09
9.	Snow Brand Milk Products	10.60	0.27	0.47	0.44	1.42	1.72	1.04	3.17	—	3.51
10.	Sapporo Beer	0.03	1.36	1.89	2.07	5.83	2.23	0.09	2.24	—	0.40
11.	Asahi Beer	0.08	2.69	0.45	4.01	0.23	—	2.66	1.86	—	0.25
12.	Kirin Beer	0.07	—	6.30	0.39	—	—	0.21	2.13	0.89	0.45
13.	Ajinomoto	2.30	0.14	6.28	—	0.13	2.23	0.40	—	—	1.23
14.	Toyobo	0.39	0.67	8.41	2.10	0.48	5.99	2.95	2.35	—	1.23
15.	Kanebo	0.33	5.21	3.09	1.59	2.67	0.22	1.15	2.48	—	4.41
16.	Nichibo	0.08	0.50	0.94	1.71	1.67	—	3.27	1.05	—	0.19
17.	Kurabo Industries	0.28	1.62	0.63	1.14	6.93	0.53	0.90	0.92	—	0.16
18.	Kurehabo	1.61	0.40	1.00	9.76	1.83	0.53	0.35	3.14	1.66	0.55
19.	Nittobo	0.23	3.45	0.13	0.13	3.63	1.68	—	14.83	0.10	3.90
20.	Teijin	0.49	0.72	0.89	1.29	—	—	6.83	3.16	—	2.84
21.	Toyo Rayon	0.15	4.92	1.52	1.55	0.87	0.37	1.98	3.99	0.95	1.40
22.	Kurashiki Rayon	2.32	0.54	1.56	1.95	1.39	—	1.45	9.42	—	0.48
23.	Nippon Rayon	0.15	0.50	0.87	2.07	0.14	0.38	7.39	5.65	—	4.91
24.	Asahi Chemical	0.29	0.29	2.40	7.00	1.52	1.43	1.35	3.90	—	0.16
25.	Sanyo Pulp	2.96	0.37	3.26	0.94	4.40	0.98	1.09	9.42	—	0.68

Financial Groups

	1	2	3	4	5	6	7	8	9	10
26. Nippon Pulp Indus.	5.66	5.12	5.47	—	—	1.33	0.90	4.56	4.39	1.55
27. Kokusaku Pulp	1.38	4.05	11.91	0.51	0.02	7.49	0.14	0.30	0.02	8.51
28. Tohoku Pulp	—	—	—	0.68	0.95	—	0.37	4.15	6.02	3.29
29. Oji Paper	0.52	2.72	5.30	0.54	2.11	0.18	3.93	0.85	7.03	5.23
30. Honshu Paper	0.61	—	5.09	0.35	0.13	1.09	3.81	1.58	5.01	5.48
31. Jujo Paper	0.77	—	5.68	2.61	0.93	3.41	2.22	3.75	5.01	2.75
32. Daishowa Paper	3.26	0.87	—	0.25	3.57	1.49	7.87	1.50	1.26	7.26
33. Toyo Koatsu	0.38	4.37	7.29	—	0.34	0.22	0.37	0.86	8.12	7.33
34. Nitto Chemical	2.22	—	12.25	0.57	11.96	1.26	0.72	1.61	1.12	8.05
35. Showa Denko	2.88	0.08	3.26	2.77	1.25	7.82	1.74	0.46	0.98	1.06
36. Sumitomo Chemical	0.22	—	7.88	0.36	—	0.43	11.98	1.06	0.39	2.55
37. Mitsubishi Chem. Indus.	—	—	—	—	—	0.47	—	8.34	—	1.08
38. Denki Kagaku (Electric Chemical Industrial Co.)	0.11	0.14	5.82	0.15	—	0.60	1.54	2.36	0.21	3.92
39. Mitsui Chemical	—	0.20	15.39	—	1.23	—	0.45	1.16	5.31	0.66
40. Sekisui Chemical	1.31	1.72	3.37	0.92	0.11	0.54	0.22	0.81	0.74	1.93
41. Ube Industries	3.67	—	5.74	6.53	0.89	0.19	0.77	0.92	1.14	3.71
42. Takeda Chem. Indus.	0.60	—	3.86	6.45	0.06	1.60	0.30	2.78	0.44	—
43. Nippon Oil	0.80	—	0.74	2.05	0.18	5.45	6.35	0.30	0.91	0.04
44. Showa Oil	0.48	2.72	4.53	0.21	4.45	1.31	—	0.36	5.50	0.96
45. Maruzen Oil	1.18	—	2.98	0.77	3.79	1.18	0.07	0.35	0.16	0.24
46. Mitsubishi Oil	1.54	—	2.73	0.60	0.15	10.88	0.98	8.52	0.36	0.08
47. Toa Nenryo	—	4.10	2.51	—	—	1.07	1.18	6.03	—	—
48. Daikyo Oil	1.57	—	12.92	0.26	—	1.97	—	1.66	0.16	0.12
49. Yokohama Rubber	9.72	1.64	4.76	—	4.56	2.45	3.39	2.79	—	0.06
50. Bridgestone Tire	0.47	1.38	5.52	0.22	0.65	1.68	—	2.31	0.55	0.64
51. Asahi Glass	0.72	3.31	2.70	0.25	0.10	11.93	5.96	6.39	1.61	0.77
52. Nihon Cement	0.94	—	2.91	0.40	0.24	0.38	0.39	0.71	—	2.26
53. Onoda Cement	2.97	—	5.58	0.43	0.02	—	0.84	2.09	7.49	0.41
54. Sumitomo Cement	1.87	—	7.79	2.99	—	—	3.74	3.98	4.09	0.24
55. Yawata Steel	0.34	0.01	8.67	3.46	0.42	4.47	4.14	3.85	1.64	0.21
56. Fuji Steel	1.22	—	8.32	2.48	0.23	1.84	3.76	2.85	2.45	0.25
57. Kawasaki Steel	1.77	—	3.34	2.06	1.12	0.92	2.16	1.73	1.57	0.72
58. Nippon Kokan	0.56	—	4.86	1.08	0.25	7.19	1.70	1.51	0.58	2.87
59. Kobe Steel	1.55	—	3.10	0.32	2.20	1.85	1.34	1.94	0.76	1.28
60. Nisshin Steel	0.99	—	4.49	6.70	0.10	0.97	0.90	2.32	0.53	0.45

Table 1 (continued)

Total Asset Dependence Coefficients

| No. Firm* | | Financial Groups | | | | | | | | % |
	Government	Mitsui	Mitsubishi	Sumitomo	Yasuda	Daiichi	Sanwa	Long-Term Credit Bank	Hypothec Bank	Other
61. Daido Steel	1.85	1.26	4.80	1.75	1.09	0.35	0.13	0.67	7.95	5.50
62. Kubota Steel	0.25	0.34	1.52	5.84	2.92	—	1.14	1.77	—	2.08
63. Japan Steel Works	1.82	11.14	1.60	1.33	0.67	0.62	0.64	—	—	3.44
64. Amagasaki Steel	0.67	0.07	0.96	0.08	0.16	1.40	12.32	4.90	—	4.75
65. Nippon Light Metal	—	0.83	1.46	1.05	0.20	3.11	1.86	4.40	—	2.19
66. Mitsui Mining & Smelting	1.94	7.23	1.15	—	0.07	—	—	—	—	—
67. Mitsubishi Metal Mining	3.89	0.17	9.65	0.33	—	0.02	0.17	2.76	—	0.09
68. Nippon Mining	1.31	4.04	0.70	0.93	1.88	—	—	2.70	1.05	1.46
69. Sumitomo Metal Mining	0.86	—	0.02	16.41	0.01	—	1.87	6.44	—	0.20
70. Furukawa Electric	0.08	—	1.82	0.20	2.46	8.27	—	3.65	—	2.41
71. Sumitomo Electric	0.24	0.22	1.45	16.39	0.64	—	0.27	8.62	—	0.27
72. Sumitomo Metal	0.16	1.06	1.60	12.44	1.19	0.07	0.28	4.47	—	0.53
73. Komatsu Ltd.	0.61	0.64	0.93	6.27	2.74	0.39	0.29	5.01	—	2.01
74. Hitachi Ltd.	1.46	1.20	2.72	2.05	3.38	2.41	2.66	1.17	0.73	1.01
75. Toshiba	0.14	5.68	1.69	1.43	1.57	1.38	3.23	4.53	—	2.62
76. Mitsubishi Electric	0.16	2.65	8.58	1.29	0.52	—	1.85	3.90	2.22	0.32
77. Nippon Electric	0.91	0.17	1.74	17.51	0.13	0.36	0.87	0.01	—	0.01
78. Fuji Electric	0.03	0.49	3.69	2.18	4.31	6.36	—	7.18	—	3.86
79. Oki Electric	0.18	0.37	3.77	0.36	15.33	0.32	0.78	3.19	—	3.15
80. Matsushita, Electric Indus.	0.11	—	0.96	2.12	0.26	—	0.70	5.07	—	—
81. Mitsubishi Heavy Indus.	6.26	0.54	9.03	2.22	0.76	0.14	0.51	4.24	—	1.88
82. Mitsui Shipbuilding	11.29	7.91	0.58	—	0.02	—	0.77	2.85	3.97	0.19
83. Hitachi Shipbuilding	13.12	0.36	0.46	1.26	1.77	—	0.50	2.12	—	1.83
84. Kawasaki Heavy Indus.	6.21	0.51	0.50	2.07	0.59	4.26	6.16	3.94	—	4.46

	C1	C2	C3	C4	C5	C6	C7	C8	C9	C10
85. Ishikawajima-Harima Heavy Indus.	10.19	0.09	0.29	0.95	0.18	3.24	1.11	2.65	—	5.58
86. Nissan Motor	0.34	0.86	1.83	1.53	2.25	0.01	1.07	3.83	—	0.51
87. Isuzu Motor	0.03	0.26	0.70	0.59	0.43	0.64	1.67	1.34	—	0.24
88. Toyota Motor	0.12	1.91	1.52	0.92	0.32	—	2.44	4.19	—	1.65
89. Prince Motor	—	0.19	1.26	2.33	0.31	0.55	—	5.48	—	0.33
90. Toyo Kogyo	0.04	1.22	2.29	4.69	0.86	0.18	2.23	3.20	—	0.35
91. Daihatsu Kogyo	—	—	0.56	0.16	—	—	9.69	3.05	—	8.26
92. Honda Motor	—	0.84	10.39	4.06	3.84	2.66	0.12	0.78	—	3.13
93. C. Itoh	1.28	0.07	0.29	2.79	1.60	0.07	1.19	0.01	1.06	2.21
94. Marubeni	4.21	0.32	0.44	0.34	5.83	0.89	6.12	0.01	—	3.88
95. Nichimen	2.07	0.19	1.21	1.09	0.52	0.71	—	0.02	0.07	4.45
96. Mitsui Bussan	0.78	4.96	0.42	12.43	2.26	—	1.71	—	—	2.15
97. Sumitomo Shoji	0.52	0.03	0.86	0.41	0.31	0.31	0.91	0.06	1.18	2.52
98. Mitsubishi Shoji	1.35	0.10	6.52	0.08	0.58	0.33	0.75	0.02	0.39	2.81
99. Mitsui Real Estate	0.11	17.23	1.25	0.38	0.86	—	—	2.39	0.01	3.25
100. Mitsubishi Estate	0.08	—	16.11	1.30	6.79	—	9.17	0.06	—	1.81
101. Tobu Railway	1.08	4.14	5.59	1.16	1.69	0.78	5.18	0.42	—	0.11
102. Keisei Elec. Railway	1.77	5.44	3.05	3.20	0.55	0.17	11.30	2.84	1.59	0.42
103. Kinki Nippon Railway	1.08	0.16	0.10	11.04	0.07	0.04	0.53	1.38	—	3.99
104. Hankyu (Kei-Han-Shin Kyuko Railway)	1.45	3.01	0.29	3.29	1.95	—	5.64	9.65	—	1.31
105. Nagoya Railroad	0.03	0.64	3.20	0.52	1.98	0.02	0.05	4.24	4.17	6.68
106. Nippon Express	—	1.84	3.20	0.35	0.99	2.16	0.31	3.30	0.02	0.67
107. Nippon Yusen	25.61	0.21	4.92	2.09	0.69	0.22	7.29	2.52	—	0.50
108. Mitsui O.S.K. Lines	26.31	2.31	0.69	0.40	1.13	0.11	0.20	3.39	—	0.29
109. Yamashita Shin Nihon Steamship Co.	28.73	0.02	1.65	0.53	0.66	—	0.07	6.30	—	1.11
110. Kawasaki Kisen	27.17	0.06	1.07	0.58	1.30	1.18	0.59	6.52	—	1.11
111. Shinwa Kaiun	21.59	0.40	2.86	0.37	0.75	1.37	—	10.79	—	0.86
112. Iino Kaiun	18.76	0.54	1.33	—	—	2.20	—	6.55	—	0.80

*[Translator's note: English names of firms are as reported in company directories.]

Table 2

Business Groupings

Government	Mitsui	Mitsubishi	Sumitomo	Long-Term Credit Banks
A	A	A	A	A
4 Mitsui Mining	39 Mitsui Chem.	92 Honda Motor	69 Sumitomo Metal Mining	7 Teikoku Oil
5 Mitsubishi Mining	63 Japan Steel Works	100 Mitsubishi Estate	71 Sumitomo Electric	19 Nittobo
9 Snow Brand Milk Products	99 Mitsui Real Estate	C	97 Sumitomo Shoji	27 Kokusaku Pulp
82 Mitsui Shipbuilding	C	5 Mitsubishi Mining	B	34 Nitto Chem.
83 Hitachi Shipbuilding	4 Mitsui Mining	12 Kirin Beer	36 Sumitomo Chem.	38 Denki Kagaku
85 Ishikawajima-Harima Heavy Indus.	28 Tohoku Pulp	13 Ajinomoto	72 Sumitomo Metal	B
108 Mitsui OSK Lines	29 Oji Paper	37 Mitsubishi Chem. Indus.	77 Nippon Electric	2 Nippon Suisan
109 Yamashita Shin-Nihon	33 Toyo Koatsu	46 Mitsubishi Oil	C	3 Taiyo Fishery
110 Kawasaki Kisen	66 Mitsui Mining & Smelting	51 Asahi Glass	24 Asahi Chemical	22 Kurashiki Rayon
111 Shinwa Kaiun	82 Mitsui Shipbuilding	67 Mitsubishi Metal Mining		25 Sanyo Pulp
112 Iino Kaiun		76 Mitsubishi Electric		31 Jujo Paper
107 Nippon Yusen		98 Mitsubishi Shoji		48 Daikyo Oil
		81 Mitsubishi Heavy Indus.		54 Sumitomo Cement
				55 Yawata Steel
				56 Fuji Steel
				68 Nippon Mining
				70 Furukawa Elec.
				89 Prince Motor

B
6 Hokkaido Colliery & Steamship
30 Honshu Paper
84 Kawasaki Heavy Indus.

	Yasuda	Sanwa	Daiichi	Hypothec Bank	Other
A	52 Nihon Cement	64 Amagasaki Steel			1 Kyokuyo Hogei
B	79 Oki Electric		34 Nitto Chem.	61 Daido Steel	
C	58 Nippon Kokan	23 Nippon Rayon, 40 Sekisui Chem., 41 Ube Industries, 60 Nisshin Steel, 95 Nichimen	70 Furukawa Elec.		85 Ishikawajima-Harima Heavy Industries

Notes: Rank A: the largest i for k such that $\rho_{ik} > 10$

Rank B: the largest i for k such that $5 < \rho_{ik} < 10$ or the second largest i for k such that $\rho_{ik} > 10$ when the largest i belongs to the Government or Long-Term Credit Bank groups.

Rank C: i such that $\rho_{ik} > 5$ and the sum for other k (excluding those belonging to the Government or Long-Term Credit Bank groups) is less than 5.

as to the relationships between financial groups and nonfinancial firms.

a) The Government Financial Group and the Long-Term Credit Bank Financial Group have greater influence on private firms than other commercial-bank financial groups have. This can be confirmed from the following three points. First of all, it is evident from the number of firms shown in Table 2. The number of firms listed is 15 for the Government Group and 17 for the Long-Term Credit Bank Group; these are far larger than those for all other commercial bank groups. We must note that this difference does not depend on differences in size of outstanding deposits. As far as the value of deposit balances is concerned, Mitsubishi is the leader with 2.297 trillion yen, followed by Sumitomo, Long-Term Credit Bank, Fuji, Sanwa, Mitsui, the Government Group, and Daiichi (but excluding "other"). Moreover, we should pay attention to the fact that, by the nature of our standards of classification, it is less probable for a certain firm to be listed with the Government or Long-Term Credit Bank groups than with a commercial bank group.

Second, the same point can be confirmed from the percentages of assets in Table 3. While the Mitsubishi group has the largest percentage, 15.4%, the Long-Term Credit Bank and Government groups follow it with 12.4% and 7.8% respectively.

Third, one can look at the influence coefficients, also shown in Table 3. For both the Government and Long-Term Credit Bank groups, these are on the order of 0.2, values clearly distinguishable from those of others. This means that outstanding deposits of the Government and Long-Term Credit Bank groups circulate more effectively among firms than those of other commercial banks do.

We can conclude from these three points that the Government and Long-Term Credit Bank groups exert stronger financial influence than commercial banks do on nonfinancial private firms. An especially important point is that the strength of this influence is verified in three aspects: the number of firms, the scale of firms, and the effectiveness of flow-of-funds. (9)

Table 3

Business Group Characteristics

	Percentage of Assets Held (%)	Influence Coefficient (10^{-4})
Government Group	7.8	2,394
Mitsui Group	3.8	1,463
Mitsubishi Group	15.4	1,518
Sumitomo Group	6.7	1,553
Yasuda Group	3.1	1,362
Daiichi Group	0.8	1,145
Sanwa Group	4.1	1,180
Long-Term Credit Bank Group	12.4	2,267
Hypothec Bank Group	0.5	770
Other	1.7	614
Remainder	47.3	

This tells, in a broad sense, how deeply state capital permeates into private firms; but it would be rash to conclude just from this observation that the Japanese economy has reached the stage of state monopoly capitalism. To reach such a conclusion, it is essential to look from other points of view at things like the role that state capital has played in the reproductive structure of the economy. Nevertheless, it cannot be denied that our analytical findings give an important basis for judgment.

b) Characteristics of three financial groups: Mitsui, Mitsubishi, and Sumitomo.

Below, we spotlight three representative financial groups, Mitsui, Mitsubishi, and Sumitomo. We can present the following observations on the characteristics of their influence on nonfinancial private firms.

While the Mitsui group contains nine firms, which are more than seven firms of the Sumitomo group as shown in Table 2, its percentage of assets and influence are the lowest of the three financial groups. Thus, we conclude that the influence which the Mitsui Financial Group exerts on nonfinancial private firms is none too large, either quantitatively or qualitatively.

Since there are twelve firms included in the Mitsubishi Financial Group in Table 2, and since its percentage of assets is 15.4%, its most remarkable feature is the fact that its influence on nonfinancial private firms is the largest in scale.

As for the Sumitomo Financial Group, we find that its influence is qualitatively strong. In other words, its main feature lies in the strongest linkage between the financial group and nonfinancial firms. This is clear from the fact that not only its influence coefficient is the largest in value among the three financial groups but, compared with other financial groups, it has the largest number of firms included in ranks A and B in Table 2.

2) Interfirm Relationships Within Business Groups

In what follows, we consider the so-called business groups and examine relationships in which individual firms stand to each other within these groups.

We take up here the six business groups, Mitsui, Mitsubishi, Sumitomo, Yasuda, Daiichi, and Sanwa. There is a problem of how to assign firms to particular business groups. Our criterion in this regard is not simply close connections with financial institutions but also one based on strong mutual relationships within groups of firms. The data in Table 4, which provide the basis of our inquiry, are developed as follows. We make an initial list of firms for each business group including those firms appearing in Table 2 but also others, which are usually assigned to each business group, and then impute a partial inverse matrix for them. Next, on the basis of the values of b_{ij} from this matrix we extract only those which show relatively close interfirm relationships. We then construct the inverse matrix for each business group as reported in Table 4.

In our examination of this table, we can classify our six business groups into the following three patterns according to the strength of interfirm linkage within groups. The first pattern is the one in which almost all elements of the matrix in Table 4 have relatively large values. In this, interfirm linkage is not only quite close but also applies to all firms alike. This pattern is associated with what is considered as the business group in the true sense of the word. Of our six groups, we can assign Mitsubishi, Sumitomo, and (although there are some doubts) Mitsui to this pattern.

Of these three, interfirm linkage is the strongest and most universal in the Sumitomo business group and weak and less universal in the Mitsui group. This point is verified if we examine the degree of interfirm linkage by calculating the averages of the elements in Table 4 (omitting the first rows and first columns). These averages are 3080 for Sumitomo and 810 for Mitsubishi, but only 223 for Mitsui. Also, the universality of interfirm association may be measured by dividing the standard deviation of the matrix elements by their mean (which we call the coefficient of variation). It is 0.94 for Sumitomo and 1.84 for Mitsubishi, but 2.67 for Mitsui.

The second pattern has a formal structure such that elements in the rows and columns corresponding to banks (the first rows and columns in Table 4) are large, but all other elements are very small. In this form, nonfinancial firms within the group are closely tied to the financial group, but very weakly associated among themselves. Thus, it is more appropriate to regard these firms as a collection of firms centered around the financial groups, rather than to call them a business group in the true sense of the word. Yasuda and Sanwa fit this pattern. We note that the means and coefficients of variation of the matrix elements are (99,2.32) for Yasuda and (196,2.14) for Sanwa (by these values, perhaps we should place Mitsui in between the first and second patterns. It is for this reason that we mentioned some doubt about including Mitsui in the first pattern).

The third pattern is a type in which two business groups

Table 4

Interfirm Linkage Coefficients

(10⁻⁶)

1. Mitsui Business Group

No. Firm	114	99	82	39	108	96	66	21	33	63	4
114 Mitsui Bank	*	6,752	1,996	5	—	1,415	1,508	1	4,540	2	—
99 Mitsui Real Estate	5,285	*	432	347	—	151	635	—	24	176	—
82 Mitsui Shipbuilding	3,242	352	*	—	—	763	5	—	15	—	—
39 Mitsui Chemical	4,235	1,305	188	*	—	285	459	417	732	—	—
108 Mitsui OSK Lines	1,406	349	3,190	372	*	133	595	—	7	—	—
96 Mitsui Bussan	18,636	127	436	118	48	*	216	361	817	—	—
66 Mitsui Mining & Smelting	2,511	336	5	83	—	112	*	—	12	—	—
21 Toyo Rayon	6,188	999	371	372	—	172	10	*	28	—	—
33 Toyo Koatsu	3,050	21	238	425	—	231	5	—	*	—	—
63 Japan Steel Works	3,444	2,199	8	1	—	5	7	—	16	*	—
4 Mitsui Mining	3,390	379	7	207	—	5	711	—	16	—	*

2. Mitsubishi Business Group

No. Firm	115	5	37	98	100	51	81	107	76	67	46
115 Mitsubishi Bank	*	31	2,450	378	8	9	1,806	4	1,581	5	1
5 Mitsubishi Mining	1,554	*	2,702	217	1,211	9	160	957	5	1,086	1
37 Mitsubishi Chem Indus.	4,453	11,301	*	287	1,484	678	13	453	462	784	1
98 Mitsubishi Shoji	12,875	3,658	1,515	*	1,917	2,158	1,877	4,682	1,593	1,292	2,043
100 Mitsubishi Estate	5,524	2,149	1,489	214	*	5,219	639	788	397	433	1
51 Asahi Glass	2,339	6	324	111	637	*	161	1	612	1	—

81 Mitsubishi Heavy Indus.	24,903	308	558	987	1,400	3,434	*	436	476	1,189	2
107 Nippon Yusen	1,533	829	6	1	2	2	641	*	3	2	202
76 Mitsubishi Electric	8,569	676	861	361	955	407	17	3	*	584	1
67 Mitsubishi Metal Mining	2,456	1,243	10	171	2	—	5	2	4	*	—
46 Mitsubishi Oil	2,451	463	8	295	1	1	6	644	4	1	*

3. Sumitomo Business Group

No. Firm	116	77	69	72	71	97	36
116 Sumitomo Bank	*	7,889	3,541	3,163	3,103	792	6,068
77 Nippon Electric	8,197	*	7,508	908	10,667	1,027	937
69 Sumitomo Metal Mining	2,767	1,773	*	14	1,432	1,367	503
72 Sumitomo Metal	13,277	6,798	10,002	*	3,855	5,826	2,730
71 Sumitomo Electric	5,264	5,985	4,882	572	*	571	658
97 Sumitomo Shoji	11,132	2,077	6,954	1,946	3,462	*	3,714
36 Sumitomo Chemical	7,928	1,923	1,766	30	1,285	1,239	*

4. Yasuda Business Group

No. Firm	117	58	94	52	35	79
117 Fuji Bank	*	2,402	1,383	6,582	4,945	1,820
58 Nippon Kokan	11,636	*	936	600	58	21
94 Marubeni	10,604	30	*	19	52	19
52 Nihon Cement	4,032	12	6	*	20	7
35 Showa Denko	992	14	86	34	*	9
79 Oki Electric	3,511	9	5	23	17	*

Table 4 (continued)

5. Daiichi Business Group

No. Firm \ No.	118	110	112	84	57	70	78	49
118 Daiichi Bank	*	13	3	2,795	1,995	4,988	3,399	7
110 Kawasaki Kisen	720	*	45,288	19,795	891	13	4	—
112 Iino Kaiun	507	22,176	*	438	21	3	12	—
84 Kawasaki Heavy Indus.	3,518	422	85	*	465	485	14	—
57 Kawasaki Steel	2,586	5,672	1,142	5,330	*	626	1,535	3
70 Furukawa Electric	5,792	—	—	17	12	*	2,283	933
78 Fuji Electric	6,616	—	—	20	14	12,422	*	755
49 Yokohama Rubber	1,921	—	—	5	4	8,575	26	*

6. Sanwa Business Group

No. Firm \ No.	119	95	23	45	64	60	20	41
119 Sanwa Bank	*	13	5,214	8	—	3,976	4,084	4,767
95 Nichimen	6,162	*	2,176	487	146	538	494	30
23 Nippon Rayon	2,796	1,272	*	1	—	12	12	13
45 Maruzen Oil	347	1,233	4	*	—	2	2	517
64 Amagasaki Steel	3,793	180	20	—	*	15	26	18
60 Nisshin Steel	2,905	566	17	—	—	*	12	14
20 Teijin	4,892	189	—	—	—	20	*	23
41 Ube Industries	3,490	126	18	—	—	14	14	*

which have huge industrial capital at their cores are tied together through the intermediation of financial institutions. In
terms of matrix structure, while the rows and columns corresponding to the financial group have large elements, the rest
of the matrix is divided into four submatrices B_{ij} $(i, j = 1, 2)$
of which relatively large values appear only in B_{ii}, and B_{ij},
$i \neq j$, are virtually zero matrices. As is clear in section 5 of
Table 4, the Daiichi Bank Group corresponds to this pattern.
It is evident that the two industrial-capital groups, Kawasaki
and Furukawa, are connected through the Daiichi Financial
Group. As a matter of fact, the coefficient of variation is 1.57
for Kawasaki and 1.12 for Furukawa but is raised to 2.57 when
the two groups are combined.

Thus, what are usually considered as business groups with
financial institutions at their cores can be divided into these
three types as our detailed analysis has revealed. We believe
that this classification provides a viewpoint indispensable in
discussing business groups.

3) Interdependent Relationships Among All
   Nonfinancial Firms

Finally, let us take up the 112 nonfinancial firms under study
as a whole and examine their interdependence relationships.
The influence coefficients, the influence susceptibility coefficients, and the interfirm linkage coefficients are the bases for
our examination. Table 5 shows the top ten firms for which
the first two of these coefficients have the largest values.
Figure 1 shows the interfirm relationships for which the b_{ij}^{*}
are greater than 0.001. Now we can indicate the existence of
the following characteristics.

First, as far as the influence coefficient goes, we notice that
more of the firms appearing here belong to industrial capital
business groups than to such business groups as Mitsui, Mitsubishi, or Sumitomo which center around financial institutions.
This must be because nonfinancial firms in the industrial capital groups must assume the role that banks play in tying together

Table 5

Top Ten Firms by Size of the Influence
and Influence Susceptibility Coefficients

Influence Coefficient	Influence Susceptibility Coefficient
1 Iino Kaiun	1 Kawasaki Kisen
2 Sumitomo Metal Mining	2 Iino Kaiun
3 Furukawa Electric	3 Shinwa Kaiun
4 Kawasaki Heavy Industries	4 Amagasaki Steel
5 Kawasaki Kisen	5 Teikoku Oil
6 Kobe Steel	6 Yamashita-Shinnihon Steamship
7 Nippon Electric	7 Nippon Electric
8 Sumitomo Electric	8 Nitto Chemical
9 Mitsubishi Mining	9 Nippon Yusen
10 Sumitomo Chemical	10 Yokohama Rubber

member firms in groups like Mitsui, Mitsubishi, and Sumitomo.

Second, we can point out that of the Mitsui, Mitsubishi, and Sumitomo business groups, Sumitomo firms are more frequently included in this table. This is just a reflection of the fact that the Sumitomo group is strongly united.

As for the influence susceptibility coefficient, we note that five of the ten firms listed here are marine transportation companies. But it is more important to compare this table with Table 2. Then we find that this table includes many of the firms which are assigned to the Government and Long-Term Credit Bank groups in Table 2. This fact is, of course, not unrelated to the characteristics of the Government and Long-Term Credit Bank Financial groups.

Finally, we touch briefly on Figure 1. Seventy-eight of the 112 firms, or 70%, are included in the chart (10). Linkages among these firms show, first of all, that there are no lines across the Mitsui, Mitsubishi, and Sumitomo groups except for

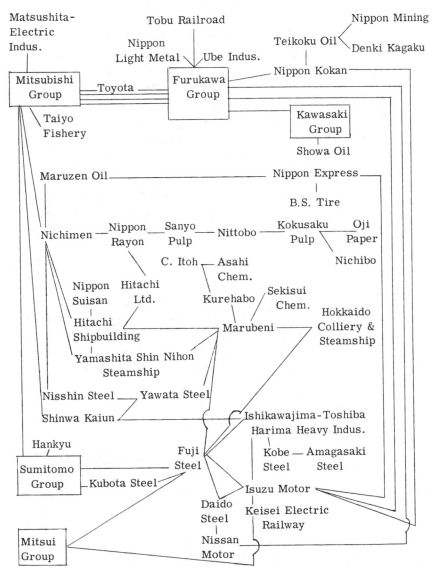

Fig. 1. Interfirm relationships.

Note: To simplify the chart, figures within business groups
(see Table 4) are not shown individually.

the one between Mitsubishi Chemical Industries (No. 37) and
Sumitomo Metals (No. 72). Thus, we can consider these three
groups to be independent of one another.

Second, we can speculate that interfirm linkages shown here
may be similar to relationships of technological transactions.
For example, this is clear in the relationships of Fuji Steel
with Hokkaido Colliery and Steamship, Kubota Steel, and Daido
Steel, and those of the Nippon Express with Maruzen Oil,
Bridgestone Tire, and Isuzu Motors. To be sure, it goes without saying that more comprehensive analysis beyond such case
studies is needed to decide whether, in general, interfirm flows-
of-funds relationships correspond to this sort of technological
relationships. (11)

Notes

1) This is true of all available works in this field, including
the excellent analysis of business groups by Yoshikazu Miya-
zaki, "Kigyō shūdan bunseki no igi to hōhō" [Significance and
Methods of Business Group Analysis] in Shigeto Tsuru, ed.,
Atarashii Seiji Keizaigaku o motomete, 1 [In Search of a New
Political Economy, Vol. 1], 1966.

2) Therefore, this calculation can be performed as many
times as the number of banks under study.

3) Of course, $c_{ij} + h_{ij} = a_{ij}$

4) In the method described in this section, one of the main
issues is evidently stability of the flow-of-funds coefficients. It is
highly likely that these coefficients would change as the date of measurement changes in view of the fact that interfirm relationships
are mobile. However, one can make no a priori judgment on the
direction and magnitude of these changes. This means that we must
start from measuring flow-of-funds coefficients themselves if we
want to measure interfirm relationships at different dates. It
seems to be risky to replace values of the exogenous variables
only. This point is left for further research.

5) Theoretically, we should take all existing firms, but
since their number is so large, limitation is inevitable. In

choosing the 112 firms, we have relied on the study of Miya-zaki, op. cit.

6) The reason we say "in principle" is that balance sheets for some firms are not as of this date. In such cases we have chosen the nearest date.

7) This is not due to a theoretical reason but due to the limitation of computer capacity.

8) That is, the column sums excluding the elements corresponding to the financial groups in the inverse matrix.

9) A view analogous to the present one already appears in the work of Professor Miyazaki. However, the reader should note that a qualitative aspect of the effectiveness of flows-of-funds is added to Miyazaki's approach from the so-to-speak purely quantitative aspect.

10) Besides these, Ajinomoto (No. 13) and Showa Denko (No. 35) satisfy the $b_{ij}^{*} > 0.001$ requirement. However, as they are independent of other firms, they are not included in the chart.

11) On this point see the author's "Kabushiki no mochiai ni mirareru kigyōkan kankei" [Interfirm Relationships Seen in Shareholding], Kobe College of Commerce, Shodai Ronshu, Vol. 18, No. 6 (February 1967), in which the author demonstrates that this correspondence is comparatively universal.

IV.

INDUSTRIAL POLICY

10

THE CONCEPTION AND EVALUATION
OF JAPANESE INDUSTRIAL POLICY

Hiroya Ueno*

A nation's economy is a living matter that functions according
to national and natural conditions, historical institutions, culture, and customs. Because national and natural conditions do
not change easily, and initial historical conditions have a his-
toricist effect over a long period, it is natural that countries
differ in economic structure and economic behavior. It is also
not at all strange that they neither follow the same methods of

---

This paper includes the following acknowledgment: This article
was written as an introduction to "A Study of Japan's Economic System (Economic Legislation and Economic Administration) and
Its Effectiveness." I am grateful to my co-researcher Mr. S.
Hoshino, who is a planning officer in the Economic Planning
Agency, for his cooperation in the writing of this study. I would
also like to express my thanks to Professor Y. Kanazawa, Fac-
ulty of Law, Seikei University, for frequent and valuable assistance that I received in the course of this study.

*Hiroya Ueno, "Wagakuni Sangyo Seisaku no Hasso to Hyoka."
Kikan Gendai Keizai, No. 20 (Winter 1975), 6-38. Appendix
omitted by agreement with the author. Translated by Jun
Uramatsu Smith.

This translation originally appeared in Japanese Economic
Studies, V (Winter 1976-77), 3-63. See the author's book,
Nihon no Keizai Seido [Japanese Economic System] (Tokyo:
Nihon Keizai Shimbun Sha, 1978).

economic planning and administration nor pursue the same
ideal for economic policy, nor go through the same process of
policy-making.

In fact, after World War II, the principles of capitalist free
society and the principles of economic democracy were introduced to Japan, and many Western institutions, new technologies,
managerial strategies, and ideologies were imported and transplanted one after another, but they have not completely changed
Japan's soil or climate, or decisively transformed its national
character. On the contrary, in the long-range perspective corresponding to climate, historicity, and national character something uniquely Japanese and incomprehensible to Westerners
has taken root in the course of the three decades after the war
following the traditions inherited from the Meiji era, with respect to the conception of policy, the system of economic institutions and economic policy, the policy-making processes and
the workings of the whole system.

We hasten to take note that some of these deep-rooted institutions and practices are out of keeping with the times or lack-
ing in internationalism. But it is too doctrinaire to compare
the Japanese systems with the Western, especially American,
systems and to place indiscriminate emphasis upon the ills of
the former on the basis of textbook analysis of the American
type, as many "modern" economists used to do. On the other
hand, it is too opportunistic and too much of a hindsight to look
at once upon neoclassical economic theory as impracticable and
sterile because it has become inarticulate in regard to modern
socioeconomic problems.

What is important when discussing the merits and demerits
of systems and policies is to judge their effectiveness and to
evaluate them based on theoretical and empirical analyses of
the relationship between the environment and goals, the relationship between ends and means, and factual relationships.
Also, when drawing an inference on systems and policies, it is
essential that this inference be based on empirical practicabil-
ity that enables us to discover the unknown from known facts
and to make reform proposals. An inference derived from

empty theories or fancies is meaningless realistically and practically. (1)

A Conception of Japanese Industrial Policy

The existence of something uniquely Japanese in the organization and working of Japan's economic system and economic policy has its own major reason. Japan, environmentally and historically, has constantly been confronted with the following two basic economic problems and has always had to cope with overcoming them.

The first is that Japan is a country in which a homogeneous population of 100 million live in a territory not blessed with land and resources, that is, a small and weak nation just in those terms. It has a land area of 370 thousand square kilometers and population density of about 290 per square kilometers, which comes to about 40 times that of America when the area is limited to flatland; its self-sufficiency rate is 75% for food, 0.3% for petroleum, and about 15% for all energy.

The second is that as the inevitable result of these conditions Japan depends on foreign sources for most of the resources needed to maintain its economic activities and must export overseas goods processed out of these imported resources. Consequently, the international division of labor and international cooperation have crucial importance for Japan's economic development.

Consequences of Land and Resource Limitations

An important economic implication of the first basic problem is that in Japan land and resources have the actual or potential character of scarce goods or factors of production. However, its limited supply does not make land a scarce commodity unless there is persistent excess demand for it. Similarly, resources are not scarce goods unless the country is forced to self-sufficiency in national emergencies like war or to quantitative import restrictions or to severe supply restrictions from

exporters like the OPEC. But in the case of a particularly scarce
commodity with extremely limited domestic supply, supply shortage or excess demand, when it develops once for some reason,
forces the economically weak to drop out of the market as they
are unable to pay for sharply risen prices because suppliers
take advantage of the excess demand to increase their own profits by increasing supply prices in the free market mechanism
in which prices serve as signals. Accordingly, when specific
scarce goods become the most limitational factors of production, resource allocation and income distribution are, ceteris
paribus, completely determined by the ownership of these
scarce goods as is often seen in less developed countries. In
this instance, neither efficiency in resource allocation nor
equity in income distribution is guaranteed, and only social in-
justice increases sharply.

When an evil effect like this is anticipated, either planning
or regulation is needed on the ownership or utilization of those
scarce goods that are factors of production essential for economic activities, and as we know from long experience, this becomes a necessity. That is, in Japan, greatly limited in land
and resources, there is reason to call for the planned utilization of national land, the regulation of landownership and utilization, and the selection and planned utilization of imported resources as substantive issues for the sake of economic development, effective utilization of resources, and public welfare. (2)

Nevertheless, with regard to landownership and utilization,
be they factory locations or residential locations, there has
been very little of direct and stringent planning and social regulation from the standpoint of public welfare. It is only since
the 1969 Urban Redevelopment Act, the 1970 revision of the
land tax system, the 1972 Industrial Relocation Promotion Act,
and the 1973 National Land Utilization Planning Act, that a full-
scale planning of national land utilization and the strengthening
of the land tax system came to be expected for the sake of public
welfare and social justice. (3) Until then, in the planning of
land utilization, even when the Compulsory Purchase of Land

Act was applied, direct regulation by state power was avoided
as much as possible. (This law is two-sided in that it provides
for the protection of private rights and compulsory acquisition
by public power.) The required regulation was carried out by
other instruments such as the distribution of funds indirectly
through fiscal policy (taxation, public work expenditure, and
subsidies) and monetary policy (low interest-rate policy and
selective lending).

In this sense, the system which preserved the framework and
practice of the most capitalistic system in the organization of
Japan's postwar capitalist free society is probably the land
system, which incorporated most faithfully the provisions of
Article 29 (the guarantee of property rights) of the Constitution.

The three main principles of capitalist free society are in
production to recognize the pursuit of profits by individual enterprises, in distribution to permit property income, and in expenditure to sanction savings, that is, not to usurp surplus income. They take form as actual legislation in the guarantee of
property rights and the realization of property income. The important point here is that scarce commodities have value as
long as property rights are guaranteed, and their financial value
increases as the demand for it rises. In effect, as Commons
noted, what is scarcity in economics is property rights in juris-
prudence, and the rightful responsibility of property is the legal
regulation of the sovereignty that governs scarcity. [5] Scarce
commodities have scarcity value only because they are scarce,
and scarcity value is attached to the property rights of things
which are either already scarce or anticipated to be scarce.
Despite the fact that it required fundamentally more planning
and regulation than other countries with regard to land utilization, Japan's conservative government insisted on private landownership and was very reluctant to institute strong regulations
on its rightful obligations, because it clung not only to the cause
of capitalism but also to the proprietary scarcity inherent in land.
It was for this reason that land prices rose steeply for so many
years and speculative demand for land was formed out of the
anticipation for further rises in land value. Urban land value

skyrocketed persistently since the high growth period of the mid-fifties, so much so that land value in 1972 was about twenty times that of 1955, or about seventeen times the wholesale price index.

While land and resources were scarce, Japan possessed a large homogeneous population rich in vitality, in other words, a superior and abundant labor force. But Japan was extremely short of both capital and modern industrial technology, without which this abundant labor force could not be utilized. Its negative side is the overabundance of population, but its positive side is the significant potentiality of economic development, once the labor force can be deployed in an efficient combination with capital that is to be accumulated since there can be a market sufficiently large to ensure development. At the same time, these circumstances effectively determined the direction and raison d'etre of Japan's economic planning and economic policy. The scale and prospect of the market make the market-economy regime more appropriate than the central planning regime. But some sort of planning or regulation is indispensable for the allocation and efficient utilization of scarce productive factors. The ease of government intervention in the market economy as well as the historical characteristics of the intervention system make it difficult to decide between the principles of central planning and market economy. (4) Moreover, the dual structure or the coexistence of an efficient modern productive segment capable of mass production and an inefficient anti-modern productive segment incapable of mass production made it initially difficult in reality to manage the economy explicitly in accordance with the models and principles that appear in modern economics. That is, abundance and efficiency stand opposite to scarcity and market valuation, but in Japan the two elements are always intermixed as problems both in actuality and policy.

Then, what principles of efficiency and selection were actually considered when three factors of production — land, resources, and capital — were scarce and only labor was an abundant factor? Efficiency criteria are usually found in the input-output coefficients (physical productivity or productive efficiency) determined by technology and the outlay-income ratio (efficiency of funds and capital, profit rate, etc.) determined by overall economic valuation. In this case, short-run, statics of economic theory would have recommended specialization in labor-intensive industries in accordance with the theory of comparative advantage or comparative cost. But viewed in terms of population size and market scale as well as the long-run efficiency of production and funds, this kind of specialization was not a rational choice. For the sake of rapid economic development and improvement of the standard of living, it was imperative to make production decisions and industry selections in accordance with the theory of dynamic comparative advantage, accepting Western economies as the model to be followed.

Importance of the International Division of Labor

The second basic problem mentioned above becomes important in deciding on the kinds of goods to produce and choosing industries. First, the lack of resources forced Japan to export fabricated goods in order to finance the importation of raw materials. This implied that protection of infant industries must go beyond the stage of import substitution and into export promotion. Granting its selfishness, Japan had to restrict imports of competing foreign goods and to erect tariff and nontariff barriers while key infant industries were being protected. And yet, once these industries grew up, they had to be able to sell their products in free overseas markets unencumbered by trade restrictions abroad. Second, in terms of marketability and the efficient use of funds or capital, these commodities ought to have been those for which a substantial increase in domestic and world demand was anticipated and which could be handled by mass production and mass sales. Third, there must have been a fair prospect that the industries could win in the severe competition in the international division of labor. Fourth, it was desirable to make the industrial structure more sophisticated, while maintaining full employment, by selecting industries subject to particularly strong increasing returns to scale in the presence of the abundant labor force.

Based on these criteria, the government — especially the Ministry of International Trade and Industry (MITI) which was in charge — decided to establish relatively soon after the war capital-intensive and technology-intensive industries, namely, iron and steel, petroleum refining, petrochemicals, automobiles, industrial machinery, electronics, electronic machinery, and the like as key industries, all of which seemed to be the most inappropriate industries for Japan then in the eyes of the static theory of comparative cost.

But by no means was this initial policy to protect key industries decided on without a contest. For instance, on September 13, 1949, the government, with regard to the Cabinet decision on "the case of industrial rationalization," worked out a guideline that specified the relative position of each industry in the prospective industrial structure. But there were two opposing views as to what position the automobile industry should occupy. One regarded the automobile industry as being useless. This position was taken notably by the then governor of the Bank of Japan Ichimada, who asserted that export promotion must conform to the principle of the international division of labor and that, from that point of view, it made no sense to strive to nurture the automobile industry in Japan. The other argued for protecting and nurturing the industry. For instance, the MITI believed that developing the automobile industry would benefit the machine industry and, through that route, industry in general. For this reason, the MITI hoped that Japan's automobile industry would concentrate its efforts on improving productivity as much as possible in order to strengthen its international competitive power, and thereby contribute to substantial sophistication of the national economy of Japan in alignment with the advanced countries. (5) This contest was finally won by the MITI. We must honor the MITI for its foresightedness. A point worth noting here is the fact that the conception and promotion of key industries was carried out not by private enterprises but under the initiative of the MITI. From this time

on, the leadership in industrial policy has been taken almost
completely by the MITI, and as key industries achieved success
after success during the period of high growth, industrial policy
has come to take the lead in Japan's public policy. (6)

All industries that the MITI judged to be either strategic or
growth industries were large-scale "facilitating" industries.
These industries are characterized by large initial fixed capital investment calling for an enormous sum for setting up
facilities. Production scale has to be sizable in order to pay
for the capital cost. But once the operation has been launched,
these industries satisfy the law of increasing returns to scale
in the long run. That is, an equiproportionate increase in all
inputs leads to a greater increase in output. The average cost
of production therefore is lowered as the scale of output increases. Such industries have no long-run limitation to production so long as demand continues to increase at a stable rate.
Furthermore, because the industrial organization is improved
substantially and its overall function develops as production
increases, the industries in question and industries related to
them enjoy both external and internal economies to a considerable extent. Though there is no general rule that increasing-
returns industries necessarily bring about a rise in their profit
rate, it is quite probable that those enterprises that expand their
scale and capture significant internal economies specific to
themselves can realize increasing returns and rising profitability at the same time. (Marshall [8])

When increasing returns to scale are expected, government
intervention is justified in order to nurture the industries concerned through special measures in taxes, subsidies, and in-
vestment-fund allotments. (7) Moreover, in a capitalist economy these types of protectionist and interventionist policies
tend to be more readily accepted when increasing-returns industries can also enjoy a rise in the profit rate.

In the foregoing sense, the basic principles that the government adopted for its industrial policy in order to establish cap-
ital- and technology-intensive industries were the planned market economy formula that allows the government to intervene

in the market economy as the needs arise. (8)

The first of the principles is to institute a well-defined "heavy and chemical industrialization plan." It is typically exemplified by the "National-Income Doubling Plan" (1960), which set up two explicit indicative targets in the income plan and the industrialization plan. The former was for the support of and guidance to public opinion, while the latter consisted of industrial policy needed for specific individual industries to enforce its heavy and chemical industrialization plan. In other words, in this plan, industrial policy was placed at the center of overall economic planning. (9)

The second is that the fundamental of this strategy was a policy to concentrate funds or capital in key industries. For this purpose, in addition to utilizing public financial institutions, private financial institutions were placed under the strict control of the Ministry of Finance. While tacitly establishing a principle that banks would neither be bankrupted nor go bankrupt, it regulated and directed financial activities so as to conform to industrial policy. A significant point in this policy of concentrating and distributing funds is that, in giving out industrial loans, private financial institutions decided on strategic industries and growth enterprises, most fundamentally along the judgment of the MITI. This was tantamount to a governmental guarantee.

The third is that key industries and enterprises were not only protected by import restrictions through foreign currency allocations, protective tariffs, the regulation of foreign capital, the regulation of the induction of foreign technology, nontariff barriers such as discriminatory commodity taxes, and the like, but also given various incentives, such as cheap credit, subsidy grants, and special taxation measures.

This type of industrial policy took deep root in the period of high growth that succeeded the postwar economic recovery, and according to the conception and design of industrial policy, an economic plan was established, and economic legislation and administrative systems were steadily prepared. Consequently, as I will show below, it is undeniable that most of Japan's economic legislation is for the sake of industrial policy and that emphasis in administration is placed on industrial administration.

The bias in favor of industrial policy in economic or public policy, economic planning, and legal and administrative systems has been subjected to much censure and criticism from within and without. Three types of criticism may be noted. The first type is critical of the bias itself and censures the idée fixe of public policy. The second one criticizes Japan's industrial policy for its violation of the basic principles of capitalist free society, free competition, and free market mechanism. The third one criticizes Japan's delay in making changes in conception and policy and in reforming institutions despite the fact that Japan's economic circumstances, structure, and objectives have changed.

In what follows, we shall evaluate the merits and demerits of industrial policy by means of our attempt at a macroeconomic efficiency analysis of the system that clarifies the systemic realities of industrial policy.

Institutional Realities of Industrial Structure Policy

Industrial structure shows how labor, capital, and other resources are allocated among various industries and what are the demand-supply relations of outputs and inputs in individual industries. There are a number of factors that circumscribe the industrial structure. The following is a usual list of them: (1) the structure of final demands covering personal consumption, private fixed capital formation, exports, and government expenditure; (2) the structure of technology that produces goods and services corresponding to fiscal demand and the distribution of firms that undertake production; (3) the endowments of factors of production, such as land, resources, labor, capital, and the sectoral distribution thereof; (4) the market structure that determines how outputs and factors are allocated; (5) institutional factors, such as the government's regulation or promotion of private economic activities and direct and indirect intervention in the flow of goods or money (e.g., economic legislation, pollution control standards, taxation and subsidy systems, credit control, selective lending, and public utility charges).

Item (3) roughly corresponds to the natural and historical environmental conditions indicated previously, (4) to industrial organization, and (5) to industrial policy. But these factors are intertwined to form demand for and supply of products and factors of production in individual industries. Altogether, they determine industrial structure.

Policies that influence these factors are fiscal, monetary, tax, subsidy, exchange and trade, technology development, antitrust, manpower, and environmental policies. But anyone of them alone cannot alter industrial structure unless it is extremely powerful.

For example, the sectoral composition of production in current prices was 19.8% (primary), 32.8% (secondary), and 47.4% (tertiary) in 1955, and 6.5% (primary), 42.3% (secondary), and 51.2% (tertiary) in 1970. The primary sector thus was reduced to the level found in advanced countries. Moreover, the ratio of heavy and chemical industries in manufacturing rose from 49.6% to 66% over the same period, clearly indicating the success of industrial policy in the "heavy and chemical industrialization plan." But one should note that it took fifteen years to accomplish this much sophistication in the industrial structure in spite of the full play that the government gave to its role as a promoter.

In a liberal economic system, production and circulation of goods and money are achieved through the self-regulating action (legally, the freedom of contract) of supply and demand. Prices are freely determined through the interaction of demand and supply. But as I already pointed out, the free enterprise system in Japan is merely a principle and not a reality. In actuality, the government tends to intervene in various economic activities by means of State Power in place of the Invisible Hand and to try to achieve a specific economic order or structure along the tradition of industrial policy since the Meiji era and with a certain stance in policy to enhance national or public interest. Moreover, there is a national character of the Japanese that makes enterprises, unless the capitalist or free-

enterprise system is overturned, cooperate with the policy design of the government and strive to achieve any goal whatsoever with the government and people as one body.

It goes without saying that economic and industrial structures
tend to change autonomously in the process of economic development, and to resist general or specific policy control except
in the Soviet-type economic system, which can enforce a materials mobilization plan, because they are subject to the price
and quantity of interindustry mechanisms. Therefore, Japan's
industrial-structure policy or industrial policy attempts to
achieve the goals of industrial structure through the govenment-
enterprise interaction in planning, intervention, and competition, namely, through mutual stimulus and response. It does
not follow the principle of a free enterprise economy as in the
United States or the principle of a centrally planned economy as
in the Soviet Union and Eastern Europe. (10)

Direct Government Interventions:
How They Are Now

In Appendix Table 1 [not reproduced here], we summarize the
present state of the government's direct and legal interventions
in enterprises and commodities with respect to business, quantity, price, capacity, etc., with the exception of those applicable
only in economic emergencies like the price control ordinance,
the anti-profiteering ordinance, the speculation prevention law,
the oil supply and demand rationalization law, and the national
life stabilization emergency measure. Also excluded are interventions via the direct regulation of foreign goods and services
for the sake of exchange and trade policy (Foreign Exchange
and Trade Control Laws, Foreign Investment Law, etc.), the
interest-rate control of public financial institutions, the legal
control of the fees charged by administrative organs, and the
legal exceptions from the Antitrust Act.

We note that the government intervenes directly in a very extensive way in agriculture, transportation and communications,
services and finance. As regards agricultural products, manu-

facturing and marketing of most food items, and service industries, government interventions are essential in protecting
farmers and small businesses though they are of a public character in a few instances. On the other hand, transportation and
communications, electricity, gas, waterworks, and education
are public-utility industries that are publicly regulated. Government regulation and intervention of this type belong to industrial
policy in a broad sense, with some bearing on industrial structure, but they differ in character from the aggressive industrial
policy implemented for rapidly advancing industrial structure.
They are derived more from a passive protective, public policy
and differ little in essence from the systems seen in the West
in terms of goals and character.

Noteworthy in this connection is aggressive industrial structure policy in the manufacturing sector and the banking, insurance, and securities sector.

Not too many of manufactured goods (under the jurisdiction
of the MITI) are subject to direct government intervention. Most
conspicuous are coal and petroleum products, textile goods,
chemical fertilizers, machinery, and shipbuilding (under the
jurisdiction of the Ministry of Transportation). Of these, however, textile goods and coal products are excluded as the government intervention with them has now assumed the character
of a passive protective policy; ordinance is an industry of a
special character. Thus, manufactures important in industrial
policy are petroleum products, chemical fertilizers, aircraft,
specific machinery, and shipbuilding. Petroleum products and
chemical fertilizers, along with textile products, receive considerable government intervention, while subsidies play a bigger
role in the machinery industry. A subsidy is important in itself, but it is more important as a signal indicating that the industry or the product receiving the subsidy is publicly recognized as the one under government protection.

The banking, insurance, and securities industry is in the private hands seeking profits but it seems like an industry under
public regulation as much as the public utility industry. It is
well known, for instance, that banks are under the strict control

and guidance of the Ministry of Finance regarding interest rates on deposits and loans, dividend rates, and office facilities. This control forces Japanese banks to compete, quite abnormally, only for market shares in deposits and loans.

This kind of competition for market shares, however, induces the banks to solicit deposits from the public as much as possible and to select growth industries and enterprises as customers for loans in order to keep bank management most efficient and profitable. This kind of bank behavior very much fits the policy that aimed at developing the industrial structure to a higher level.

Enacting Basic Laws and Establishing a
Policy for Economic Planning

A salient feature of the system of the economic legislation that sanctioned and systematized Japan's economic policy is the method, first of all, of giving the government a long-term guideline for economic management and a keynote of national policy and, on the basis of them, concretely preparing legislation such as government regulation, intervention, promotion, subsidy, and the like. Of course, there are exceptions, and in some instances, the order is reversed in terms of the timing of the legislation. Setting these aside, however, the order that we have referred to gives us a convenient framework in which to consider economic legislation in terms of ends and means and to evaluate the effectiveness of concrete economic policy through economic legislation. Typical of them are the relationship of the Agricultural Fundamental Law to specific laws concerning agriculture such as the Agricultural Cooperative Act, the Agricultural Improvement Funds Assistance Act, the Agricultural Modernization Funds Assistance Act, the Land Improvement Act, and the Farm Produce Price Stabilization Act; the relationship of the medium-sized and small Enterprises Fundamental Act to a number of specific laws concerning medium-sized and small enterprises with respect to their collective organizations, cooperative societies, and modernization

promotion; the relationship of the Basic Law for Environmental
Pollution Control to a host of pollution control laws; and the relationship of the Basic Law for Consumer Protection to many
related laws.

However, there is no basic law that outlines the conception of
industrial policy for the sake of sophisticating the industrial
structure. Somewhat approaching it in spirit are the two bills —
"Measures for the Promotion of Specified Industries" introduced
by the MITI in 1958 in order to establish the three-way cooperative system of government, industry and finance, and "Measures for the Promotion of the Conversion of Industrial Structure" conceived by the MITI in 1974. But neither saw the light
of day.

The role of the basic law for industrial structure policy was
played, however, by a series of economic plans prepared through
the consultation between representatives of business, specialists
and bureaucrats of the Economic Planning Agency, the Ministry
of Finance, and the MITI. Economic plans themselves had
neither a sufficient legal basis nor legal sanction. Just like the
basic laws referred to, plans had no legal binding force unless
further specific legislative measures were put into force. (11)
Plans were important, however, in the sense that they indicated
the direction in which government policy was moving and thereby led private economic activities toward a definite goal, while
providing enterprises with an outlook on activities and countermeasures in advance. In a way, both economic plans and basic
laws are equivalent to a party platform or an administrative
policy speech; they provide long-term guidelines for the government and business in the name of national consensus and restrict the course of private activities within a large framework.

When a policy decision is made on an economic plan with a
given goal, or when a basic law that prescribes a specific objective comes into legal existence, it is legislated in more
concrete and specific terms, and a variety of administrative
systems and measures are prepared on the basis of this series
of laws.

Types of Government Intervention —
Classification by Aims and Actions

Interference or intervention by the government in private economic activities may be broadly divided by aims and actions into passive interference (restriction of rights or freedom) and active interference (protective aid), and by methods of interference into authoritative and nonauthoritative interference (including administrative guidance). The actual forms of interference or regulation are combinations of the above. (12)

Passive authoritative interference is the method of directly and generally (in principle) forbidding some economic action according to the law and entrusting its approval (prohibition in general and in principle), authorization (consent of the government), and license (government permission for specific actions and items) to executive authority. The approval and authorization of businesses, the authorization of prices and fares, restrictions on new capacity, and the like are all in this category. The registration system for capacity according to the Law for Temporary Measures for the Improvement of the Structure of the Textile Industry (formerly the Law for Temporary Measures for the Equipment of the Textile Industry) is also a system that conforms to this. The Foreign Exchange and Foreign Trade Control Laws, enacted for the sake of the balance-of-payments policy and the trade protection policy, and the administrative measures thereof are major authoritative restrictions.

Active authoritative interference includes many legal systems. The first of these is a system which, in order to attain the goals of economic plans and public policy, establishes public financial institutions like the Japan Development Bank ("Japan Development Bank Law," 1951) and the Export-Import Bank of Japan ("Japan Export-Import Bank Law," 1950) and special public utilities like the Japan Highway Public Corporation and invests large sums of state funds and supplies goods and services to the private economic sector through these public organs. Government financial institutions, for instance, were established

for the purpose of appropriating public funds toward the promotion of industry in the form of low-interest and selective loans.
Loans for specific industries are designated in separate laws
such as the "Law for Temporary Measures to Promote Specified
Machine Industries."

Second, another channel of investment of public funds in specified industries is the government subsidy system (subsidies,
grants, bounties), called legal assistance and budget assistance,
which is almost permanently institutionalized. Subsidies to industry are mainly in agriculture, forestry, fishing, food processing, coal and petroleum mining, small business, water service
for industrial use, machine tools, electronic equipment, and
marine transport and shipbuilding.

In addition to those mentioned above, one can cite tariffs, discriminatory excises, and special depreciation charges (as tax
credits) to protect trade and specified industries. In these, the
government interferes deliberately on the basis of the Customs
Act and the Excise Act. Also, the power rates of the govern-
ment-regulated electric power industry are approved as public
utility charges by the Public Utilities Division of the Agency
of Natural Resources and Energy of the MITI, and the rates
for large industrial users have until now been kept preferen-
tially low.

The Antitrust Act, as far as its character is concerned, comes
under passive authoritative interference by the government. This
is because the Antitrust Act restricts the freedom of contract,
economic activities, and business conduct and generally prohibits collusive acts (cartel) by enterprises, monopolistic acts,
unfair trade restrictions, and the like as violations of economic
democracy and public interest. But ever since the 1953 reform
that relaxed government interference, authorized cartel agreements, or acts have been more important in Japan in conjunction
with industrial policy. This is because it involved not only passive approval by the authorities concerned (e.g., the MITI and
the Fair Trade Commission) of depression cartels or rationalization cartels, but also because laws by which the government
actively instructs manufacturers to engage in certain types of

cartel agreements within the scope determined by the law were
expanded as a force that lends support to industrial policy.

We have compiled a list of major commodities and industries
which have been frequently exempted from the Antitrust Act [in
Appendix Table 2, which is not reproduced here]. A few cartels
were approved, especially for the sake of industrial policy. They
include the agreement on interest rates based on the "Temporary
Interest Rates Adjustment Law" in order to provide low interest
loans for businesses and collusive acts regarding production
and sales, prices, capacity, technology, and purchasing methods
of raw materials approved by a number of laws that the MITI
legislated, e.g., the "Law for Temporary Measures for Textile
Industry Equipment," the "Law for Temporary Measures to Promote the Machine Industry," the "Law for Temporary Measures
to Promote the Electronics Industry," and the "Law for Temporary Measures to Stabilize Fertilizer Price." Incorporated
cartels are approved in the same vein by the "Environmental
Sanitation Act," the "Import-Export Transactions Act," the
"Small Enterprises Organization Act," etc. These cartels are
mostly made up of small businesses. By contrast, "recession"
cartels and "rationalization" cartels are mainly in textiles,
iron and steel, chemicals, and petroleum products manufactured
mostly by big business.

This legislative maneuvering takes into account the fact that
Japan's postwar acceptance of the principles of American economic democracy, particularly the antitrust principle, obligates
the government to prohibit cartels. It is a legal ingenuity so
devised as to make the government avoid fully or semicompul-
sory regulatory methods like government decrees ordering establishing cartels, restricting production, or restraining capacity increases in violation of the above principles.

Finally, there are two types of nonauthoritative interference
by the government — administrative guidance unique to Japan
and the injection of public work funds into the private sector.

Administrative guidance is usually conveyed in the form of a
"communication," based on "recommendation" (13), but the directives, advices, wishes, notifications, opinions, etc., of public

agencies like the Ministry of Finance, the MITI, the Ministries
of Transportation, Construction, and Agriculture and Forestry
to private enterprises concerned often constitute administrative
guidance in a broad sense, and these, too, in fact frequently
achieve the objectives of regulation and promotion. This type
of nonauthoritative administrative guidance is often carried out
in Japan's economic administration for two reasons: a flexible
adaptation to economic realities and an expectation of practical
results.

Administrative guidance at times has a direct legal basis,
but generally it does not require direct legal authority. Actually, it is either related to laws designed for authoritative interference or is carried out as administrative power or duty
based on the law that established each ministry. For instance,
Article 3 of the law that established the Ministry of International Trade and Industry expressly states that "the Ministry
of International Trade and Industry shall be an administrative
organ that will assume the responsibility of carrying out as one
body the following national administrative affairs and activities:
(1) the promotion and regulation of commerce and the supervision of foreign exchange accompanying commerce; (2) the
promotion, improvement, regulation, and inspection of the production, distribution, and consumption of mineral and industrial
goods; (3) ..."; Article 9 of the said law defines the duties of
the Industrial Policy Bureau thus: "The following affairs shall
be administered by the Industrial Policy Bureau: (1) devising
policies and plans related to the overall supply and demand of
goods that are handled within the domain of the MITI as well
as basic policies and plans related to commerce, mining,
and manufacturing; (2) improving the industrial structure concerned with operations handled within the domain of the MITI
and, in addition, matters related to the rationalization of enterprises...." Thus, the MITI has extremely broad powers to
carry out its administrative duties, but, as provided in Article 4,
the exercise of these powers must be in accordance with the
law (including orders based on it). But the administrative guidance that each ministry and agency carries out by notification,

recommendation, or instruction is at times inconsistent with the provisions of general economic laws so that the question as to which has priority becomes an issue. Typical examples of administrative guidance that frequently aroused public discussion in relation to the Antitrust Act are MITI recommendations for curtailed production in spinning, iron and steel, chemical fertilizers, vinyl chloride, etc., in the 1950s, open sales of iron and steel (14), and the guidance of major industries in their investment plans, capacity adjustment, and capacity control.

Despite legal problems in administrative guidance or the dissatisfaction of private enterprises with it, each ministry can normally bring pressure to bear on private enterprises by virtue of its power to approve, to authorize, to pass judgments, and to supervise on the basis of laws that enpower the ministry with authoritative interference. Private enterprises in almost all cases comply with administrative guidance, thereby making it a success. In other words, administrative guidance is also rooted in state power. In Japan's political system and practice, there does not exist in administrative guidance — except for very few precedents — administrative disposition that could be contested in court substantively and practically (in administrative or civil suits). Thus, it lacks the prerequisites of administrative relief, and there being no means for the protection of rights, there is a danger of its abuse. (15)

In fact, Japan's economic and industrial policies are not directly based on the law, and there are many cases in which the government, without depending on the application of the law, makes a specific plan with a certain outlook and demands and forces compliance from the people. In practice, the function of this type of administrative guidance occupies an important place in Japan's economic policy. For instance, between 1952 and 1965, while 58 laws (excluding revisions) related to trade and industry policy came into being, as many as 50 administrative directives of some effective consequences were effected by the MITI. [17] It is for these reasons that foreign countries regard Japan's public policy as essentially being industrial policy, and voice a cynical criticism that industrial policy is policy conducted by the MITI.

Another kind of nonauthoritative interference is the disburse-
ment of state funds in the form of public works expenditure,
which is carried out, as a rule, nonauthoritatively and follows
civil law via buying and selling, contractual work, employment,
and the like. It has two important functions for economic policy.
One is its function as a fiscal policy for stabilization of demand
and promoting growth; the injection of public funds in the private
sector increases effective demand and employment. The other
is the supply of public goods which have significant effects on
growth policy and industrial policy. The public works expenditure, allocated chiefly to projects like forestry conservation,
river improvement, roads and harbors, transport and communications facilities, water supply and drainage, and irrigation and
land improvements, provides the basis for industrial development,
gives to the private sector a direct and indirect productivity
effect that includes the effect of external economies, and
through industrial locations and the maintenance of the environment induces industrial investment and housing investment.

The Effect of the Selective Allocation of Funds

As already stated, the economic objective that was the persistent theme of economic plans during the high growth period
of 1955-1970 was the expanding equilibrium of growth, full employment, and the balance of payments. This objective was to
be achieved through planning for heavy and chemical industrialization, choosing in particular the following three types of industries — (1) those found in advanced industrial nations which
have great weights in production and employment and in which
demand is expected to grow faster than income; (2) those which
will bring about expansion and technological progress in related
industries; and (3) those which are expected to become export
industries.

The theory underlying the industrial structure policy for this
purpose was to place undeveloped domestic industries with
little competitive power under the government's active interference and to build up a large-scale production system, while

limiting entry into the domestic market of foreign enterprises
with already established mass production systems and restricting the competition of foreign manufacturers in the domestic
market. Concrete protective and nurturing policies adopted on
the basis of this theory may be summed up as follows: for the former
(1) protective tariffs, (2) a commodity tax system favorable to
home-produced goods, (3) import restrictions by means of foreign exchange allocation, and (4) the regulation of foreign exchange; for the latter, (1) selective low-interest credit supply
by public and private financial institutions, (2) subsidy grants,
(3) a special depreciation system under the Special Taxation
Measures Law, (4) exemption from import duties on essential
machinery and equipment, (5) authorization to import necessary
foreign technology, (6) improving land conditions for industrial
plants by means of public works, and (7) administrative guidance
by the MITI.

The Effects of Protective and Nurturing Policies

First, let us examine changes in Japan's industrial structure in
relation to the choice of industries (1) and (3) [see p. 24]. Changes
in the industrial structure are represented by changes in industrial compositions of employment, gross production, real value
added, and exports between 1955 and 1970. (They are shown in
Appendix Table 3 [not reproduced here].) The data reveal the
fact that the industrial structure attains its sophistication via
establishing heavy and chemical industries during the late sixties,
so much so that by 1970 heavy and chemical industries accounted
for a higher proportion of production and exports in Japan than
in Western European countries.

Income and price elasticities of domestic demand for consumption and of demand for leading export commodities between
1960 and 1971 are reported in Table 1. [18]

They indicate that it proved to be appropriate to select key commodities and industries in the light of high income elasticities.

It is, however, extremely difficult to make a quantitative de-
composition of the sophistication of Japan's industrial structure

Table 1

Income and Price Elasticities of Demand

	Income elasticity	Price elasticity
Domestic consumption		
Food	0.376	−0.681
Textiles	0.605	−0.802
Consumer durables	1.523	−1.413
Exports		
Textiles	0.483	−0.624
Chemicals	3.046	−
Iron and steel	3.249	−1.232
Metal products	1.426	−2.235
Machinery	1.448	−1.457
Automobiles	1.945	−2.554

in order to determine the net effect of each of the protective and nurturing policies mentioned above.

Therefore, from what we have observed, we propose a hypothesis that the most decisive factors in facilitating sophistication of the industrial structure were nurturing policies (1) and (6), namely, the selective credit allocation by public financial institutions and public works expenditures. In what follows we examine how this selective allocation of capital worked. We should note, however, that it was effective under the multiple barriers of tariffs, discriminating commodity taxes, and import restrictions involving a foreign exchange allocation system. (16)

Table 2 shows changes in the quinquennial sum of real public investment. The ratio of real gross investment to real gross domestic product, which determines Japan's productive capacity rose rapidly from 17.2% in 1955-1959 to 24.8% in 1960-1964 and 28.4% in 1965-1969. In this surge of overall investment, priority in public investment was given to road and port facilities, transport and communications facilities, and the like, which build up the economic overhead capital ahead of demand. This type of investment grew as much as 2.92 times from 1955-1959 to 1960-

Table 2

Public Investment in Constant Prices(b)

(billions of 1965 yen)

	Gross domestic product (1)	Gross domestic investment in plant and equipment(a) (2)	(2)/(1) (%) (3)	Private investment in plant and equipment (4)	Public investment (5)	Public investment in the industrial overhead (6)	Public investment in the living overhead (7)	(5)/(4) (%) (8)	(6)/(5) (%) (9)	(7)/(5) (%) (10)
1955-59	78,923	13,594	17.2	9,039	4,555	2,177	2,378	50.4	47.8	52.2
1960-64	132,711	32,856	24.8	22,102 (2.44)	10,754 (2.36)	6,355 (2.92)	4,399 (1.85)	48.7	59.1	40.9
1965-70	268,794	76,298	28.4	52,862 (2.39)	23,436 (2.18)	13,608 (2.14)	9,828 (2.23)	44.3	58.1	41.9

a) Excluding private residential construction and inventory investment.

b) Figures in parentheses are the rates of expansion over the preceding period.

1964. It was followed immediately by private investment in plant and equipment at almost the same rate. This fact indicates that the government considered the preparation of the industrial base essential for realizing its industrialization plan. In fact, as much as 59.1% in 1960-1964 and 58.1% in 1965-1970 of public investment was devoted to building the industrial base. This made it inevitable for public investment to lag behind in the areas of improving living conditions, namely, environmental hygiene, welfare facilities, and pollution control measures.

The Realities and Significance of Nurturing Key Industries

Next, let us examine how funds were selectively allocated for the purpose of nurturing key industries through various financial institutions — nine public financial institutions, e.g., the Japan Development Bank, the Export-Import Bank of Japan, the Agriculture, Forestry, and Fisheries Financial Corporation, the Small Business Finance Corporation, and the People's Finance Corporation, commercial banks (city banks, local banks, trust banks, and the long-term credit bank), small-business financial institutions (mutual loans and savings banks, credit associations, the Central Bank for Commerce and Industry, credit unions, etc.), agriculture, forestry, and fisheries financial institutions (Central Cooperative Bank for Agriculture and Forestry, Credit Federation of Agricultural Cooperatives, agricultural cooperative associations, Credit Federation of Fishery Cooperatives, fisheries cooperative associations, etc.), securities financial institutions (securities finance corporations, security corporations), and insurance companies (life insurance companies, indemnities insurance companies). The allocation of funds determines the capital stock of industrial equipment, which in turn determines the productive capacity of the industrial sector. Since the industrial composition of the capital stock is by and large decided upon by this fund allocation, the industrial composition of the employment, production, and value added are also determined. In other words, the credit allocation is a decisive factor in advancing the industrial structure.

Table 3, showing changes in public loans by industry (net of double counting), reveals clearly the government's financial policy in this respect. Both the industrial composition and the rates of increase from 1960-1965 to 1966-1970 indicate that priority was placed in public fund allocation on key industries like primary metals, metal products, and machinery, on agriculture, forestry, and fisheries for the sake of protection and modernization, on basic overhead industries like transport and electric power, which require colossal funds, and on tertiary industries for the sake of protection and modernization of small business (especially in distributive trades).

We can get a broad idea of how emphasis shifted in public financing policy from examining various laws, certificates of incorporation, and annual reports of public financial institutions. A clearer view, however, can be obtained from inspecting works of the Japan Development Bank which played a leading role in industrial financing. Its major projects from 1951 to 1974 are listed in Appendix Table 4 [not reproduced here]. Table 4 shows changes in the amounts of its new loans, outstanding loans, and the number of borrowing firms by industry. It reveals that priority was given to basic overhead industries like electric power and transport until 1960, shifted gradually to key industries like metals, chemicals, and machinery by 1970, and has now moved to urban redevelopment, regional development, pollution control, technical development, and the modernization of distribution. Within key industries, the emphasis is being shifted to electronic computers, now that older ones have been fully developed.

Nevertheless, public industrial loans are less than one-tenth of the total financial requirement. Therefore, the significance of selective allocation of public funds is found in officially designating certain industries as key or growth industries and in guiding private financial institutions to extend credit actively to these industries. Another important feature is low interest rates charged on public loans as compared to private loans. Once a decision was made by public financial institutions to

Table 3

Industrial Loans(a) by Public Financial Institutions
(billions of yen)

Period / Industry	1960-65	Composition (%)	1966-70	Composition (%)	The rate of expansion over the preceding period	1971-72	Composition (%)
Agriculture, forestry, and fisheries	298 (15.6)(b)	13.5	601 (15.7)	13.8	2.02	373 (14.7)	12.5
Mining	91 (4.8)	4.1	46 (1.2)	1.1	0.51	28 (1.1)	0.9
Textiles	67 (3.5)	3.1	90 (2.4)	2.1	1.34	105 (4.2)	3.5
Chemicals	67 (3.5)	3.0	72 (1.9)	1.7	1.08	22 (0.9)	0.8
Primary metals and metal products	83 (4.4)	3.8	180 (4.7)	4.1	2.16	97 (3.8)	3.2
Machinery	290 (15.1)	13.1	582 (15.2)	13.4	2.01	123 (4.9)	4.1
Paper and pulp	31 (1.6)	1.4	25 (0.7)	0.6	0.83	25 (1.0)	0.8
Other manufacturing	155 (8.1)	7.0	220 (5.8)	5.1	1.42	219 (8.6)	7.3
Construction	38 (2.0)	1.7	101 (2.6)	2.3	2.66	103 (4.1)	3.4
Transportation, communications, trade, finance, and services	794 (41.4)	36.0	1,909 (49.8)	44.0	2.40	1,442 (56.7)	48.1
All industries	1,917 (100.0)	100.0	3,830 (100.0)	100.0	2.00	2,540 (100.0)	
Individuals	292	13.3	511	11.8	1.75	461	15.4
Grand total	2,210	100.0	4,341	100.0	1.96	3,002	100.0

Notes: a) Net loans, including long-term and short-term loans (excluding those which are purely for the short-term). In Japan, short-term loans serve very often as long-term loans because they are repeatedly renewed.
b) Figures in parentheses are the percentages of the total for all industries.
Source: Based on the author's tentative estimates.

finance an industry or an enterprise, private financial institutions competed with one another in financing them with almost no investigation. If a single bank was unable to take care of matters, banks formed a syndicate to raise funds. As for the interest rates of public financial institutions, the Agriculture, Forestry and Fishery Finance Corporation makes some loans at 3.5% and 4.5% in accordance with its legal stipulation. Most of them are about 8-9% as against the official discount rate of 9%. As is well known, city banks were engaged in forcing borrowers to maintain compensatory balances under conditions of excess demand for credit. It can be surmised that city banks' effective rates were higher than the rates charged by public financial institutions by 3 to 4 percentage points. In other words, public loans subsidized key industries in the form of cheap credit.

Table 5 gives the industrial composition of loans by private financial institutions. A comparison with Table 4, which shows the industrial composition of public loans, readily reveals that our hypothesis on the allocation of funds is empirically supported in the long run. Therefore, broadly speaking, the total supply of funds in Japan was controlled by the Bank of Japan, the level and structure of interest rates were artificially regulated by the Ministry of Finance, and private funds were allocated, under the guidance of public financial institutions, by city banks which competed for market shares. In this process, the Bank of Japan followed the guidelines of the Economic Planning Agency and the MITI and determined the total amount of funds so as to satisfy the demands of growth industries. At the same time, the Ministry of Finance maintained the low interest policy inasmuch as the policy did not lead to large deficits in the balance of payments or to sharp price rises.

This semi-artificial system of fund supply worked well during the period of high growth when the industrialization plan was in force. This was because, as Table 6 shows, the operating profit rate on total assets was relatively high in key industries in conformity with the capitalistic principle of profit maximization. Hence, both lenders and borrowers benefited from the arrangement.

404

Table 4

The Japan Development Bank: New Loans, Outstanding Loans, and
the Number of Borrowing Firms by Industry
(millions of yen)

Year / Industry	1955						1960						1965					
	New loans	Composition (%)	Outstanding loans	Composition (%)	Number of firms	Composition (%)	New loans	Composition (%)	Outstanding loans	Composition (%)	Number of firms	Composition (%)	New loans	Composition (%)	Outstanding loans	Composition (%)	Number of firms	Composition (%)
Electric power	22,305	45.1	188,003	50.0	30	2.8	21,350	32.8	277,499	51.0	18	1.6	18,897	9.5	335,878	35.2	25	1.3
Transportation	16,492	33.3	120,181	32.0	244	23.1	16,505	25.3	177,203	32.6	180	15.9	100,153	50.4	323,235	33.8	316	17.0
Mining	4,375	8.9	35,694	9.5	320	30.3	6,918	10.6	31,819	5.9	152	13.4	18,319	9.2	80,811	8.5	108	5.8
Metal manufacturing	475	1.0	11,395	3.0	37	3.5	2,984	4.6	11,108	2.1	112	9.9	4,020	2.0	18,706	2.0	156	8.4
Chemicals	1,070	2.2	5,677	1.5	61	5.8	4,690	7.2	17,529	3.2	55	4.8	15,835	7.9	62,009	6.5	132	7.1
Machinery	2,930	5.9	3,817	1.0	86	8.1	3,537	5.4	9,737	1.8	288	25.4	12,610	6.3	39,801	4.2	465	24.9
Agriculture, forestry, and fisheries	230	0.5	2,607	0.7	101	9.6	825	1.3	1,802	0.3	37	3.3	602	0.3	1,890	0.2	23	1.2
Textiles	200	0.4	4,174	1.1	76	7.2	290	0.4	1,825	0.3	43	3.8	5,446	2.7	14,270	1.5	124	6.7
Others	1,345	2.7	4,335	1.2	102	9.6	8,072	12.4	15,440	2.8	249	21.9	23,386	11.7	77,436	8.1	515	27.6
Total	49,422	100.0	375,883	100.0	1,057	100.0	65,171	100.0	543,962	100.0	1,134	100.0	199,678	100.0	954,036	100.0	1,864	100.0

Year / Industry	1970 New loans	(%) Composition	1970 Outstanding loans	(%) Composition	1970 Number of firms	(%) Composition	1974 New loans	(%) Composition	1974 Outstanding loans	(%) Composition	1974 Number of firms	(%) Composition
Electric power	26,971	7.9	359,635	20.4	30	1.6	79,625	12.6	488,932	16.3	26	1.3
Transportation	151,301	44.3	754,514	42.7	353	18.6	144,408	22.9	1,120,327	37.4	333	16.0
Mining	4,160	1.2	101,538	5.8	69	3.6	4,800	0.8	80,007	2.7	49	2.4
Metal manufacturing	16,185	4.7	53,307	3.0	161	8.5	48,903	7.7	160,416	5.4	205	9.8
Chemicals	28,245	8.3	106,572	6.5	156	8.2	76,510	12.1	179,948	6.0	179	8.6
Machinery	23,365	6.8	80,306	4.5	356	18.8	35,930	5.7	119,302	4.0	330	15.8
Agriculture, forestry, and fisheries	3,890	1.1	8,741	0.5	35	1.8	1,968	0.3	17,155	0.6	25	1.2
Textiles	9,265	2.7	27,278	1.5	129	6.8	8,165	1.3	49,942	1.7	130	6.2
Others	78,502	23.0	274,572	15.6	609	32.1	231,345	36.6	774,750	25.9	807	38.7
Total	341,884	100.0	1,766,463	100.0	1,898	100.0	631,654	100.0	2,990,779	100.0	2,084	100.0

Source: The Japan Development Bank.

Table 5

Industrial Loans(a) by Private Financial Institutions
(billions of yen)

Period / Industry	1960-65	Composition (%)	1966-70	Composition (%)	The rate of expansion over the preceding period	1971-72	Composition (%)
Agriculture, forestry, and fisheries	1,575 (7.8)(b)	7.5	3,436 (9.7)	9.0	2.18	2,225 (6.9)	6.1
Mining	154 (0.8)	0.7	77 (0.2)	0.2	0.50	160 (0.5)	0.4
Textiles	1,007 (5.0)	4.8	1,192 (3.4)	3.1	1.18	1,055 (3.3)	2.9
Chemicals	1,268 (6.3)	6.0	1,734 (4.9)	4.6	1.37	1,076 (3.4)	2.9
Primary metals and metal products	1,611 (8.0)	7.7	2,985 (8.5)	7.9	1.85	2,108 (6.6)	5.8
Machinery	2,955 (14.6)	14.0	4,603 (13.1)	12.1	1.56	1,749 (5.5)	4.8
Paper and pulp	290 (1.4)	1.4	440 (1.3)	1.2	1.52	406 (1.3)	1.1
Other manufacturing	2,213 (10.9)	10.5	3,289 (9.3)	8.7	1.49	2,926 (9.2)	8.0
Construction	1,248 (6.2)	5.9	1,896 (5.4)	5.0	1.52	2,998 (9.4)	8.2
Transportation, communications, trade, finance, and services	7,892 (39.0)	37.5	15,591 (44.2)	41.1	1.98	17,186 (53.9)	47.0
All industries	20,219 (100.0)		35,247 (100.0)		1.74	31,892 (100.0)	
Individuals	852	4.0	2,706	7.1	3.18	4,672	12.8
Grand total	21,071	100.0	37,954	100.0	1.80	36,565	100.0

Notes: a) See note (a) of Table 3.
b) See note (b) of Table 3.
Source: Based on the author's tentative estimates.

Table 6

Operating Profit Rate on Total Assets
(%)

Period Industry	1956-60 average	1961-65 average	1966-70 average
Textiles	8.8	6.0	6.8
Chemicals	11.0	8.8	9.2
Iron and steel	10.0	7.2	8.6
Machinery	11.9	8.9	8.6
Transport equipment[a]	9.9	9.2	8.7
Metal products	11.7	8.7	9.8
Paper and pulp	9.0	6.9	6.9
Other manufacturing	9.7	7.7	8.2
Construction	6.4	7.1	6.7
Services	5.7	7.0	7.4

Note: a) Excluding shipbuilding.
Source: Annual and Quarterly Reports of Corporate Enterprise Statistics [Hojin Kigyo Tokei].

Other Determinants of the Industrial Structure

Tables 7 and 8 show what kind of industrial structure of investment and capital stock resulted from this fund allocation. The tables give a strong support to our hypotheses that connects the fund allocation and the industrial composition of capital stock. However, we note that the industrial compositions of employment, production, and value added do not necessarily correspond to those of funds and capital stock. This indicates the fact that the industrial structure is not determined by the credit allocation mechanism alone but is greatly dependent upon initial conditions, production technology, final demands, and market organization. Just a single policy measure cannot achieve a multitude of targets. The industrial structure cannot be changed easily in a short time.

Table 7

Private Investment in Plant and Equipment
(billions of yen)

Industry	1955-59	Composition (%)	1960-65	Composition (%)	Rate of expansion over the preceding period	1966-70	Composition (%)	Rate of expansion over the preceding period	1971-72	Composition (%)
Agriculture, forestry, and fisheries	983	12.9	2,380	9.3	2.42	4,978	10.3	2.09	2,732	9.1
Mining	226	3.0	651	2.6	2.88	963	2.0	1.48	404	1.3
Textiles	310	4.0	681	2.7	2.20	1,208	2.5	1.77	764	2.5
Chemicals	591	7.7	2,047	8.0	3.46	3,369	7.0	1.65	1,631	5.4
Primary metals and metal products	637	8.3	2,939	11.5	4.61	5,295	11.0	1.80	2,845	9.4
Machinery	612	8.0	3,107	12.1	5.07	5,716	11.8	1.84	2,952	9.8
Paper and pulp	197	2.6	556	2.2	2.82	845	1.8	1.52	494	1.6
Other manufacturing	504	6.6	1,943	7.6	3.85	3,888	8.0	2.00	2,503	8.3
Construction	172	2.3	983	3.8	5.69	2,077	4.3	2.11	1,648	5.5
Transportation, communications, trade, finance, and services	3,409	44.6	10,286	40.2	3.02	19,923	41.3	1.94	14,206	47.1
Total	7,646	100.0	25,578	100.0	3.35	48,266	100.0	1.89	30,184	100.0

Table 8

Private Capital Stock in Plant and Equipment
(billions of 1965 yen)

Year / Industry	(1) 1960	Composition (%)	(2) 1965	Composition (%)	(2)/(1)	(3) 1970	Composition (%)	(3)/(2)	(4) 1973	Composition (%)
Agriculture, forestry, and fisheries	5,310	19.2	7,544	15.9	1.42	11,942	14.2	1.58	14,452	12.5
Mining	459	1.7	812	1.7	1.77	1,307	1.6	1.61	1,643	1.4
Textiles	1,668	6.0	2,430	5.1	1.46	3,743	4.5	1.54	4,635	4.0
Chemicals	1,117	4.0	2,277	4.8	2.04	4,301	5.1	1.89	5,368	4.6
Primary metals and metal products	1,738	6.3	3,806	8.0	2.19	7,720	9.2	2.03	10,272	8.9
Machinery	1,863	6.8	3,990	8.5	2.14	8,097	9.6	2.03	12,223	10.5
Paper and pulp	422	1.5	813	1.7	1.92	1,430	1.7	1.76	2,110	1.8
Other manufacturing	2,605	9.4	4,762	10.0	1.83	8,748	10.4	1.84	12,680	10.9
Construction	440	1.6	1,134	2.4	2.58	2,720	3.2	2.40	4,232	3.6
Transportation, communications, trade, finance, and services	12,039	43.5	19,823	41.8	1.65	33,901	40.4	1.71	48,413	41.7
Total	27,664	100.0	47,394	100.0	1.71	83,913	100.0	1.77	116,031	100.0

For example, the goal of promoting heavy and chemical industries has been achieved by concentrating funds in these industries, but the goal of modernizing agriculture, forestry, and fisheries and tertiary industries has not been too well accomplished despite heavy injections of public and private loans and grants-in-aid from the government. The labor productivity index (the volume of production per person engaged in production) increased from 1955 to 1970 as follows: 3.1 in agriculture, forestry, and fisheries, 2.5 in tertiary industries, 5.4 in the chemical industry, 4.3 in the metal and metal products industry, and 7.2 in the machine industry. The first two industries contain many nonmodern enterprises, but labor productivity rose significantly because of increases in capital intensity, of technological progress, and of internal and external economies. However, its increase is much less than that experienced in heavy and chemical industries. As of 1970, the labor productivity in the traditional industries was less than one-seventh that in the heavy and chemical industries. As the Japanese economy expanded over the decade and a half under review, funds invested in agriculture and tertiary industries were relatively inefficient; their efficiency is estimated to be one-third to one-fourth that in heavy and chemical industries. The same tendency is observed also in the textile industry, and it is undeniable that funds were invested in these industries for the sake of protection and relief based on political and social considerations.

Effectiveness of Mass Production System —
Cost and Price Reductions

I have mentioned several times that priority was given to key industries in order to create international competitive power through the mass production system that would bring about cost and price reductions and thereby establish heavy and chemical industries as export industries. I also took note that as long as economies of the large scale operate and the law of increasing returns works, government intervention through subsidization and fund allocation is justified. Economies of scale, how-

ever, are internal and external and there are many kinds of
these. This gives rise to a controversy between economists
and industrialists whenever enterprise mergers come to be a
political issue. I will not touch upon this subject here and limit
my discussion to the effectiveness of cost reduction arising
from mass production in mechanical industries. For instance,
consider a number of studies on the optimum plant size in the
automobile industry, referring not only to production but also
to sales.

While it is necessary to define international competitive power,
we believe that it is reflected in price and quality. In what follows, we deal with cost and price only, leaving the discussion of
quality to another occasion.

First, Table 9 broadly indicates the international competitive
power of Japan's industrial products. The table shows changes
in the unit values of industrial exports and in the market shares
of major industrial countries. The American unit value rose by
22%, 7%, and 12.4% in the three sub-periods between 1953 and
1970, resulting in the American loss of market share by 7.8 percentage points. By contrast, Japan had falls in its export unit value by
11% and 3% during the first two sub-periods. This price competition enabled Japan to increase its market share by 7.5 percentage points by 1970. We may conclude that the international
competitive power of Japan's industrial goods increased sharply
over seventeen years until 1970, producing favorable results.

But we should note that between 1967 and 1970 Japan's export
prices rose sharply in step with those of the U.S., West Germany, and Italy. There are a number of reasons for this price
increase. Of these, three principal ones are the end of cost reduction through the system of large-scale production, the rising
trend in wages due to the end of excess supply of labor, and the
emergence of downward price rigidity associated with the formation of an oligopolistic system. What at least comes into
question here is the possibility that by 1970 the mass production system was no longer capable to reduce prime cost.

Figure 1 illustrates movements of the average prime cost,
producer price, and export price in iron and steel, automobiles,

412

Table 9

Export Unit Values and Market Shares of Industrial Goods(a)

	The rate of change in the export unit value of industrial goods (%)			Market shares of individual countries in the total industrial exports of the 12 advanced countries(a) (%)			
	1953-62	1963-66	1967-70	1953	1963	1966	1970
U.S.	22	7	12.4	26.2	21.8	20.3	18.4
U.K.	17	10	5.3	15.2	14.2	12.7	10.2
W. Germany	6	4	11.1	13.4	19.9	19.1	19.2
Italy	-20	-1	9.9	3.3	5.8	6.8	6.9
Japan	-11	-3	11.1	3.8	7.7	9.6	11.3

Note: a) Consisting of U.S., U.K., W. Germany, France, Sweden, Netherlands, Belgium, Italy, Canada, Austria, Switzerland, and Japan.
Sources: Data from OECD and UN sources.

nonferrous metals and metal products, machinery, and chemicals. The figure indicates that it was roughly in 1963 that the end or slowdown in the rate of cost reduction became evident. There is a clear indication that these prices became rigid downward and flexible upward after 1963. The phenomenon appeared first in iron and steel and nonferrous metals, which are intermediate products and last in automobiles, which are final goods. Changes in the average prime cost in the automobile industry until 1963 resembles the Silverstone curve or the average cost curve that often appears in economics textbooks. Producer and export prices decreased in about the same way as the average cost but started to rise in 1967. Therefore, 1967 seems to have marked a clear end to the effectiveness of industrial policy.

To judge international competitiveness, however, we have to look at international parity. Kravis and Lipsey [22], in order to measure accurately international price competition among advanced industrial countries, computed international parity indices by country and by commodity, based on actual prices or prices offered rather than on unit values obtained from trade statistics. Table 10 summarizes their results with regard to iron and steel, metal products, and machinery. The indices computed up to 1964 for the U.K., the EEC, West Germany, and Japan relative to the United States represent very well the actual status of international competitiveness.

The table enables us to judge that Japan was fully competitive in international markets of iron and steel, metal products, and electrical machinery by 1963. Thus, in these products, Japanese industries had been securely established as export industries, supporting our foregoing time-series observations.

Unfortunately, the Kravis-Lipsey indices are not available beyond 1964. Limited time and resources do not permit me to extend the indices for later years. However, changes in the export unit value indices reported in Table 9 suggest that Japan strengthened its international competitive power in major industrial products until 1966. It is probable that Japan maintained its strong competitive position until 1970, despite all-round price increases of Japanese industrial products after

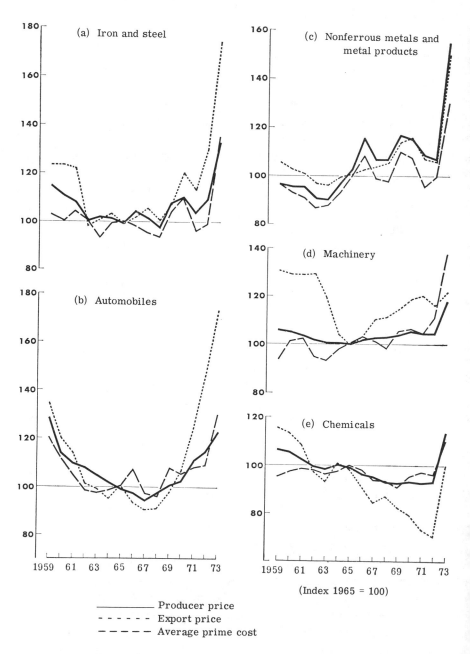

Figure 1. Average prime cost, producer price, and export price in heavy and chemical industries.

1967 because its competitors' prices rose also at about the
same rate. It is for this reason that Japan's exports of heavy
and chemical products grew markedly during the late sixties,
enlarging its market share. One might say that this was a period during which Japan was drunk with the spectacular results
of its industrialization plan and industrial policy.

Had we had the benefit of correct foresight, however, we
would have seen this period as a crucial period of transition in
which we should have immediately come to grips with a turn-
about in policy and reforms in the system. We should have
recognized that industrial policy, which had been justified until
then, and systems adopted on its behalf had already finished
playing their roles; reorganized the legal administrative system, fiscal and monetary system, and protective system adopted
in the interest of industrial policy in the light of the basic principles of economic policy and the fundamental changes in Japan's
economic structure; and devised a plan and system of competition to deal with new socioeconomic problems.

The Aftereffects of Industrial Policy

Special policies and systems for achieving specific goals re-
semble specific medicines. Specific medicines prove effective
when they are used for certain therapeutic goals and for the
purpose of improving physical constitution, and if they are used
intensively during a given period, their benefits increase
markedly. But because specific medicines are not panaceas,
they have many side effects and are dangerous if used in a big
dose for extended periods. These side effects are hardly noticed
at first because of the eye-catching effect of the medicines, but
as they accumulate, they show their results in due course, changing physical constitution for the worse and debilitating the body
in the long run. Another annoying problem with specific medicines is that even if the harm of side effects comes into the
open or is noticed, it is not easy to restore a person's physical
constitution to the original state. Industrial policy and its specific systems have the same character and function as specific
medicines.

Table 10

International Parity Indices by Commodity

(U.S. = 100)

	1953	1957	1961	1962	1963	1964
Iron and steel (SITC 67)						
U.S.	100 (84)(a)	100 (101)	100 (102)	100 (100)	100 (99)	100 (100)
U.K.	92	85	79	78	76	82
EEC	88	87	76	74	72	78
W. Germany	85	83	77	76	73	78
Japan	NA	NA	75	70	70	70
Metal products (SITC 69)						
U.S.	100 (86)	100 (98)	100 (98)	100 (100)	100 (100)	100 (102)
U.K.	97	95	97	92	92	92
EEC	97	96	97	96	93	91
W. Germany	90	87	92	92	91	90
Japan	NA	NA	74	74	69	73
Electrical machinery (SITC 72)						
U.S.	100 (102)	100 (108)	100 (104)	100 (100)	100 (97)	100 (97)
U.K.	97	94	102	103	108	106
EEC	90	86	91	94	97	95
W. Germany	90	87	93	96	98	97
Japan	NA	103	91	89	90	91

417

Shipbuilding (SITC 735)						
U.S.	100 (98)	100 (116)	100 (101)	100 (100)	100 (96)	100 (97)
EEC	68	66	58	59	56	55
W. Germany	62	60	53	56	54	53
Japan	59	62	50	51	46	46
Precision instruments (SITC 861)						
U.S.	100 (86)	100 (93)	100 (99)	100 (100)	100 (100)	100 (102)
U.K.	76	85	89	88	87	91
W. Germany	86	86	87	88	88	88
Japan	NA	NA	83	82	84	83

Note: a) U.S. figures in parentheses are price indices with 1962 = 100.
Source: I. B. Kravis and R. E. Lipsey, Price Competitiveness in World Trade (New York: NBER, 1971).

Japan's industrial policy, too, has had many side effects. The two that stand out in the long run, doing the most harm, are pollution (industrial pollution and accumulated urban pollution) and oligopolistic price rises. Each involves a risk of weakening the Japanese economy.

With regard to pollution, I am not ready to present detailed analysis of either its actual state or the effect of regulatory measures. Therefore, I will limit myself here to merely pointing out a few examples and problems.

It has been some time since the question of pollution, especially industrial pollution, was raised around 1959 by a few informed persons and local residents. It is common knowledge that all along industrial development involving continued expansion of production, concentration of factories in limited areas, and agglomeration of urban population was leading to a marked increase in both industrial pollution and urban pollution. There is no doubt, therefore, that pollution is a negative by-product of industrialization that directly harms human society and is an illegitimate child of industrial policy.

Nevertheless, it is only since the enactment of the "Basic Law for Environmental Pollution Control" in 1967 that the control of pollution by the government began as a systematic legal administrative system. And it is only after the amendment of February 1970 which deleted the "stipulation for harmony with the healthy development of the economy" from the Basic Law that the government launched full-scale pollution regulations, placing a greater importance on pollution control over industrial production in a society which has had an industry-first policy. Thus, there was nearly ten years' delay in taking measures against the harmful side effects of industrial policy. This is clearly noted in the first appearance in 1970-71 of "pollution control" as a major item in the Japan Development Bank's loans. Another clear evidence is the establishment of the Environmental Agency on May 31, 1971.

Consequently, we are completely ignorant as to just how industrial and urban pollution have increased quantitatively as industrialization and urbanization proceeded. It is only from

1970 onward that it finally became possible to estimate the approximate quantity of various pollutants generated, the effectiveness of regulatory measures based on the legal administrative system, and the extent to which investment in pollution control has increased. For instance, among pollutants, those for which the estimation of the quantities generated and treated appear to be comparatively easy and in which control seems to have been effective are sulfur dioxide (SO_2), biochemical oxygen demand (BOD), and suspended substances (SS). The effectiveness of pollution control with regard to these factors as estimated by the Japan Economic Research Center is shown in Table 11.

In Table 11, the volume of exhaust (1) is the estimated volume of exhaust under conditions that industries, under present pollution control measures, engaged in pollution control activities, such as the installation of equipment for desulfurizing exhaust gas, and carried out the disposal of pollutants. The volume of exhaust (2) is the estimated volume of exhaust under conditions that pollution control measures did not exist and that industry did not make the effort to control pollution as they are doing now. We can conclude from the table that the rate of improvement in recent years has gone up and that pollution control has become more effective. Nonetheless, the total volume of discharged pollutants is as large as ever, suggesting that the increase in industrial activities will lead to a continued increase in the total volume of exhaust.

Ordinarily, drastic antipollution measures are not easily implemented in a capitalist industrial society. This is because investment in pollution control does not improve productive efficiency and is not lucrative. It is essentially the same with respect to those public goods that are required for improving living conditions for the sake of welfare. Therefore, there is no way to promote antipollution measures other than through coercion to strengthen regulatory measures, supplemented by subsidies and special financing. But the strengthening of regulatory measures will require a huge amount of pollution control investment, which has no productivity effect, and make

Table 11

Effects of Pollution Control

Rate of improvement $= \dfrac{\text{Absence of control} - \text{Presence of control}}{\text{Absence of control}} \times 100$

Industry (Amount discharged)	1965	BOD (Biochemical Oxygen Demand)						SS (Suspended Substances)...			
		1970: Efforts to control pollution			1973: Efforts to control pollution			1965	1970: Efforts to control pollution		
		Present	Absent	Rate of improvement	Present	Absent	Rate of improvement		Present	Absent	Rate of improvement
	10^3 tons	10^3 tons	10^3 tons	%	10^3 tons	10^3 tons	%	10^3 tons	10^3 tons	10^3 tons	%
Textiles	1,076.9	1,280.0	1,688.9	24.2	1,120.3	1,818.4	38.4	538.4	658.0	844.5	22.1
Paper and pulp	2,640.0	3,979.7	5,943.6	33.0	4,404.3	7,606.9	42.1	1,650.0	2,383.2	3,566.2	33.2
Chemicals	13,124.0	17,680.0	19,595.0	9.8	22,342.9	24,113.2	7.3	3,281.0	6,367.9	6,999.1	9.0
Petroleum and coal products	238.0	562.3	673.0	16.4	762.3	780.0	2.3	31.0	73.6	87.8	16.2
Clay and stone products	73.7	90.0	156.9	42.6	90.0	187.5	52.0	30,700.0	36,891.0	65,360.0	43.6
Food processing	1,255.4	1,700.0	2,288.3	25.7	1,857.8	2,747.6	32.4	1,506.5	2,041.0	2,746.0	25.7
Other manufacturing	1,401.0	2,037.4	2,613.6	22.0	2,188.0	3,648.3	12.6	1,635.0	2,388.0	3,049.2	21.7
Nonferrous and metal products	114	29.0	–	–	44.0	–	–	399.0	912.3	970.3	6.0
Iron and steel	245.0	472.0	539.8	12.6	593.8	695.2	14.6	5,671.0	10,848.0	12,522.3	13.4
Machinery	113.0	163.0	323.1	49.6	223.7	487.7	54.1	135.6	180.2	387.8	53.5
Automobiles	80.8	118.9	221.5	46.3	133.8	270.6	50.6	96.9	145.1	265.7	45.4
Mining	13.2	12.0	17.9	33.0	11.0	17.1	35.7	6,611.0	5,873.0	8,935.0	34.3
Electric power	1.7	4.0	–	–	5.0	–	–	86.0	200.0	–	–
Total	20,274.0	28,128.3	34,095.0	17.5	33,777.0	42,417.1	20.4	52,341.4	68,961.3	105,894.5	34.9

	...SS (Suspended Substances)			SO₂ (Sulfur Dioxide)						
	1973: Efforts to control pollution			1965	1970: Efforts to control pollution			1973: Efforts to control pollution		
Industry Amount discharged	Present	Absent	Rate of improvement		Present	Absent	Rate of improvement	Present	Absent	Rate of improvement
	10^3 tons	10^3 tons	%	10^3 tons	10^3 tons	10^3 tons	%	10^3 tons	10^3 tons	%
Textiles	671.5	909.2	26.1	122.7	183.2	192.5	4.8	147.8	207.4	28.3
Paper and pulp	2,613.9	4,564.1	42.7	178.2	260.3	321.2	19.0	223.3	411.1	45.7
Chemicals	8,218.4	8,611.9	4.6	373.2	535.1	796.4	32.8	442.3	979.9	54.9
Petroleum and coal products	100.1	101.7	1.6	209.3	278.6	354.8	21.5	226.3	549.5	58.8
Clay and stone products	34,216.5	78,122.5	56.2	301.7	404.5	640.4	36.8	324.5	765.5	57.6
Food processing	2,238.3	3,297.1	32.1	137.1	125.5	249.9	49.8	105.3	300.1	64.9
Other manufacturing	2,631.3	4,256.4	38.2	65.6	53.4	122.7	56.5	36.0	171.2	79.0
Nonferrous and metal products	1,151.6	1,412.8	18.5	68.8	106.6	167.6	36.4	75.9	244.1	68.9
Iron and steel	13,303.4	16,129.3	17.5	750.0	1,582.6	1,655.9	4.4	1,642.4	2,132.9	23.0
Machinery	279.9	585.3	52.2	32.2	79.2	91.6	13.5	70.1	138.2	49.3
Automobiles	167.1	324.7	48.5	11.4	29.6	31.1	4.8	23.0	38.0	39.5
Mining	4,374.0	8,543.0	48.8	49.3	40.9	66.5	38.5	20.3	63.6	68.1
Electric power	231.0	-		1,029.0	1,888.9	1,921.6	1.7	1,558.3	2,494.8	37.5
Total	70,197.0	127,066.5	29.0	3,328.6	5,668.4	6,612.2	15.8	4,895.5	8,496.3	42.4

Table 12

Cartel Violations by Industry

Industry	1965	1966	1967	1968	1969	1970	1971	1972	1973	Total
Manufacturing										
Food processing	2 (1)(a)			4 (1)	(4)	2	1		3	12
Textiles		(1)						1	1	1
Clothing and apparel	1	1								2
Lumber and wood products										2
Pulp, paper, and paper products					1	5	1	1	5	13
Printing and publishing			(1)			3	3			6
Chemicals		1		1			6	7	11	26
Petroleum and coal products	(4)	1 (1)	1 (2)	(3)	1 (7)	1 (17)	(12)	(3)	3 (16)	6
Rubber products			(1)		1	(6)	2			3
Clay and stone products		1	1 (1)	1	2	1	2 (4)	5	9	22
Iron and steel									4	4
Nonferrous metals									5	5
Metal products				1		1	1			3
Electrical machinery		(2)								
General machinery									2	2
Transport equipment				(1)	1		1			2
Precision instruments		(1)								
Other manufacturing				1		1			4	6
Subtotal	3	4	2	8	6	14	17	14	47	115
Construction									1	1
Wholesale and retail trade	(5)	(5)	(5)	(8)	(12)	(23)	(16)	(3)	(16)	(94)
Services	6	5	3	4	3	5	2	2	3	30
Total	14	14	8	20	21	42	35	19	67	240

Note: a) Cartels in wholesale and retail trade are in parentheses.

Source: Minokata, K., "A Thorough Study of Cartels — In Search of a New Development in Antitrust Policy" [Cartel no Tetteiteki Kenkyu — Dokkin Seisaku no Atarashii Tenkai o Motomete] Kikan Chuo Koron, Fall 1975.

locational conditions increasingly poor as well. Thus, we must conclude that this aftereffect of industrial policy will continue to remain serious in this respect for a long time. (17)

The second aftereffect of industrial policy is concerned with the constitution of an oligopolistic system. Heavy and chemical industries expanded during the period of rapid growth. This gave rise to the formation of an oligopolistic system in these industries. However, initially, economies of scale brought about price reduction. These called forth competition in investment, in cost reduction, and, at times, even in prices, in an attempt to enlarge the market shares. Therefore, during this period, work-able competition prevailed. The oligopolistic system was growth-oriented and competitive. In this sense, industrial policy had more merits than demerits until about 1965.

There were two adverse side effects at work in this process, however. One is, as we have already noted, that an oligopolistic system was gradually formed in heavy and chemical industries. The other is that the productivity differentials grew larger be-tween high-productivity industries like heavy and chemical in-dustries subject to economies of scale and low-productivity in-dustries like agriculture, trade, and services with very little economies of scale and between big and small business. Big business placed small businesses under control through busi-ness groupings and subcontracting in order to successfully com-pete in cost reduction.

As a result, in the manufacturing industries controlled by big business, particularly in the heavy and chemical industrial sec-tor, there emerged — coupled with the administrative guidance of the MITI — the practice of taking joint action regarding price, volume, and equipment investment in order to avoid excessive competition in capacity expansion in a recession with sluggish demand. This practice is inherent in the oligopolistic system. As growth slows down or slow growth continues, this tendency becomes stronger and the oligopolistic system becomes stag-nant and collusive. It is for this reason that depression cartels are formed in many products of heavy and chemical industries controlled by big business. Table 12 shows that cartel viola-

Table 13

Employers' Associations: the Number of Registrations(a) and the Cumulated Total

Industry	Registrations in 1974			Effective increase (A-B)	Number in existence at the end of 1973	Number in existence at the end of 1974
	Approved (A)	Amended	Dissolved (B)			
Voluntary associations						
Agriculture					3,185	3,185
Forestry	5			5	907	912
Fisheries		2			502	502
Mining	3	4	2	1	123	124
Construction	21		1	20	279	299
Manufacturing	114	52	11	103	3,944	4,047
Trade	1,703	53	5	1,698	4,661	6,359
Finance and insurances	12	23		12	444	456
Transportation, communications, and public utility	10	11	1	9	1,099	1,108
Services	9	5		9	778	787
General	8		1	7	2,203	2,210
Subtotal	1,885	151	21	1,864	18,125	19,989

Associations based on legislation

Commercial and industrial associations	75	31	1	74	915	989
Import and export associations	1	7		1	48	49
Alcoholic beverage industry associations	3	17		3	773	776
Export fisheries associations	3	17		3	773	776
Environmental sanitation associations					7	7
Coastal shipping associations	14	21		14	426	440
Fisheries production regulation associations					114	114
Mining and manufacturing technical research associations					9	9
Shopping district promotion associations	8	1		8	14	22
	2			2	8	10
Others	107	59		107	114	221
Subtotal	210	136	1	209	2,428	2,637
Grand total	2,095	287	22	2,073	20,553	22,626

Note: a) Registrations required by Section 2, Article 8 of the Antitrust Act.

Source: Secretariat, Fair Trade Commission.

tions have increased in the manufacturing sector in recent years.

On the other hand, in order to protect and modernize agriculture, forestry, and fisheries and tertiary industries, which cannot adapt themselves to drastic changes in output demand and in factor supply in the course of rapid growth, and in order to protect small business from and enable them to oppose the oligopolistic system of big business, the government engages in direct intervention in prices, volumes, capacity, and entry and to enlarge exemptions from the Antitrust Act. This is based on the idea of protecting the weak and creating countervailing power against the formation of oligopolies in heavy and chemical industries. It is for this reason that many industries and commodities in agriculture, forestry, and fisheries, trade and services, textiles, etc., are found to be subject to government intervention and to be exempted from the Antitrust Act.

Oligopolistic systems, collusive actions, federations of the weak, and countervailing power all require collectivization of those with some common interest. Collective, organized group action is necessary in order to achieve objectives effectively. In this sense, John R. Commons, the institutionalist, was right when he asserted in The Economics of Collective Action that the twentieth century is the age of collective action.

Business enterprises join together to form enterprise associations in order to promote their joint interest. These associations began to increase during the period of rapid economic growth and grew rapidly since the mid-sixties. By now, these associations are formed in nearly all industries, their total number having reached 22,626 as of 1974. Their distribution by industry is given in Table 13. They are particularly numerous in commerce, manufacturing, and agriculture, presumably for the aforesaid reasons. There are many employers' associations in important manufacturing industries, such as the Japan Iron and Steel Federation, the Japan Automobile Manufacturers' Association, the Japan Electrical Manufacturers' Association, the Japan Perfumers Association, the Japan Machinery Federation, and the Cement Association. While this associations are, by their nature, clearly for the common benefit of private enterprise, they are organized as nonprofit foundations because of vestiges of an era in which industrial policy was representative of public policy.

These associations are called into question because they help to serve as a breeding ground for stagnant, collusive oligopoly systems and as an intervening instrument for cartel action and administered pricing. In fact, we witness an increase in illegal cartels formed by big business, and there are indications that many cartels of this type were behind-the-scene schemes of these associations. Even if a certain employers' association had been created as a counterforce of the weak against the strong, it is still likely that disadvantages will be shifted from the strong to the weak, while advantages are shifted from the weak to the strong, reflecting the balance of power among these associations. [23] It is for these reasons that vertical or horizontal countervailing power, organized for defensive purposes, ultimately forces the consumers, the weakest group, to take the brunt of price rises, and to suffer the most.

With respect to the formation of prices, a large number of commodities is presently in danger of having free price formation obstructed at either the production or sales stage mainly by direct systemic intervention (including the approval of cartel action) or cartel or cartel-like action, as seen from past experience. Table 14 counts the number of such commodities from among those covered in the wholesale price index of the Bank of Japan. Table 15 reports the same computation with regard to the consumer price index in the Tokyo Metropolitan area.

The two tables show that commodities in danger of having their free price formation obstructed mainly by some institutional factor or by cartel action or administered pricing action are about 43% at the wholesale price stage and about 54% at the consumer price stage.

In Conclusion

Most of these systems and practices, which are largely re-

Table 14

Proportion of Commodities Affected by Systemic Factors in
the Wholesale Price Index of the Bank of Japan

	Total number of commodities	Commodities under systemic intervention (1)		Commodities threatened by cartel action (2)		Total (3) = (1) + (2)	
		number	ratio (%)	number	ratio (%)	number	ratio (%)
Foodstuffs	111	35	31.5	11	9.9	46	41.4
Nonfood agricultural products	30	4	13.3	21	70.0	25	83.3
Textile products	104	90	86.5	–	–	90	86.5
Lumber and wood products	42	–	–	25	59.5	25	59.5
Metallic materials	15	–	–	5	33.0	5	33.0
Iron and steel	63	–	–	39	61.9	39	61.9
Metal products	46	–	–	2	4.3	2	4.3
Electric machinery	67	14	20.9	5	7.5	19	28.4
General and precision machinery	100	–	–	22	22.0	22	22.0
Chemicals	119	5	4.2	50	42.0	55	46.2
Petroleum and coal products	27	27	100.0	–	–	27	100.0
Ceramic products	45	–	–	17	37.8	17	37.8
Miscellaneous products	65	6	9.2	7	10.8	13	20.0
All combined	928	181	19.5	204	22.0	385	41.4
Perishable foods	67	3	4.5	37	55.2	40	59.7

Table 15

Number of Commodities Affected by Systemic Factors in the
Consumer Price Index (Tokyo Metropolitan Area)

	Total number of commodities	Commodities under systemic intervention (1)		Commodities threatened by cartel action (2)		Total (1) + (2)	
		number	ratio (%)	number	ratio (%)	number	ratio (%)
Food	160	17	10.6	42	26.3	59	36.9
Housing	59	5	8.5	12	20.3	17	28.8
Fuel and light	7	7	100.0	–	–	7	100.0
Clothing	81	–	–	57	70.4	57	70.4
Miscellaneous	114	47	41.2	41	36.0	88	77.2
Total	421	76	18.0	152	36.1	228	54.2

sponsible for Japan's current pricing problems, came into being
in the process of heavy and chemical industrialization. With the
collusive oligopoly system prevailing in heavy and chemical industries, they may — as we know from America's experience —
become even more prolonged and troublesome aftereffects for
the Japanese economy. The reason is that, as a general political
rule, a system, once established, cannot be dissolved or reformed
unless a revolutionary event or considerable abuse takes place.
It means that groups and organizations that were artificially
created to meet the need of a specific system tend to grow with
this system into powerful champions or political pressure groups
that can no longer be controlled by this system. In that respect,
economic systems and economic actions are generally irreversible.

Competitive investment behavior of a growth- and competion-
oriented oligopoly system during the period of rapid economic
growth promoted, on the whole, growth and progress of the economy, so long as workable competition was maintained in essence, even though some restraints were placed on price competition and resource allocation in connection with the industrial
policy. However, a stagnant, collusive oligopoly system in the
slow growth period tends to curtail competitive and efficient investment activity — the more so if the greater heavy and chemical industries are in the manufacturing sector. This in turn
weakens increases in demand for capital goods and producer
goods. It may result in a vicious cycle of reducing effective aggregate demand. In heavy and chemical industries, unlike light
industries such as the spinning industry, shutting down operations of individual plants or factories as a whole or promoting
the scrapping of giant plants is infeasible because of excessive capital loss. But it is also impossible for the government
to purchase idle equipment in these heavy industries in view of
the colossal fund requirement.

Thus, in the sense that every aftereffect of industrial policy
serves not as a stimulant to capitalist enterprises and banks
but makes oligopolistic business groups and employers' associations more conservative, it makes institutional reform in a period of slow growth all the more difficult.

Notes

1) On this point, see Myrdal [1], Simon [2], Peirce [3], Ueno [4].

2) If one regards land, space, and environment as public goods, one can understand better why the principles of economic planning or economic control are needed in addition to the principles of free economy dependent only on the price and market mechanism.

3) The effects of land legislation and land taxation are outside of the scope of this article. Their importance calls for a separate, detailed analysis.

4) On this point, see my comments presented at an international conference on the procedures and practices of economic planning, Ueno [6].

5) On the protective policies toward the automobile industry, see Ueno and Muto [7].

6) The MITI was often given leadership in industrial policy and administration, even after enterprises in key industries became sufficiently strong, because, for one, it was convenient for promoting harmony within the industries concerned and because, for another, it was a means of winning favorable public opinion, as it gave the appearance of coinciding with public interest.

7) See Marshall [8] and Aoki [9, 10].

8) [11] is an important official position paper that concisely explains the needs and features of Japan's industrial policy. The paper points out the need for a planned system of supply and demand that either replaces or partly revises the market mechanism via the government participation.

9) The MITI, Sangyo Kozo no Choki Vision [Long-Range Vision of Industrial Structure] (1974) takes note of a need for the renewed "introduction of a planned market economy," but its industrial policy practiced heretofore has all been of this category.

10) See, e.g., Peterson [12] on main features of Japan's economic system and economic policy as seen by foreigners.

11) See Kanazawa [13] for the relationship between planning and legislation. It is said that Japan's economic planning resembles that of France. The latter, however, has a much clearer

legal and administrative basis and plays a more definite role.
See, for example, Ridley et al. [14] for France's overall legal
system and administrative structure.

12)' The point of view regarding regulation in economic legislation is based entirely on Kanazawa [15].

13) There is a huge number of "notifications" issued by each
ministry. It may take several years just to examine these notifications for the sake of an efficiency analysis of the system.

14) This system went into effect in June 1958 in the form of
the MITI's administrative guidance in order to stabilize prices
of iron and steel by price maintenance and production cutbacks.
The open sale system was set up by the MITI in its "Main Principles of the Measure to Guarantee Iron and Steel Price Stabilization" (July 25, 1960), with respect to six types of ordinary
steel materials. This guideline provides for the reporting and
public announcement of the sales prices by individual enterprises, the reporting of the expected production and sales volumes, the implementation of simultaneous sale, price recommendations, official instructions on production volume, the
creation of a steel marketing committee and a monitoring committee. A 1963 subcommittee report by the Industrial Structure
Council is of great interest in revealing the points of view held
by the steel industry and the MITI regarding this system. "The
open sales system is neither a cartel of industrial enterprises
nor a government regulation. All cartels, except depression
cartels and rationalization cartels, are forbidden by the Antitrust Act. The open sales system manages matters through
the cooperation of the government and the steel industry in the
form of administrative guidance in order to bring about price
stabilization while avoiding the abuses of cartels and regulation.
With regard to price, this system is fundamentally based on the
principles of free competition and leaves it, as a rule, to the
discretion of individual enterprises. The MITI intervenes actively only when there is a danger of price fluctuations beyond
a certain limit. Therefore, the idea is to limit price fluctuations within the narrowest range possible and not to freeze
prices completely." That a point of view such as this was cur-

rent in those days is, in fact, tantamount to the Antitrust Act
having been ignored.

15) See Narita [16] for legal problems related to administrative guidance.

16) It is difficult to evaluate the effects of tariff and non-
tariff barriers and other trade policy measures. It requires
a separate, detailed analysis. Here, I assume that foreign-
made key commodities were effectively barred from the domestic market. See Watanabe [19, 20], Kojima and Komiya, eds.
[21], and Ueno and Muto [7].

17) It was in 1972 that the "Industrial Relocation Promotion
Act," aiming at the simultaneous solution of overpopulation and
depopulation, was enacted, and it was in 1974 that the "National
Land Utilization Planning Act" was established. One might estimate the delay in institutional reform in this aspect to be also
roughly ten years.

References

[1] Myrdal, G., The Political Element in the Development
of Economic Theory (1955).

[2] Simon, H. A., Models of Man (1957).

[3] Peirce, C. S. S., Studies in Logic (Little Brown, 1883).

[4] Ueno, H., "Keiryo Keizaigaku no Hitsuyosei to Yukosei"
[The Necessity and Validity of Econometrics], Kikan Gendai
Keizai, No. 1 (June 1971).

[5] Commons, J. R., The Economics of Collective Action (1951).

[6] Ueno, H., "Comments on the Papers Presented at the
Quantitative Techniques for Planning Session," September 1970.

[7] Ueno, H., and H. Muto, "The Automobile Industry of
Japan," Japanese Economic Studies, III (Fall 1974).

[8] Marshall, A., Principles of Economics (1890, 8th ed., 1920).

[9] Aoki, M., "Increasing Returns to Scale and Market Mechanisms," Technical Report, No. 6, Stanford University, November 1967.

[10] Aoki, M., "Dynamic Processes and Social Planning
under Increasing Returns," Technical Report, No. 15, Stanford
University, June 1968.

[11] Address by the vice-minister of international trade and industry to the industrial committee of OECD, "Basic Philosophy of Japanese Industrial Policy," June 1970.

[12] Peterson, P. G., A Foreign Economic Perspective, 1971, especially IX, "The Japanese Economic Miracle — A Special Review."

[13] Kanazawa, Y., "Keizaiho ni okeru Keikaku" [Planning in Economic Legislation], Hokudai Hogaku Ronshu, Vol. 16.

[14] Ridley, F., and J. Blondel, Public Administration in France (1969).

[15] Kanazawa, Y., Keizaiho [Economic Legislation] (revised) (Tokyo: Yuhikaku, 1967).

[16] Narita, Y., "Gyosei Shido" [Administrative Guidance], I. Ogawa and S. Takayanagi, eds., Gendaiho 4 — Gendai no Gyosei [Modern Legislation 4 — Modern Administration] (Tokyo: Iwanami Shoten, 1966).

[17] See MITI, Tsusho Sangyo Sho Nijunen-shi [Twenty-year History of the Ministry of International Trade and Industry] (1969), ibid., Tsusho Sangyo Sho Gyosei Shihanseiki no Ayumi — Tsusho Sangyo Sho Niju-gonen Shi [A Quarter Century of Progress in International Trade and Industrial Administration — Twenty-five Year History of MITI] (1975).

[18] Ueno, H., et al., "Simulation Experiments with the JERC Inter-Industry Econometric Model," mimeographed, 1975.

[19] Watanabe, F., "Sangyo Kozo to Kanzei Taikei" [Industrial Structure and the Tariff System], H. Niida and A. Ono, eds., Nihon no Sangyo Soshiki [Japan's Industrial Organization], (Tokyo: Iwanami Shoten, 1969).

[20] Watanabe, F., "Nihon no Boeki" [Japan's Trade], T. Negishi and F. Watanabe, eds., Nihon no Boeki [Japan's Trade], (Tokyo: Iwanami Shoten, 1971).

[21] Kojima, K. and R. Komiya, Nihon no NTB [Japan's Non-Tariff Barriers] (Tokyo: Nihon Keizai Shimbun Sha, 1971).

[22] Kravis, I. B., and R. E. Lipsey, Price Competitiveness in World Trade (New York: NBER, 1971).

[23] Scherer, F. M., Industrial Pricing Theory and Evidence (1970).

V.

BIBLIOGRAPHIC STUDIES

11

INDUSTRY STUDIES OF JAPAN: A SURVEY

Toshimasa Tsuruta*

Lineage of Industry Studies

As a branch of empirical research, industry studies attempt to analyze various problems of the times impinging upon industry. We have a considerable accumulation of such studies. Even before World War II there were outstanding works on agriculture, cotton textiles, and other industries. For instance, Minoru Toyosaki's Nihon Kikai Kogyo no Kiso Kozo [The basic structure of Japan's machine industry] (Nihon Hyoron Sha) is a classic in industrial research. Prewar industry studies have a special characteristic in that they went down to the industry level to analyze the reproduction structure of Japanese capitalism. In particular, Toyosaki concluded from his research

―――――――――
*Toshimasa Tsuruta, "Sangyo Ron no Keifu to Genzaiteki Shikaku" [Survey of Literature on Industry Studies and Contemporary Viewpoints], Keizai Seminar, No. 224 (November 1973), 122-127. Reprinted in English by permission of the author and publisher. Translated by Irvin Schenkman.

This translation originally appeared in Japanese Economic Studies, III (Winter 1974-75), 68-81 (68-69 omitted in this reprint).

on the machine industry that Japan would be unable to survive
a long-term war. It is a distinguished book written under conditions of severe repression of thought.

There is also a tremendous accumulation of individual industry studies in the postwar period. Among them the following three works are representative in that they give a systematic analysis of a number of industries from certain specific
points of view.

The first, Gendai Nihon Sangyo Koza [A course on contemporary industry of Japan] (Tokyo: Iwanami Shoten, 1959), appeared in eight volumes under the editorship of Hiromi
Arisawa, Professor Emeritus of the University of Tokyo.
Economists and industry specialists who were active in research at the time contributed to this Course, which presented
a painstaking analysis of the processes of formation and expansion of modern industry. It is becoming a classic in this
field.

The second work is Gendai no Sangyo [Contemporary in-
dustry] (Tokyo: Toyo Keizai Shimpo Sha, 1967), which appeared
in nine volumes under the editorship of five scholars, Masao
Sakisaka, Yasuo Takeyama, Yoshiro Hoshino, Buhei Miyashita,
and Ryozo Yamada. It is regrettable that only nine volumes
have been published out of the originally planned twelve, with
three volumes dealing with plastics, industrial machinery, and
machine tools yet to appear.

The third work is Nihon no Sangyo Soshiki [Industrial organization of Japan] (Tokyo: Chuo Koron, 1973 and 1974),
which appeared in three volumes under the editorship of
Professor Hisao Kumagai of Osaka University. Two volumes
have already been published. [Volume three was published in
1976 — K.S.]

It is hardly necessary to mention that besides these three
works a good many others have been published that comprehensively treat many industries, for example, Gendai Sangyo
Keieishi Taikei [History of contemporary industrial manage-
ment]. These three, however, stand out as the representative

general works, since they deal with problems of the times in
industrial economics and cover important industries. However,
with regard to analytical approaches, the Course of 1959 and
Contemporary Industry of 1967 are completely different from
the Industrial Organization of 1973. While the two earlier
works apply general analysis to industry, the last one is based
on the theory of industrial organization, which is established
as an application of price theory. I shall now examine the problems and the contemporary background these studies attempted
to analyze. By noting changes in problems discussed in these
three series of industry study, I will identify contemporary
tasks of industry studies.

Emphasis on Productivity in the "Course"

Around 1960, when the Course was published, the Japanese
economy was experiencing a tremendous upsurge owing to
technological innovations and the consumption revolution;
clusters of modern industries were being formed and expanded.
There were two types of technical innovations. The first was
changes in existing industries, such as electric power, iron
and steel, and automobiles. Typical among them are, in the
case of electric power, development of large-scale dams for
hydroelectric generation of electric power and a conversion
from hydro to thermal power; in the case of iron and steel,
introduction of large-scale blast furnaces, conversion from
open-hearth to LD-type converters, and adoption of hot-strip
mill rolling; and in the case of automobiles, mechanical auto-
mation, represented by transfer machines.

The second type is associated with the formation and development of completely new industries like petrochemicals and
electronics. The petrochemical complex that was established
in 1957 changed materials of synthetic fibers from coal to oil
and created new industries manufacturing many varieties of
plastics, synthetic rubber, and synthetic detergents. The industrial complex, which is now regarded as the arch-culprit

of pollution, was the star of technological innovations then.
Yet another symbol of innovations was transistorization in the
electronics industry. Furthermore, black-and-white TV, electric washers, and refrigerators (known popularly as the three
great "boons") familiarized people for the first time with the
benefits of consumer durables; their diffusion process therefore
was called the consumption revolution.

Thus the late fifties, when the Course was published, were
probably the period in which the Japanese economy really flour-
ished for the first time in history. The main theme of the
Course, therefore, was to explain the modernization of the
Japanese economy and the development of productivity. The
editor, Arisawa, contributed a general introduction to the first
volume of the series (October 1959) and made the following
statement:

> Having been swept by waves of technological innovations,
> Japanese industry has had a new birth and shown sensa-
> tional development. A great upheaval has taken place in
> our consumption itself, which is now called the "consump-
> tion revolution." ... The most essential contemporary
> problem cast by the boundless progress of modern science
> and technology is what kind of existence our industry ought
> to assume. We have to reexamine the directions of busi-
> ness management, institutional reforms, the functions of
> the nation-state, and the orientations of policy. Industry
> studies provide basic materials for solving these contem-
> porary problems. In any other way, they have no contem-
> porary raison d'être.
>
> A number of viewpoints are possible in industry studies.
> There is a view that studies of product prices should be
> the central theme of industry studies. But we have de-
> cided to focus more generally on specific studies of pro-
> ductivity developments. This point of view is not only al-
> ways fundamental to industry studies but also should be
> emphasized particularly in this period of technological

innovations....Furthermore, if technological change plays
the leading role in current productivity developments, we
have to highlight the technological aspects [my emphasis —
T. T.].

This long quote brings out the basic viewpoint of the editor
of the Course. It is also clearly expressed in the section on
editorial policy in the first volume of the work.   Accordingly,
the Course was prepared throughout as a joint work of economists and technologists. At the present moment, however, the
productivity point of view can no longer be the basic one in
industry studies. As we shall note later, productivity growth
has given rise to many problems, including that of pollution.
It seems that the emphasis on productivity not only reflected
actual rapid transformation of industries at the time, as we
mentioned earlier, but also was proposed subconsciously as a
contraposition to the "dual structure" thesis of those who stress
production relations — that the existence of a relative surplus
population would stand in the way of the development of
Japanese capitalism.

The International Approach in
Contemporary Industry

The nineteen sixties witnessed trade liberalization in the
Japanese economy, with foreign exchange restrictions partially
removed. In contrast to the "hothouse" atmosphere up to the
end of the fifties, industry studies shifted their focus to Japan's
international competitiveness. Of especial importance in this
regard is the industrial policy which aimed at increasing industrial concentration and promoting mergers in order to cope
with impending liberalization of trade. Yoshihiko Morozumi,
then MITI section chief in charge of the policy, wrote as
follows:

From the point of view of industrial organization,

Japanese enterprises could develop international competitiveness in liberalized trade by pursuing economies of
scale to the fullest extent, in which they have usually been
weak. To be more specific, this requires merger and
integration of enterprises and concentration and specialization of production [my emphasis — T. T.].*

Against this stand of the policy authorities for merger and
reorganization, many counterarguments were presented in
connection with the Antimonopoly Law. However, by the late
sixties when Contemporary Industry was published, trade liberalization was nearly over. Liberalization of capital was now the
main problem for the Japanese economy. The policy-makers were
again presenting their thesis of industrial reorganization, albeit
in a new dress. Under these circumstances, Contemporary Industry placed special emphasis on appraising Japan's competitive strength in the international setting. In its first volume the editors made the following statement on editorial
policy:

The time is now to internationalize everything from
trade liberalization to capital liberalization. Japanese
industry has entered the export stage with some firms
already going overseas. Under these circumstances, it
is important to clarify the international position of Japanese
industry in various aspects and to explore its prospects
for the future. For this purpose it is essential not only to
appraise its international competitiveness at the moment
with respect to prices and technology but to investigate
general and specific characteristics of industrial development.

---

*Y. Morozumi, "Sangyo Taisei Ron — Tsusan Sho gawa no Ichi
Teian" [Industrial system — a proposal from the MITI], in
Nihon Keizai no Genjo to Kadai [The present state and tasks
of the Japanese economy] , Vol. 4 (Sangyo Taisei no Saihensei
[Restructuring the industrial system])(Tokyo: Shunju Sha, 1963).

Thus, in contrast to the Course which described the process
of technical progress in relation to market conditions from
the productivity point of view — that the Japanese economy
would be modernized through productivity advances — Contemporary Industry, stressing the international aspects of the
Japanese economy, intended to place Japan's industrial modernization and development in the perspectives of world industrial development, thereby clarifying both the generality and
the specificity of Japan's modernization process and evaluating
Japan's industrial competitive strength through international
comparisons.

Today, following the revaluation of the yen toward the end
of 1971 and the adoption of the fluctuating exchange-rate system in February 1973, which was virtually another revaluation
of the yen, it is already behind times to conduct industry studies
from the point of view of international competitiveness, since a
consensus of opinion has already been reached as to the international competitive strength of Japanese industry. However,
we must note that in the mid-sixties Japan's trade was barely
balanced and that the low ceiling of the balance of payments
was still considered to be a constraint on growth. It was thus
natural that these historical circumstances should claim researchers' attention. It was also natural that their attention
should be attracted to the history of industrial development in
major advanced nations in order to learn a few lessons as to
what consequences impending liberalization of capital would
bring to Japanese industry.

Diversified Points of View

In the late sixties there were abrupt changes in problems
and concerns as to industrial organization. Although the Course
and Contemporary Industry addressed themselves to different
questions, both shared the productivity point of view in that
developments of industrial productivity were connected to the
modernization of the economy in the former and to the strengthening of international competitiveness in the latter, in spite of

changes in historical circumstances between the two series.

However, since the late sixties ills accompanying rapid industrial productivity expansion began to appear; the main themes of industry studies were again shifted. We list six of them below.

First, strengthened international competitiveness resulted in a huge accumulation of foreign exchanges under the fixed exchange-rate system, thus intensifying international conflicts. Japanese merchandise was being boycotted abroad, and the move was visible overseas for protection of trade. Japan's accumulation of dollars aggravated international currency complications, and Japan had to go through two exchange-rate adjustments.

Second, there is the question of industrial oligopolization. As a result of the industrial policy that favored concentration and merger, large firms attempted merger in almost all industries; symbolic of this movement is the Yawata-Fuji merger into Nippon Steel Corporation, the world's largest. Non-Marxian economists opposed this merger on the grounds that the merger would bring about restrictions in competition in the steel industry, form extreme oligopoly, and induce collusion among enterprises. Consumer campaigns were also increasing against oligopoly control of industry. Thus industry studies also shifted more toward the industrial organization point of view; these studies deal with what sort of public policy, in particular concerning the Antimonopoly Law, is desirable in order to improve market performances of industry. As we shall note in the next section, Industrial Organization of Japan is the compendium of industry studies based on this point of view.

Third, the environmental pollution problem suddenly appeared,* e.g., the mercury poisoning in Minamata Bay and the

---

*The first case of the Minamata disease was reported in 1953; industrial-complex pollution was known already in the late fifties. What I mean here is that these problems came to be discussed as serious social problems only in the late sixties — T. T.

Agano River (Niigata), the bone disease from cadmium in the
Toyama Mountain District, and the pollution caused by industrial complexes in Yokkaichi and elsewhere. These events
made many people realize for the first time that productivity
advances that had brought the "light" of industrial development,
as emphasized in the Course, had at the same time caused environmental pollution and endangered human survival. Hence
the appraisal of technological innovations stressed their
"light" side in the late fifties and their "dark" side in the
late sixties. It was recognized that contemporary pollution
is due to a problem inherent in the modern production system,
namely, the fact that it is not a closed but an open system,
which does not recycle fumes and contaminated water inside
the plant but simply discharges them outside. This awareness
has completely changed the point of view in industry studies,
which is particularly advocated by members of the Gendai
Gijutsu Shi Kenkyukai [Study group on history of contemporary
technology] led by Yoshiro Hoshino and Kan'ichi Kondo.

Fourth, Japan's direct investments abroad started to increase rapidly in the late sixties. Japanese enterprises
started to go overseas especially after the first revaluation of
the yen. This has manifested itself in changes in the patterns
of international specialization — the process of multinationalization of Japanese firms. So far, multinational corporations
have been studied mainly in the U.S. and Europe, but now research in this area has extended to Japanese firms. Of particular concern in this connection is the enactment of international
antimonopoly regulations in order to control MNCs' activities
for the sake of maintaining economic order in most countries.

Fifth, resource and food problems have come back. As for
resources, Japan can no longer be treated as a "small country" in
the world resource markets now that the Japanese economy has
become so gigantic, and Japan's shares in world trade of resources
have become so high.* It is only natural that Japan's high

---

*In 1970 Japan's import shares in total imports of devel-
oped nations were 18.9% for crude oil; 37.5% for coal; 36.3%
for iron ore; 13.6% for bauxite; 78.5% for copper ore; 27.7%

growth tightens the world resource markets, resulting in sharp rises in resource prices. From the standpoint of industry, Japan's overseas investments for the sake of resource development imply vertical integration of Japanese industry. It has also become necessary to reevaluate agriculture in the setting of the worldwide food crisis.

Sixth, there is the problem of industry rotations. As heavy and chemical industries become gigantic and reach maturity, clusters of new industries are being formed on their periphery. The "venture business" thesis, energetically propounded by Professor H. Nakamura of Senshu University and Professor T. Kiyonari of Hosei University, is an empirical attempt to demonstrate how new social divisions of labor are being formed, as well as the transfer of technologies.

Market Mechanism and Public Policy in "Industrial Organization of Japan"

We have just seen how industry studies changed approaches in the late sixties. Industrial Organization of Japan, while it examines the same industries on earlier studies, also views market structure and market behavior from the point of view of the theory of industrial organization, evaluates market performances of various industries, and presents recommendations for necessary public policy measures.

One could trace the ancestry of the theory of industrial organization to the Principles of Economics by Alfred Marshall. However, a strong impetus was given by The Theory of Monopolistic Competition (1933) by E. H. Chamberlin and The Modern Corporation and Private Property (1932) by A. A. Berle and G. C. Means. Joe S. Bain organized these ideas into a systematic theory of industrial organization in his two-volume Industrial Organization. We may note that the American tradition of industry studies differs from Japan's in that it has been closely

---

for zinc ore. In particular, Japan imported 24 or 25% of world production of iron and copper ore — T. T.

related to the antitrust policy since the Sherman Act of 1890.

The American viewpoint was introduced and transplanted into Japan by Professor Ryutaro Komiya of the University of Tokyo through his articles since 1960.* It also seems that Japanese industry studies, along the lines of theory of industrial organization, have come into popularity, for one thing, under the influence of the public debate on the Yawata-Fuji steel merger and, for another, by a pioneering study by Professor K. Imai of Hitotsubashi University on Japan's petroleum refining industry.**

Industrial Organization of Japan, originally carried by Chuo Koron magazine, covers household electric appliances, pharmaceutical drugs, automobiles, shipbuilding, ball bearings, banking, iron and steel, aluminum, cameras, synthetic fibers, housing, rice distribution, petroleum refining, and so on. The common approach in this series is an empirical analysis as seen from the theory of industrial organization. Professor Hisao Kumagai emphasizes this point of view in his editorial introduction as follows:

In contemporary economics under the capitalistic mixed system, the government-public sector plays an important role in the management of the national economy. There is

---

*See, e.g., R. Tachi and R. Komiya, Keizai Seisaku no Riron [The theory of economic policy](Tokyo: Keiso Shobo, 1964); R. Komiya, "Nihon ni okeru Dokusen to Kigyo Rijun" [Monopoly and profits in Japan], T. Nakamura et al., eds., Kigyo Keizai Bunseki [Economic analysis of business firms: essays in honor of Professor Y. Wakimura] (Tokyo: Iwanami Shoten, 1962).

**K. Imai, "Sangyo Soshiki Ron kara mita Enerugi Sangyo" [Energy industry as seen from the theory of industrial organization], in H. Niida and A. Ono, eds., Nihon no Sangyo Soshiki [Industrial organization of Japan](Tokyo: Iwanami Shoten, 1969). [This volume is the proceedings of the annual Zushi Conference — K. S.]

no doubt that this role is gaining in importance. However, the preponderance of economic activities of an economy is still directly in the private sector. Most economic problems are solved in the private sector through free decisions made by individual economic units and through control of the market mechanism. In Japan government purchases of goods and services (current purchases and capital formation) are nearly 20% of GNP, but they are mostly directed toward goods and services produced by private industries. Government activities reflected in the proposition of "public administration" in net national product originating from industry is less than 5%. Therefore, economic activities in the private sector, particularly organization of production activities by private enterprises, are of decisive importance to the basic problem as to how national resources are to be employed and what is to be produced by how much and for whom [my emphasis — T. T.] .

The theory of industrial organization is an applied field of economics which conducts industry studies in particular reference to how to regulate the market in order to maximize the economic welfare of the nation. It is at this point that the approach basically differs from earlier industry studies. To be sure, this approach has invited criticism for not paying sufficient attention to the analysis of technological aspects of various factors that determine dynamic changes in basic conditions and market structure. However, what is essential to industry studies at the present stage is that they introduce the market-regulation point of view. The conventional view that industrial development raises national welfare has already reached the limits of its usefulness.

Contemporary Points of View in Industrial Studies

The point raised above is related to the anti-industrialism movement which has recently been in vogue; it is also the basic problem of contemporary industry. We now see many proposals and announcements from business leaders and groups concerning norms for business activity. There are also theses on "the social responsibility of business" or reform plans for industrial structure. They are counterproposals to the antipollution or consumer movements and to social disapproval of land speculation by developers and commodity speculation by trading firms. One ought to question the social responsibility of those enterprises that generate pollution or offer defective goods. The Yokkaichi court decision made it perfectly clear how far the social responsibility of an enterprise with regard to pollution goes.

The basic problem of industry today, however, is not limited to enforcing the social responsibility of enterprises; it is fundamentally tied to the management of institutions and policy as to how to regulate activities of enterprises and industries. With regard to pollution, the first step of its solution is to counter the covert sabotage by enterprises and to strive for elimination of pollution through official intervention that raises environmental standards. As for the exclusive market control by big business, antitrust policy should be more strictly enforced; in particular, it is important to restore the clause concerning division of enterprises which was deleted in 1953. As for the housing problem, without adequate formulation of a comprehensive land policy, it will be impossible to plan efficient utilization of land and to eliminate unequal distribution of wealth. Official intervention in the market is necessary to establish standards for activities of multinational firms. In short, the basic problems of contemporary industry require certain regulations of the market mechanism, without which neither resource allocation nor income distribution can be improved.

Until now, Japan's industrial policy has emphasized fostering and promoting industry, setting aside market regulations. This attitude still prevails. Through the sixties industry studies were primarily based on the productivity point of view, precisely because of the industry-first principle. It is now high time for industry studies to prompt a basic change in public policy.

JAPANESE STUDIES
OF INDUSTRIAL ORGANIZATION

Kazunori Echigo*

Industrial organization is an applied field of microeconomics; its main task is to conduct empirical testing of the resource allocating function of the price mechanism and to clarify its policy implications. It covers not only organization of individual industries but also issues of public policy, so that it is difficult to draw a well-defined boundary between it and other fields of economics. We limit this survey, however, to the fields listed in the Journal of Economic Literature as "industrial organization and market structure" and "public policy toward monopoly and competition." Earlier surveys of industrial organization by Hiroshi Niida and Ken'ichi Imai [1], Kojiro Niino [2], and Masao Baba [3], [4] also place emphasis on these fields, though they differ somewhat in coverage.

This limitation of coverage, however, gives rise to a few problems, particularly in excluding those industry studies and policy analyses conducted on theoretical bases and problem-setting alien from our theory of industrial organization. There are a number of outstanding Marxian studies among those exclusions as Niino [2] notes in his survey. Most of them are not mentioned in the present survey.

*Kazunori Echigo, "Sangyo Soshikiron." Nihon Keizai Gakkai Rengo [The Union of the National Economic Associations in Japan], ed., Keizaigaku no Doko [Survey of the State of Economic Studies in Japan] (Tokyo: Toyo Keizai Shimpo Sha, 1975, Vol. II, Chap. 5, pp. 33-40, 64-68. Translated by permission of the author and publisher. Translated by Kazuo Sato.

1. History of Japanese Studies of Industrial Organization

It is only in the last ten years or so that "industrial organization" has been established as a discipline in Japan. Hisao Kumagai [5] states that industrial organization was "developed as a discipline mainly in the United States," that "it is relatively recently that the field was formed as an established discipline" even there, and that "it was through a number of articles written by Ryutaro Komiya in 1960 and later that the American theory of industrial organization came to be effectively transplanted in Japan for the first time, even though there had been many empirical studies of the 'dual structure' and 'business groupings' from the viewpoint of the Marxian concept of 'monopoly capitalism.'"

The tradition of antimonopoly policy did not exist in Japan, unlike the United States. The resource allocating function of the price mechanism was suppressed or distorted under the zaibatsu's control of industry and the government's economic control before and during World War II. In the reconstruction period after the war, the industrial policy placed chemical and heavy industries under heavy protection. Consequently, the maintenance and promotion of competition was made little of as public policy. However, the zaibatsu were abolished, the antitrust law was enacted, and other industrial institutions were brought into force; technological innovations were introduced into every industrial field; new industries rose and old industries were improved with entry of new firms under the stimulus of competition and with the expansion of the competitive mechanism. Along with those developments, the people concerned became very aware of the effects that the competitive character of industrial organization has upon effective resource allocation and economic progress.

Rapid economic growth of Japan in the early 1960s created a climate in which Japan for the first time "opened its eyes" on the competitive mechanism and the price system. It is no coincidence that theory of industrial organization was introduced and established in Japan at precisely this moment. Komiya, in

his paper [6] published in Sekai, severely criticized the traditional misconception on the relation between firm size and the
profit rate and much other conventional wisdom. This, along
with his other papers [7] , [8] , impressed Japanese economists with the importance of empirical studies of industrial
organization.

Around 1960, theory of industrial organization was given a
general analytical framework by the significant work of Joe S.
Bain [9] in the United States. This Bain book and a later book
by Richard Caves [10] , both of which were translated into Japanese, exerted a strong influence on Japanese students in this
field.

Thus, the 1960s witnessed Japanese economists busily engaged in introducing and digesting American-style theory of
industrial organization. Kumagai, in his celebrated work
Principles of Economic Policy [11] , placed industrial policy
within the general framework of economic policy on the basis
of his lifelong study of the subject. Komiya summarized theory
of industrial organization in a 1964 book [8] he co-authored
with Ryuichiro Tachi. Subsequently, a great deal of effort was
made to introduce theory of industrial organization into Japan
by a number of economists — Kazunori Echigo [12] , Tetsuya
Ichisugi [13] , Tadao Konishi [14, 15] , Kojiro Niino [16, 17] ,
Kenichi Imai [18] , Yoshihiro Kobayashi [19] , and Baba and
Niino [20] . An excellent textbook [21] was recently published by Komiya, Imai, et al. Another one was edited by
Echigo [22] . It is judged that, as regards the systematic introduction of the subject, Japan has now reached an adequate
level.

2. Oligopolies and Industry Reorganization

At the time theory of industrial organization was transplanted
into Japan, active interfirm competition broke out in major
Japanese industries, particularly chemical and heavy industries. The competitive stimulus helped Japanese industries
to improve themselves and to reinforce their international

competitiveness. This development gave rise to a great many discussions on how to assess and evaluate the active oligopolistic competition. A notable example is the thesis of "excessive competition" [kato kyoso]. Industry reorganization was put forth on the basis of this thesis. Mergers of big firms, which peaked with the establishment of the Nippon Steel Corporation, were subjected to a heated debate. This debate as well as that of commercial trade policy and capital liberalization drew economists' attention at this time. The infant theory of industrial organization faced its first challenge in these debates.

These discussions are adequately summarized in a paper by Hideichiro Nakamura [23] and a survey by Konishi [24]. In this connection, Yoshikazu Miyazaki [25] raised a sharp question as to the characteristics of Japanese oligopolies. He and Hitoshi Misonoo [26] analyzed capital concentration and monopolization in Japanese industry and highlighted the problem of keiretsu or business groupings. Their works, as well as a pioneering study by Yoshio Kobayashi et al. [27], are worthy of note.

In the meantime, the Japan Economic Research Council [Nihon Keizai Chosa Kyogikai] [28] and Yoshihiko Morozumi [29] developed the thesis of "excessive competition" and advocated the need for industry reorganization. Komiya, however, criticized this thesis in his "Direct Investment and Industrial Policy" contained in [30] and other papers. Kumagai [31] clarified theoretical issues involved in the theses of too small firm size and of excessive competition. Other noteworthy studies on this topic are [32] ~ [35] and an article by Toshio Kimura [36].

In the 1960s, no inflexible oligopolistic control was established in Japanese industry. Rather, competitive oligoply was prevalent. It is therefore interesting to note that discussions by non-Marxian economists gradually made it clear that "excessive competition" was really monopolistic or oligopolistic competition and what were regarded as its evils were actually owing to the lack of competition. Of studies on this topic, [37] by Nakamura, Sugioka, and Takenaka is worthy of mention as a significant study that clearly and correctly interpreted Japanese industrial organization as that of competitive oligopoly. Alongside these studies, an attempt began in the late 1960s to deepen oligopoly theory to account for big-business mergers and industry reorganization. Tatsuji Yamatose [38],[39] have full-fledged studies of the subject. Oligopolies are studied in the framework of industrial organization by [16] and [40]. An overall analysis of the oligopolistic economy is attempted in [20],[41] ~[43]. Fully articulated empirical works are undertaken by Kobayashi [44]~[46]. Meticulous studies of workable competition by Konishi [47] and others [48] may also be noted.

3. Studies in Individual Fields

References cited above contain textbook-type works, and not all of them are scholarly enough. This situation is perhaps unavoidable when theory of industrial organization was being imported and transplanted. Many of the nearly high-level studies in this field are reprinted in the readings edited by Baba and Taguchi [49]. We therefore mention book-length studies that are not included in the readings.

Data on industrial concentration and the degree of concentration are contained in [50] ~[55] compiled by the Economic Department of the Secretariat of the Fair Trade Commission, which played an important role in conducting surveys of the degree of concentration and in disseminating statistics thereof. As regards growth and size of firms, consult studies by Imai [56], Baba [57], and Nishikawa et al. [58].

Studies of economies of scale in Japan had long been under the strong influence of E. A. G. Robinson [59]. But the need to measure effective economies of scale was keenly felt when discussions of industry reorganization were put forth; there is almost no mentionable study of this topic except for an incomplete interim report edited by Echigo [60].

As regards price behavior, a systematic analysis of cartels [61] was published in the early 1960s. In the late 1960s, attention was focused on the administered prices in connection with the problem of inflation. Oligopolistic, administered prices were studied by Sekio Sugioka in his pioneering fact-finding study [62] and later by Kobayashi, Miyazaki, and others [63] ~ [66]. Nonetheless, because of the lack of data, analysis of oligopoly price behavior is far from developed. More work is required. Resale price maintenance is studied by Hasegawa [67] and the Fair Trade Commission [68] from the viewpoint of comparative systems. There are a large number of empirical studies of nonprice competition, but we may note a theoretical study by Yasuta Fujimoto [69].

A recent advance in studies of industrial organization is represented by econometric studies of the relation between the market structure and market performance by Baba [57], Kobayashi [44] ~ [46], and Imai [56], [70]. The relation between the degree of concentration and the profit rate is examined by Kazuo Matsushiro, reprinted in the readings [49], Takehiko Musashi, and Masu Uekusa [71]. Research and development activities are examined by Uekusa [72] and a series of papers by Imai, e.g., [70]. Echigo examines arguments on the Schumpeter-Galbraith hypothesis in a paper contained in [49] and [73].

Industry policy and antitrust policy are studied in [17], [29], [47], and [74], but there are almost no case studies of applications of the antitrust law. Japan is clearly far behind the U.S. which has many meticulous case studies of this sort. [75] deals with history of antitrust policy and is useful as a data source.

4. Small Business and Industry Studies

Analysis of small business in Japan belongs to a field separate from that of industrial organization. It has been developed on its own and with its own problems. However, this survey must make a brief excursion into this field. An article by Kimihiro Masamura [76] gives a concise summary of how the small-business problem evolved in the postwar period. As

can be surmised from the bibliographies in Fujita and Takeuchi
[77], references in this field are too numerous to mention in
the limited space available here. [78]~[83] are cited as a
few representative works in successive periods. We should
note that they include meticulous and thoroughgoing studies of
individual traditional industries like [84]. Generally speaking,
to reexamine and reassess the tremendous number of research
materials and studies accumulated in this field from the point
of view of industrial organization theory still remains as part
of the agenda.

The same point applies to industry studies. There is an
enormous accumulation of individual industry studies as listed
in the book edited by Buhei Miyashita [85]. Outstanding studies
are not limited to Japan's major industries like the one by
Mikio Sumiya et al. [86] but also cover foreign industries like
the study by Tetsuo Takahashi [87]. Space limitation does not
allow us to mention them here.

Theory of industrial organization is most effective in industry studies in which interrelations between market structure,
market behavior, and market performance are examined. It
goes without saying that this theory cannot perform its real
function of providing economic criteria for public policy without studying individual industries. Many available industry
studies are not necessarily of this type except for a few works
like the paper by Imai contained in [49]. But the three-volume
essays edited by Kumagai [5] finally published industry studies
of the desired type, and these represent the level of academic
sophistication attained in Japan at the present moment.

References

[1]   Niida, H. and Imai, K., "Kasen no Jisshoteki Bunseki,
Tembo" [Empirical Analyses of Oligopoly: A Survey], Keizai
Kenkyu (Hitotsubashi University), 20 (1969).
[2]   K. Niino, "Saikin no Wagakuni ni okeru Sangyo Soshikiron no Tenkai," [Recent Developments in Theory of Industrial Organization in Japan], Nihon Keizai Seisaku Gakkai

<u>Nempo</u> [Annual Proceedings of the Japan Economic Policy Association] , Vol. XVII (Tokyo: Keiso Shobo, 1969).

[3]   Baba, M., "Sangyo Soshikiron ni okeru Jisshoteki Kenkyu, Tembo" [Empirical Analyses in Industry Organization: A Survey] , Discussion Paper of the Institute of Economic Research, Kyoto University, 1970.

[4]   Baba, M., "Sangyo Soshikiron ni okeru Keiryoteki Kenkyu, Tembo" [Econometric Analyses in Industrial Organization: A Survey] , <u>Economic Studies Quarterly</u>, 21 (1971).

[5]   Kumagai, H., ed., <u>Nihon no Sangyo Soshiki</u> [Industrial Organization in Japan] (Tokyo: Chuo Koron Sha, 1973, 1974, 1976), Vol. I, II, III.

[6]   Komiya, R., "Dokusen Shihon to Shotoku Saibumpai Seisaku" ["Monopoly Capital" and Income Redistribution Policy] , <u>Sekai</u>, March 1961.

[7]   _____, "Nihon ni okeru Dokusen to Kigyo Rijun" [Monopoly and Profits in Japan] , Nakamura, T., et al., eds., <u>Kigyo Bunseki</u> [Business Analysis] (Tokyo: Iwanami Shoten, 1962).

[8]   Tachi, R. and Komiya, R., <u>Keizai Seisaku no Riron</u> [Theory of Economic Policy] (Tokyo: Keiso Shobo, 1964).

[9]   Bain, J. S., <u>Industrial Organization</u> (New York: John Wiley and Sons, 1959, 2nd ed.).

[10]   Caves, R., <u>American Industry: Structure, Conduct, Performance</u> (New York: Prentice-Hall, 1964).

[11]   Kumagai, H., <u>Keizai Seisaku Genri</u> [Principles of Economic Policy] (Tokyo: Iwanami Shoten, 1964).

[12]   Echigo, K., <u>Kogyo Keizai — Sangyo Soshikiron</u> [Industrial Economy — Industrial Organization] (Tokyo: Mineruva Shobo, 1965).

[13]   Ichisugi, T., "Sangyo Soshiki" [Industrial Organization] , Miyazawa, K., ed., <u>Sangyo Kozo Bunseki Nyumon</u> [Introduction to Analysis of Industrial Structure] (Tokyo: Yuhikaku, 1966).

[14]   Konishi, T., "Sangyo Soshiki no Seisaku" [Policy of Industrial Organization] , Chigusa, Y., ed., <u>Keizai Seisaku</u> [Economic Policy] (Tokyo: Yuhikaku, 1967).

[15] _____, "Sangyo Soshiki" [Industrial Organization], Kato, H., et al., eds., <u>Keizai Seisaku</u> [Economic Policy], Vol. 3 (Tokyo: Yuhikaku, 1971).

[16]   Niino, K., <u>Gendai Shijo Kozo no Riron</u> [Theory of Modern Market Structure] (Tokyo: Shinhyoron Sha, 1968).

[17] _____, <u>Sangyo Soshiki Seisaku</u> [Policy of Industrial Organization] (Tokyo: Shinhyoron Sha, 1970).

[18]   Imai, K., "Sangyo Soshiki" [Industrial Organization], Kumagai, H., et al., eds., <u>Kindai Keizaigaku</u> [Modern Economics], Vol. 2 (Tokyo: Yuhikaku, 1970).

[19]   Kobayashi, Y., "Kasen Bunseki to Sangyo Soshikiron" [Analysis of Oligopoly and Theory of Industrial Organization], Niino, K., et al., eds., <u>Kasen Keizai Ron</u> [Oligopolistic Economy] (Tokyo: Yuhikaku, 1970).

[20]   Baba, M. and Niino, K., eds., <u>Kasen no Keizaigaku</u> [Economics of Oligopoly] (Tokyo: Nihon Keizai Shimbun Sha, 1969).

[21]   Imai, K., Uzawa, H., Komiya, R., Negishi, T., Murakami, Y., <u>Kakaku Riron</u> [Price Theory], Vol. III (Tokyo: Iwanami Shoten, 1972).

[22]   Echigo, K., ed., <u>Sangyo Soshikiron</u> [Industrial Organization] (Tokyo: Yuhikaku, 1963).

[23]   Nakumura, H., "Shihon Jiyuka to Sangyo Saihensei" [Capital Liberalization and Industry Reorganization], Urabe, T., et al., eds., <u>Sangyo Saihensei to Kigyo Senryaku</u> [Industry Reorganization and Business Strategy] (Tokyo: Nihon Keiei Shuppankai, 1968).

[24]   Konishi, T., "Saikin no Wagakuni ni okeru Sangyo Saihensei Ronso no Ichi Tembo" [A Survey of the Recent Controversy on Industry Reorganization in Japan], <u>Nihon Keizai Seisaku Gakkai Nempo</u> [Annual Proceedings of the Japan Economic Policy Association], Vol. XVIII (Tokyo: Keiso Shobo, 1970).

[25]   Miyazaki, Y., <u>Sengo Nihon no Keizai Kiko</u> [The Economic Mechanism of Postwar Japan] (Tokyo: Shinhyoron Sha, 1966).

[26]   Misonoo, H., <u>Nihon no Dokusen — Saihensei no Jittai</u>

[Monopoly in Japan — Facts on Industry Reorganization] (Tokyo: Shiseido, 1965, rev. ed.).

[27]   Kobayashi, Y., ed., Kigyo Keiretsu no Jittai [Facts on Business Groupings] (Tokyo: Toyo Keizai Shimpo Sha, 1958).

[28]   Nihon Keizai Chosa Kyogi Kai, ed., Nihon no Sangyo Saihensei [Industry Reorganization] (Tokyo: Shiseido, 1967).

[29]   Morozumi, Y., Sangyo Seisaku no Riron [Theory of Industrial Policy] (Tokyo: Nihon Keizai Shimbun Sha, 1966).

[30]   Niida, H. and Ono, A., eds., Nihon no Sangyo Soshiki [Industrial Organization of Japan] (Tokyo: Iwanami Shoten, 1969).

[31]   Kumagai, Y., ed., Shijo Kozo to Keizai Koritsu [Market Structure and Economic Efficiency] (Tokyo: Yuhikaku, 1968).

[32]   Morozumi, Y., et al., eds. Sangyo Taisei no Saihensei [Reorganization of the Industrial System] (Tokyo: Shunjusha, 1963).

[33]   The Institute of Economic Research, Osaka City University, ed., Sangyo Saihensei to Kigyo Gappei [Industry Reorganization and Business Mergers] (Tokyo: Nihon Hyoron Sha, 1967).

[34]   Fujisawa, S., and Omori, S., "Shijo ni okeru Kyoso Joken" [Conditions of Competition in Markets], Kanamori, H., ed., Keizai Seicho to Kigyo Keiei [Economic Growth and Business Management] (Tokyo: Shunjusha, 1966).

[35]   The Institute of Economic Research, Chuo University, ed., Kigyo Shuchu to Sangyo Saihensei [Business Concentration and Industry Reorganization] (Tokyo: Toyo Keizai Shimpo Sha, 1971).

[36]   Kimura, T., "Kyodai Kigyo no Seicho to Kasen Taisei no Keisei" [Growth of Giant Firms and Formation of the Oligopoly System], Koza Nihon Shihon Shugi Hattatsushiron [Lectures on History of Development of Japanese Capitalism], Vol. V (Tokyo: Nihon Hyoron Sha, 1969).

[37]   Nakamura, H., Sugioka, S., and Takenaka, I., eds., Nihon Sangyo to Kasen Taisei [Japanese Industry and the Oligopoly System] (Tokyo: Shinhyoron Sha, 1966).

[38]   Yamatose, T., Kasen Keizai Riron no Kozo [Structure of the Economic Theory of Oligopoly] (Tokyo: Shinhyoron Sha, 1970).

[39]   Yamatose, T. and Inoue, T., Kasen no Keizai Riron [Economic Theory of Oliogopoly] (Tokyo: Diamond Sha, 1972).

[40]   Echigo, K., Kasen Keizai no Kiso Kozo [Basic Structure of the Oligopoly Economy] (Tokyo: Shinhyoron Sha, 1969).

[41]   Abe, K. and Kobayashi, Y., Gendai Kasen Keizai Ron [Modern Economics of Oligopoly] (Tokyo: Toyo Keizai Shimbun Sha, 1967).

[42]   Momo, Y., Gendai Shihon Shugi to Kasen Keizai [Modern Capitalism and Oligopoly Economy] (Tokyo: Toyo Keizai Shimbun Sha, 1969).

[43]   Niino, K. and Ito, M., Kasen Keizai Ron [Oligopolistic Economy] (Tokyo: Yuhikaku, 1970).

[44]   Kobayashi, Y., Kasen Keizai no Dotai Bunseki [Dynamic Analysis of Oligopoly Economy] (Tokyo: Koseikaku, 1970).

[45]   _____, Kasen Kigyo no Kodo Bunseki [Behavioral Analysis of Oligopolies] (Tokyo: Shunjusha, 1971).

[46]   _____, Nihon Keizai no Kasen Kiko [The Oligopoly System of the Japanese Economy] (Tokyo: Shinhyoron Sha, 1971).

[47]   Konishi, T., Handokusen Seisaku to Yuko Kyoso [Antitrust Policy and Workable Competition] (Tokyo: Yuhikaku, 1967).

[48]   Cho, M., Kasen to Yuko Kyoso [Oligopoly and Workable Competition] (Tokyo: Chuo University Press, 1967).

[49]   Baba, M. and Taguchi, M., eds., Sangyo Soshiki — Readings [Readings on Industrial Organization] (Tokyo: Nihon Keizai Shimbun Sha, 1970).

[50]   Holding Company Liquidation Commission, Nihon Zaibatsu to sono Kaltai [Japan's Zaibatsu and Their Dissolution], data volume (1950) textbook volume (1951).

[51]   Secretariat, Fair Trade Commission, ed., Nihon ni okeru Keizairyoku Shuchu no Jittai [Reality of Economic Concentration in Japan] (Tokyo: Jitsugyo no Nihon Sha, 1951).

[52] _____, Nihon no Sangyo Shuchu no Jittai [Realities of Industrial Concentration in Japan] (Tokyo: Toyo Keizai Shimpo Sha, 1957).

[53] _____, Nihon no Sangyo Shuchu [Industrial Concentration in Japan] (Tokyo: Toyo Keizai Shimpo Sha, 1964).

[54] _____, Nihon no Sangyo Shuchu — Showa 38-41 [Industrial Concentration in Japan, 1963-66] (Tokyo: Toyo Keizai Shimpo Sha, 1969).

[55] _____, Nihon no Kigyo Shuchu — Daikigyo niyoru Shihon Shuchu, Kabushiki Shoyu, Gappei no Jittai [Business Concentration in Japan — Capital Concentration, Stock Ownership, and Mergers by Big Business] (Tokyo: Government Printing Office, 1971).

[56] Imai, K., "Kigyo Seicho to Sangyo Soshiki" [Business Growth and Industrial Organization], Miyazawa, K., ed., Sangyo Kiko [Industrial Structure] (Tokyo: Chikuma Shobo, 1971).

[57] Baba, M., "Kigyo Kibo, Sangyo Shuchu, Rijunritsu" [Firm Size, Industrial Concentration, and Profit Rates], Discussion Paper, the Institute of Economic Research, Kyoto University, 1971.

[58] Nishikawa, S., et al., "Sangyo Shuchu ni kansuru Tokeiteki Kenkyu" [Statistical Study of Industrial Concentration], Keizai Bunseki, No. 15 (1965).

[59] Robinson, E. A. G., Structure of Competitive Industry (Cambridge: Cambridge University Press, 1931).

[60] Echigo, K., ed., Kibo no Keizaisei [Economies of Scale] (Tokyo: Shinhyoron Sha, 1969).

[61] Yoshida, N., ed., Nihon no Karuteru [Japanese Cartels] (Tokyo: Toyo Keizai Shimpo Sha, 1964).

[62] Sugioka, S., Kasen Kakaku [Oligopolistic Prices] (Tokyo: Nihon Hyoron Sha, 1966).

[63] Misonoo, H. and Nitta, S., Dokusen Kakaku [Monopolistic Prices] (Tokyo: Nihon Hyoron Sha, 1967).

[64] Secretariat, Fair Trade Commission, ed., Kanri Kakaku [Administered Prices], Vols. I and II (Tokyo: Government Printing Office, 1970, 1972).

[65] Kobayashi, Y., Kanri Kakaku [Administered Prices] (Tokyo: Diamond Sha, 1971).

[66]   Miyazaki, Y. and Niino, K., eds., <u>Kanri Kakaku</u> [Administered Prices] (Tokyo: Yuhikaku, 1972).

[67]   Hasegawa, F., <u>Saihambai Kakaku Iji Seido</u> [System of Resale Price Maintenance] (Tokyo: Shoji Homu Kenkyu Kai, 1969).

[68]   Secretariat, Fair Trade Commission, <u>Saihan Seido</u> [System of Retail Price Maintenance] (Tokyo: Government Printing Office, 1971).

[69]   Fujimoto, Y., <u>Hikakaku Kyoso no Riron</u> [Theory of Nonprice Competition] (Tokyo: Toyo Keizai Shimpo Sha, 1965).

[70]   Imai, K., "Joho, Gijutsu, Kigyo Kibo" [Information, Technology, and Firm Size], Imai, K., et al., eds., <u>Joho to Gijutsu no Keizai Bunseki</u> [Economic Analysis of Information and Technology] (Tokyo: Japan Economic Research Center, 1970).

[71]   Uekusa, M., "Rijunritsu to Shijo Kozo Shoyoin, Nichibei ni kansuru Jissho Kenkyu" [Profit Rates and Factors of Market Structure: Empirical Analysis of Japan and the U.S.], <u>Mita Gakkai Zasshi</u>, 63 (July 1970).

[72]   _____, "Sangyo Soshiki to Innovation" [Industrial Organization and Innovations], Hijikata, B. and Miyakawa, K., eds., <u>Kigyo Kodo to Innovation</u> [Business Behavior and Innovations] (Tokyo: Nihon Keizai Shimbun Sha, 1973).

[73]   Echigo, K., "Nozomashii Gijutsu Shimpo to Sangyo Soshiki" [Desirable Technical Progress and Industrial Organization], <u>Toyo Keizai</u>, No. 3690 (1972).

[74]   _____, <u>Handokusen Seisaku Ron — Amerika no Hantorasuto Seisaku</u> [Antitrust Policy of the United States] (Tokyo: Mineruva Shobo, 1965).

[75]   Fair Trade Commission, ed., <u>Dokusen Kinshi Seisaku Nijunen Shi</u> [Twenty-year History of Antimonopoly Policy] (Tokyo: Government Printing Office, 1968).

[76]   Masamura, K., "Sengo ni okeru Chusho Kigyo Mondai no Hatten Katei" [Postwar Developments of the Small-Business Problem], <u>Koza Nihon Shihon Shugi Hattatsushiron</u> [Lectures on History of Development of Japanese Capitalism], Vol. IV (Tokyo: Nihon Hyoron Sha, 1969).

[77]   Fujita, K. and Takeuchi, M., eds., Chusho Kigyo Ron [Small Business] (Tokyo: Yuhikaku, 1968).

[78]   Ito, T., Chusho Kigyo Ron [Small Business] (Tokyo: Nihon Hyoron Sha, 1957).

[79]   Fujita, K., Nihon Sangyo Kozo to Chusho Kigyo [Industrial Structure and Small Business in Japan] (Tokyo: Iwanami Shoten, 1965).

[80]   Takizawa, K., Kodo Seicho to Kigyo Seicho [Rapid Growth and Business Expansion] (Tokyo: Toyo Keizai Shimpo Sha, 1973).

[81]   Nakamura, H., Chuken Kigyo Ron [Medium-size Firms] (Tokyo: Toyo Keizai Shimpo Sha, 1964, 1972 [2d ed.]).

[82]   Kiyonari, T., Nihon Chusho Kigyo no Kozo Hendo [Structural Change of Japanese Small Business] (Tokyo: Shinhyoron Sha, 1970).

[83]   Kiyonari, T., Nakamura, H., and Hirao, M., Venture Business (Tokyo: Nihon Keizai Shimbun Sha, 1971).

[84]   Kokusho, I., ed., Nishijin Kigyo no Kenkyu [Silk Weaving Industry at Nishinjin] (Tokyo: Mineruva Shobo, 1965).

[85]   Miyashita, B., Nihon Sangyo Ron [Japanese Industry] (Tokyo: Yuhikaku, 1971).

[86]   Sumiya, M., ed., Nihon Sekitan Sangyo Bunseki [Analysis of Japanese Coal Industry] (Tokyo: Iwanami Shoten, 1968).

[87]   Takahashi, T., Igirisu Tekko Dokusen no Kenkyu [Study of Monopoly in English Iron and Steel Industry] (Tokyo: Mineruva Shobo, 1967).

CONTRIBUTORS

Kazunori Echigo, Shiga University

Yusaku Futatsugi, Kobe University

Ken'ichi Imai, Hitotsubashi University

Tadao Kiyonari, Hosei University

Ryutaro Komiya, University of Tokyo

Yoshikazu Miyazaki, Kyoto University

Ken'ichi Miyazawa, Hitotsubashi University

Hiromichi Muto, Japan Economic Research Center

Hideichiro Nakamura, Senshu University

Kazuo Sato, State University of New York at Buffalo

Toshimasa Tsuruta, Institute of National Economic Research

Hiroya Ueno, Seikei University